British Women Writing Fiction

Edited by Abby H. P. Werlock

Foreword by Regina Barreca

THE UNIVERSITY OF ALABAMA PRESS

Tuscaloosa and London

Copyright © 2000
The University of Alabama Press
Tuscaloosa, Alabama 35487-0380
All rights reserved
Manufactured in the United States of America
1 2 3 4 5 6 7 8 9 • 08 07 06 05 04 03 02 01 00

∞

The paper on which this book is printed meets the minimum requirements of
American National Standard for Information Science–Permanence of Paper for
Printed Library Materials, ANSI Z39.48-1984.

Library of Congress Cataloging-in-Publication Data

British women writing fiction / edited by Abby H. P. Werlock;
foreword by Regina Barreca.
    p. cm.
  Includes bibliographical references (p.) and index.
  ISBN 0-8173-0982-9 (alk. paper)
  ISBN 0-8173-0981-0 (pbk. : alk. paper)
  1. English fiction—Women authors—History and criticism.
2. Women and literature—Great Britain—History—20th century.
3. English fiction—20th century—History and criticism. I. Werlock,
Abby H. P.
  PR830.W6 B75 2000
  823'.914099287—dc21
       99-6471

British Library Cataloguing-in-Publication Data available

To
Frank and Ethel
Who shared with me
their love of England
and their love of words

Contents

Foreword

Regina Barreca

"Atmosphere plainly is a very mighty power. Atmosphere not only changes the sizes and shapes of things; it affects solid bodies, like salaries, which might have been thought impervious to atmosphere. An epic poem might be written about atmosphere, or a novel in ten or fifteen volumes. . . . [L]et us confine ourselves to the plain statement that atmosphere is one of the most powerful, partly because it is one of the most impalpable, of the enemies with which the daughters of educated men have to fight." So declares the narrator in Virginia Woolf's 1938 treatise, *Three Guineas.* The significance of Woolf's passage delineates the position that the ways in which women write and the larger cultural context within which they write need to be connected. That belief is the reason for the great significance of the essays collected here: they establish, collectively and individually, the need to see British women writers of fiction as defining themselves against an accepted series of conventions—an "atmosphere" of British life and culture—even as they struggle for their own identity and art. The critics brought together under Werlock's aegis all examine these issues in light of larger principles of power, writing, and resistance in a world still uncertain about the place of the strong woman's voice, or the woman's strong voice, or (pretty much, let's face it) the voice of any woman at all.

Establishing context is necessary—particularly necessary, we can argue—for those writers whose main business seems to be removing the boundaries and rewriting the very definition of culture. One of the distinctive features of the contributions to Werlock's collection is the fact that the essays point to areas of connection as well as differences among the authors, connections and differences reflecting the distinct historical, political, and personal moments in the lives of the writers, as well as their particular sexual, class, and artistic concerns. Reading the book as a whole, then, we are compelled to recognize inescapable patterns of similarity: we see the struggle to understand political as well as familial history; we see the conflict between the powerful and oppressive influences of the dominant culture and the desire of the characters for autonomy and self-expression; we see the textual exploration and uses of anger, humor, insurgence, reverence, respect, and rebellion.

In addition to the stimulating critical readings and various theoretical perspectives the essays offer concerning individual texts or authors, one of the best things about the collection is the way it insists on bringing together interesting intellectual matings. In other words, because many feminist, psychological, economic, deconstructive, and reader-response issues resonate across the works under consideration, the book ends up making fascinating points concerning our definition of every word in the title: after all, what does it mean to be a British woman writing fiction?

This useful and important collection of original essays is founded on the belief that women have different stories to tell from their male counterparts and contemporaries. Little is taken for granted: issues surrounding sexual identity, desire, and preference are examined, as are issues of race, age, religion, and cultural imperialism. Although the texts under discussion offer their insights and pleasures to both male and female readers, the criticism collected here reflects an important vision of the function of literature: that there are methodologies and mappings particular to the woman writer. The finite, tightly closed-off limits of traditional narrative are erased by the decentering, dislocating aspects of women's writing in the twentieth century. Even while assuming ostensible conventionality, women's narratives inevitably but subtly undercut the defining features of the very genres they seem to embody in order to repudiate the repressive nature of those limitations. By calling the definitions into question, women's narratives alter the compass of the question itself, depicting, finally, the ideological foundations embodied and perpetuated by conventional narrative, which often disregards or debases women's experience.

A shared fund of secrets, laughter, silences, and truths belong to those who have developed as women writers under the influence of modern British life, where the experience of being a woman is erased, written over, or devalued. Werlock's collection adds a series of powerfully provocative, convincing, and intelligent voices to the discussion of every aspect of the central issues and by so doing increases the impact and reach of the writers' missions.

Acknowledgments

In addition to the scholars in England and the United States whose expertise made this book possible, numerous librarians and editors provided invaluable assistance. In particular, I wish to thank Larry L. Nesbitt, Director, Library Information Resources, and the Mansfield University Library staff for generously helping me acquire interlibrary loan sources and for extending to me the full range of their computer and bibliographical services. Professor Laurie Howell Hime of the Miami Dade Community College, Kendall Campus Library, provided timely bibliographical support; and the St. Olaf College Rolvaag Library staff, particularly Professors Bryn Geffert and Mary Sue Lovett and Visiting Instructor Anne C. R. Friederichs, responded immediately to last-minute citation queries. Helpful too were the services of the Florida State University Strozier Library and the State Library of Florida. I am grateful to Sue Ann Oines, St. Olaf College, for outstanding secretarial services; Paul Marino, computer consultant, for help with numerous technical questions; Jonathan M. Lawrence for meticulous editing; Lee Cobb for careful proofreading; and the talented staff at the University of Alabama Press. Nicole Mitchell, Director, and Curtis L. Clark, Assistant Director and Editor in Chief, made numerous suggestions and wise decisions throughout the progress of this book. I owe special thanks to Joe

Abbott for his impressive editorial expertise, efficiency, and unfailing attention to detail and to Mindy Wilson, Assistant Acquisitions Editor, who kept track of all the parameters of this project.

Finally, I am grateful to Abby and Tom Potter for making Woodburn and the Lake Bradford house available during summer and winter alike, Jean and Marshall Case for opening their eighteenth century log house to me, Jennifer and John Winton and Dewey Potter for their continuous and generous encouragement, and Mickey Pearlman for her unflagging support throughout this entire undertaking. Jim Werlock, as always, sustained me through his belief in the value of my work and this book.

British Women Writing Fiction

Introduction

Abby H. P. Werlock

The fiction published by British women during the last half of this century is impressive, important, individual, and, not infrequently, iconoclastic and irreverent. However, although in England several significant books, collections of critical essays, and personal interviews with the authors have been published, in the United States most of these books are not widely available other than in university libraries. Excepting the American professoriat who specialize in contemporary British fiction (and their numbers are small), readers of American literature in this country typically appear abashed and discomfited when approached about their readings of the many British women writing today. Too often they respond that the authors' names sound familiar, but their books remain unread. The ordinary educated American reader knows the names of Margaret Drabble and Doris Lessing, and of Muriel Spark's *The Prime of Miss Jean Brodie.* In the 1990s the success of A. S. Byatt's *Possession* and Jeanette Winterson's *Oranges Are Not the Only Fruit,* for instance, has whetted the appetites of readers of British fiction by women, yet many feel bewildered about where to begin or how to ground themselves. Readers who feel confidently versed in the great women writers of the nineteenth century, readers who—regardless of cultural differences—respond eagerly to a host of American contemporary writers, exhibit a certain timidity about plunging into the unknown waters of contemporary British women writers.

Evidently, part of the dilemma inheres in the ways in which we American educators construct our courses and parcel out our reading lists. Virtually no high school teachers with whom I have spoken use books by twentieth-century British women writers other than Virginia Woolf. Moreover, although university faculty certainly offer courses in "modern" British literature, few move beyond that period, and—if and when they do embrace the "postmodern"—their classes are composed of self-selected "Brit. Lit." majors or women's studies majors. Thus the majority of educated Americans apparently graduate from college without having been introduced to contemporary British writers, particularly women. Correspondingly, the bookstores I queried in major cities in several states—New York, Florida, Minnesota, Washington—shelve few if any books that could serve as an introduction to the world of contemporary British women writing fiction.

This collection of essays—partly inspired by my work with Mickey Pearlman, who edited *American Women Writing Fiction* (1989) and *Canadian Women Writing Fiction* (1993)—has been especially commissioned to introduce readers to the wealth of fiction being written by British women. In this volume both American and British scholars examine work by Anita Brookner, A. S. Byatt, Angela Carter, Margaret Drabble, Buchi Emecheta, Elaine Feinstein, P. D. James, Ruth Prawer Jhabvala, Doris Lessing, Iris Murdoch, Joan Riley, Michèle Roberts, Muriel Spark, Emma Tennant, Fay Weldon, and Jeanette Winterson. With the exceptions of Angela Carter and Iris Murdoch, who died while this work was in progress, all these writers are very much alive, well, and actively continuing to write. All were either brought up in England or make their home there now; in their writing all use British subjects and themes, sometimes from radically differing perspectives. Several, daughters of immigrants to England, see themselves as outsiders, people writing on the margins.

Notwithstanding these nominally shared backgrounds, however, this book, in a deliberate resistance to classification or thematization, positions these writers chronologically and encourages readers to perceive each writer on her own merits. In commissioning these essays I made no attempt to impose either a "theme" or uniform theoretical approach for the collection; indeed, the only major guideline was that each contributor keep critical jargon to a minimum. Further, all contributors independently selected the works they wished to examine, works that could profitably be interpreted either for newcomers to British contemporary fiction or for those wishing to widen their area of reading. The overriding purpose of this book, then, is to bring together in one volume discussions of a wide range of women authors in Britain today, and to provide a background against which each writer may usefully be read.

Ultimately, this book tries to achieve a balance among those who have been writing since the 1950s and 1960s, those who have attracted critical attention during the 1970s and 1980s, and those who have entered the literary scene fairly recently. A significant number have won such prizes as the prestigious Booker Prize or have received other honors and awards, many are currently the subject of scholarly research, and all have appeared recently in collected interviews.[1] Some have not received the attention they deserve, and some are near the beginning of their careers. All write in English; some write with a consciousness of an English tradition, some try to revise it, and others experiment with alternate ways to expand or redefine this tradition.

Some are profoundly conscious of themselves as "women writers," others are not; nearly all call themselves "feminists" to some degree, although, as in the real world, they define feminism along an entire spectrum. As Nicci Gerrard observes, "feminism is now so fragmented and dispersed that it is hard to perceive any sense of a common purpose" (5).[2] For the writers of the 1980s and beyond, "there are as many feminisms as there are feminists—and so the word's meaning implodes" (7). Naturally, a number of these writers appear controversial, depending on the reader's perspective; indeed, in addition to finding these essays challenging and informative, I hope readers will find at least some of these essays controversial as well.

Of course, real similarities and differences exist among such a diverse group of writers. For the most part, however, I have deliberately avoided the sorts of "lists" that detail, for example, those writers influenced by their grandmothers, by Jane Austen, by Plato, by Freud. Rather, the fullness of the information contained in the individual essays provides ample material on these and a stimulating range of other topics, encouraging readers to participate as they draw their own conclusions, provide their own parallels, and compile their own predilections.

Nonetheless, these essays raise some intriguing questions about British women writing today, and suggest some original ways to view them. "No other race of women," said an Argentinean psychiatrist of Fay Weldon's acquaintance, is "so determined to underrate" themselves and their rights and achievements (Weldon 161). Paradoxically, this observation about British women rang true for Weldon when she recorded it in 1983, the same year Margaret Drabble proclaimed that "never before, perhaps, have women had so much to say" (161).[3] The link between the two statements proves instructive, for they reflect both the difficulties and the challenges for women writing in the five decades since World War II.

The writing of contemporary women may be seen as an evolving response to questions and anxieties in the wake of World War II, which, as Alison Light suggests, "provided a new heroic stage for a British people" no longer seen as "a race of empire builders or natural warriors, but rather as . . . little, ordinary people at home, 'muddling through'" (154). In the past, as Cairns Craig explains, the study of English literature was designed to promote harmony in a class-structured society by offering a single national identity to which all could subscribe, and to promote for the peoples of the Empire an ideal of English civilization and values to which, in theory, all could aspire. As modernization swept the world, and as the wars of the twentieth century broke down and reconstructed nations, the old belief in an England of homogeneous cultural and linguistic tradition became more and more removed from reality (Craig 7). Chief among the postwar issues was "a deep structural crisis over what masculinity and femininity might be" (Light 176).

Rosalind Miles articulates the difficulties for the contemporary woman writer who grapples with those questions: "Does she choose to live within her sex, undergoing all the personal, social, and educational restrictions that that can entail, or does she make the bid for full selfhood and equal partnership in human affairs?" (202). In the broadest sense, her answer—whether she writes of the lived lives of millions of women, or of their increasingly expanding possibilities, or of the two combined— helped determine her technique. A closely allied question arose vis-à-vis technique: should she tell her story in the traditional ways of either the nineteenth or the twentieth century? That is, women writing from the 1950s and 1960s to the present have had to determine whether to use realism, romance, comedy, and other traditional forms, or to experiment with alternative techniques.[4] Recently emerging is "a view of the woman writer less contentedly keeping to her separate sphere—and a particular kind of fiction—than powerfully straining against the boundaries that hem her in" (Anderson, *Plotting Change* vii).[5]

Indeed, in the decades since World War II, as women writers pondered the issues of subject matter and narrative technique, the women who opted for using traditional modes have—as Marguerite Alexander notes—"revitalized" those techniques (17). For instance, Drabble, Emecheta, Feinstein, Murdoch, and Riley—and even the early Carter and Roberts—use realism to illustrate the actuality of women's lives as well as of their social era. Brookner views romanticism in a somberly realistic way as she demonstrates its restriction of female potential, while Byatt reenvisions it from a woman's perspective. Carter, Murdoch, Spark, and Weldon use various comedic techniques to examine moral issues. Equally exciting is the experimental rewriting of fairy tale and myth from a feminist perspective, as in the work of Carter, Tennant, Weldon, and Winterson, or of male-authored novels, as in those of Byatt, Tennant, and James, the latter updating the detective story with a woman detective and psychological insights.[6] Olga Kenyon points out that Tennant is "multifaceted," using many genres to look at adolescent girls and comment on England today, and that Roberts depicts female experience using original metaphors and innovative structures to extend the potential of fiction (4).

Clearly, both the realistic and more experimental approaches have value as women define themselves and paint their stories on the literary canvas. In Gerrard's view, referring to such writers as Lessing, Murdoch, and Drabble, realism was significant to women writers and readers in the 1960s and 1970s: "We needed novels to 'tell it like it is,' showing the way that women lived, exploring personal and sharply contemporary issues." The books of Lessing, Drabble, and Murdoch treated women's experiences as "central and significant: it mattered that daily and domestic details were recorded; that shopping and cooking, nappies and sleepless nights, menstruation and sexual desire, heterosexual and homosexual relationships were written about from a woman's point of view" (111–12).

On both sides of the Atlantic, authors, publishers, and editors have underscored the need to replace "domestic realism" with "something less insular" (Gerrard 108), and the majority of writers, both the older and more established as well as the younger and emerging ones, have responded in intriguing blends of subject matter and technique. Certainly we see fewer "women-as-victim" novels (Gerrard 14) and more forthright portrayals of a whole range of gender-related issues. As Paulina Palmer points out, "these include critiques of patriarchal power and male violence, analyses of mother-daughter relations and women's community, and debates about sex and relations between women" ("Feminist Fiction" 43). Positing the 1960s as the turning point for both feminism and experimental fiction, Ellen Friedman and Barbara Fuchs note that on the whole, experimental women writers have adopted a more "subversive stance than that taken by male experimentalists" and offer a "hopeful alternative (rather than a mournful alternative, as is the case with much male experimentation) to the failed master narrative" (27).

Thus there is room for both realism and other forms. Women can use the old methods to include themselves, and new methods in which they invent their own stories. Although it is tempting—and in many cases valid—to see a movement away from old forms and subjects as we look from the older to the younger, it is worth noting that older writers keep experimenting with technique, too: Drabble, for instance, has ranged far afield since her early works, literally moving from London to Cambodia in a recent novel; Lessing, after moving to outer space in her most radically experimental fiction, has recently returned to realism; and Spark, to use John Glavin's phrase, keeps "beginning again." "Experimental" writers such as Carter share "split subject" techniques with both Lessing and Drabble.[7] Ultimately, perhaps, as Randall Stevenson suggests, both traditional realism and either modernism or postmodernism "have seemed appealing, often simultaneously" (230).

In the wake of Britain's final disconnection from Empire, Craig notes, writers "turned increasingly to American exemplars, not as models to be imitated, but as the foremost exponents of an English no longer tied to sounds of English speech" (8), an English metamorphosed into myriad varieties of accent and dialect and alternative language. And in this sense all these writers are affected. Buchi Emecheta and Joan Riley, as literal émigrés, share a sense of "exile" or "outsider status" with a remarkable number of the other women writers in this book, including Brookner, Carter, Jhabvala, Spark, Feinstein, Lessing, Murdoch, Roberts, and Weldon.

Not surprisingly, then, a certain international quality inheres in the subjects these authors write about, beginning with their settings, which range from all five continents to the mythical cosmos of Shikasta, from the Caribbean to Nigeria to Cambodia, from London and Paris to Jerusalem and New York. Moreover, as these women write, many declare their awareness of the contributions of writers from the so-called Third World. Indeed, the last two decades have produced some highly significant work by "post-colonial" women of color who have until recently been underrepresented in literary discussions and collections. Angela Carter's words may serve to speak for several of the writers in this collection: "I personally feel much more in common with certain Third World writers, both female and male, who are transforming actual fictional forms to both reflect and to precipitate changes in the way people feel about themselves" (77).

Noting a similarity between Muriel Spark (b. 1918) and Iris Murdoch (1919–1999), Richard Kane points to the "odd combination of the moral and the macabre" in both women's fiction (37). Just as Spark, of Anglo-Jewish parentage, feels "exiled" from Edinburgh, Murdoch has observed that, growing up, "I scarcely knew my Irish relations. I feel as I grow older that we were wanderers, and I've only recently realized that I'm a kind of exile, a displaced person. I identify with exiles" (Haffenden 201). Nonetheless, she describes her books as "full of happiness" (204), for she believes that through "great comic art the sorrows of human life can be truthfully conveyed; one is moved by the spectacle, and feels that something truthful has been told in a magical way" (Kenyon 145).

In the first essay in this volume, Roberta White comments that, as in the traditional nineteenth-century novel, Murdoch invents serious characters, substantial settings, and old-fashioned, complicated plots. As a modern author, however, she creates characters notable for their rootlessness, their uncertain identities, and their darkly comic erotic lives as they relentlessly seek values in a world without God. Focusing on love, which White calls the "stuff" of Murdoch's novels, she notes that "Murdoch seldom describes the workaday world; her settings, London and the English countryside, are heightened and energized by desire. In all its varieties, perverse and possessive to ennobling, love obsesses her characters and drives her plots; love is also one of the supreme, problematic concepts—love and the good—which she attempts to illuminate in both her philosophical writings and her novels." Yet according to White, although Murdoch weaves her fiction from the failures and frustrations of everyday life, in all its comedy and its bleak ironies, one still senses an urgent search for genuine values underlying Murdoch's fiction.

While Iris Murdoch declares herself less interested in the "female viewpoint" than in the universally human one, some writers find themselves "trapped by their own reputation as women writers" (Kenyon 29). According to Margaret Drabble, Doris Lessing (b. 1919) "achieved fame, indeed notoriety for *The Golden Notebook* in 1962. She became spokesperson for the American Women's movement, without her consent" (Kenyon 29). And while her movement away from realism may not be fueled by her position as a woman, no one questions that Lessing has radically evolved in her fictional focus and techniques. In Linda Anderson's words, "The alternative to change is bleak for Lessing; if we do not change we may not survive and her fiction has taken on a strongly prophetic character" (*Plotting Change* viii). Further, as Ruth Whitaker says, Lessing's emphasis on personal change is related to her interest in the Sufi religion and her belief that "to prevent ourselves from annihilating most of the population of this planet, or to cope with survival after such a catastrophe," we must cultivate these humanistic qualities (9–10).

In her essay on Lessing, Susan Rowland points out that *Canopus in Argos: Archives* has provoked diverse critical reactions and contends that "the galactic empires of *Canopus in Argos* constitute precise examinations of political, psychic, and artistic colonization literally going 'beyond' but expressing Lessing's persistent theme of Empire." The resisting reader, Rowland argues, may well see Canopus as yet another imperial metaphor aimed at actual domination. Rowland believes, however, that *Canopus in Argos* "colonizes" nonresisting readers. Readers of *Shikasta* are translators, and Lessing forces us into constant translation so that we can make sense of "this outrageously fragmented text." Thus Rowland concludes that by translating Shikasta into Earth, the reader actually colonizes the novel. Rowland also identifies Lessing's uses of Jungian ideas to illuminate the tropes of empire and colonization that dominate our understanding of history. Ultimately, then, Rowland suggests that Lessing's space novels invite readers to develop alternate perspectives of events.

The widely admired and highly successful P. D. James (b. 1920) sees herself as a contemporary writer who—unlike the detective fiction writers of the 1930s whose novels conclude with a restoration of order—writes novels that neither "restore Eden" nor provide order and justice

(Kenyon 118). James has commented, "I don't feel I want to free language. But I did want to free the classical detective story of some of its constraints. . . . You need to free the form to be truthful about sexual and other matters" (121). Indeed, James, a pioneer in this traditionally male form, invented both the sensitive male detective poet and the talented young woman detective cautiously infiltrating the domain (Gerrard 124). In his essay on James's *The Skull Beneath the Skin*, Eric Nelson describes Cordelia Gray as the "anima" to the male inspector Adam Dalgliesh. Yet unlike Kathleen Gregory Klein, who finds Cordelia "too young, too sweet and sincere, too unsure of her ability" (155), Nelson finds that by the end of the novel Cordelia "has at last come of age."[8]

Noting both the psychological acuity and ontological depth of James's work, Nelson suggests that James's ultimate purpose is to lead the reader to the challenging questions that lie beyond mere textual analysis. Rather than escape or deny the innate artificiality of the mystery genre, James "draws attention to it, pushing the reader, in a Brechtian move, to a critical distance from the genre's conventions. If her strategy seems coy, her intention is serious: to plumb the human soul." Like T. S. Eliot, James uses her forensics lab to put the human soul "under her knife, like a patient etherized upon a table." Briefly surveying famous sleuths in earlier detective fiction, Nelson points out the way they sever the connection between feeling and thought. This "dissociation of sensibility," as Eliot termed it, connects Adam Dalgliesh to modernist male characters whose suppression of feeling leads to depression and exhaustion; Dalgliesh, however, does not die: in Nelson's view, he "carries on," because "that is what the British do in these latter days of imperial decline."

Linda Anderson notes that "women's writing has always existed illegitimately; the official story—the version that passes into history—is the one written by male writers." The woman writer, because she inherits "a plot which is not her own," must discover "ways of contesting her own silencing" (*Plotting Change* vii). Ruth Prawer Jhabvala (b. 1927) illustrates this point, focusing increasingly in her novels on characters who appear as outsiders and as rootless or displaced persons.

So noting in her essay on Jhabvala, Judie Newman examines two different novels and offers an original interpretation of Jhabvala's meaning. Newman confronts head-on the commonplace criticism of Jhabvala as an apologist for the Empire, observing that only at first glance might Jhabvala appear as part of "the retrofitting process"—especially in relation to the widely successful *Heat and Dust*. However, observes Newman, it would "be surprising, to say the least," if Jhabvala participated in rewriting the history of Empire to in any way obscure its horrors. To the contrary, Newman argues, Jhabvala's fiction reveals a keen sensitivity to a history fraught with trauma. As a German-Jewish Holocaust survivor who lost forty family members and who emigrated to Britain in 1939, to a newly partitioned India after her marriage in 1951, and finally to the United States in 1975, Jhabvala emphasizes themes of loss, disinheritance, exile, alienation, and the fragmentation of identity. Indeed, says Newman, "Jhabvala has described her childhood in terms which suggest an experience of such profound trauma that it remains almost entirely blocked from consciousness."

Drawing on Cathy Caruth's research on trauma victims, Newman suggests that Jhabvala's reactions to a "literally unspeakable history" parallel the reactions of those suffering from trauma. In examining the issue, Newman finds that Jhabvala imagistically emphasizes "the image of the female body in pain" through sati and a host of other practices that victimize women. Ultimately, Newman argues, "Jhabvala makes the point that we should never lose sight of past trauma—whether it results from European or Indian agency—however difficult or painful it may be to articulate it."

When Anita Brookner (b. 1928) received the Booker Prize in 1984, one reviewer called her "probably the best-known and most popular exponent of 'domestic realism' in Britain who has steadily been turning out novels about the plight of the plain young woman with passions hidden beneath beautifully appropriate behaviour."[9] The daughter of immigrant Polish Jews, Brookner views herself as an outsider, "a grown-up orphan" and a "lapsed Jew—if such a thing were conceivable, but it isn't. Jewishness is a terrible religion, for its relentlessness, its bad-tempered god, its inability to learn anything at all, its self-obsessed quality" (Haffenden 63, 67). A self-admitted "observer" (Kenyon 14), Brookner is sometimes criticized for her passive heroines, but she holds her ground: "People always say I'm so serious and depressing, but it seems to me that the English are *never* serious—they are flippant, complacent, ineffable, but never serious—and this is maddening" (Haffenden 61).

In answer to whether she will ever depict a strong active heroine, Brookner responds, "If I knew one, I would" (Haffenden 62). Romanticism, she insists, "is not just a mode; it literally eats into every life. Women will never get rid of just waiting for the right man" (Kenyon 15).[10] Yet as Nicci Gerrard points out, Brookner raises central questions, and feminists cannot simply dismiss her writing: "She conveys a sense that life is hostile to happiness, a view shared by many women" (110).[11]

Affirming Brookner's distinguished, productive, and multifaceted career, Kate Fullbrook in her essay sees Brookner as a quintessential London novelist: "To the chill and grey of London and her Londoners, she contrasts the sun and warmth of southern Europe," moving to the Riviera as the geographical foil to the bleak northern cold. Despite critics who find her limply passive heroines tiresome, observes Fullbrook, Brookner's point is that late-twentieth-century malaise is part of a debilitated culture as yet unable to find substitutes for the romantic paradigms that still direct our ideals and dreams. Fullbrook shrewdly notes that the real heroism of anti-romanticism is stoicism: "the Brookner tale will not be exhausted any sooner than the power of the Romantic myths which she so surgically dissects."

Noting among many women writers of Brookner's generation a general "dissatisfaction" with the constrictions of traditional modes of storytelling, Gerrard observes a simultaneous "sense that the times require cultural spokeswomen: truth-tellers and soothsayers" (151). In her essay on Elaine Feinstein (b. 1930) Phyllis Lassner makes a strong case for Feinstein's search for new ways of telling "other" sorts of English truths. Feinstein's literary identity—like her writing—is shaped by disturbing but revealing travels in time and space: "Rather than blending her Leicester childhood, Cambridge education and Russian Jewish heritage, she expresses their tense relations through her characters' sense of exile." Thus, Lassner demonstrates the ways that Feinstein joins the dislocations of immigrant experience to the English literary tradition. Lassner reminds us, however, that "no matter how settled in their Englishness, they remain subject to memories of an historic identity that destabilize the self, memories that materialize as imagined odysseys to medieval Europe or real ones that recall war-torn Europe or involve them in a tumultuous Middle East." Feinstein's women, too, fragmented and disconnected, seek their place in the world. Lassner argues that Feinstein's women struggle with memory, Jewish identity, and the way to realign that identity with a sense of Englishness. Ultimately, because she leaves her women with indeterminate endings, Lassner suggests that for Feinstein, "the discourse of Jewish history and continuity remains an ongoing process of revision and discovery."

This concern with women's consciousness occurs in the irreverent novels of Fay Weldon (b. 1931). Although Palmer has pointed to an "atmosphere of a privileged, upper-middle-class existence of a particularly British kind" (*Women's Fiction* 101–2) in Weldon's novels, Patricia Juliana Smith opens her essay by celebrating Weldon's subversive and disruptive intent in those novels in the wake of the "Swinging Sixties": "A veritable postmodern Jane Austen, Weldon chronicles the disintegration of the patriarchy and middle-class respectability with acerbic wit and gleeful malice." Smith notes that Weldon often positions lesbians—or the concept of lesbianism—in the midst of her narratives' sexual chaos and explores "the subversive significance" of her lesbian characters. By examining three novels from Weldon's so-called middle (and feminist) period, Smith demonstrates that Weldon's ironic wit augments rather than detracts from her subversive art. By treating her lesbian characters with the same scrutiny that her heterosexual characters receive, Weldon creates lesbian figures who stand on their own as individuals with identifiable strengths and weaknesses. Thus, says Smith, "by treating them as she does other women, she humanizes and, to the extent that it is at all possible, 'normalizes' the lesbian."

Part of a late-twentieth-century effort to "examine the ways the procreative/creative mother can potentially give birth to newfound lands and legends" (Gilbert and Gubar 379–80) is Antonia Byatt (b. 1936). For Byatt, "the English novel, the small novel about class and the home, is finished simply because 'there have been too many of them—nobody except the English are interested in this small form'" (Gerrard 108). In her essay, Deborah Denenholz Morse correspondingly sees Byatt's bestselling novel, *Possession: A Romance,* as "a feminist reinscription of the Romantic vision of the poet." In this novel, Byatt demonstrates her radical and feminist view of Victorian limitations. Morse points out that "the canonized English Romantic poets were all male," but Byatt creates two women, a nineteenth-century poet and her descendent. Morse decodes and interprets Byatt's literal, figurative and allusive words in this novel to reveal her creation of "a fully creative mother and a fully empowering literary matrilineage" (Gilbert and Gubar 386).[12] Ultimately, Morse points out, Byatt "shows us that through the poet's words—the words of male and female artist—we are in true possession of our sacred lives."

Like Byatt and many other writers, Emma Tennant (b. 1937) asserts her intentionality in revising traditional forms: women writers, she believes, should "take, magpie-like, anything they please from anywhere, and produce a subversive text out of the scraps; out of the patriarchal or any kind of material they can get in their beaks" (Kenyon 176). Tennant has written novels of "poetic intensity, visionary power, wit and thrilling penetration of psychology" (Haffenden 281). Noting her strong belief in feminism, Tennant comments that "some of Virginia Woolf's extraordinary writings are among the best things that have ever been said" (Haffenden 292–93). She also believes in the significance of her Scottish roots, saying, "The concept of the split personality is particularly appealing to Scottish writers because the doubleness of national identity has been there for so long" (Haffenden 292). Although she acknowledges the significance of "post-imperialist" or "third-world" literature, Tennant also believes that "in terms of novel-writing the hardest thing of all is to write the traditional English novel, which is what the English have always been good at, the novel of character and feeling. It's only too easy to say that we've reached the end, the post-imperialist stage" (Haffenden 293). She defends all modes of writing, from surrealism and allegory to realism (Kenyon 180).

Marilyn Wesley, in her essay on Tennant, acknowledges her often avant-garde style but points out that in her best novels Tennant achieves "a radically politicized but touchingly intimate portrayal of the psychological predicament of the young woman." Wesley uses Tennant's *The Ghost Child* to demonstrate the supernatural influence on Tennant's portrayal of young women: "it is, after all, not ghosts that invent stories, but stories that introduce ghosts, define them, and tell what tales can be told about them." Indeed, Wesley suggests that in this sense, all of Tennant's fiction may be viewed as a complex ghost story. Despite the ordinariness of her characters, the commonplace aura of her settings, and the routine nature of the action, these characters are haunted by the influential ghosts of other stories. Thus Tennant employs the ghosts of culture to explore such feminine preoccupations as family and space, memory and identity. Wesley illuminates "the feminist project evident throughout Emma Tennant's oeuvre: girls, too, have secret lives worthy of fiction."

Speaking of Margaret Drabble (b. 1939), Tennant has declared, "I couldn't do what Margaret Drabble does" in Drabble's much noted detailing of the British social situation (Kenyon 189). Drabble, often compared to Charles Dickens in the scope of her attention, likes to think "I write books which might contribute to a way of seeing British society" (34), writing of a "domestic" world that "other people hadn't written much about" (4). Thus while acknowledging the usefulness of magical realism, for instance, used by such writers as Carter and Weldon (Kenyon 39–40), Drabble is known for her realism. Ironically, though, as Mary Rose Sullivan notes in her essay on Drabble, "this very skill—for rendering ordinary events with precision—has led some feminist critics to charge Drabble with a lack of seriousness." Now, however, having read such recent works as *The Gates of Ivory,* we can look back and see that her work consistently contains Drabble's conviction that we must make peace with the past, forge connections with others, and respond to the larger needs of the community and of society.

Sullivan points out that Drabble's most recent work allows her to portray characters who develop against both historical and sociological backdrops. Moreover, by focusing her narrative on the power and sustenance of women's friendship, Drabble emphasizes her concern with the human need to forge personal and communal bonds. On finishing a recent book, says Sullivan, Drabble "expressed the hope of growing old like her fellow novelist Doris Lessing who, in her seventies, is still changing and 'moving on.'"[13] And so she is: remarkable in her output, Drabble continues to write as novelist, as literary critic, as editor, as coauthor.

Like many of her contemporaries, Angela Carter (b. 1940) rewrites and reinscribes older stories and myths and has expressed her aim to turn language on its head. In an interview, Carter revealed that, in addition to "decolonialising our language and basic habits of thought" (Haffenden 93), she uses both Freud and Bruno Bettelheim[14] to her own ends and in her own way; and she has commented that "some of the stories in *The Bloody Chamber* are the result of quarrelling furiously with Bettelheim" (Haffenden 82–83). In the same interview she notes, "I have always used a very wide number of references because of tending to regard all of western Europe as a great scrap yard from which you can assemble all sorts of new vehicles" (92). Carter believed that "British society is one in which most values are determined by a specific sex and a specific class, and I think that's unjust: that's all" (95).

Haffenden (82) points out that Carter has been using magic realism for twenty years, long before Gabriel Garcia Marquez; and Dee Goertz, in her essay in this volume, suggests that "by using magical realism with a feminist edge, she makes up for the rarity of the female perspective in initiation myths and quests for self-discovery." Moreover, according to Goertz, in Carter's employment of female characters from fairy tale and fantasy, ranging from vampires to puppets to sleeping beauties, she portrays young women facing male and female sexual desires, male attitudes toward women, and self-knowledge. Her young women constantly navigate a perilous road, learning that the dangers sometimes lead even to death. Ultimately, says Goertz, "Carter does not posit a world where women are free from the male gaze and their own objectifications of themselves, but rather worlds where women learn to deal with this inevitability."

Carter's experiments with language and her recognition of class and gender discrimination led to her declaration of empathy with Third World writers who "don't tell people what to do" (Gerrard 167). Similarly, Michèle Roberts (b. 1949) believes that "women are moving out of that period of modernism when the preoccupation was with the breakdown of language and form" and that, like the many Third World writers with whom she feels an affinity, "we are in a postmodernist, confident phase; we are putting the bits together again, working with the fragments, the splits and breaks and making new myths" (Kenyon 166).[15]

In her essay on Roberts, Clare Hanson agrees that her fiction addresses a number of the significant issues facing women today, but Roberts writes from the viewpoint of a half-English, half-French woman, "split between nations and identities." Hanson places Roberts in the generation of British women authors notably influenced by the second wave of feminism in the 1960s and 1970s. Like Carter, Roberts sees an inseparable connection between her writing identity and her feminism. Yet despite their similarities, Hanson sees Roberts "as a kind of antithesis to Carter," for Roberts "emphasizes the ways in which 'feminine' values have been suppressed in our culture. Just as women have, historically and physically, been oppressed in Western culture, so, she suggests, the qualities which have traditionally been associated with them have been derogated and downgraded."

Roberts, like Jeanette Winterson (b. 1959), believes that "the writer should struggle to be bisexual and learn from the father as well as the mother" (Kenyon 172). Similarly, in her essay on Winterson, Jan Rosemergy observes that because "Truth" belongs to no one person, Winterson finds essential the multiple perspectives that she represents in fiction through dual narrators of different genders.

According to Rosemergy, Winterson "portrays the journey into the external world where oppressive institutions of family, religion, and gender stereotypes limit the self." Among Winterson's metaphors for self-distorting social forces are walls, pollution, and water imagery, through which passion and imagination can liberate one's identity. Rosemergy sees that for Winterson, "a child of the 1980s," (Gerrard 167–68), the actual creation of fiction reveals the many ways that socially constructed gender roles build a wall around a person's identity. Rosemergy identifies storytelling—including fairy tale, fantasy, history, satire, and myth—as Winterson's creative device that will enable both characters and readers to change "ourselves and the world."

Focusing on the black woman writer's experience as émigré in England, Laura Niesen de Abruña examines the writing of the two major groups of immigrants, women from Africa and from the Caribbean, and pays particular attention to the Nigerian Buchi Emecheta (b. 1944) and the Jamaican Joan Riley (b. 1950). De Abruña notes that the past twenty years have seen a marked increase in the creative productivity of African and Caribbean women writers in Africa, Canada, the Caribbean, the United States, and England. She further notes that West Indians, especially, differ from the émigrés to the United States or Canada because of their profound feeling of betrayal by England, the "mother country." When they arrived in England, black families found themselves viewed as a "marginalized and victimized minority," and thus a sense of exile, race, and class discrimination became the paramount problems to surmount.

Buchi Emecheta, one of the most significant diaspora writers, creates her fiction "from a rich texture of the context of black women writers in England." In her novels that feature characters who, like herself, move from Nigeria to England, Emecheta foregrounds the issues behind the struggle of black women to establish an individual identity. Emecheta employs a realistic technique to explore many women's issues from motherhood to abortion to incest and other physical abuse.

Both Emecheta and Riley use the metaphor of the house to convey their views of women as trapped and violated. Riley's fiction covers the entire female life span and investigates such issues as child abuse, rape, marital relations, sexism, and the erosion of respect for older women. A good deal of her writing "constitutes a wrenching indictment of the insidious racism and the inherent betrayal of England, as well as of the way that hatred is displaced onto women and children, the most vulnerable and therefore the most common scapegoats." Riley seems to speak for a majority of émigrés in her recognition of the difficulties of coming "to terms with the past" and creating "new memories" that will help sustain them in the present. Both she and Emecheta demonstrate the ability of their women characters to resist their ill treatment and survive.

Chronologically speaking, Muriel Spark (b. 1918) is the first of the writers in this book, but because, in John Glavin's words, she tends to keep "beginning again," her work may serve to illustrate the myriad possibilities and achievements of British women writers. Glavin sees Sparks's "own trauma, her own primal scene . . . depicting the 'many screams in the night'" as the source of her constant rebeginnings: "This primal memory conceives male sexuality as inherently brutal, naturally duplicitous, and always a threat, perhaps even a deadly threat," but Glavin suggests that "if a woman begins again, over and over, she might avoid being entrapped in the conditions heterosexuality commonly places on her sex." Thus Glavin believes that in her current fiction Spark has accumulated the experience and confidence to move from stories of the unbearable to stories she delights to tell: Spark is not only an excellent storyteller, but an excellent story herself. In his essay, Glavin sets Spark against Virginia Woolf and her ideal of *A Room of One's Own*. As Glavin sees it, Muriel Spark's entire career testifies that a room of one's own never really has a good view; conversely, the search to find a room belonging to somebody else, that one can rent on a temporary basis, is a more worthwhile endeavor: such a concept serves as a metaphor for Spark's own work, which alights in one place for a while and then moves onward. The source of her talent lies in her ability to convert and on her continuing tendency to begin again.

Choosing writers for inclusion in this book has been, as for any selective collection, extremely difficult. Considerations of space have naturally circumscribed selection, and, regrettably, a number of fine writers could not be included. Indeed, because the writers represented in this collection are not intended to constitute a complete canon, I hope that this book will stimulate the publication of still further examinations of British women writing fiction.

Finally, among the wealth of emerging views on the changing faces of British writing, three in particular—from Alison Light, Linda Anderson, and Bernice Johnson Reagon—not only seem especially pertinent to this book but also provide thought-provoking directions for its readers. Alison Light prefaces her courageous and insightful work *Forever England* (1991) with words that cannot be ignored, at least among those who remember World War II:

> As someone who once played on bombsites and listened avidly to stories of the Blitz and of "our finest hour," maybe my own sadness has seeped into the writing: a sort of melancholy recognition that those ways of being English, foolish and even vicious as they often were, were a form of identity and community in which I too was brought up, and whose disappearance, however welcome, is also bound to hurt. . . . [Light's ellipses]. But these thoughts are perhaps more fitting to a peroration than a prologue. (19)

In her book *Plotting Change: Contemporary Women's Fiction* (1990), Linda Anderson—reckoning that today's woman writer strains valiantly "against the boundaries that hem her in"—notes the advantages of writing in today's England: "The contemporary woman novelist may be able to unravel her situation with far greater clarity than of old: what she may be clearer about, however, is the entanglement of masculine fictions of desire and power in the constitution of what we take as universal truth. Her own truth-telling may depend on her acumen in seeing through stories as well as on her ability to make up new ones of her own" (vii).

Ultimately, the world of British women who write fiction proves both generous and capacious. It contains space for all writers of talent, whether they favor the realism and humanism of Drabble, Murdoch, and Brookner or the imaginative experimentation of Carter, Roberts, and Weldon, from the characters of Brookner to the outer-space dwellers of Lessing to the bravely struggling personae of Joan Riley. Yet new and perhaps unexpected parallels keep emerging as authors of the earlier generation continue to write and to develop at the end of the century. For instance, in Spark's resistance to Virginia Woolf's room of her own, she shares in the concepts of "community" posited in the works of such different writers as Buchi Emecheta and Fay Weldon. In the words of Bernice Johnson Reagon: "We've pretty much come to the end of a time when you can have a space that is 'yours only'—just for the people you want to be there. . . . There is no hiding place. There is nowhere you can go and only be with people who are like you. It's over. Give it up" (357).

These original, previously unpublished essays aim to provide an introduction to, and whet our appetite for, the excellent works issuing from these writers. As Emma Tennant has wryly commented, "Now that England is split between an aircraft landing ground for America and not knowing what it is, new kinds of writing are causing excitement here" (Kenyon 185). Except for Murdoch and Carter (who advocated "putting new wine in old bottles, especially if the pressure of the new wine makes the old bottles explode" [69]), both of whose works continue to grow in significance, these British women continue to write fiction, to experiment, and to show us innovative ways not merely of seeing but of comprehending the multifarious perspectives of gender and geography.

NOTES

1. See, for example, Haffenden, *Novelists in Interview;* Kenyon, *Women Writers Talk;* and Wandor, *On Gender and Writing.*

2. Gerrard also writes: "The splits, bitter arguments and developing factions were inevitable. Now we have radical feminists, separatist feminists, Christian feminists, social feminists, Marxist feminists, New Wave Feminists, post-feminist feminists and the 'I'm-not-a-feminist-but . . . ' feminists. . . . By the end of the 1970s and the early 1980s there was a kind of frictional diversity which, if sometimes bruising to individuals and lacerating to the women's movement's reputation, was nevertheless vital, committed and robust" (6–7).

3. Drabble also says critics should not "sneer" at the writers who choose to write on women's subjects ("A Woman Writer" 161). Rosalind Miles agrees: women are "freer than they have ever been historically to write what they want in the way that they want" (200).

4. "The fear that poststructuralist theory could be disabling for women, making history disappear even before we have had a chance to write ourselves into it, needs to be set against another danger: the constant danger that by using categories and genres which are implicated in patriarchal ideology we are simply re-writing our own oppression" (Anderson, "Re-Imagining" 134).

5. Regarding the covert influence of women, Anderson states that "women's

writing has always existed illegitimately; the official story—the version that passes into history—is the one written by male writers. . . . [I]nheriting a plot which is not her own, she must find ways of contesting her own silencing" (*Plotting Change* vii).

6. "Crime writing is a perfect example of how the feminist consciousness can infiltrate and invigorate a familiar and much-loved form, but also of how feminism itself is challenged in the process" (Gerrard 122).

7. See also Stevenson 159.

8. Klein continues, "the second novel's revelation of Cordelia's limitations is far less subtle," as James "puts her on a level with her two temporary typists as employer, tea maker, and finder of lost animals," providing thereby "a sharp contrast between the presentation of a woman detective and the male model" (157–58).

9. Haffenden 58, quoting Antony Beevor in *Literary Review* (September 1984). See also Gerrard 109.

10. Although Brookner has numerous women friends, she continues to believe that "there is a certain inborn competitiveness among women which is a little bit murky, and it has to do with success with men. . . . [I]t's an area in which friendships can become strained. . . . I love being with women, but I [p]refer men's conversation. Mixed company is best, can't we agree on that?" (Kenyon 21). Regarding her own work, Brookner says, "You'd have to be crouching in your burrow to see my novels in a feminist way. I do not believe in the all-men-are-swine programme" (Haffenden 70).

11. Further, says Gerrard, Brookner believes that "women are separate beings who have been abandoned by men and by time, that feminism has often betrayed them, that 'something has gone wrong.'" This belief strikes a chord with many women who echo Brookner's complaints: "The women's movement has often disregarded the emotions, anxieties and desires of an inarticulate majority" (110).

12. Crediting Toni Morrison and A. S. Byatt with "veering from a more conventional daughterly perspective to a maternal one," Gilbert and Gubar (379–80) place Morrison's *Beloved* and Byatt's *Possession* in the tradition of Kingston's *Woman Warrior* (1976), Emecheta's *The Joys of Motherhood* (1979), and Caryl Churchill's *Top Girls* (1982).

13. "I thought I had a whole new world that other people hadn't written much about," Drabble has said. "That encouraged me to carry on, so did the letters I received, and reading Doris Lessing" (Kenyon 4). As Gerrard points out, "there is a way in which these older generation of women writers have taken

upon themselves the role of cultural scientists and historians of the age. Doris Lessing has gradually deserted the solid and reassuring firmness of realism" (151).

14. Bruno Bettelheim, *The Uses of Enchantment* (New York: Knopf, 1976).

15. Roberts also notes that "as imperialism falls apart, there's this great surge of writing," and names Morrison and Walker as ones she most admires (Kenyon 166).

Works Cited

Alexander, Marguerite. *Flights from Realism: Themes and Strategies in Postmodernist British and American Fiction.* London: Edward Arnold, 1990.

Anderson, Linda, ed. *Plotting Change: Contemporary Women's Fiction.* London: Edward Arnold, 1990.

———. "The Re-Imagining of History in Contemporary Women's Fiction." *Plotting Change: Contemporary Women's Fiction.* Ed. Linda Anderson. London: Edward Arnold, 1990. 129–41.

Carter, Angela. "Notes from the Front Line." *On Gender and Writing.* Ed. Michelene Wandor. London: Pandora Press, 1983. 69–77.

Craig, Cairns. "Twentieth Century Scottish Literature: An Introduction." *The History of Scottish Literature.* Vol. 4: *Twentieth Century.* Ed. Cairns Craig. Aberdeen: Aberdeen UP, 1987. 1–9.

Drabble, Margaret. "A Woman Writer." *On Gender and Writing.* Ed. Michelene Wandor. London: Pandora Press, 1983. 156–59.

Friedman, Ellen G., and Miriam Fuchs. "Contexts and Continuities: An Introduction to Women's Experimental Fiction in English." *Breaking the Sequence: Women's Experimental Fiction.* Ed. Ellen G. Friedman and Miriam Fuchs. Princeton: Princeton UP, 1989. 3–51.

Gerrard, Nicci. *Into the Mainstream.* London: Pandora Press, 1989.

Gilbert, Sandra M., and Susan Gubar. *No Man's Land: The Place of the Woman Writer in the Twentieth Century.* Vol. 3: *Letters from the Front.* New Haven: Yale UP, 1994.

Haffenden, John. *Novelists in Interview.* London: Methuen, 1985.

Kane, Richard C. "Didactic Demons in Contemporary British Fiction." *University of Mississippi Studies in English* ns 8 (1990): 36–57.

Kenyon, Olga. *Women Writers Talk: Interviews with Ten Women Writers.* Oxford: Lennard Publishing, 1989.

Klein, Kathleen Gregory. *The Woman Detective: Gender and Genre.* Urbana: U of Illinois P, 1988.

Light, Alison. *Forever England: Femininity, Literature, and Conservatism between the Wars.* London: Routledge, 1991.

Miles, Rosalind. *The Female Form: Women Writers and the Conquest of the Novel.* London: Routledge & Kegan Paul, 1987.

Palmer, Paulina. "Contemporary Lesbian Feminist Fiction: Texts for Everywoman." *Plotting Change: Contemporary Women's Fiction.* Ed. Linda Anderson. London: Edward Arnold, 1990. 43–62.

———. *Contemporary Women's Fiction: Narrative Practice and Feminist Theory.* London: Harvester Wheatsheaf, 1989.

Reagon, Bernice Johnson. "Coalition Politics." *Home Girls: A Black Feminist Anthology.* Ed. Barbara Smith. New York: Kitchen Table, 1983. 250–57.

Stevenson, Randall. *The British Novel since the Thirties: An Introduction.* London: B. T. Batsford, 1986.

Wandor, Michelene, ed. *On Gender and Writing.* London: Pandora Press, 1983.

Weldon, Fay. "Me and My Shadows." *On Gender and Writing.* Ed. Michelene Wandor. London: Pandora Press, 1983. 162–65.

Whitaker, Ruth. "Doris Lessing and the Means of Change." Anderson, *Plotting Change* 1–16.

I

Iris Murdoch: Mapping the Country of Desire

Roberta S. White

> [Murdoch] uses love the way some Arab tribes in North Africa used mud
> to build whole cities. Sometimes she uses it as various agricultural people
> use fire to clear the land.
>
> ANATOLE BROYARD[1]

Love is the stuff of Iris Murdoch's twenty-four novels, out of which she
erects her fictional structures. Love is also a narrative strategy she uses
to burn off her own talkiness and tendency to abstraction, blasting away
her characters' assumptions about themselves and making way for new
growth. Murdoch seldom describes the workaday world; her settings,
London and the English countryside, are heightened and energized by
desire. In all its varieties, perverse and possessive to ennobling, love obsesses her characters and drives her plots; love is also one of the supreme,
problematic concepts—love and the good—which she attempts to illuminate in both her philosophical writings and her novels.

Murdoch evidently conceives of her fiction as new space to be opened
up and explored. In her first novel, *Under the Net* (1954), Jake observes
that a novel is like a natural landscape: "Starting a novel is opening a
door on a misty landscape: you can see very little but you can smell the
earth and feel the wind blowing" (177–78). Fiction provides space for the

discovery of experience and the testing of ideas. In the grand tradition of the nineteenth-century novel, Murdoch creates serious-minded characters, ample settings, and big old-fashioned plots with many twists. Her modernity manifests itself in the rootlessness of her characters, their uncertainty of identity, the dark comedy of their erotic life, and their sometimes desperate search for values in a world from which God is conspicuously absent.

Despite the length of her novels, Murdoch has no interest in producing histories or sagas. One therefore need not observe chronology in exploring her anatomy of love. Her novels resemble a series of experiments performed to reveal moral, psychological, and spiritual aspects of human behavior. Frequently she puts in motion an instance of obsessive love or desire and then scrutinizes, in a sympathetic but rather clinical way, the psychological and moral states induced in the lover, who is usually male and rather weak. The results often prove comic, but only because Murdoch judges humans by the highest standards of behavior; her novels are suffused with human sympathy as well as high intelligence. Moreover, according to Murdoch's Platonic philosophy, sexual love, for all its inherent comedy, is also a powerful energy capable of assuming higher forms. In her book on Plato and art, *The Fire and the Sun* (1977), she claims that "Plato's Eros is a principle which connects the commonest human desire to the highest morality and to the pattern of divine creativity in the universe" (33). The event of falling in love, she writes, "is for many people the most extraordinary and most revealing experience of their lives, whereby the centre of significance is suddenly ripped out of the self, and the dreamy ego is shocked into awareness of an entirely separate reality" (36). On yet another level, the literary artist, like Plato's Demiurge, creates worlds out of a love that resembles the lower forms of love, with all the usual attendant dangers of egotism and delusion.

Instances of obsessive love in Murdoch's novels range across a wide spectrum. At one extreme, revelation of hidden perversity, such as the sibling incest in *A Severed Head* (1961) or the father-daughter incest in *The Time of the Angels* (1966), impels melodramatic plots in which unsuspecting persons are abruptly exposed to the breaking of taboos. A revelation of Dionysian forces rends the screen of civilized behavior, and the onlooker's world turns upside down. This is not to label these novels themselves Dionysian; they do not provide steamy reading. On the contrary, Murdoch emphasizes not the gratification of desire, but the aching experience of desire and the dislocations it causes in the psyche. Despite her various experiments with gothic horror—additional examples include *The Unicorn* (1963) and *The Italian Girl* (1964)—Murdoch's fictional mode remains Apollonian and comic. In no more than four or five of her twenty-four novels does death, betrayal, or unfathomable evil overwhelm the potential for comedy, and even in these novels the dailiness of life frequently asserts itself in comic fashion.

At the other extreme looms a higher, selfless, transcendent Eros, more often pointed to as an ideal or felt in moments of epiphany than actually practiced; as Jake learns from his pursuit of Anna in *Under the Net,* such ideal love would mark the end of desire and even of longing to know the other person. It would amount to full acceptance of the otherness of the other, "and this too is one of the guises of love" (268). Ideally, as Murdoch writes in *The Fire in the Sun,* "Carnal love teaches that what we want is always 'beyond,' and it gives us an energy which can be transformed into creative virtue" (34). But the path to creative virtue is rarely taken, and usually Murdoch deals with more common themes—love triangles, adultery, unreciprocated desire—though often with a bizarre twist, such as sixty-year-old Charles Arrowby's obsession with Hartley in *The Sea, the Sea* (1978). Long ago Hartley was his youthful sweetheart, "the jewel of the world" to him; she continues to obsess Charles to such an extent that he kidnaps her and holds her as a prisoner of love even though she is now a confused and rather decrepit old woman.

In Murdoch's novels love proves so capricious, unpredictable, irrational, and contrary to the conscious wishes and intents of the ego and practical needs of the self as to seem like an external force. As Hugh Balfounder insists in *Under the Net,* "anyone can love anyone, or prefer anyone to anyone" (255). A memorable instance of this arbitrariness occurs in *The Book and the Brotherhood* (1987). Gerard Hernshaw experienced the most intense love of his life at age eleven, a passion whose object was a small parrot named Grey with clever yellow eyes and scarlet wing tips. Although he symbolically equates his lifelong grief for the absence of Grey with his sorrow for his dead lover Sinclair and for "all the agony and helpless suffering of created things" (590), it is nonetheless Grey whom Gerard so poignantly and rather ludicrously mourns, the particular other being, beautiful and replete.

Desire portrayed as a force contrary to the will of the ego invites Freudian interpretation. But in *The Sacred and Profane Love Machine* (1974),

Blaise Gavender, a psychotherapist, finds that his understanding of Freudian mechanisms neither helps nor inhibits the treatment of his patients any more than it offers him the least guidance in his own wayward love life, which entangles him in the usual messes. One might just as well call upon any old notions or superstitions to explain the inexplicable phenomenon of love's arbitrariness. In *The Black Prince* (1973), one of her finest novels, Murdoch amusingly draws upon the psychology of love in Shakespeare's time, when, for example, Robert Burton diagnosed love as a melancholic disease of the liver that drives lovers "headlong like so many brute beasts." Despite all the counsels of reason, "they will do it," Burton writes in his *Anatomy of Melancholy* "they will do it, and become at last void of sense; degenerate into dogs, hogs, asses."[2]

In *The Black Prince,* Bradley Pearson narrates, from prison, the story of his ill-fated love for Julian Baffin, a young woman nearly forty years his junior. Julian's mother, Rachel, herself in pursuit of Bradley, warns him, "it's nearly midsummer and you are, perhaps, reaching the age when men make asses of themselves" (239). Even before the publication of *The Black Prince,* critic Robert Hoskins noted that several of Murdoch's novels resemble midsummer night's dreams, comic novels of love gone awry in summery settings.[3] Here Bradley, a writer and serious intellectual, ironically plays the role of Bottom. Bradley's life is already complicated by three other women—Rachel, his suicidal sister Priscilla, and his ex-wife Christian—when he feels helplessly drawn to Julian in a fetishistic way: her legs, feet, body smells, and hair overwhelm and madden him. From the moment he falls for her in the middle of their *Hamlet* tutorial, his stomach feels hollow, his knees dissolve, his teeth chatter, and his face takes on a waxen smile (172). This aging lover comically experiences transcendence, anxiety, longing, jealousy ("like a red-hot knitting needle thrust into the liver"), desire, humiliation, and so on (209). Murdoch details every phase of love's foolishness. Bradley confesses his love to Julian only after listening to the opening of *Der Rosenkavalier,* and then vomiting in Covent Garden out of sheer lovesickness. When he loses Julian and goes to prison for a crime that Rachel commits, the bludgeoning of Julian's father, Bradley narrates his story in a posthumous novel within the novel, *The Black Prince,* subtitled "A Celebration of Love," edited by P. Loxias (Apollo in disguise).

In *The Black Prince* we thus have the curious situation, often repeated in Murdoch's novels, of a woman novelist anatomizing and memorializing the erotic features of a woman character through the transfixing gaze of an adoring male. (A useful study could be made of the importance of *hair* in her novels as an erotic and aesthetic display of the vital, enticing "otherness" of the adored person.) This intertwining of genders, reminiscent of Shakespeare's playfulness with gender-shifting characters like Rosalind and Olivia (male actors playing women who play men), produces startlingly actual and vivid views of women—they seem wholly present. Murdoch supports the feminist movement, but she rarely brings feminist issues into her fiction; rather, she sets out to break down what she sees as arbitrary and limiting definitions of gender and of love. Delicate males and boyish women with androgynous names abound in her work; not just homosexuals and bisexuals, but virtually everyone is capable of same-sex love, often hovering somewhere between friendship and Eros. Like Virginia Woolf before her, Murdoch sets out to define and hence legitimize varieties of human attraction previously undefined and therefore unacknowledged.

Ambivalence about gender abounds in *The Black Prince*. When Bradley first sees Julian strewing bits of love letters in the street, he thinks she is a boy in dark trousers and jacket. He becomes aroused by her when she is wearing his socks, and he cannot make love until she dons her Hamlet costume, breeches, tunic, and chain. The comedy of the gender-bending and the lovesickness is at once dark, funny, and tragic because the first-person narration traps us inside Bradley's confession and his pain.

A self-conscious narrator, Bradley also theorizes about his own dilemma and its relation to his writing. Like Stephen Dedalus in *Ulysses*, Bradley presents a theory of *Hamlet* at the center of *The Black Prince*, that is, in the tutorial scene with Julian. *Hamlet* is postmodern in its intricate self-reflexiveness. Bradley describes it as "a work endlessly reflecting upon itself . . . in its very substance, a Chinese box of words . . . a meditation upon the bottomless trickery of consciousness and the redemptive role of words in the lives of those without identity, that is human beings" (166). Yet paradoxically *Hamlet* also reveals Shakespeare's deepest beliefs: "He is speaking as few artists can speak, in the first person and yet at the pinnacle of artifice" (166). Here Murdoch gives us a clue to her own work: *The Black Prince* is an intricate fiction within a fiction, and yet we may assume that, as Shakespeare revealed himself most when most disguised, so Murdoch speaks most candidly when artfully hidden in the guise of Bradley Pearson (BP, Black Prince, B.

Person). Bradley comments: "Almost any tale of our doings is comic. We are bottomlessly comic to each other. Even the most adored and beloved person is comic to his lover. The novel is a comic form, and makes jokes in its sleep [as Bradley has just made a pun on Bottom]. . . . Yet it is also the case that life is horrible, without metaphysical sense, wrecked by chance, pain and the close prospect of death. Out of this is born irony, our dangerous and necessary tool" (58). Irony is dangerous because it kills sentiment, and a necessary tool because it converts life's horrors into something bearable, a dark joke, a rhetorical gesture, or a work of literary art that distances us one step away from the pain, allowing us to contemplate it. More recently, in her philosophical lectures entitled *Metaphysics as a Guide to Morals* (1992), Murdoch argues that "Novels are, however sad or catastrophic, essentially comic" (97). The novel is an "open" form that embraces more of life's ordinariness than other genres do: "Characters in novels partake of the funniness and absurdity and contingent incompleteness and lack of dignity of people in ordinary life" (97).

The comedy of ordinary life often arises in Murdoch's novels when, like Bottom, people delude themselves with dreams of romance. As Joyce Carol Oates notes in a review, "Murdoch's philosophical position is austere, classical, rigorously unromantic, and pessimistic. Not that the pessimism precludes comedy: on the contrary, it is probably the basis of the comic spirit."[4] In *An Unofficial Rose* (1962) the traditional plot device of the love triangle, an unstable situation always conducive to irony, is repeated in three generations of would-be lovers, representing a continuity of foolishness that seems as ingrained as original sin. As the novel opens, Hugh Peronette, a retired civil servant aged sixty-seven, realizes at his wife's funeral that "he had not really known what was in her heart" (20). Ignorance of the hearts of others repeats itself, realistically, in virtually every relationship in this novel and throughout Murdoch's work, leading to possibilities of both illusion and disenchantment. In this most Jamesian of Murdoch's novels, Hugh feels an unpleasant touch of complicity in his desire to help his son Randall leave his dutiful wife Ann and daughter Miranda to run off with the big blonde Lindsay Rimmer. Randall, once a talented horticulturist now given to drink and self-indulgence, feels, probably rightly, that Ann's unselfishness is ruinous to him; she lacks "form," lives too much for others, and seems amorphous. His father, Hugh, who failed to make his own leap to "freedom" in an affair with Emma Sands many years ago, sells his treasured Tintoretto to finance Randall's high-style elopement with Lindsay, thus freeing Emma, so Hugh hopes, from her own involvement with Lindsay, her secretary and "gaiety girl." In the third generation, Hugh's grandson Penn imagines himself the courtly lover of his cousin Miranda, a demonic pubescent girl-woman who plays with dolls but cherishes a secret crush on her mother's admirer Felix Meecham.

Randall's love for Lindsay, like his father's love for Emma and his nephew's love for Miranda, is delusory and romantic in the extreme: "Randall's love for Lindsay has come violently and suddenly, the entire transformation of the world in a second, a wild cry after a long silence, the plunge of a still stream into a deep ravine" (65). Randall understands neither Emma's lesbian interest in Lindsay nor her control of Lindsay through the purse strings, and not until after the elopement does he learn what is in Lindsay's heart, mainly self-interest and vulgar avarice. Having taken the plunge, he will soon tire of her and move on to other aimless affairs. And Hugh, no better off for having abetted Randall, loses Emma, who finds herself another "gaiety girl," Jocelyn.

Randall's rose nursery at Grayhallock, which once provided meaningful work for him, no longer holds meaning, and the pervasive motif of the rose symbolizes disenchantment rather than love. *An Unofficial Rose* is Murdoch's anti-romance of the rose, a work of comic irony in which three types of characters disastrously interact. The manipulators, who, like Emma Sands and young Miranda, resemble the Medusa-women in several of Murdoch's novels, keep their hearts to themselves, act in their own self-interest, and sometimes manage to attain their desires. The selfish fools, or erotic dreamers, Hugh, Randall, and Penn, obsessed and deluded with love, always act in their own self-interest yet ironically fail to attain their desires. Unselfish fools, like Ann, act against their own self-interest, convinced they serve a higher good. When soldier Felix offers to Ann his love and a more felicitous life, she bungles her own chance for happiness by concealing her feelings from him, imagining herself attached forever to the worthless Randall and letting herself be manipulated by her daughter Miranda. An interesting variation on the unselfish fool is Hugh's old friend Mildred, an amiable, elderly woman married to a suspected pederast, who wants Hugh for herself but acts against her own interest by encouraging him to sell the Tintoretto, thus freeing Ann for marriage to Felix, Mildred's brother. Mildred's unselfishness pays off in the end because, although her matchmaking fails, she gets Hugh to herself on a slow boat to India.

The notion of a romantic setting, of spaces made sacred for love, also receives comic treatment in *An Unofficial Rose*. Randall's foolish flight to Rome with Lindsay creates a virtual map of erotic excess: "Randall made of Rome a sort of map of love, a series of lovepilgrimages where places were identified by embraces and ecstasy. . . . He took Lindsay to the Appian Way and made love to her behind the Tomb of Caecilia Metella. He took her to the Palatine and made love to her in the Temple of Cybele. . . . He took her to the Catacombs. He took her to the English Cemetery and would have made love to her on Keats's grave, only some American ladies arrived" (308–9).

The idea of a map of love is not a joke, however, in *Nuns and Soldiers* (1981). Sacred places in the warm south, in this case natural features of the French countryside, have the power to redeem, to transform, and to make a space for love. Whereas *An Unofficial Rose* comically exposes the folly of romance, *Nuns and Soldiers* tests the possibility of authentic love. More deeply concerned with the moral life, *Nuns and Soldiers* is comic in the traditional sense with its happy ending in which love triumphs over, in this case, class distinctions, disapproving relatives, and clashing values.

Again a death sets the plot in motion. Guy Openshaw, the cohesive intellectual and moral force in both his marriage and his extended family ("*les cousins et les tantes*"), dies prematurely after urging his wife, Gertrude, to seek happiness with another man such as his upright friend the Count. Gertrude's grief turns to love, some would say hastily—the *Hamlet* theme appears all on the surface here—when at her summer home in France she falls in love with Tim Reede, an indifferent painter and amiable hedonist whose irresponsibility and moral laxity most vividly contrast him to Guy. (Guy was the sort of stern agnostic who longed for an afterlife only so that he might be judged.) In her relationship with Tim, Gertrude has all the advantages: maturity, money, upper-bourgeois status, and a firmer moral sense. The crucial question is whether Tim can rise to the occasion of their love. In fact, both Gertrude and Tim have doubts as to whether their love might be a midsummer delusion. Tim wails, "We're under a spell. But when we go away it will fade. You'll see I'm just a dull fellow with ass's ears. Gertrude, you are deluded, you can't love me, I'm not educated, I'm not clever, I can't paint, I'm going bald"

(188). Such irony and doubt are in themselves saving graces. And the "sacred" places in the French countryside which Tim encounters and sketches, a daunting old rock face and a pure crystal pool, are ritual markers of his emotional growth, preparing him for the new, serious love of Gertrude. But when they marry, Tim conceals from Gertrude his longtime affair with the hapless artist Daisy Barrett. When Gertrude learns the truth, Tim, having little faith in himself and their love, returns to Daisy. Tim and Gertrude are reunited at last, in France, after Tim undergoes a literal test by water and symbolic rebirth in which he is nearly drowned in a rushing underground canal and spewed into the sunlight again. These adventures are an objective correlative for the journey to truth and openness essential to their marriage. The transformative factor, purging love of its delusional folly for Gertrude and Tim, is the presence of the genuine Eros, which makes itself felt in their first moments of dancing, wine, and lovemaking: "There was no doubt about the *fact* of her being in love with Tim and Tim being in love with her. This was the real, the indubitable and authoritative Eros: that unmistakable seismic shock, that total concentration of everything into one necessary being, mysterious, uncanny, unique, one of the strangest phenomena in the world" (194).

The magic of Eros is counterbalanced by the secondary characters and their loveless fates. Anne Cavidge and the Count, a lapsed nun and a soldier "in the army of the moral law" (42), ultimately lose out in the love triangles of Tim-Gertrude-Count and Anne-Count-Gertrude. Anne keeps her love for the Count secret, selflessly urging his suit with Gertrude, and finally immigrates to America, "the spy of a non-existent God" (62). And the Count permits himself to be co-opted when Gertrude offers him a "love-treaty" allowing him to remain a special member of her inner circle and live on the scraps of love she dispenses to him in the name of friendship. For the sake of avoiding romantic fantasy in *Nuns and Soldiers,* Murdoch surrounds her warm, rather Lawrentian love story (true Eros) with these cool, Jamesian ironies, and the reader feels the chill.

Murdoch, like Virginia Woolf, frequently views sexual identity as ambiguous and heterosexual orientation as provisional. Moreover, she follows both Woolf and Rosamond Lehmann in treating homosexuality sympathetically and naturally within the context of her mainstream fiction. Homosexual, bisexual, and lesbian characters abound in her novels, in and out of their closets, some of them noble and lonely, some treacherous, some silly, about like everyone else. In *A Fairly Honorable Defeat* (1970), Julius King (emperor-ruler?), a serious mischief-maker, performs a cruel experiment on Murdoch's behalf: he sets out to destroy both a stable, well-established marriage and a similar monogamous homosexual relationship. Julius calls his trick "a midsummer enchantment, with two asses!" (255). In a scarcely believable plot twist, Julius turns out to have been both a scientist working on biological weapons and, before that, a survivor of Belsen—and yet it makes thematic sense that one who has suffered and perpetrated two of the most unthinkable horrors of the twentieth century should play the role the cynic who idly wishes to prove love illusory. The experiment yields mixed results, a fairly honorable defeat. The heterosexual marriage ends in disaster: using falsely planted letters, Julius manipulates Rupert Foster and his unstable sister-in-law Morgan into a romantic affair, after which Rupert and his wife break up and Rupert drowns in the backyard pool under ambiguous circumstances. But the homosexual couple, Simon Foster and Axel Nilsson, manage to survive the suspicions Julius disseminates between them when Julius manufactures evidence of an affair between Simon and himself. Actually, Axel never doubts Simon's faithfulness, but he feels deeply hurt by the lies that Simon tells in order to cover up the *appearance* of his guilt. In the end, Axel and Simon are united by their honesty and the presence of the true Eros; like Gertrude and Tim in *Nuns and Soldiers*, they will remain in their challenging marriage. As his name implies, Axel is the more stable of the two men; the relationship revolves around him. Detesting the loose promiscuity of the underground gay scene, Axel has moderate opinions on love halfway between those of the cynic Julius and the optimist Rupert, who drowns believing in love as an absolute. Axel tells Simon that "Almost all human love is bloody selfish. If one has anything to hang onto at all one clings to it relentlessly. . . . To take refuge in love is an instinct and not a disreputable one" (424). Whereas Axel brings to the marriage intellectual power and unvarnished truth, simpler Simon is closer in his nature to the spirit of Eros. At the end we see Simon and Axel together in an authentic midsummer dream, on holiday in France, drinking wine in a sunny garden among the vine leaves, anticipating happiness.

Homosexuality is also crucial to the moral and spiritual problems presented in *The Bell* (1958). The novel's two most dynamic characters, the conscious seekers of self-understanding, are Dora Greenfield, who faces choices between values of flesh and spirit, and Michael Meade, a homosexual lay preacher, who has difficulty reconciling his erotic needs with the higher callings of the spirit. Murdoch's rural setting establishes a clear demarcation between the naturally pagan surroundings of woods and lakes, where erotic trysts occur, and the ascetic life of the Anglican Benedictine nuns, cloistered until death in their abbey. Just outside the abbey walls lies Imber Court, which Michael has established as a lay community for people who can live neither in the world nor out of it. Dora, unhappily married to a rather rigid, judgmental art historian, is in her spontaneity and careless ways allied—as her name implies—with the pagan green world, and she detests "the spiritual ruling class" of Imber Court. She gains a new sense of autonomy by participating in the mischievous adventure of retrieving an ancient monastic bell from the lake, a bell whose symbolic associations are related more to aesthetic and sexual knowledge than to the spirit. In a moment of revelation, the Botticellis, Pieros, and Gainsboroughs in the National Gallery also strengthen Dora's inner being; she is not so much dumb Dora as an inarticulate woman who experiences wordlessly the calm, the conferred dignity, and the consolation of great art, "and her heart was filled with love for the pictures" (191). By the end of the novel Dora feels ready to leave behind both her dry husband and her loosely hedonistic summer lover and move forward to begin a new life in Bath.

Whereas Dora appears to arrive at an aesthetic synthesis of spirit and flesh through art, Michael seems more deeply torn and more deeply made to suffer by society because of his hidden homosexuality and his attraction to young men. Being gay kept Michael from the priesthood. Some years earlier, Michael, then a schoolmaster, fell passionately in love with a student, Nick Fawley, and although the idyll amounted to nothing more than holding hands and bestowing light caresses, Nick cruelly betrayed Michael to the headmaster, implying that more serious behavior had occurred. History repeats itself. Nick is present at Imber Court, and so is Toby Gashe, a charming, callow boy who looks like Donatello's *David*. When Michael kisses Toby in the woods after drinking too much cider in the village, satanic Nick betrays Michael a second time by inducing Toby to "confess" the story to Michael's colleague James Tayper Pace, a hard-nosed moralist and homophobe. Thus, Michael's sexual preferences are revealed and the community of Imber Court dissolved.

Despite its melancholy ending, *The Bell* is often comic, its implications positive. The emergence of a stronger Dora and a wiser Michael at the end actually endorses the values they embody: her healthy paganism and his deeply thoughtful spiritual questing. Whereas James Tayper Pace preaches a Calvinistic Christianity that insists upon the preeminence of moral legalism, Michael Meade, as his name suggests, preaches a mediate path of realistic striving toward perfection starting with an affirmation of one's identities and abilities, a pilgrimage that Murdoch clearly endorses.

The pattern of an inner journey or pilgrimage occurs with increasing frequency in Murdoch's novels, always carrying the possibility of a movement toward enlightenment. Joyce Carol Oates proposes, "the work that is central to an understanding of Murdoch's oeuvre is Plato's allegory of the cave: I suggest that all of Murdoch's novels are commentaries on it" (31). While one might argue that nearly any serious work of fiction aims at extricating ourselves from the cave, Murdoch's novels explicitly allude to Plato's allegorical setting. In *Metaphysics as a Guide to Morals* she insists, "We must transform base egoistic energy and vision (low Eros) into high spiritual energy and vision (high Eros)" (24). "Eros" she defines as "the continuous operation of spiritual *energy*, desire, intellect, love . . . the force of magnetism and attraction which joins us to the world. . . . It gives sense to the idea of loving good, something absolute and unique" (496). This notion of love as a transformable magnetic energy binding us to the world, and possibly to the good, helps to explain some crucial dramatic moments in her novels.

For example, Charles Arrowby in *The Sea, the Sea* misinterprets Plato's myth and inverts the meaning of the cave when he imagines his love for the illusive long-lost Hartley to be the genuine article, mistaking his desire for reality: "O my darling, how clearly I can see you now. Surely this is perception, not imagination. The light in the cavern is daylight, not fire" (79). Clearly, Bottom's dream is also the dream of the prisoner in Plato's cave. By the end of the novel, after several disastrous encounters with Hartley and her family, Charles somewhat more willingly acknowledges Hartley's existence as another human being, apart from his desires, and though scarcely enlightened, he is better prepared to confront whatever comes next in his "demon-ridden pilgrimage" (502).

A literal cave serves as the means to enlightenment in *The Nice and the Good* (1968) when John Ducane, a good man who fancies himself capable of judging others, undergoes a series of moral crises while investigating the suicide of a colleague. The climax occurs when John becomes trapped in a rapidly flooding sea cave at high tide while attempting to rescue Pierce, son of the widow Mary Clothier, and Pierce's dog Mingo. In the icy cold Ducane manages to guide Pierce and the dog up through a narrow rock chimney and finally out into the light and safety. Such physical ordeals constitute a means of moral testing in Murdoch's novels, just as the features of Plato's cave constitute metaphors for states of the soul's enlightenment. First Ducane learns to acknowledge his own pitiful, self-preoccupied mortality: stranded in a flooding shaft, he sees himself as "a little rat, a busy little scurrying rat" (263). Then, vowing to kill the rat in himself, he thinks "If I ever get out of here I will be no man's judge" (263). And finally he reaches an understanding that "To love and to reconcile and to forgive, only this matters. All power is sin and all law frailty. Love is the only justice" (263). Mary, fearing her son drowned, carries this understanding one step further; she feels "a love so impersonal and so cold it can scarcely be recognized, a love devoid of beauty" (265), a love that she can feel for the dead, like Gabriel Conroy in Joyce's story "The Dead."

A momentary glimpse of this same selfless love is granted to Effingham Cooper in *The Unicorn*. Facing imminent death, mired in a liquid hole of mud in a bog that literally sucks him down into the earth, Effingham sees that, given the extinction of the self, "What was left was everything else, all that was not himself, that object which he had never before seen and upon which he now gazed with the passion of a lover" (167). Effingham sees "with a clarity which was one with the increasing light, that with the death of the self the world becomes quite automatically the object of a perfect love" (176). Although Effingham survives, he fails to bring his vision of love of the world down to the realm of lower Eros, for he is an ineffectual bureaucrat enmeshed in the irresistible mechanism of a gothic horror plot.

Even without Murdoch's writings on Plato, a quasi-Platonic pattern reveals itself in the fiction, a pattern variously influenced by the mysticism of Eastern religions, the psychological insights of existentialism, and the moral teachings of Christianity. Advancing beyond illusions about the self and others and beyond the demands of the self, the soul (mind) on its way to enlightenment must experience the death of the ego, learn to love others in all their incomprehensible otherness, and learn to love the world without the self, thus perhaps attaining a glimpse of *the* good. Successful pilgrimages like this are rare, and they do not make very good fiction anyway. Murdoch wisely chooses to weave her fiction from the failures and compromises of ordinary life, its comedy and grim ironies, but the underlying presence, not so much of a value system as of a systematic pursuit of value, makes itself urgently felt in her work.

The nightmare experience of a life utterly lacking in love is beautifully portrayed in *A Word Child* (1975), arguably Murdoch's finest novel. The narrator, Hilary Burde, presents himself to the reader as a man made irredeemably brutal, harsh, and unlovable by the burden of remorse and self-loathing he carries as a result of having caused the death of Anne Jopling, wife of his friend Gunnar, when the two men were young Oxford dons. Rising out of the most abject origins through serious linguistic study, Hilary managed to ruin his academic career by falling in love with Anne and then causing the motor accident in which she died even as she was trying to break off her affair with Hilary. He regards himself as a murderer, his life blackened forever. In this winter's tale of rain, fog, mist, and snow, Hilary's extreme pessimism creates a dark cosmos around him; rendered in the light of Hilary's brutally precise language, his London emits a stark, almost splendid, misery. Barely existing in a deadening government job, Hilary rigidly parcels out his weeks into "days" when he dines with various people, including his hapless mistress Thomasina and his half-sister Crystal, a very plain and simple soul and the object of his only (tense and possessive) affection. His particular hellish cave is the Inner Circle of the Underground, where he likes to ride round and round until the station bars open.

In *A Word Child* Murdoch employs a favorite device, the twice-told plot, enacted first as tragedy and second as tragicomedy. Hilary's past redounds upon him when Gunnar's second wife, Lady Kitty, "courts" Hilary through her maid, a mysterious Indian girl called Biscuit, in order to enlist Hilary's help in exorcising Gunnar's own obsession with the past and the ghost of Anne. Hilary eventually reconciles with Gunnar until he learns of Hilary's infatuation with Kitty. A scuffle on a jetty leads to Kitty's death in the freezing Thames and Hilary's near-death ordeal in the rushing water.

Murdoch powerfully engages the reader in *A Word Child* not only by her direct, forceful style and suspenseful plot, but also through the particular tone of Hilary's narration and the relation it establishes with the reader. We are invited to engage deeply in Hilary's story, but not allowed to love him: the excessiveness of his remorse and the brutality of his candor leave room for neither pity nor love. Hilary cannot live within the circle of humanity until he finally comprehends that his remorse need not be infinite, since it is not logical. Having "raged at the accidental," Hilary has nonetheless insisted "upon being the author of everything," a victim of the gods himself playing God (382). In the denouement, which occurs in T. S. Eliot's church, Hilary learns to weep and "to conjugate the verb of love" (380). His painful and reluctant journey out of his cave is dramatized within the reader, through one's slow, unwilling process of identification with this dark, recalcitrant character.

Murdoch's recent novels continue to hold out the possibility of metaphysical discovery. As their titles imply, *The Philosopher's Pupil* (1983), *The Good Apprentice* (1985), *The Book and the Brotherhood* (1987), and *The Message to the Planet* (1989), all long, ambitious novels, demonstrate Murdoch's increasing preoccupation with searching out truth, apprenticing oneself to it, and inscribing and imparting it. Even more prominently than in her earlier work, magical places in these novels—the underground hot springs of Ennistone in *The Philosopher's Pupil,* the mysterious towered house Seegard in *The Good Apprentice,* or the garden at Ballmain with the mysterious Axel Stone in *The Message to the Planet*—exert a force field, transforming the characters who enter them in a way that parallels love's transformations of the ego. From her early experiments with the gothic, Murdoch learned to use atmospheric settings as pervading presences that could manifest enchantments or inflictions of the soul, like Hannah Crean-Smith's castle Gaze in *The Unicorn.* In these later novels, the "sacred" spaces seem to promise revelations from a place beyond the self to searchers like Edward in *The Good Apprentice* or Alfred Ludens in *The Message to the Planet.* Frustratingly, and realistically, however, Murdoch always stops short of revelation, bringing us back to the realm of lower Eros.

In *The Message to the Planet,* for example, Ludens, whose gloomy nature belies his name, loves and loses the young Irini, daughter of his friend Marcus Vallar (valor?). But the one Ludens really loves is Marcus, a mysterious charismatic figure and modern-day prophet without a religion who, having advanced, like Dr. Faustus, through various forms of learning—mathematics, art, philosophy—finally turns to forms of mysticism. Marcus commits suicide after preaching to a multitude of New Age believers who have followed him to Ballmain, a rural mental institution, and who end up stoning him. Christian, Jewish, and pagan themes and symbols so deeply infuse this novel that much seems at stake—at least to his disciple Ludens—in Marcus's quest for truth, some universal understanding, perhaps. The disappointment to both Ludens and the reader occurs as Marcus's papers are burned, the meaning of his final act is indecipherable, and the planet must go on without receiving the message. *The Message to the Planet* is a fine novel, a satisfying "read," but it nonetheless leaves the reader profoundly unsatisfied about the religious and metaphysical questions it raises. This dissatisfaction is obviously deliberate, a lesson. Murdoch raises frustrating questions about the existence of God and the nature of reality. One has no choice but to reexamine and to doubt the faith one has placed, as a reader, in both Marcus and Iris Murdoch's novel, a self-examination that continues after the novel is put aside.

Another messianic figure makes an appearance in London and later dies in a mental hospital in *The Green Knight* (1993), but in this case Peter Mir, a Russian Jewish Buddhist whose name means "world" and "peace," manages to carry out a series of morally significant actions before his mysterious demise. Physically intervening in a Cain-and-Abel struggle between two brothers, Lucas and Clement, Peter accidentally receives the blow to the head meant for Clement and then serves as the bearer of both justice and mercy for Lucas by administering a symbolic nick to Lucas's flesh, as the Green Knight did to Gawain. Successive chapter titles—"Justice," "Mercy," and "Eros"—suggest an upward moral progression, as do the several allusions to Dante's *Purgatorio* and the work of the Pearl Poet. With its bright imagery of medievalism and pervasive references to art and magic, *The Green Knight* is more festive in tone than Murdoch's several previous novels. She hints at a splendid dream of universal love, never to be synthesized or realized, but perceived only in scattered form among the great religious traditions and the stories and arts of East and West.

"Art, especially literature," Murdoch writes in *The Fire and the Sun*, "is a great hall of reflection where we can all meet and where anything under the sun can be examined and considered" (86). The house of fiction, with its many mansions, represents for Murdoch a place where teaching and learning about human nature can naturally occur; she opens up fictional spaces for that reflective purpose. The novelty and pleasure of her novels—the suspense, adventure, and wild twists of plot—keep the enterprise from ever seeming academic. Murdoch has a fine power of storytelling, and she fabricates her narratives out of love as she defines it: the energy that binds mortal fools to one another and to their world.

Notes

1. Anatole Broyard, "In the Emergency Ward of the Mind," *New York Times Book Review* 4 Feb. 1990: 3.

2. Robert Burton, *The Anatomy of Melancholy* (6th ed., 1651; New York: Farrar and Rinehart, 1927), 737.

3. Robert Hoskins, "Iris Murdoch's Midsummer Nightmare," *Twentieth Century Literature* 18.3 (July 1972): 191–98.

4. Joyce Carol Oates, "The Novelists: Iris Murdoch," rev. of *The Sea, the Sea,* by Iris Murdoch, *New Republic* 18 Nov. 1978: 28. Further page references are given in the text.

Selected Works by Iris Murdoch

The Bell. New York: Viking, 1958.

The Black Prince. New York: Viking, 1973.

The Book and the Brotherhood. London: Chatto & Windus, 1987.

Existentialists and Mystics: Writings on Philosophy and Literature. Ed. Iris Murdoch, Peter J. Conradi, and George Steiner. New York: Allen Lane/Penguin Press, 1998.

A Fairly Honorable Defeat. New York: Viking, 1970.

The Fire and the Sun: Why Plato Banished the Artists. Oxford: Clarendon Press, 1977.

The Good Apprentice. New York: Viking, 1985.

The Green Knight. 1993. New York: Viking, 1994.

Jackson's Dilemma. New York: Viking, 1996.

The Message to the Planet. London: Chatto & Windus, 1989.

Metaphysics as a Guide to Morals. New York: Viking Penguin, 1992.

The Nice and the Good. New York: Viking, 1968.

Nuns and Soldiers. New York: Viking, 1981.

The Philosopher's Pupil. London: Chatto & Windus, Hogarth Press, 1983.

The Sea, the Sea. New York: Viking, 1978.

Under the Net. New York: Viking, 1954.
The Unicorn. New York: Viking, 1963.
An Unofficial Rose. New York: Viking, 1962.
A Word Child. New York: Viking, 1975.

Selected Works about Iris Murdoch

(Compiled by Sarah Mackey and Roberta S. White)

Baldanza, Frank. *Iris Murdoch.* New York: Twayne Publishers, 1974.

Bayley, John. *Elegy for Iris.* New York: St. Martins Press, 1999.

Begnal, Kate. *Iris Murdoch: A Reference Guide.* Boston: G. K. Hall, 1987.

Bellamy, Michael O. "An Interview with Iris Murdoch." *Contemporary Literature* 18 (1977): 129–40.

Biles, Jack I. "An Interview with Iris Murdoch." *British Novelists since 1900.* Ed. Jack I. Biles. New York: AMS, 1987. 299–310.

Bloom, Harold, ed. *Iris Murdoch: Modern Critical Views.* New York: Chelsea House, 1986.

Bove, Cheryl Browning. *A Character Index and Guide to the Fiction of Iris Murdoch.* New York: Garland, 1986.

Byatt, A. S. *Degrees of Freedom: The Novels of Iris Murdoch.* London: Chatto & Windus, 1965.

Gerstenberger, Donna. *Iris Murdoch.* Lewisburg, PA: Bucknell UP, 1975.

Glover, Stephen. "An Interview with Iris Murdoch." *New Review* 3 (November 1976): 56–59.

Haffenden, John. "John Haffenden Talks to Iris Murdoch." *Literary Review* (London) 58 (April 1983): 31–35.

Hague, Angela. *Iris Murdoch's Comic Vision.* Selinsgrove, PA: Susquehanna UP, 1983.

Heyd, Ruth. "An Interview with Iris Murdoch." *Windsor Review* 1 (1965): 138–43.

Meyers, Jeffrey. "An Interview with Iris Murdoch." *Denver Quarterly* 26 (Summer 1991): 102–11.

Modern Fiction Studies 15.3: Iris Murdoch Special Number (Autumn 1969).

Rabinovitz, Rubin. *Iris Murdoch.* New York: Columbia University Publications, 1968.

Rose, W. K. "An Interview with Iris Murdoch." *Shenandoah* 19.2 (1968): 3–22.

Sage, Lorna. "Female Fictions: The Women Novelists." *The Contemporary English Novel.* Ed. Malcolm Bradbury and David Palmer. New York: Holmes and Meier, 1980. 67–87.

Slaymaker, William E. "An Interview with Iris Murdoch." *Papers on Language and Literature: A Journal for Scholars and Critics of Language and Literature* 21 (Fall 1985): 425–32.

Todd, Richard. *Iris Murdoch: The Shakespearean Interest.* New York: Barnes and Noble, 1979.

Wolfe, Peter. *The Disciplined Heart: Iris Murdoch and Her Novels.* Columbia: U of Missouri P, 1966.

2

"Transformed and Translated": The Colonized Reader of Doris Lessing's Canopus in Argos *Space Fiction*

Susan Rowland

Doris Lessing's fiction has always regarded artistic representation as a political act. From the very first novel, *The Grass Is Singing* (1950), which sets a Mary who failed to bear a redemptive child on the regressive white colonial road until a black Moses leads her to the promised land of death, she has tested the extent to which any particular society can bear to be represented. The *Children of Violence* series (1952–69) interposed a female bildungsroman to contest a colonial and patriarchal culture (*Martha Quest* [1952], *A Proper Marriage* [1954]), and used the resources of the realist novel, lauded in *The Small Personal Voice* (1957) as "the highest form of prose writing" (8), to fragment the impersonal claims of Communist theory in *A Ripple from the Storm* (1958). Lessing then turned to reexamine the realist novel's own representational capacities as she moved toward Sufi beliefs concerning the interconnected potentialities of higher consciousness in *The Four-Gated City* (1969). Her most acclaimed novel, *The Golden Notebook* (1962), challenged the representability of experience under pressure of breakdown, both mental and political, by fracturing the traditional form and thus providing a devastating analysis of Western women's social, economic, and psychic frictions. This novel, above all of Lessing's others, has generated profound feminist readings.

Thereafter Lessing mediated between the appeal of realism and metafictional or metaphysical needs until the writing of the *Canopus in Argos* space fiction (1979–83), which seemed to produce a deterministic and alienated universe. *Canopus in Argos* has provoked diverse critical reactions,[1] and it is worth considering the distance it has strayed from Lessing's political and artistic conceptions of "representation" described in "A Small Personal Voice." The most urgent political message of this essay (first published in 1957) is the universal threat of nuclear war, "the kinship of possible destruction" (13) that might be sparked by a "Chairman [who] will say: 'I represent the people.' And the people is the brown man sitting under the tree . . . the people is me" (14). Interestingly, the collective threat appears to be figured in a metaphor of white colonization, culminating in Lessing's necessary identification with the colonized (since nuclear war is not *local*). I say "appears" because we are not given the race of the "Chairman," though the implication in 1957 is surely white and male. At the end of the same essay, Lessing makes a claim for the artist to "represent" the people, arguing that literary form has a political extension: "one is a writer at all because one represents, makes articulate, is continuously and invisibly fed by, numbers of people who are inarticulate, to whom one belongs, to whom one is responsible" (24). One could argue that Lessing uses nuclear terror to submerge her position as a white colonizer (as a British subject but also one who grew up in the then Southern Rhodesia, now Zimbabwe, however opposed to the regime) and allow her identification with "the people" in a politicized artistic role. I contend that the galactic empires of *Canopus in Argos* constitute precise examinations of political, psychic, and artistic colonization literally going "beyond" but expressing Lessing's persistent theme of Empire.

The Small Personal Voice lacks the territories of the psyche first explored in *The Golden Notebook,* particularly in the role of the Jungian analyst, Mrs. Marks, and the mental record of the Blue Notebook. Lessing, an interested but not uncritical reader of Jung, considers him "limited. But useful as far as he went,"[2] and Jungian studies have been the route of much successful critical analysis of Lessing's work[3] in tracing archetypes and individuation patterns (whereby consciousness is deconstructed by the active unconscious into a continuing "marriage" or relationship). Such criticism tends to be apolitical, since Jung's theory of archetypes as inherited psychic potentials appears to discount cultural differences. So far, few critics have paid attention to Jungian ideas in *Canopus in Argos.*

However, even a cursory reading of the first volume, *Shikasta,* can reveal resemblances between Lessing's Canopeans, who have been "crystallized, into forms as different as snowflakes" (17), and Jung's archetypes, which "are not determined as regards their content, but only as regards their form and then only to a very limited degree. . . . Its form . . . might perhaps be compared to the axial system of a crystal, which, as it were, preforms the crystalline structure in the mother liquid, although it has no material existence of its own."[4] Canopeans are, like archetypes, "androgynous" (142), and they use "crystalline" (43) spacecraft. *Shikasta*'s chief Canopean representative is Johor, which means "pearl" in Arabic (Caracciolo 15), a frequent Jungian sign for the archetype of the "self,"[5] an unconscious structure to which the ego becomes a subject in individuation. Yet the Canopeans cannot be "represented" as archetypes because, as Jung's definition suggests, archetypes themselves are irrepresentable and can be posited only from their derivatives, archetypal images. The crystalline archetype or Canopean can be represented only as incarnated or imaged: such images will be colored or animated by local cultural conditions. Thus Canopeans visit as members of local species as Johor manifests himself as a native on Shikasta, or are born into a particular culture stripped of other identity and memory except for the crystalline imprint of the Signature from Canopus that they must discover within. Therefore Taufiq becomes John Brent-Oxford and Johor becomes George Sherban. Canopeans enter Shikasta and realist fiction as "characters" bearing traces of a psychic colonization that they can choose to ignore as Taufiq/John does and Johor/George does not. Johor's selected documents tell us that the main cause of fruitful Rohanda's change to broken Shikasta was a "disaster" (35), a fault in the stars recalling the frequent depiction of archetypes as a star-filled heaven.[6]

This deterministic universe displeases many critics. Lorna Sage, in her powerful essay "The Available Space," calls the Canopeans "remarkably pure figures of power" and states that she, as a reader, feels "'colonized' by a benevolent . . . authority" (31). To a certain extent, this is an inevitable reaction to novels based on ideological premises not shared by the critic. Lessing's Jungian, alchemical, Sufi, and mystical ideas of the essential oneness of created reality are explored in terms of physics in *The Making of the Representative for Planet 8*. All is "a unity . . . patterns of matter, matter of a kind, since everything is—webs of matter . . . intermingling" (158). A reader unwilling to transfer ideas current in physics, such as chaos theory, to psychic and social structures, as Lessing does in

Canopus in Argos, will likely view Canopus as yet another imperial trope aiming solely at literal domination or, as Johor puts it, ensuring "the creation of ever-evolving Sons and Daughters of the Purpose" (52). Canopus, in this sense, is an exaggerated version of the Jungian principle that privileges unconscious meaningful potential over a selfish, limited ego, a structure now dangerously hardened into literal domination by an alien Other. This harsh stance is not softened by the Canopean method of activating unconscious paradigms within, thereby apparently offering choice. Johor tries to recall John Brent-Oxford to his superior but unconscious knowledge, through messages from his unconscious, including dreams (106–7), but real choice is circumscribed in a *dis-asterous* universe.

The colonized reader is a dispirited one, but *Canopus in Argos* colonizes the reader in two senses: first, as Sage observes, by the Canopean ideology itself, and second, by the way Lessing positions the reader within the texts. The reader of *Shikasta* is a translator. Opening with a partial and nonchronological selection of documents, mainly authored by Johor, and followed by the diary of Rachel Sherban (sister to George/Johor) and other documents, the novel through its structure and Shikastan perspective defamiliarizes Earth history and its "alien" reality. The name "Earth" is never used, and virtually no terrestrial terms appear in the "Canopean" part of Shikasta, but because Lessing saturates readers with tropes and structures from Earth history and sacred literature, she forces us into a continual translation of this outrageously fragmented text (e.g., "SEE History of Shikasta, VOLS. 2955–3015" [100]). Part two does employ Earth names while eschewing the word "Earth" itself, yet the unfamiliar future setting and the charismatic presence of George, whom we know to be Johor, forces a continual retranslation into the imperial Canopean ideology of part one, especially as, through the sympathetic Rachel, the reader feels constantly challenged to read beyond the realist novel to the extra-terrestrial, extra-representational elements of *Shikasta.* In this novel, reading as translation is completely inescapable and highly problematic. Through the difficulties Lessing introduces— such as the paucity of clues in part one, the requirement to remember the geographical schemes of "North West Fringes" (Europe) and "Isolated Northern Continent" (United States)—the reader must constantly translate between two separate ideological perceptions of reality, the science fictional Canopean empire of psyche and matter, versus the reader's own supported by Rachel, who prefers personal relationships and writes from the domain of traditional realism. Thus Lessing builds into the reading experience of *Shikasta* the difficulty and impossibility of "pure" translation between different cultural perceptions. The novel encodes competing discourses, so by translating Shikasta into Earth, the reader endorses a power relationship within the text, appropriating Earth history in Shikastan terms: the reader is *colonizing* the novel.

This manipulation into the Canopean position is further compromised by the implications of reading Shikasta as Earth. Such a reading transports the reader from simply seeing with the crystalline clarity of the Canopean perspective to actually becoming a citizen of Shikasta, a polluted degraded planet: Shikastan citizens are utterly incapable of clear thinking, for their world has been hopelessly colonized by aliens, both biologically and psychically. We learn that pure natives, themselves reshaped by Canopus, die out in favor of the extra-terrestrial Giant-native "cross" (127), and that genes from the space empires of Shammat, Sirius, and Canopus have contributed to the heterogeneous stock.

Consequently, because readers cannot find secure positions either as colonizers/translators of the text or as colonized citizens, we therefore view ourselves as mentally inadequate captives. We read that Canopean colonization "raises" natives, whereas the evil empire, Shammat, causes minds to degrade, but we have yet to explore whether Lessing can convincingly distinguish between the imperial discourses of the two empires. What is apparent so far is Lessing's depiction of the inescapability of the imperial trope for her readers (expected to be mainly white Western?) represented here in the reading experience. *Shikasta* reproduces this dynamic of the colonizing/colonized reader in the description of the Trial of the White Races (374–419) conveyed in the reports of the Chinese, the latest colonial rulers of a future "Europe."

At a time of mass starvation and overpopulation, anger at the historic cruelty of the white races reaches genocidal proportions and focuses on the drama of the Mock Trial. Typically, George Sherban acquires a key role as chief prosecutor for the dark races, but because he has only an Indian grandmother and in fact looks entirely white, his position becomes a joke during the trial (379). In fact, we realize that someone, presumably George, has avoided the appearance of black/white polarization by mixing the races on both sides of the room and by complicating the lighting at this trial, which, notably, takes place at night. Throughout *Shikasta*, Lessing's techniques, characters, and incidents invite the reader to develop other perspectives of events. In addition to the broad invitation to guess George's Canopean agency, Lessing here provides the problematic situation of the narrator, a Chinese colonial official whose summaries of reports gradually force him to read unmentionable analysis of the new Chinese empire with its unstated policy of population reduction through starvation and through its encouragement of racial hostility. The trial describes the reality behind the British policy of "benevolence" (403) in Africa, but ironically, the Chinese use the term "Benevolent Rule" to justify their empire. When Chen Lui tries to direct the dangerous word (and the reader) to other meanings, his superiors decide that he has translated enough to secure "beneficent correction" (419) until his death. Although Chen Lui ostensibly writes for a reader within the novel, Ku Yuang, he essentially encourages the external reader to question the term "benevolent rule," for it is that concept, though differently expressed, that the Canopeans claim. If Chen Lui can translate his empire into an-other culture, then the reader can translate the *difference* in the Canopean way. But the difference, the untranslatable residue between British and Chinese cruelty and Canopean nurture, in fact proves unstable. We also see a *similarity* in language, in roles, while unavoidably remembering that we perceive the Canopean imperial trope from the positions of degraded, muddled, colonized, and colonizing Shikastans. The novel allows the reading of the Canopeans as the literal, dominant empire while insisting that the reader recognize this as an act of translation made not from a neutral position, a crystalline clear vision, but from a culturally contaminated perspective. The reader must recognize such a reading as a translation into the literal or the "proper," the term preceding the literal which, as Eric Cheyfitz argues in *The Poetics of Imperialism,* is related to seizing property, and is a trope of aggressive colonization: "The notion of the *proper,* I argue, must be understood in relation to European notions of property and identity. As for the *literal* . . . its figurative use for the notion of the *proper* has historically taken on a metaphysical force that naturalises writing, concealing it as technology—that is, as a form of politics" (xviii). Colonizing the text in the terms of our own fictions of cultural identity, the reader translates Canopeans into a literal empire. Lessing does not argue that this is an incorrect reading, but she makes us realize that it is a political reading.

Yet just as Lessing invites and problematizes translation, she spreads it into modes other than the literal. This methodology suggests itself

particularly in the use of fictions in imperial discourses with the Canopeans who have Sufi, a superior system of teaching stories to develop the
desired cosmic consciousness. In fact, fictions and metaphors provide
most of our information about Canopus: we learn about the androgynous archetypal Canopeans only through their incarnations as culturally
specific archetypal images, and through the use of stories and metaphors
in developing civilizations. Once Shikasta has fallen into individualistic
Shammat, Johor tries to maintain some ghost of Canopus with his metaphor of SOWF, "Substance Of We Feeling" (96), which, we are told, he
has devised because damaged Shikastan brains can hope to retain nothing else. The sheer difficulty of literal translation into Earth concepts,
its politicization, and the persistence of Canopean fictions rather than
Canopean facts encourage the reader to maintain *also* a sense of the fictionality of the Canopean empire within the experience of reading in this
explicitly science fiction novel. The structure of the text, and the constant
demands that characters within the narrative strive for other readings,
fosters and encourages external readers to perceive the Canopeans as also
fictions (residing in incompleteness of translation, for if Shikasta is also
not Earth, then we are aware of *Shikasta* as fiction), to perceive them as
Other voices as well as imperial agents.

If the Canopeans are also read metaphorically, then *Shikasta* adopts an
air of postmodernity, interrogating its own fictional ideology. Reinforc-
ing this postmodern role is the perception of *Shikasta* as a fictional macrocosm of Lessing's entire oeuvre, a metatext, that not only reexamines
old themes of racial oppression, female subordination, and class conflict
but also discerns future fictions, as in Johor's "case histories," which function as seeds for novels. The enumeration of terrorist types anticipates
The Good Terrorist (1985), problem children, *The Fifth Child* (1988). In addition, early Lessing characters reappear, redefined in science fiction,
most notably Lynda Coldridge from *The Four-Gated City* as a Canopean
agent (226, 230–39, 431). The entire *Canopus in Argos* series develops this
role as not only a fictional space of ideological empires, to form a *canopy*
over Lessing's work, but also as textual space, reprising and extending her
thematical concerns.

The encoded sense of the fictionality of the Canopeans receives still
further support through continued readings of envoys such as Johor as
archetypal images of unrepresentable crystalline archetypes. *Shikasta* operates two poles of an unstable reading process: first, a reading that trans-

lates the reader into a Shikastan so under the literal authority of the Canopeans/archetypal images, and second, a reading aware of the resistance to translation with the Canopeans as fictional metaphors of Otherness. These readings together reproduce the Jungian structure of individuation whereby the ego makes meaning or "reads reality" by a continual dialogue with archetypal images. The Jungian ego is conceived as imperious: it desires to translate unconscious material into its own terms, the literal, or in Cheyfitz's words, to make "proper" the unassimilable realm of the unconscious, to translate it into the ego's property.[7] Therefore the reader of *Shikasta* as a colonizer, appropriating Earth's political and sacred history and situating him- or herself as a Shikastan who confronts a literal Canopean empire, experiences one Jungian mode of understanding—but one always in tension with, and inseparable from, the unconscious reshaping of the ego by revealing the literal translation as inadequate, as an inauthentic fantasy of dominance. In Jungian individuation, deconstruction of the ego occurs by also reading archetypal images as fictional, metaphorical, provisional, culturally colored manifestations of a plural psyche not open to conquest. *Shikasta's* situating of the reader reproduces Jungian individuation as a way of politicizing reading experience, thus revealing the inescapability of the imperial trope for readers within Western culture. It also engenders a re-cognition using the Jungian structure of encounter with the Other that aims to develop the reader's consciousness in the manner of a Sufi teaching story.

Jung's typical narrative of individuation is one of "sacred marriage," union with an-other that remains untranslatable into the *same*.[8] The second volume of *Canopus in Argos, The Marriages between Zones Three, Four, and Five* (1980), seizes upon this structure and attempts to move beyond the duality of the marriage plot and to explore issues of psychic and physical colonizing of Other realms. The zones start in mutual hostility, declining in fertility. The order from the "Providers" (12), presumed to be Canopeans, decrees that Al.Ith, the queen of agrarian, utopian Zone Three, must marry Ben Ata, the king of patriarchal, militaristic Zone Four. This union initiates beneficial movements between zones, renewing cultures and stimulating personal individuation. However this positive cultural exchange eludes "pure" translation, again revealed as a myth. Although Al.Ith asks for a dictionary to define the Zone Four use of the word "love" (117), she can never completely express her Zone Three self in her husband's land. Equally, she realizes that she perceives Zone Two through the filter of her Zone Three culture: what she sees as blue may in fact be "an iridescence of flames" (236). Encountering the Other in this Jungian "marriage" structure results in process, but resists a hierarchical discourse of colonial dominance. It is Zone Five, apparently the "lowest" culture, that produces the key to the movement into the highest, Zone Two (280).

Like Al.Ith, exposing the impossibility of pure translation, the narrator Lusik claims the impossibility of pure representation because artists of Zones Three and Four produce different images for different cultural resonances. Lusik and Al.Ith are almost split Canopeans from *Shikasta*, with Al.Ith taking the incarnated role and Lusik the role of one who makes meanings for a specific culture. Like the Canopeans, Lusik draws fictionality, here the constructed quality of this fable, into the reading experience. He also forces the reader to address the darker side of authorship, the use of fiction in oppressive power structures, just as Jungian individuation contains the concept of the shadow, the destructive side. To represent violent impulses is not to control them: "Describing, we become. We even—and I've seen it and have shuddered—summon" (243).

Although *The Marriages* contains comparatively little to shudder at, issues of representation, first articulated in *The Small Personal Voice* (the male dictator claiming to represent the people in the political sphere and the author representing the silent in the artistic), do cast a long shadow. As embodiments of their realms, Al.Ith and Ben Ata are extensions of Lusik—the artist as shaper—into the text, thereby dispersing the autocratic functions of rule to the Providers whose very non-appearance contributes to the fictive feel of the text. As female head of a cooperative society, Al.Ith appears the antithesis of the male dictator, but, interestingly, these ideal "representative" rulers have been contaminated by the threat of weapons of mass destruction. Zone Four's "death ray fortresses," suggested by "strangers" (122), promote antagonism between zones. The very language of "death ray fortresses" plunges us into "science fiction," and Lessing simultaneously reveals them as fictions, designed to intimidate, thus demonstrating that even ideal ruler-authors cannot entirely divest themselves of the shadow side of their *authority*.

Similarly, in *Shikasta*, the archetypal Canopeans attempt to disperse Lessing's own authorship, her authority, but they find themselves in continual battle with Shammat, clearly the hideous progeny of the white male dictator in *The Small Personal Voice*. Shammat is *different* from

Canopus: the two types of representatives are different but, in their imperial discourse, not entirely *separate,* just as the representative author never remains wholly free of the colonizing, imperial shadow. Lessing's two types of representation in the early essay become two imperial discourses, the metaphorical authorial Canopeans and the literal dictatorship of Shammat: different but not separable, as demonstrated by the persistence of the literal mode of understanding the Canopean empire, which draws it close to Shammat in its appearance of power. The empires exist in a Jungian trope of deconstruction between ego translation (colonizing the novel into literal empires that simultaneously and ideologically colonize the reader) and archetypal representation (metaphorical, recognizing the inauthenticity of translation). It is not possible to have one way of representing without a shadow of the Other. In addition to the Canopeans' roles as authors of teaching stories, as fictional archetypal images, a literal reading of the Canopeans inescapably establishes their role as an empire of control and authority. The Shammat empire, functioning both to resemble and to differ enormously from Canopus, simultaneously offers and problematizes analogy.

The reproduction of Jungian individuation in the reading process politicizes this literal dictator/fictional author dialectic by making the reader conscious of the shadow of colonial history structuring her perceptions. Eric Cheyfitz argues that metaphor, being inseparable from the literal, also constitutes a colonial mode of reading: "I do not agree that metaphor is a privileged place, located 'outside' of or 'beyond' or 'above' the colonial and imperial politics of language" (108).

Lessing's use of Jung here apparently endorses such a conclusion while asserting the difference encoded within metaphor. If we remember that Sufi teachers, like archetypal images, work with cultural material rather than outside it, then Lessing's Sufi ideology clearly desires the difference of metaphor to provide an alternative reading of empire, while not pretending to be outside or to escape colonial culture and structures of thinking.

Significantly, Lessing depicts Al.Ith's final destination, Zone Two, as a place of "crystalline yet liquid" (237) earth, where her thoughts are "the creatures of this unfamiliar place" (238). It is a place of image where she can almost see people "as if flames trembled into being," and where she feels most strongly "at home" (238). Zone Two appears to be the realm of the archetypal imagination that recalls the crystalline Canopeans. Another designation of it, however, could be death. From the perspective of Zone Three it is blue, the color of mourning in that zone,[9] and Al.Ith hopes to find her dead horse Yori "there, but a transformed and translated version of him . . . so dreamed Al.Ith" (242). Virtually the only use of the word "translated" in *Canopus in Argos,* it here returns to an earlier sense of "translated to heaven." Only in the realm of the plural archetypal psyche can translation occur *differently* to the political appropriation reproduced elsewhere. Nevertheless, this difference does not take it outside the topos of colonization explored in the whole novel series. Al.Ith's move to Zone Two is part of the cultural exchanges contained within the individuation narratives figured elsewhere in this text as "marriage."

Lessing has dispersed her authority behind the archetypal Canopeans in order to colonize Earth history for *Canopus in Argos.* As with any imperial discourse, she gives back to the colonized (the readers) a mistranslated, ideologically biased history. Her envoys, or archetypal images, are culturally colored by her mode of debunking religious and political myths. For example, Johor/George's early encounter with a Miriam (278) reminds us that, by the end of *Shikasta,* he is a Moses leading survivors to a promised land of new sacred cities; moreover, in his incarnation he suggests Jesus. At the same time, established religions receive criticism as perversions of Canopean truths. In *The Sirian Experiments* we learn that Canopeans employ "subtle technology" (62), and as Lessing's subtle empire they embody their author's technology in individuating the readers, reshaping interpretations. Lessing uses such Jungian ideas as archetypes, individuation, and sacred marriage to illuminate the tropes of empire and colonization that dominate not only our history but also our structures of understanding. We cannot escape reading the crystalline Canopeans as a literal empire, not securely distant from the dictator of *The Small Personal Voice,* but we remain conscious that this reading is filtered by our translating ourselves into Shikastans, so entering the colonizing process by occupying the text. By becoming Shikastan, we are told that we pollute our vision. Thus Lessing's technique, inviting readers to Other readings, endeavors to raise our consciousness as we view Canopeans as also fictive, and listen to storytelling Sufi teachers who warn that Shikasta can use their words against them, hardening them "into dogma" (145). Lessing thus enables our recognition of Shikasta as the author's fictional macrocosm and of the possibility of reading empire differently, but not separately, from the political.

In Jung's view, an unsophisticated mind perceives the psyche as "removed from and alien to the ego" (p. 13); and Lessing's subtle empire explores the political potential of Jungian ideas just as it uses Jung to demonstrate the psychic persistence of politics. If Shammat is the shadow of Canopus as literal/political empire, it is part of a continual displacement of authority (from Lessing to Canopeans, Canopeans to Shammat) that aims to offer a textual space to empire as metaphor, using Jungian paradigms that allow the reader to be colonized also by Otherness, to participate through the author's fictional use of the teaching story.

Stars signify the deterministic universe, sign of the Canopean empire as literal or "proper." Ultimately all becomes the stars' property as Al.Ith muses: "stars are what we are made of, what we are subject to" (*Canopus in Argos* 14); so, fittingly, "Canopus" and "Sirius" are terrestrial names for stars, and as such an obvious projection, another trace of science *fiction* in the texts. Not for nothing did Jung, quoting an alchemical text,[10] call the imagination the star in man. The Canopeans are messengers from the stars *and* images from the archetypal imagination. By powerfully demonstrating the way we make fictions within political and colonial tropes, Lessing's *Canopus in Argos* bids us beware how we trespass in our imaginative space (*Canopus in Argos* 14).

NOTES

1. Diverse critical reactions to *Canopus in Argos* include Kaplan and Rose, *Doris Lessing: The Alchemy of Survival,* especially Carey Kaplan's "Britain's Imperialist Past in Doris Lessing's Futuristic Fiction"; Ward Jouve, "Of Mud and Other Matter," in *White Woman Speaks with Forked Tongue;* and Fishburn, *The Unexpected Universe of Doris Lessing.*

2. Lessing in a letter to Roberta Rubenstein, quoted in Rubenstein 230–31.

3. Notable studies of Lessing using Jungian ideas include Rubenstein, *The Novelistic Vision of Doris Lessing;* Singleton, *The City and the Veld;* and Cederstrom, *Fine-Tuning the Feminine Psyche.*

4. C. G. Jung, *The Collected Works of C. G. Jung, Volume 9, pt. 1,* trans. R. F. C. Hull (London: Routledge & Kegan Paul, 1959), 79. In *The Collected Works of C. G. Jung,* ed. Sir Herbert Read, Michael Fordham, M.D., M.R.C.P., and Gerhard Adler, Ph.D., trans. R. F. C. Hull, 19 vols. (London: Routledge & Kegan Paul, 1953–77).

5. Jung, *Collected Works* 9 i, p. 160.

6. Erich Neumann, *The Origins and History of Consciousness,* trans. R. F. C. Hull (London: Routledge & Kegan Paul, 1949), 437–38.

7. Lessing, "If You Knew Sufi . . . " 12.

8. Jung, *Collected Works* 14: 469.

9. Jung, *Collected Works* 14: 300.

10. Jung, *Collected Works* 12: 277.

SELECTED WORKS BY DORIS LESSING

Canopus in Argos: Archives, Re: Colonised Planet 5, Shikasta. London: Jonathan Cape, 1979.

Canopus in Argos: Archives, The Marriages between Zones Three, Four, and Five. London: Jonathan Cape, 1980.

Canopus in Argos: Archives, The Sirian Experiments. London: Jonathan Cape, 1981.

Canopus in Argos: Archives, The Making of the Representative for Planet 8. London: Jonathan Cape, 1982.

The Fifth Child. London: Jonathan Cape, 1988.

The Four-Gated City. London: MacGibbon & Kee, 1969.

Going Home. New York: HarperPerennial Library, 1996.

The Golden Notebook. 1962. New edition with author's introduction. London: Michael Joseph, 1972.

The Good Terrorist. London: Jonathan Cape, 1985.

The Grass Is Singing. London: Michael Joseph, 1950.

"If You Knew Sufi . . . " *Guardian* 8 Jan. 1975.

Love, Again. New York: HarperPerennial Library, 1997.

Mara and Dann: An Adventure. New York: HarperFlamingo, 1999.

Martha Quest. London: Michael Joseph, 1952.

Memories of Water. New York: HarperCollins, forthcoming in 2000.

A Proper Marriage. London: Michael Joseph, 1954.

A Ripple from the Storm. London: Michael Joseph, 1958.

"A Small Personal Voice." *The Small Personal Voice: Essays, Reviews, Interviews.* 1974. Ed. and intro. Paul Schlueter. Rpt. London: Flamingo, 1994.

Under My Skin: Volume One of My Autobiography to 1949. New York: HarperPerennial Library, 1995.

Walking in the Shade: Volume Two of My Autobiography, 1949–1962. New York: HarperPerennial Library, 1998.

Selected Works about Doris Lessing

Caracciolo, Peter. "What's in a Canopean Name?" *Doris Lessing Newsletter* 8.1 (1984): 15.

Cederstrom, Lorelei. *Fine-Tuning the Feminine Psyche: Jungian Patterns in the Novels of Doris Lessing.* New York: Peter Lang, 1990.

Cheyfitz, Eric. *The Poetics of Imperialism: Translation and Colonization from "The Tempest" to "Tarzan."* New York: Oxford UP, 1991.

Fishburn, Katherine. *The Unexpected Universe of Doris Lessing: A Study in Narrative Technique.* Westport, CT: Greenwood Press, 1985.

Galin, Muge. *Between East and West: Sufism in the Novels of Doris Lessing.* Albany: State U of New York P, 1997.

Kaplan, Carey, and Ellen Cronan Rose, eds. *Doris Lessing: The Alchemy of Survival.* Athens: Ohio UP, 1988.

Rubenstein, Roberta. *The Novelistic Vision of Doris Lessing: Breaking the Forms of Consciousness.* Urbana: U of Illinois P, 1979.

Sage, Lorna. "The Available Space." *Women's Writing: A Challenge to Theory.* Ed. Moira Monteith. London: Harvester Press, 1986. 15–33.

Singleton, Mary Ann. *The City and the Veld: The Fiction of Doris Lessing.* London: Associated University Presses, 1977.

Ward Jouve, Nicole. *White Woman Speaks with Forked Tongue: Criticism as Autobiography.* London: Routledge, 1991.

3

P. D. James and the Dissociation of Sensibility

Eric Nelson

"Detection is, or ought to be, an exact science," Sherlock Holmes tells Dr. Watson in Sir Arthur Conan Doyle's *The Sign of Four,* "and should be treated in the same cold and unemotional manner. You have attempted to tinge it with romanticism, which produces much the same effect as if you worked a love-story or an elopement into the fifth proposition of Euclid."[1] Sergeant Cuff, in Wilkie Collins's *The Moonstone,* shares that remarkable capacity for detachment. In his case it seems rooted in a deeper disillusion. "His eyes," Gabriel Betteredge tells us, "of a steely grey, had a very disconcerting trick, when they encountered your eyes, of looking as if they expected more from you than you were aware of yourself."[2] That observation might easily apply to P. D. James's Adam Dalgliesh. This dispassion goes all the way back to Poe's Dupin. Not that these early detectives were without passions, or even pathologies. What distinguished them was their ability to sever at will the connection between thought and feeling. This "dissociation of sensibility,"[3] as T. S. Eliot called it, may be of enormous advantage to a detective.

The necessity for this dissociation is explained in an exchange between Cordelia Grey, journeyman private detective, and an experienced professional, Grogan, in *The Skull Beneath the Skin.* After Ms. Grey has inventoried her impressions of a murder scene, Grogan registers surprise at Cordelia's lack of shock or hysteria on finding the body; to the contrary, she displays a remarkably calm demeanor and meticulous powers of observation. Cordelia admits that her response has surprised her too. She reasons that she could not have stood the impact of the feelings that would have engulfed her; to succumb emotionally would have meant admitting the full horror of her discovery that a human life had been brutally and wantonly terminated. Perhaps fortuately, she says, her "intellect took over" and transformed the scene into a "detective puzzle" that allowed her to examine the crime scene in dispassionate detail (178). Comparing her reactions to those of doctors at the scene of an accident, she understands the necessity of concentrating on fact, evidence, and procedural techniques to keep at bay the ultimate horror of murder.

Grogan's assistant, Sergeant Buckley, chimes in, pointing out that trained policemen respond to accidents—or murders—in the same clinically detached way. In this view, there is nothing personal in the detective's impersonal manner in his work. Off duty he may have a passion for gardening (Cuff) or a passionless garden-variety marriage (Maigret). He may be deeply neurotic (Holmes) or incorrigibly sane (Father Brown). On the job, however, he *is* his job. For the true genius—your Holmes, your Dalgliesh—his job is, alas, his life. For these unhappy few the price of genius is melancholy and bouts of despair. Interestingly, the brilliant detective is often drawn to one less in control of his emotions, as Holmes is to Watson and Cuff is to Betteredge. Perhaps on some level they long for a "normal" life—a life, that is, where thought and feeling are never separable, an integrated life however inept and confused. Certainly, crime seems to isolate the detective fully as much as the criminal from restorative intimacy. Ironically, this paradox, in some detectives, may be the source of a strong sexual appeal, as it is in Dalgliesh.

In the fiction of P. D. James, however, this dissociation of sensibility is much more than a defining feature of her celebrated sleuth. It is often a defining feature of the world she portrays. To illustrate, I will look at *The Skull Beneath the Skin*, where the sleuth is not Dalgliesh but Cordelia Grey. In part I choose this book because Grey is the central detective. Cordelia is, if you will, Dalgliesh's anima (to borrow Jung's term). She is one who has serious difficulty severing thought from feeling, even on the job. This may be a function of her youth or her gender, or both. In any event, when we encounter the dissociation of thought and feeling in *The Skull Beneath the Skin,* as we do throughout the book, we cannot attribute the division to an internal schism in the narrative's detective.

To begin with, the controlling conceit of the novel is theatrical. An aging actress prepares to perform in a production of *The Duchess of Malfi* in a restored Victorian theater on the island of a wealthy friend. It will be a one-time performance for a select audience. The actress has been receiving poison pen letters containing quotations from Shakespeare and Webster that are veiled death threats. Her husband hires Cordelia Grey to watch over his wife during the weekend of the performance. When the actress is brutally murdered, the usual suspects do not need to be rounded up, for they are already sequestered on the island. It is the classic Agatha Christie paradigm. Each of the suspects has a motive, all are forced by circumstances into playing a role in the unfolding drama. And it is a situation that will inevitably divide thought from feeling in all of them.

Some of these "actors" already start with literary names: Clarissa (the murdered victim) and Cordelia herself. Some have odd names that sound literary: Ivo Whittingham, Ambrose Gorringe. In the throes of a crisis they will respond with a bon mot or an aria. Late in the novel, one suspect, a middle-aged spinster named Roma, learns that her lover is throwing her over. Cordelia worries that she is so distraught she may do herself harm. Distraught she may be, but even on the brink of hysteria she is not without powers of self-expression G. B. Shaw might envy. Predicting her future with grimly wry cynicism, Roma demonstrates an impressive comprehension of the dull reality of her situation and promises not to behave "stupidly" (279). With Clarissa's money, she says, she can sell her shop, purchase a London flat, find part-time employment, and take occasional trips abroad with a "woman friend" in order to avoid solitary travel. They will probably not like each other much but will invent such "little treats" for themselves as attending plays, visiting art galleries, and dining at the sorts of restaurants that "don't treat solitary women as pariahs" (279). On her return to London she will enroll in pottery or architecture courses, growing progressively more prudish and conservative— and "a little more lonely, a little more dead" (280). Though this is not, the context makes clear, a "performance," Roma acts as if it were and apologizes to Cordelia for her "disgusting exhibition" (278). When Roma tells her that she can have love at any time, Cordelia cries, "That isn't true; not of me, not of anyone!" (278).

This sense of artifice is reinforced by the tendency of everyone, not just the poison pen writer, to speak in literary quotations. Gorringe, acknowledging his complicity in the destruction of Clarissa, says that on coming to the island as a sixteen-year-old boy, he suddenly understood that he differed from most ambitious young men in that he desired none of the usual trappings of power, success, or sex, whether with women or men: that, he says, in an allusion to the Shakespeare sonnet, has always seemed to him "an expense of spirit in a waste of shame" (305). Sir George, confessing to Cordelia his pain at his wife's death, asks her who first observed that "we owe god a death." "I can't remember," she tells him. "Someone in Shakespeare's *Henry the Fifth*" (262).

When Grogan, the self-educated investigator, condescends to Cordelia, he does so through an allusion to French literature—"*On doit des égards aux vivants; on ne doit aux morts que la vérité*—challenging her as a woman of education and intelligence to understand the quotation. She does indeed. "'We owe respect to the living; to the dead we owe only the truth.' It's Voltaire, isn't it? But I was taught a different pronunciation" (177–78). Even butlers in the better houses mine the classics. Munter, Mr. Gorringe's butler, recalls that when his employer told them of the murder, Munter's first response was that it couldn't have happened in "our house." "Quite Shakespearean," our Voltaire-quoting investigator replies. "The Macbeth touch. And no doubt Mr. Gorringe could riposte with 'Too awful anywhere'?" (189). The exchange recalls the acerbic lines from Eliot's *The Waste Land:*

OOOOO that Shakespearean rag—
It's so elegant
So intelligent[4]

The many allusions to Elizabethan and Jacobean literature in *The Skull Beneath the Skin* function much as they do in Eliot's *The Waste Land.* Ironic evocations of a more robust time, they emphasize the dissociated emptiness of contemporary life. Gorringe's island mansion, filled with ornate decor and overwrought prose, is not unlike the opening setting of "A Game of Chess" in Eliot's poem:

The Chair she sat in, like a burnished throne,
Glowed on the marble, where the glass
Held up by standards wrought with fruited vines
From which a golden Cupidon peeped out
(Another hid his eyes behind his wing)
Doubled the flames of sevenbranched candelabra
Reflecting light upon the table as
The glitter of her jewels rose to meet it,
From satin cases poured in rich profusion. (ll. 77–85)

In the following passage, James's highly wrought deception evokes precisely the same overloaded synesthetic delirium rendered in Eliot's lines:

The six candles in their branched entwined stems seemed to burn less brightly than on their first evening so that their features, half-shadowed, were sharpened into caricatures of their daytime selves. Pale etiolated hands reached out to the fruit bowl, to furred and flushed peaches, the curved shininess of bananas, apples burnished so that they looked as artificial as Ambrose's candlelit skin. (237)

The hysterical outbursts of the wealthy woman in "A Game of Chess" might be spliced seamlessly into James's novel.

"My nerves are bad to-night. Yes, bad. Stay with me.
"Speak to me. Why do you never speak. Speak.
"What are you thinking of? What thinking? What?
"I never know what you are thinking. Think." (ll. 111–14)

The characters' sense of their own insubstantiality is reflected in their self-reflexive suggestions that they are mere fictive figures in a whodunit. When Munter dies, his employer remarks that the death is altogether too convenient: the deceased suspect obviously cannot communicate, and the butler cannot be the murderer because, even in literature, his role has become a cliché. Elsewhere Gorring says that popular fiction has taught him caution: one should always try to avoid being the person who discovers the corpse. This chief villain in the book, who has himself written a best-selling mystery, compliments himself on inventing a plot in "this real life mystery" nearly as ingenious as the one he created in his book (310). This coy collapsing of "art" into "life" implies that crime and punishment are just another silly game, even to the dour investigator in charge of the case. "And if Miss Roma Lisle's story is less than convincing, it's not the only one," he remarks. "Consider the curious reticence of the lady's maid. It sounds like the chapter heading for one of those snobbish thirties thrillers" (213).

The mystery genre, of course, especially the classical cozy, is by definition artificial. James does not attempt to escape this limitation but draws attention to it, pushing the reader, in a Brechtian move, to a critical distance from the genre's conventions. If her strategy seems coy, her intention is serious: to plumb the human soul. There are those (John Cawelti, Dennis Porter, Martin Priestman, Robin Winks)[5] who argue that the mystery genre can accommodate high aspirations.

For Winks, James's novels are clearly of this order; in his view she is a writer in the classical sense (216). "Rarely since [Dorothy] Sayers has a writer of thrillers diagnosed existing society with such microscopic precision [or] dissected human character with such relentlessness" (128). Bernard Benstock praises her social and psychological acuity. For Erlene Hubly, James's books have not just psychological depth but ontological depth as well, for they reveal to us "a world that is very different from that of the classical detective story. Unlike that world, James's world . . . is one in which all things do not tend toward order, is one in which all things cannot be known or proved. . . . For at every turn James seems to be saying that man, with his limited and erring intelligence, cannot fully understand the reality around him" (515).

James has repeatedly indicated that she sees her oeuvre as more than a series of best-selling potboilers. "I write detective stories," she told Julian Symons. "I hope they are novels, too, and I don't see any contradiction in that. But if I felt there *was* a contradiction, if the detective element got in the way of the novel and I had to sacrifice one or the other, then the detective element would have to go. I hope and believe I shan't have to make such a choice" (qtd. in Benstock, "P. D. James" 2, 227). The hint of a doubt in this declaration of faith in her chosen form ("if I felt there *was* a contradiction") can be found in even the most passionate celebrations of the detective genre. "For every person who argues that detective fiction is the diet of the noblest minds, there is another who finds it wasteful of time and degrading to the intellect. Detection fiction is seldom submitted to the scrutiny of a Leavis (or a Harold Bloom), perhaps because such critics feel it could not withstand such an intense light, perhaps because they would be accused of slumming were they to take it seriously, perhaps because they have simply never thought to do so" (Winks, "Introduction" 1).

James's "hidden agenda" is to lead the reader through analysis to difficulties beyond analysis. Case in point: Cordelia and the butler's wife. Cordelia, sensitive to the inequities of the British class system, muses on her own difficulties and ponders the even greater problems suffered by those who lack even her privilege, education, and eloquence. How, she asks herself, do they manage to face the utterly unfeeling technicalities of the bureaucratic legal system? When she tries to offer sympathy and help to the butler's wife, she fails to cross the social gulf that divides her from the working class. She admits her ignorance of the details of their lives and seeks consolation in the words of Henry James, "Never believe that you know the last word about the human heart."

From James it is a short step to her sense of inadequacy in her ability to solve this murder case: painfully aware of her youth, her dearth of experience, and her apparently minuscule amount of wisdom, she nearly despairs of measuring her limited assets "against the immense mysteriousness of the human heart" (274). Very quickly, however, Cordelia attempts to give this mystery the narrower focus her genre requires. As she tries to imagine Ivo and Tolly's relationship, she wonders about the expectations they might have had of and for each other. Had Ivo been attempting to wound Clarissa or avenge himself of some deep wound of his own? Could Tolly have been the type of woman whose consuming desire for a baby rendered the husband irrelevant? Even had her pregnancy been accidental, Tolly must have planned the delivery of the baby Viccy. Even as Cordelia thinks about these complicated relations, she realizes that the relationship is none of her business. More than any other aspect of human relationships, the "sexual act" was the most complicated, perhaps the most unfathomable (275). Because her profession has little tolerance for the inexplicable, Cordelia must draw back from "the immense mysteriousness of the human heart" to probe probable motives in one or two specific people, a case that might be argued in court.

In the fiction of P. D. James, moral and spiritual mysteries are exposed through the devices of a mystery that often dissociates thought from feeling. For that is the effect of all the histrionic posturing and literary referencing in *The Skull Beneath the Skin:* the self-protective artifice is finally ruthlessly revealing. This effect derives not only from rhetoric but from the shaping of scene and character. One example—admittedly the most egregious—may serve to illustrate. Late in the novel the butler dies in circumstances that incriminate one of the suspects. Another suspect proposes to the rest that they withhold much of the incriminating information from the police. Everyone must cooperate in this suppression or it will fail disastrously; the deception also entails not only silence but the invention of a few lies. The group argues about the wisdom of this course of action, so it is proposed that the issue be decided by secret ballot; a majority vote will commit all of them to either a truthful account or a misleading one. The balloting is done with a precious artifact, Princess Victoria's solitaire board. The five people vote by closing their eyes, taking a marble, and dropping it into the cup on the left if they favor the option of lying, the cup on the right if they favor the option of truth telling. Because of Roma's absence from dinner, a tied vote is out of the question. The results of the final vote: three for truth, two for deception.

These are five adults, none of them uneducated in the esoteric machinery of the law; one of them is dying of a terminal disease, another is our stalwart detective herself. They consent to surrender their moral responsibility (an act with serious legal repercussions) to a group none of them likes or trusts. What in Agatha Christie would be a silly plot device ("Then we close our eyes—no peeping, I implore you") is here a trope of ethical self-betrayal that functions much as the game of chess does in *The Waste Land*. The players become detached from their "moves."

The emotional detachment ubiquitous in *The Skull Beneath the Skin* is frequently noted by the characters themselves. Two examples, one from early in the novel and one from late in it, will serve. In the first, Whittingham, diagnosed with a terminal illness, considers asking his doctors about the amount of time remaining to him. He knows that his life is "depressingly" in order, following his divorce from his wife and his estrangement from his children five years earlier. Acknowledging the solitary tidiness of his flat and his uncluttered bachelor existence, he admits to only a "mild curiosity" about his condition and the length of time he will live. Looming larger than his curiosity is his conviction of the tastelessness of the question itself; Sir James dislikes having his patients upset him with uncomfortable questions of life and death. Instead—and Whittingham is not entirely "in disagreement" with Sir James's philosophy—each patient will eventually realize that life is just fading away into oblivion. In the second example, Roma, in a furious outburst against Gorringe, demonstrates her righteous but frustrated and ultimately useless recognition of the failure to feel passion or emotion. Wildly, she accuses Gorringe of failing to care that both Clarissa and Munter are dead. Lacking the ordinary emotions of love, outrage, sadness, or regret, she says, Gorringe cares only for his own comfort and amusement. In a final jab at his own humble beginnings before his grandfather bequeathed him a fortune, Roma accuses Gorringe of lacking "even the excuse of caste for not behaving like a human being" (255).

Ironically, it is the detective in the novel, Cordelia Grey, who has the hardest time suppressing her emotions. Again and again her gestures of sympathy, springing from empathetic identification with others, are rebuffed by the recipients. Too much fellow feeling, she comes to realize, does not help others and only puts herself at risk. In the novel's concluding pages she seems to have grasped this unpleasant truth. She envies animals, which, unlike humans, face death and dying with stoicism, without the human tendency to unburden themselves or complain about their problems. The final paragraph tells us that she has at last come of age. All of a sudden she feels "inviolate. The police would have to make their decisions. She had already made hers, without hesitation and without a struggle. She would tell the truth, and she would survive." Firmly adjusting her shoulder bag, Cordelia moves "resolutely" toward the little boat that will take her away from Courey Island. Her heart beating "steadily," she moves away from death and into her own—momentarily, at least—"sunlit" future (328).

What began as a discipline of professional detachment—how policemen and doctors are trained to behave at the scenes of accidents or murder cases—has become a life lesson of how to survive emotionally in a world of competing self-interests. In a loveless society the impulse to care is a liability, an opening for manipulation, humiliation, sometimes death. What is sacrificed, of course, is intimacy. This failure of intimacy was a central theme of modernist writers as different as Eliot, Lawrence, Hemingway, and Joyce. For them it was a symptom of a larger moral and spiritual poverty, the emptiness of self-protection. In the judgment of *The Waste Land*'s conclusion:

I have heard the key
Turn in the door once and turn once only
We think of the key, each in his prison
Thinking of the key, each confirms a prison (ll. 412–15)

The suppression of feeling carries a cost, a cost one sees in Dupin, Cuff, Holmes, and Dalgliesh, and in many of the characters in James's fiction: depression. And beyond depression, exhaustion. The routine of getting up in the morning and going to work comes to seem, at times, pointless.

It is a problem Adam Dalgliesh knows only too well. At the beginning of *The Black Tower* he is in a hospital bed recovering from a misdiagnosis. He will not die of acute leukemia, as his doctors thought; rather, he will recover from an atypical mononucleosis.

> It was, he had thought, uncommonly inconsiderate if not negligent of his doctors to reconcile him so thoroughly to death and then change their minds. It was embarrassing now to recall with what little regret he had let slip his pleasures and preoccupations, the imminence of loss revealing them for what they were, at best only a solace, at worst a trivial squandering of time and energy. Now he had to lay hold of them again and believe that they were important, at least to himself. He doubted whether he would ever again believe them important to other people. No doubt, with returning strength, all that would look after itself. The physical life would re-assert itself given time. He would reconcile himself to living since there was no alternative and, this perverse fit of resentment and accidie conveniently put down to weakness, would come to believe that he had had a lucky escape. His colleagues, relieved of embarrassment, would congratulate him. . . . But, at present, he wasn't sure that he could reconcile himself to his job. Resigned as he had become to the role of spectator—and soon not even to be that—he felt ill-equipped to return to the noisy playground of the world and, if it had to be, was minded to find for himself a less violent corner of it. (10–11)

Dalgliesh does return to his job, of course, because that is what the British do in these latter days of imperial decline: they carry on. They carry on on principle, the principle here being that, on balance, it is right to protect the not-so-innocent from untimely death. Then, too, there is Voltaire's point: *on ne doit aux morts que la vérité.* After all, we will be dead someday. In the meantime one can always look on one's work, as Holmes and Dalgliesh do, as the best antidote to apply to the wound of a dissociated life. A hair of the dog that bit you.

Admirers of James frequently cite her years as a principal administrative assistant for the North West Metropolitan Regional Hospital Board in London, and later as a Civil Servant with the Department of Home Affairs (in the Criminal Department). Such experience, it is said, has given her a wealth of technical knowledge and a grasp of the milieu of professional police work that inform her novels with special authority. I would press this point even further: her years of professional experience gave her an attitude as well, a way of looking at her material, and this attitude can best be defined as clinical. The surgeon and the forensic pathologist require not only knowledge and skill to do their work, but a state of mind that is cool and detached. It is a state of mind they slip into as automatically as they put on surgical gloves; it becomes, as we say, second nature.

James's novels do not feel clinical, of course. On the contrary, her works are sometimes accused of gothic and melodramatic excess. But gothic melodrama is not incompatible with clinical detachment, as Poe's "The Murders in the Rue Morgue" makes startlingly clear. James's critics acknowledge this juxtaposition in her work. "At times the books verge on the macabre and once or twice they slip into the melodramatic, but both the icicle eye and the piece of ice at the heart quickly return" (Winks, "Sordid Truth" 215). This ice at the heart is for James the pathology under examination. James speaks as if she might easily abandon the detective genre if she chose to do so, but I am not so sure it would be that easy. It is a genre too well suited not only to her experience but to her temperament (a temperament conditioned, perhaps, by her postwar experience). James seems, in my imagination, rather like Dalgliesh, a stoical temperament with a gift for detection and poetry who has, improbably, attained a certain celebrity in both. She is a poet in the modern, metaphysical tradition. In her forensics lab it is the soul that is under her knife, like a patient etherized upon a table.

Notes

1. Arthur Conan Doyle, "The Sign of Four," *Sherlock Holmes, Selected Stories* (New York: Oxford UP, 1980), 69.

2. Wilkie Collins, *The Moonstone* (Oxford: Oxford UP, 1982), 107.

3. T. S. Eliot, "The Metaphysical Poets," *Selected Essays* (New York: Harcourt Brace, 1950), 288.

4. T. S. Eliot, "The Waste Land," *Collected Poems, 1909–1962* (New York: Harcourt Brace, 1963), ll. 128–30.

5. Cawelti, *Adventure, Mystery, and Romance;* Porter, *The Pursuit of Crime;* Priestman, *Detective Fiction and Literature;* Winks, "The Sordid Truth." Robin Winks, for example, claims

> the artificiality said to limit mystery fiction is an open invitation to create art. To be donnish for a moment and dot the page with quotations, let Keats do for us what we cannot do for ourselves, with his concept of negative capability: "that is, when a man is capable of being in uncertainties, mysteries, doubts, without any irritable reaching after fact and reason." The mystery provides us with this capability, for while the central "problem" may be satisfactorily resolved, in that the murderer is uncovered and, perhaps, justice is done, with a form of catharsis achieved for some, many mysterious elements relating to precise actions and precise motivations at precise times, as opposed to general explanations of motive, will almost certainly and properly be left unresolved. . . . That is, the formal puzzle is "solved," the "detective" does his or her job, while the mystery of human choice is left in a condition of complex plausibility, so that even the tidiest of endings remains, upon reflection, ambiguous.

Selected Works by P. D. James

"The Art of the Detective Novel." *New Welsh Review* 2.1 (Summer 1989): 4–9.

The Black Tower. 1975. New York: Scribner, 1975.

A Certain Justice. 1997. New York: Warner Books, 1999.

The Children of Men. 1992. New York: Warner Books, 1994.

Cover Her Face. 1962. New York: Warner Books, 1992.

Crime Times Three: Three Complete Novels Featuring Adam Dalgliesh of Scotland Yard. New York: Scribner, 1979.

A Dalgliesh Trilogy. London: Penguin in association with Faber & Faber, 1991.

Death of an Expert Witness. 1977. New York: Warner Books, 1992.

Devices and Desires. 1989. New York: Warner Books, 1992.

800 Years of Women's Letters [Designer]. Ed. Olga Kenyon, 1992. New York: Penguin, 1994.

In Murderous Company: Three Complete Novels Featuring Detectives Adam Dalgliesh and Cordelia Gray. 1988. Avenel, N.J.: Wings Books, 1992.

Innocent Blood. 1980. New York: Warner Books, 1992.

The Maul and the Pear Tree. Coauthor with T. A. Critchley. 1971. New York: Warner Books, 1990.

A Mind to Murder. 1963. New York: Warner Books, 1992.

Murder in Triplicate: Three Complete Novels by the Queen of Crime. New York: Scribner, 1980.

Introduction. *Mystery!: A Celebration: Stalking Public Television's Greatest Sleuths.* Ed. Ron Miller and Karen Sharpe. New York: KQED Books, 1996.

Original Sin. 1994. New York: Warner Books, 1996.

P. D. James Omnibus. 1982. London: Faber & Faber, 1990.

A Second Dalgliesh Trilogy. London: Penguin in association with Faber & Faber, 1993.

Shroud for a Nightingale. 1971. New York: Warner Books, 1992.

The Skull Beneath the Skin. 1982. New York: Warner Books, 1994.

A Taste for Death. 1986. Ballantine Books, 1999.

Trilogy of Death: Three Complete Novels: "The Skull Beneath the Skin," "Innocent Blood," "Death of an Expert Witness." London: Penguin in association with Faber & Faber, 1992.

Unnatural Causes. 1967. New York: Warner Books, 1996.

An Unsuitable Job for a Woman. 1972. New York: Warner Books, 1992.

Selected Works about P. D. James

Benstock, Bernard. "The Clinical World of P. D. James." *Twentieth-Century Women Novelists.* Ed. Thomas F. Staley. London: Macmillan, 1982. 104–29.

———. "P. D. James." *British Mystery and Thriller Writers since 1940.* First Ser. 87. Ed. Bernard Benstock and Thomas Staley. Detroit: Gale, 1989. 210–27.

Campbell, SueEllen. "The Detective Heroine and Death of Her Hero: Dorothy Sayers to P. D. James." *Feminism in Women's Detective Fiction.* Ed. Glenwood Irons. Toronto: U of Toronto P, 1995. 12–28.

Cawelti, John G. *Adventure, Mystery, and Romance: Formula Stories as Art and Popular Culture.* Chicago: U of Chicago P, 1976.

Heilbrun, Carolyn G. "The Detective Novel of Manners." *Reading and Writing Women's Lives: A Study of the Novel of Manners.* Ed. Bebe K. Bowers and Barbara Brothers. Ann Arbor: University Microfilms International Research, 1990. 157–98.

Hubly, Erlene. "The Formula Challenged: The Novels of P. D. James." *Modern Fiction Studies* 29 (Autumn 1983): 511–21.

Kotker, Joan G. "P. D. James's Adam Dalgliesh Series." *In the Beginning: First Novels in Mystery Series.* Ed. Mary Jean Demarr. Bowling Green, OH: Popular, 1995. 139–53.

———. "The Re-Imagining of Cordelia Gray." *Women Times Three: Writers, Detectives, Readers.* Ed. Kathleen Gregory Klein. Bowling Green, OH: Popular, 1995. 53–64.

Mosebach, Angje. "'A Smell of the Place Should Almost Rise from the Pages': P. D. James and London: An Interview." *Anglistick and Englischunterricht* 54 (1994): 173–86.

Nixon, Nicola. "Gray Areas: P. D. James's Unsuiting of Cordelia." *Feminism in Women's Detective Fiction.* Ed. Glenwood Irons. Toronto: U of Toronto P, 1995. 29–45.

Porter, Dennis. *The Pursuit of Crime.* New Haven: Yale UP, 1981.

Priestman, Martin. *Detective Fiction and Literature.* New York: St. Martin's, 1991.

Sizemore, Christine Wick. *A Female Vision of the City: London in the Novels of Five British Women.* Knoxville: U of Tennessee P, 1989.

Winks, Robin W. "Introduction." *Detective Fiction.* Ed. Robin Winks. Englewood Cliffs, NJ: Prentice-Hall, 1980.

———. *Modus Operandi.* Boston: David R. Godine, 1982.

———. "The Sordid Truth: Four Cases." *Detective Fiction.* Ed. Robin Winks. Englewood Cliffs, NJ: Prentice-Hall, 1980. 209–28.

4

Retrofitting the Raj: Ruth Prawer Jhabvala and the Uses and Abuses of the Past

Judie Newman

In August 1987, when Ralph Lauren opened a new Polo emporium on Rodeo Drive in Los Angeles, second in size only to his Madison Avenue flagship, the *Los Angeles Times* reported intense speculation in the design community: "How would Polo's aristocratic appeal be translated into a fantasy with which Rodeo Drive shoppers would identify?" (Price 30).[1] Perhaps unsurprisingly, given the enduring rage for the Raj, Lauren chose a "British Colonial" design concept on the basis of its appeal to nostalgia. Why the colonies? As his franchise-holder responded: "I think the atmosphere lends itself to the design of Ralph's clothes. I think people today like tradition in a world where relationships seem to be more casual and shallow" (30). Like so many latter-day white hunters, the design team promptly embarked on an antique-hunting safari, shipping back some three thousand props to be "retrofitted" (32)—converted into merchandise-display features. The new store exemplifies two disturbing features of the recent treatment of Empire: its commodification as a marketable entity, based on nostalgia for a past never-neverland (as in the success of the films of *Passage to India, Out of Africa,* and *The Far Pavilions*), and its identification with homogenized, patriarchal values. (The Polo store set out to evoke the atmosphere of "a British men's club in . . . the colonies of the British West Indies, India and Africa" [30].) In her successful film partnership with Ismail Merchant and James Ivory, Ruth Prawer Jhabvala might well appear to be implicated in the retro-fitting process, particularly in relation to *Heat and Dust,* her most suc-cessful novel to date, which was subsequently lushly filmed with all the trappings of its setting in the 1920s in an Indian princely state.

It would, however, be surprising, to say the least, if Jhabvala acceded to the rewriting of the history of Empire in any way that obscured its horrors. In fact, her fiction reveals a keen sensitivity to a past traumatic history. As a German-Jewish Holocaust survivor who reached Britain in 1939 (minus forty family members who perished), moved to a newly par-titioned India on her marriage (1951), and moved thence to America (1975), she has tended in her writing to emphasize themes of loss, disin-heritance, exile, alienation, and the fragmentation of identity in the flux of history. Jhabvala has described her childhood in terms that suggest an experience of such profound trauma that it remains almost entirely blocked from consciousness. She has spoken of it publicly only once:

> I don't feel like talking much about 1933 and after. Everyone knows what happened to German Jews first and other European Jews af-ter. Our family was no exception. . . . I have slurred over the years 1933 to 1939, from when I was six to twelve. They should have been my most formative years; maybe they were, I don't know. . . . I've never written about those years. To tell you the truth, until today I've never even mentioned them. Never spoken about them to any-one. ("Disinheritance" 6)

Jhabvala's response to a literally unspeakable history supports recent theorizations of the phenomenon of trauma as denying our usual modes of access to it. Cathy Caruth has argued that "Trauma . . . does not sim-ply serve as record of the past but precisely registers the force of an ex-perience that is not yet fully owned. . . . The trauma is the confrontation with an event that, in its unexpectedness or horror, cannot be placed within the schemes of prior knowledge."[2]

It is just such a paradoxical relation between the pervasiveness and the absence of the past that characterizes much of Jhabvala's work. In her early writing the past is everywhere evident. As a student at London University she wrote her M.A. thesis on the subject "The Short Story in England 1700–1750," and her work has consistently reflected the in-fluence of eighteenth-century writing. Essentially comedies of manners, these early Indian-centered works enclose dramas of courtship and marriage, Austen-fashion, within carefully balanced narrative structures, using the opposition of tradition to modernity as a constant theme. Despite the Austenian sense of enclosure, a historical dimension is indicated. *To Whom She Will* (1955) draws its title from the Vedic epic the *Panchatantra*, and concerns itself with Punjabi survivors of Partition, and with the ambivalent response to Westernization in Independent India (a theme also prominent in *The Nature of Passion* [1956]). *Esmond in India* (1958) introduces the topic of the European eroticization of the relationship to India, in the shape of the eponymous hero and his disenchantment with both India and his Indian wife. In a parallel treatment, *The Householder* (1960) examines a young man's slow habituation to the role of "householder," the second stage of the orthodox Hindu four-stage life pattern. With *Get Ready for Battle* (1962) the pendulum swings once more toward a harsher and more combative satire, exposing the widening gap between rich and poor, and the corruption of Indian society. The last of Jhabvala's novels to focus on the extended Indian family, it is also the last to draw its title from an Indian literary source (the *Mahabharata*).

From this point onward, Jhabvala's titles have an ironically "colonial" ring, with the focus shifting to Europeans in India, and to a reversed process of cultural domination in which Indians (particularly questionable gurus) prey upon Westerners. Themes of cultural confrontation, initiated in *A Backward Place* (1965), move to center stage. At the same time, after the balanced Augustan defensive structures of the first phase, the nightmares bred of the sleep of reason begin to take hold. Laurie Sucher, one of Jhabvala's most percipient critics, has identified a strong gothic strain running through the later works, which feature demon-lovers, willing victims, mysterious Indian palaces and ruined forts, "thriller" elements (poisoning, drug smuggling, gunrunning), and the eroticization of spirituality (with gurus standing in for sinister monks and ashrams for convents). As I have argued elsewhere,[3] the ability of gothic to retrace the unseen and unsaid of culture renders it peculiarly well adapted to articulating the untold stories of the colonial experience. Eve Kosofsky Sedgwick[4] has analyzed the gothic emphasis on the "unspeakable" both in the intensificatory sense of "nameless horrors" and in the play of narrative structure, with its stories-within-stories, secret confessions, and general difficulty in getting the story told at all. In Jhabvala's case, techniques of understatement and telling omission combine in narratives that fragment and embed themselves in intricate webs of deception. Frequently a barrier of some sort exists between teller and tale. In *A New Dominion* (1972), rational, "objective" Raymond is ironized as a neo-Forsterian spokesman, out of touch with both contemporary India and his own blocked emotions. The grand sweep of the novel, indicated in its tripartite structure (Delhi, Benares, Maupur), contrasts with the fragmented narrative that emanates from a variety of viewpoints, each providing a short scene or episode with a faux-naïf heading. These vignettes present Europeans as trapped within Augustan illusions of reason and objectivity, while below the cool surface story lies a buried melodrama. (Memorably in the example of Lee, who invites herself to stay with an Indian family and cheerfully settles down to eat, unaware that the commotion all around her concerns the rush to cremate the victim of a "dowry death" in order to destroy the evidence of poisoning.)

Jhabvala establishes a similar counterpoint of reason and passion in *Heat and Dust* (1975), which reworks Forster's *The Hill of Devi* in the light of postcolonial hindsight.[5] The stories of Olivia and her Nawab (in 1923), and of the narrator who retraces her steps fifty years later, are spliced (in Jhabvala's filmic metaphor) in order to juxtapose Imperial and Independent Indias, past and present, and to assess their relative merits. Scenic intercutting is accompanied by interpolated narratives, forming a veritable anthology of different Western textualizations of India—as horror story, epic, or romance. Sharp scene-cutting against a sweeping historical backdrop is also a feature of *In Search of Love and Beauty* (1983), in which the guru reappears amidst a group of German-Jewish refugees in New York, whose friendships are charted over three generations from the thirties on. An Augustan mock-epic quality (with characters playfully based on Greek deities) contrasts with the awareness that surface comedy conceals a deeper tragedy.

The experiences of India, Europe, and America combine in *Three Continents* (1987), a deeply disquieting tale that offers a subtle dramatization of the psychopathology of power and the vulnerability of the rational. Here the corrupt Sixth World Movement, with its militaristic drills, parades, lobotomized fealty to a leader, and air of insane righteousness, clearly looks back to the Third Reich. Myth is once more mystification. Crishi, the charismatic villain, is modeled less on Krishna than on a contemporary Asian mass murderer, and finds an exceptionally naive victim in an American heiress, whom he despoils of both honor and fortune. Both *In Search of Love and Beauty* and *Three Continents* had a mixed reception, with reviewers commenting on Jhabvala's chilly authorial detachment, the elements of masochism, and the conjunction of phallic anti-heroes with passive, drifting heroines. Her most recent novel, *Poet and Dancer* (1993), returns again to a group of German refugees in New York, and concentrates upon the Sapphic relationship between two of their children—Lara, a failed dancer, and Angel, a would-be poet. The narrator, a writer, has been approached to write Angel's life story by her mother, who desperately wishes to fill "this silence, this blank, where her daughter had once been" (6). Lara, the victim of a damaged childhood, has carried Angel with her into a joint suicide pact. Earlier Angel had underscored a favorite quotation in a medieval text: "And this, truly is what a perfect lover must always do, utterly and entirely despoiling himself of himself for the sake of the thing he loves, and that not only for a time, but everlastingly" (6). The example of Lara and Angel suggests that where creative expression is balked, Jhabvala's heroines become self-punishing and self-silencing, surrendering to self-destructive urges. Trauma, exile, and the long reach of the past come together in the reproduction of violence.

Where Western reviewers tended to concentrate upon the psychology of Jhabvala's protagonists, in India the ambivalence of her vision of India has ensured that she has rarely received the serious critical attention she deserves. When the Booker Prize was awarded to *Heat and Dust* in 1975, reaction in India was immediately hostile. For many Indians the novel represented an attempt to ridicule India, abetted by the stamp of British approval offered by the prize. Whereas British reviewers tended to see the intercultural encounter in the novel as of secondary interest, "Indian reviewers dwelt on the India of *Heat and Dust,* on the character of the Indian Nawab or Prince who has an affair with the wife of a British Civil Servant stationed in his town, and on the explicit and implicit commentary on Indian mores as well as the Indian setting. For them, there could be no separation between these and the quality of the novel, its authenticity, its literary substance."[6] In general, the Indian literary reaction was based upon mimetic, representational criteria, which it refused to sunder from the formal merits of the novel. In 1988 Upamanyu Chatterjee satirized the nature of the reaction in *English, August: An Indian Story.*[7] In the novel, Menon, the Sub-Divisional Magistrate of Rameri, offers the hero a copy of *Heat and Dust,* borrowed from the Collectorate library under the mistaken impression that "it was about an Assistant Collector's life in the British days. But it's not really about that" (39). Menon has nonetheless annotated the volume in red ballpoint in order to correct what he sees as historical misrepresentations—examples, though he does not know the term, of "retrofitting." "Not necessary these days to wear solar topee. Relic of the Raj" (39) is one such emendation. Later in the novel, in an artful allusion to Jhabvala's modern narrator's researches into the events of 1923, an Englishman, John Avery, visits the town in order to view the memorial to his grandfather, a former Collector and District Magistrate, who came to a sticky end following an attack by a tiger, also in 1923. John's girlfriend actually appears in a solar topee, to the hero's amusement: "Just in case the heat and dust get too much?" (196) he queries. Like the narrator of *Heat and Dust,* John Avery has read his grandfather's letters and has been struck by their apparent timelessness: "There is no sense of a living place. In fact all that detail somehow further deadens it. There was apparently a big clock in the dining room, and most of his letters would begin, 'It has just struck four and Baldev has brought in my tea,' 'It is now seven thirty and Natwar, the one who can never get my boots right, is at the door asking about dinner.' Everything is static, as though Richard Avery would always remain here in Madna. . . . As though nothing would ever change" (212). John recognizes in the static repetitions of the letters the potential for creating, and re-creating, a frozen, ahistorical image of India, as if the Gorgon breath of the Raj had petrified everything in its path. Chatterjee's hero, Agastya Sen, has already had to face the same problem. On arrival in Madna he is greeted with the ringing declaration that "This is India, bhai, an independent country, and not the Raj" (23), only to be immediately offered videos of *A Passage to India* and *The Jewel in the Crown.*

Is Jhabvala, then, as Chatterjee's characters suggest, complicit in the retrofitting of the Raj? Or is her historical material overtly designed *to* historicize, to abolish the image of India as timeless Orient and to restore a vital awareness of the traumas of the past? Particularly acute examples of test cases occur in *Three Continents* and *Heat and Dust,* each of which engages with one of the major colonial scare stories of India, respectively, "thuggee" and "suttee." Patrick Brantlinger has commented that "In the late 1830s . . . new revelations about a destructive offshoot of Hinduism provided another sensational focus for reformist writing, and served as the subject of the first best-selling Anglo-Indian novel, Philip

Meadows Taylor's *Confessions of a Thug* (1839)."[8] Thuggee, the secret cult of professional murderers and robbers who worshiped Kali and preyed on unsuspecting travelers, became in Taylor's hands the central theme of a highly successful crime novel—as it was also to do for Jhabvala. In 1979 Jhabvala referred to thuggee in the context of modern muggers, remarking that areas of New York were now as deserted "as though they were infested by those thugs that throttled wayfarers in the deserts of Rajasthan or the ravines of Madhya Pradesh" ("Displacement" 14).

In *Three Continents*, Jhabvala's central character, Crishi, is based upon a modern "thug," Charles Sobhraj, the Indian "drug and rob" man and serial killer who preyed upon Western travelers who had set out on the "hippy trail" in search of mystic enlightenment in the timeless East. Sobhraj's story has been told in the West in two works of "faction" and a TV miniseries, in a manner that dehistoricizes its central protagonist and essentially purveys a stereotypically Orientalist tale (Newman, "Post-Colonial Gothic"). The television series (*Shadow of the Cobra*) characterized Sobhraj as diabolical villain. The blurb to the reissued tie-in said it all: "An audience with psychopathic mass-murderer Charles Sobhraj. It was like having supper with the devil." Reviewers described Sobhraj as a "plausible, Bruce Lee style, Asian fiend," "diabolically charismatic" (Marnham 11), who took his followers on a "descent into hell."[9] The evolution of the various accounts shows the West writing and rewriting Sobhraj into the ahistorical norms of the snaky, Oriental villain, with elements of *Vathek*, Milton's Satan, and Fu Man Chu. In contrast, Jhabvala foregrounds the historical and socioeconomic dimension of the tale. Sobhraj's early life was as disturbed by Empire, as Jhabvala's was under the Reich. As the illegitimate offspring of a Vietnamese mother and an Indian father, born in Saigon when it was under Japanese occupation but Vichy French administration, he was captured by the Vietminh, rescued by the British, abandoned by his mother on the streets of Saigon, reclaimed and taken to Dakar (French West Africa), returned to France, and thence to Bombay. Stateless, at times institutionalized, Sobhraj shuttled between countries until adulthood, the victim of war, the redrawing of territorial boundaries, and the aftermath of Empire. In *her* revision of his story, Jhabvala emphasizes the traumas of the past as formative, drawing upon anthropological analysis of serial killers. Elliott Leyton describes serial killers as frequently adopted, illegitimate, or institutionalized in youth, and seeking identity in criminal celebrity.[10]

Typically their victims are drawn from a category some social bands above the killer, whose motive is to wreak revenge. Killings of this nature register a protest against exclusion from social discourse, as the killer commits "unspeakable" crimes which nonetheless provide a message that society must read.

Other factors relevant in the formation of the serial killer are a disappointed dream or ambition, and the existence of cultural forms that can mediate killer and victim in a special sense, ridding victims of humanity and killer of responsibility (e.g., the social validation of violent identity in modern film and television, or in Jhabvala's case, a totalitarian religio-political movement). In *Three Continents* mobility is thus the mark of both the Western truth seeker and the serial killer. Just as the latter links the culturally spoken and the unspeakable, so Crishi reveals in his actions the revenge of the excluded. Sobhraj, the stateless exile, killed those whose willful deracination parodied his own disappointed state, just as Crishi, who has had disinheritance forced upon him, ensures that his condition is shared. Ironically, Crishi uses the Sixth World Movement only as a blind for his activities as a smuggler of objets d'art, plundering the East to the benefit of the West. Complicit, therefore, in the very activity that allows the West to impose its own signifying practices upon the East, he supplies the props for his own victimization. In the formation of this particular "thug," colonialism and neocolonialism are decisive factors. Despite his evocation of his namesake, Krishna, Crishi merely employs the timeless image of Indian religion to his own purposes.

In *Heat and Dust,* as the setting Satipur (the place of sati) indicates, a central thematic element is sati (Western "suttee").[11] Two scenes are particularly important: the discussion of a recent case of sati in 1923, and in the 1970s the death of an elderly widow at the sati memorial stones. In introducing the topic of sati, Jhabvala could hardly expose herself more completely to the accusation of retrofitting. David Rubin, for one, has read Jhabvala as repropagating a demonic view of India, in the footsteps of earlier writers: "Jhabvala, far from being the 'Indian' novelist she is generally held to be, in fact continues the traditions of the colonial British novelists of the half-century preceding Indian independence" (*After the Raj* 70). In the earlier period, as Patrick Brantlinger has amply demonstrated, nineteenth-century utilitarian and evangelical attacks on Hinduism tended to emphasize sati as an example of the Hindu "abominations" from which the kindly Imperialists were bent on saving the Indian masses.[12] Southey's "The Curse of Kehama" (1810), for example, in-cludes a tirade against sati. India was seen as locked into patterns of im-memorial violence, a kind of horror story without a history. Oddly, how-ever, not every British writer took quite such a critical view. In "The Death of Oenone" Tennyson allows Oenone to fling herself upon her husband's pyre, in an act seen as expiating her past misdeeds.

> The morning light of happy marriage broke
> Thro' all the clouded years of widowhood,
> And muffling up her comely head, and crying
> "Husband!" she leapt upon the funeral pile,
> And mixt herself with him and past in fire.[13]

The West was, of course, always ready to appropriate an Indian practice to the Western discourse of romantic love, especially when it allowed the body of a woman to be simultaneously transcended and killed off. Ro-mantic and sentimental codes cross-fertilized here, in the ideas that a romantic lover could have no existence without the beloved, and that the wife should sacrifice herself for her husband. L.E.L. (Letitia Elizabeth Landon) actually appears to endorse the process in "A Suttee," which ends:

> The red pile blazes—let the bride ascend,
> And lay her head upon her husband's heart,
> Now in a perfect unison to blend.[14]

Clearly, sati could serve patriarchal norms as much among Imperialists as Imperialized.

Indeed, sati has become a key concern in modern debates about the relation between feminism and postcolonialism, the construction of the female subject, and the weight to be given to the past as legitimating practice.[15] In *Heat and Dust* all the different discourses on sati circulate in one key scene, set at a dinner party in 1923. Discussions of sati have tended to focus upon the degree of female autonomy involved, with apologists portraying the sati as unusual, heroic, and voluntaristic while reformers advance evidence of coercion (drugs, physical violence, family pressure, pyres designed to tip the widow into the flames or to collapse upon her). In Jhabvala's novel the discussion initially moves between the two poles of the sati as victim or as heroine, both of which preclude the possibility of complex female subjectivity.[16] The 1923 sati is presented as involuntary: "A grain merchant had died and his widow had been forced by her relatives to burn herself with him on his funeral pyre. Although Douglas [Olivia's husband] had rushed to the scene the moment information had reached him, he had arrived too late to save the woman" (55).[17] This description conforms entirely to the stereotypical British view of sati, memorably characterized by Gayatri Chakravorty Spivak as white men saving brown women from brown men: "Imperialism's image as the establisher of the good society is marked by the espousal of the woman as object of protection from her own kind."[18] The "women's issue" gave the British a justification for their own interference in India, though in most other respects they were hardly motivated by liberatory intentions. As a result, sati quickly became a focus for Indian resistance. In the novel, Douglas's action leads to unrest, as the arrested relatives are immediately turned into martyrs (57). Olivia, however, sympathizes with the Indian view: "It's part of their religion, isn't it? I thought one wasn't supposed to meddle with that" (58). The comment lays bare the problem facing the modern postcolonial feminist, unwilling to condone practices that exemplify the male abuse of women, yet also chary of appearing to criticize another culture from her own Eurocentric position. (Female circumcision is a contemporary case in point.) Sati was vigorously defended in India as sanctioned by the Vedic scriptures and by immemorial tradition. The extreme British Imperial position is represented in the novel by the outburst from Dr. Saunders in response to Olivia: "It's savagery . . . plain savagery and barbarism" (59).

In the argument that follows, Olivia has no real desire to recommend widow-burning but is motivated by her antipathy to the condescension and smug self-certainty of her fellows. At the dinner table the British exchange a whole series of anecdotes about sati, "drawn not so much from personal experience as from a rich store-house of memories that went back several generations" (57–58). The tales are recounted in a fashion designed to conceal any ideological content, as if the stories "spoke for themselves." They are presented "with no moral comment whatsoever . . . they even had that little smile of tolerance, of affection, even enjoyment that Olivia was beginning to know well: like good parents they all loved India whatever mischief she might be up to" (58). As that final feminization implies, an apparent narratorial objectivity conceals a paternalistic project designed to maintain India in a state of infantilized dependence. It also refers outward to that hegemonic discourse which

Edward Said has characterized as "Orientalism," in which the West is envisaged as male, the East as passively female, waiting to be rescued from ignorance and fertilized with the seeds of civilization by Western culture-bearers.[19] Later in the novel, when he describes India as requiring the exercise of "a virile, measured, European feeling," Major Minnies restates this particular ideological position, which depends upon the assumption that it is natural for man to dominate woman. Major Minnies "loved India so much, knew her so well, chose to spend the end of his days here! But she always remained for him an opponent" (171).

The feminization of India goes to the heart of the colonial enterprise. The British treat India itself as a sati. On the one hand, reformers generally portray the widow as weak, pitiful, frightened, and deluded, as fundamentally non-agentive. On the other, as "The Death of Oenone" reveals, the power of woman as sexual destroyer was implicitly recognized in the practice of sati, which clearly responds to a vision of woman as a danger when no longer under male control. The East was thus *either* a foolish woman who needed to be saved from herself *or* a sexual temptress who should be controlled and resisted at all costs. Appropriately, as the discussion develops, it is Major Minnies who, with a story of a sati in 1829 (as originally told by W. H. Sleeman in 1844), provides a less vulnerable image of the sati as strong-willed and voluntaristic. Although both Sleeman and the woman's relatives had attempted to dissuade her, she had persisted over several days in her intention to burn herself, declaring that if prevented she would simply starve herself to death. "She wasn't a fanatic. . . . There was something noble there," says the Major (60). Olivia's response to sati is similarly romantic. While flashing ardent glances at Douglas, she declares her own desire to accompany the beloved in death. (Olivia is conveniently unaware of the number of satis, victims of arranged child-marriages, who saw their husbands for the first time on their mutual pyre.)

Up to this point, Jhabvala appears to be keeping the arguments for and against sati evenly balanced. Significantly, however, one issue has been omitted from the public discourse: trauma. Rajeswari Sunder Rajan has commented that the rejection of the colonial discourse of sati as a women's issue, to embrace instead an earlier reading of it as an index of conjugal love and female heroism, can be fraught with dangerously regressive tendencies (8). Rajan thus displaces the traditional construction of the sati in terms of one who chooses or is forced to die, first onto questions of the embodied subject (the subject of pain) and then onto the representation of the widow who chooses to live. In an enormously important thesis, Rajan therefore shifts the issue from sati-as-death to sati-as-burning. Defenders of sati deny the woman's pain since sati depends upon the idea of the triumph of spirit over flesh. (Apologists argue not that the sati embraces pain but that she knows no pain.) Even Sleeman (in a passage carefully not included by Jhabvala in her account) describes the widow as "consumed without uttering a shriek or betraying one sign of agony."[20] Indeed, the woman's body is curiously absent from all the debates on sati. Lata Mani comments that "Even Rammohun, commonly regarded as the first modern champion of women's rights, did not base his support for abolition on the ground that sati was cruel to women."[21] And yet the pain is recognized in the custom. Thompson notes that because it is considered a bad omen to hear the groans of the sati, onlookers usually yell, sound horns, and beat drums.[22]

In anticipation of Rajan's thesis, Jhabvala restores the experience of trauma to history. Douglas has not described the 1923 sati to Olivia, "wanting to spare her the details (which were indeed very painful—he was to hear that woman's screams to the end of his days)" (58). By maintaining in the foreground of her novel the image of the female body in pain, Jhabvala also constitutes sati as typical, bolstering a whole complex of other practices that victimize women—female infanticide, child marriage, and dowry deaths ("kerosene satis"). The modern narrator describes the case of Ritu, an unhappy young wife whose precarious mental condition deteriorates as the heat of the hot season increases. The narrator comments that "I can't get used to these screams" (81). The other witness to her mental torment, Chid, a would-be Hindu sadhu, simply increases the volume of his chanting to block them out. Later "the screams broke out again, but in an entirely different way. Now they were bloodcurdling as of an animal in intense physical pain" (81).

In an attempt at exorcism by fire, Ritu is being burned by red-hot irons to drive out evil spirits. The incident constitutes a crypto-sati, with its elements of pain by burning, female victimization by marriage customs, and a religious bystander's willful disregard. Olivia's own bodily suffering is also brought into sharp focus. Although not, of course, a sati, her choice of "burning" on the plains during the heat and dust of the hot season, in order to remain with the man she loves, is described as an ordeal by fire (90). But the reference is to some degree ironic. Only a faithful wife can become a sati. By this point in the novel, Olivia has already transferred her affections to the Nawab. Olivia is last seen in acute pain following a backstreet abortion, after which she is detected by Dr. Saunders and flees to the Nawab. Appearing at the palace in native dress, pale from an enormous loss of blood, she reminds her friend Harry of a print he had once seen called *Mrs. Secombe in Flight from the Mutineers,* depicting Mrs. Secombe in native dress fleeing the mutineers at Sikrora to the safety of the British Residency at Lucknow (172). The image of the Indian Mutiny deliberately reverses the usual historical stereotype. Olivia has "gone native" to escape the British. As opposed to the Orientalist idea of the British as bearers of the seeds of culture and as protectors of women, her abortion represents the sterility and destructiveness of Imperial rule. She is in flight, not from destroying Indians, but from the hostile British. Olivia made her own choice between Douglas and the Nawab, Empire and India, but to the British she will always appear as a manipulated victim, deluded into self-destruction by a villainous Indian: "No one ever doubted that the Nawab had used Olivia as a means of revenge" (170).

In the modern plot of the novel the narrator is inclined to view sati as a thing of the past. She notes that all the sati stones look age-old (55), even the 1923 shrine. The death of Leelavati, a widow who had been driven out of her father-in-law's house and spent her life as a destitute beggar, takes place at the stones and is described in terms that appear to validate the widow-who-survives. Although the description of her death is not sparing of physical details, her attendant comments that "Leelavati had done well and had been rewarded with a good, a blessed end" (115).

Rajan has made the point that historicization combats the notion of an age-old, platonic sati. Sati may be seen as the result of local practices, and as evolving historically rather than being enjoined by ancient scriptures (17–18). Indeed, in 1817 the chief pundit of the Supreme Court argued that a woman's burning herself was an unworthy act and that a life of abstinence and chastity was preferable. Similarly, Lata Mani has argued that the discourse on sati was not a discourse in which preexisting traditions were challenged by an emergent modern consciousness, but one in which both "tradition" and "modernity" were contemporaneously produced. Thus emptied of historical resonance, the sati became the site on which tradition was debated and reformulated: "neither subject nor object but ground—such is the status of women in the discourse on sati."[23]

Importantly, in *Heat and Dust* the modern narrator spends much of her time with a group of vigorous widows who range freely about the town, gossiping, joking, and clearly having the time of their lives. Nonetheless, a warning note is struck at the sati stones when one of the widows makes reverent offerings to those who, in her view, have honored ancient custom and made the highest sacrifice. "She even seemed regretful—this merry widow!—that it had been discontinued" (55). Discussing sati in 1978, Dorothy Stein noted that "an occasional illegal sati is still reported in the newspapers, and satis of the past are still family and village saints; the places where they burned are considered sacred ground. Otherwise only the thousands of stone memorials and the stony survival of Hindu widowhood remain."[24] In fact, however, sati is exceptionally, and lamentably, contemporaneous. In 1981 Kumkum Sangari and Sudesh Vaid reported a case of sati (August 1980) and warned of the active reviving of sati in some areas for socioeconomic reasons: "Unless countermeasures are immediately undertaken at various levels, the incidence of sati in these regions is likely to continue and may even occur with greater frequency."[25] Indeed, writing in 1993, Rajan notes a particular increase in sati in the last ten years and describes the case of Roop Kanwar, married only seven months, who died voluntarily on 4 September 1987 on her husband's pyre in Deorala village, two hours' journey from Jaipur, the capital of Rajasthan. Although hundreds witnessed the event, and although sati is, of course, illegal, the state government showed no reaction until women's groups intervened. Even then, 300,000 people attended the *chunari mahotsav,* the festival marking the thirtieth day after the sati. Huge pro-sati rallies occurred in Jaipur, and the village of Deorala has developed into a prosperous pilgrim center. Nobody has yet been convicted of an offense in connection with Roop Kanwar's death, despite the passing of *The Commission of Sati (Prevention Act, 1987).*

Almost as disturbing as the act itself is the recent glorification of sati through temples and annual fairs. Rajan points out that all over Rajasthan businessmen have built temples to past satis. In this particular case, the past is being commodified not by Western but by Indian financial interests, as "the enactment of modern sati derives its features from popular cinema and political meetings rather than hallowed ritual" (18).

One representation of Roop Kanwar's death took the form of a photo-montage, using photographs taken at her wedding. As if actually immolating herself, she smiles out at the camera, apparently oblivious to pain, sitting beside her husband's body in the midst of the flames. Roop Kanwar has, in short, been comprehensively retrofitted to provide a fantasy for Indians to buy into, a fantasy that excises the pain of woman from the apparently "historical" record. It is to Jhabvala's credit that nobody who has read *Heat and Dust* could accept such a photograph as genuine. In her writing, Jhabvala makes the point that we should never lose sight of past trauma—whether it results from European or Indian agency—however difficult or painful it may be to articulate it. Indeed, it is precisely this difficulty of conscious articulation that provides a site of resistance to the forces of commodification.

NOTES

1. I am grateful to Laura E. Donaldson for drawing my attention to this item in her *Decolonizing Feminisms: Race, Gender, and Empire Building* (London: Routledge, 1992).

2. Cathy Caruth, "Introduction," *American Imago* 48.4 (Winter 1991): 417, 419.

3. Newman, "Post-Colonial Gothic."

4. Eve Kosofsky Sedgwick, *The Coherence of Gothic Conventions* (London: Methuen, 1986).

5. See Chew, "Fictions of Princely States and Empire"; Cronin, "*The Hill of Devi* and *Heat and Dust*"; and Newman, "The Untold Story and the Retold Story."

6. Nissim Ezekiel, "Cross Cultural Encounter in Literature," *The Indian P.E.N.* (November–December 1977): 5, quoted in Agarwal, "A Critical Study of *Heat and Dust*" 53.

7. Upamanyu Chatterjee, *English, August: An Indian Story* (London: Faber, 1988).

8. Patrick Brantlinger, *Rule of Darkness: British Literature and Imperialism, 1830–1914* (Ithaca: Cornell UP, 1988), 86.

9. Gerry Clarke, rev. of *Serpentine,* by Thomas Thompson, *Bestsellers* Jan. 1980: 383.

10. Elliott Leyton, *Hunting Humans: The Rise of the Modern Multiple Mur-*

derer (London: Penguin, 1989). First published as *Compulsive Killers* (New York: New York UP, 1986).

11. The term *sati* is used for both the widow and the practice.

12. Brantlinger 86.

13. T. Herbert Warren, ed., *Tennyson: Poems and Plays* (Oxford: Oxford UP, 1971), 816.

14. Letitia Elizabeth Landon, *The Poetical Works of Letitia Elizabeth Landon (L.E.L.),* ed. W. Bell Scott (London: George Routledge and Sons, 1874), 524.

15. See Mary Daly, *Gyn/Ecology* (London: Women's Press, 1979); V. C. Joshi, ed., *Rammohun Roy and the Process of Modernization in India* (Delhi: Vikas, 1975); Joanna Liddle and Rama Joshi, *Daughters of Independence: Gender, Caste and Class in India* (London: Zed, 1986); Lata Mani, "The Production of an Official Discourse of Sati in Early Nineteenth Century Bengal," *Europe and Its Others* (Proceedings of the Essex Conference on the Sociology of Literature, July 1984), ed. Francis Barker et al. (Colchester: U of Essex P, 1985), 107–28; Lata Mani, "Contentious Traditions: The Debate on Sati in Colonial India," *Recasting Women: Essays in Indian Colonial History,* ed. Kumkum Sangari and Sudesh Vaid (New Brunswick, NJ, and New Delhi: Rutgers UP and Kali for Women, 1989), 88–126; Vina Mazumdar, "Comment on Suttee," *Signs* 4.2 (Winter 1978): 269–73; Rajan, *Real and Imagined Women;* Kumkum Sangari and Sudesh Vaid, "Sati in Modern India: A Report," *Economic and Political Weekly* 1 Aug. 1981: 1284–88; Gayatri Chakravorty Spivak, "Can the Subaltern Speak?" *Marxism and the Interpretation of Culture,* ed. Cary Nelson and Lawrence Grossberg (London: Macmillan, 1988), 271–313; Dorothy K. Stein, "Women to Burn: Suttee as Normative Practice," *Signs* 4.2 (Winter 1978): 253–68. An important early source for descriptions of sati is Edward Thompson, *Suttee: A Historical and Philosophical Enquiry into the Hindu Rite of Widow Burning* (London: George Allen and Unwin, 1928).

16. Mani, "Contentious Traditions" 117.

17. For a comprehensive discussion of *Heat and Dust* see Newman, *The Ballistic Bard,* 29–50.

18. Spivak 299.

19. Edward Said, *Orientalism* (London: Routledge and Kegan Paul, 1978).

20. W. H. Sleeman, *Rambles and Recollections of an Indian Official* (London: Oxford UP, 1915), 22–23.

21. Mani, "Contentious Traditions" 110.

22. Thompson 40.

23. Mani, "Contentious Traditions" 18.

24. Stein 262.

25. Sangari and Vaid, "Sati in Modern India" 1288.

Selected Works by Ruth Prawer Jhabvala

A Backward Place. London: John Murray, 1965.

Amrita: Or to Whom She Will. New York: W. W. Norton, 1955.

"Disinheritance." *Blackwoods* April 1979: 4–14.

East into Upper East: Plain Tales from New York and New Delhi. Washington, DC: Counterpoint Press, 1998.

Esmond in India. London: George Allen and Unwin, 1958.

Get Ready for Battle. London: John Murray, 1962.

Heat and Dust. London: John Murray, 1975.

How I Became a Holy Mother and Other Stories. New York: Harper & Row, 1976.

The Householder. London: John Murray, 1960.

In Search of Love and Beauty. London: John Murray, 1983.

The Nature of Passion. London: George Allen and Unwin, 1956.

A New Dominion. London: John Murray, 1972.

Out of India: Selected Stories. New York: William Morrow, 1986.

Poet and Dancer. London: John Murray, 1993.

Shards of Memory: A Novel. New York: W. W. Norton, 1995.

A Stronger Climate: Nine Stories. New York: W. W. Norton, 1968.

Three Continents. London: John Murray, 1987.

To Whom She Will. London: George Allen and Unwin, 1955.

Travelers. New York: Simon & Schuster, 1987.

Selected Works about Ruth Prawer Jhabvala

Abel, Elizabeth. "Emerging Identities: The Dynamics of Female Friendship in Contemporary Fiction by Women." *Signs* 6.3 (Spring 1981): 413–35.

Agarwal, Ramlal G. "A Critical Study of *Heat and Dust.*" *Studies in Indian Fiction in English.* Ed. G. S. Balarama Gupta. Gulbarga, India: JIWE Publications, 1987. 53–60.

———. "The Expatriate Experience: The Novels of Ruth Prawer Jhabvala and Paul Scott." *The British and Irish Novel since 1960.* Ed. James Acheson. New York: St. Martin's, 1991. 48–61.

———. *Ruth Prawer Jhabvala: A Study of Her Fiction.* New York: Envoy, 1990.

Albertazzi, Silvia. "'Shut In, Shut Off': Ruth Prawer Jhabvala's 'Mythology of Captivity.'" *Commonwealth Essays and Studies* 8.1 (Autumn 1985): 45–55.

Bawer, Bruce. "Passage to India: The Career of Ruth Prawer Jhabvala." *New Criterion* 6.4 (December 1987): 5–19.

Bennett, Bruce, Peter Cowan, Dennis Haskell, and Susan Miller, eds. *Westerly Looks to Asia: A Selection from Westerly, 1956–1992.* Nedlands, Australia: Indian Ocean Centre for Peace Studies, 1993.

Chakravarti, Aruna. "Stepping out of the Zenana: Jhabvala's *The Nature of Passion.*" *Margins of Erasure: Purdah in the Subcontinental Novel in English.* Ed. Jasbir Jain and Amina Amin. New Delhi: Sterling, 1995. 94–105.

Chew, Shirley. "Fictions of Princely States and Empire." *Ariel* 17.3 (July 1986): 103–17.

Crane, Ralph J. "Ruth Prawer Jhabvala: A Checklist of Primary and Secondary Sources." *Journal of Commonwealth Literature* 20.1 (1985): 171–203.

——. "Ruth Prawer Jhabvala's Sky: Escape from *Heat and Dust?*" *Journal of the South Pacific Association for Commonwealth Literature and Language Studies* 24 (April 1987): 178–89.

Cronin, Richard. "*The Hill of Devi* and *Heat and Dust.*" *Essays in Criticism* 36 (April 1986): 142–59.

Dahr, T. N. "Jhabvala's 'An Experience in India': How True and Right?" *Panjab University Research Bulletin* (Arts) 21.2 (October 1990): 21–27.

Dudt, Charmazel. "Jhabvala's Fiction: The Passage from India." *Faith of a Woman Writer.* Ed. Alice Kessler-Harris. Westport, CT: Greenwood, 1988. 159–64.

Ezekiel, Nissim. "Two Readers and Their Texts." *Asian and Western Writers in Dialogue: New Cultural Identities.* Ed. Guy Amirthanayagam. London: Macmillan, 1982. 137–41.

Gooneratne, Yasmine. "Apollo, Krishna, Superman: The Image of India in Ruth Prawer Jhabvala's Ninth Novel." *Ariel* 15.2 (April 1984): 109–17.

——. "Contemporary India in the Writing of Ruth Prawer Jhabvala." *Westerly: A Quarterly Review* 28.4 (December 1983): 73–80.

——. "Film into Fiction: The Influence of Ruth Prawer Jhabvala's Early Cinema Work upon Her Fiction." *Still the Frame Holds: Essays on Women Poets and Writers.* Ed. Sheila Roberts and Yvonne Pacheco Tevis. San Bernardino: Borgo, 1993. 173–89.

——. "Images of Indian Exile in Rushdie's *The Satanic Verses* and Ruth Prawer Jhabvala's *Three Continents.*" *Literature and Exile.* Ed. David Bevan. Amsterdam: Rodopi, 1990. 7–21.

——. "Literary Influences on the Writing of Ruth Prawer Jhabvala." *Language and Literature in Multicultural Contexts*. Ed. Satendra Nandan. Suva, Fiji: U of the South Pacific, 1983. 141–68.

——. "Satirical Semi-Colon: Ruth Prawer Jhabvala's Screen Play for Bombay Talkie." *Journal of Indian Writing in English* 8.1–2 (January–July 1980): 177–81.

Hayball, Connie. "Ruth Prawer Jhabvala's India." *Journal of Indian Writing in English* 9.2 (July 1981): 42–54.

Lenta, Margaret. "Narrators and Readers: 1902 and 1975." *Ariel* 20.3 (July 1989): 19–36.

Marnham, Patrick. "Sobhraj's Slow Poison." *Books and Bookmen* Feb. 1980: 11.

McDonough, Michael. "An Interview with Ruth Prawer Jhabvala." *San Francisco Review of Books* 11.4 (Spring 1987): 5–6.

Moore, Susan. "Comic Novels about India: Neglected Masters, and Others." *Quadrant* 29 (September 1985): 76–79.

Newman, Judie. *The Ballistic Bard: Postcolonial Fictions*. London: Edward Arnold, 1995.

——. "Post-Colonial Gothic: Ruth Prawer Jhabvala and the Sobhraj Case." *Modern Fiction Studies* 40.1 (Spring 1994): 1–16.

——. "The Untold Story and the Retold Story." *Motherlands: Black Women's Writing from Africa, the Caribbean, and South Asia*. Ed. Susheila Nasta. London and New Brunswick, NJ: Women's Press and Rutgers UP, 1991. 24–42.

Price, Susan. "Images of Empire." *Los Angeles Times Magazine* 30 Aug. 1987: 30, 32.

Rai, Sudha. "Purdah: Indian and British, in Jhabvala's *Heat and Dust*." *Margins of Erasure: Purdah in the Subcontinental Novel in English*. Ed. Jasbir Jain and Amina Amin. New Delhi: Sterling, 1995. 83–93.

Rajan, Rajeswari Sunder. *Real and Imagined Women: Gender, Culture, and Postcolonialism*. London: Routledge, 1993.

Rubin, David. *After the Raj: British Novels of India since 1947*. Hanover, NH: UP of New England, 1986.

——. "Ruth Jhabvala in India." *Modern Fiction Studies* 30.4 (Winter 1984): 669–83.

Shahani, Vasant A. "An Artist's Experience of India: Ruth Prawer Jhabvala's Fiction." *English and India*. Ed. M. Manuel. Madras: Wasani for Macmillan, 1978. 1–15.

Shepherd, Ron. "The Need to Suffer: Crisis of Identity in the Fiction of Ruth Prawer Jhabvala." *Commonwealth Review* 2.1–2 (1990–91): 196–203.

Singh, Brijraj. "Ruth Prawer Jhabvala: *Heat and Dust*." *Major Indian Novels: An*

Evaluation. Ed. N. S. Pradham. Atlantic Highlands, NJ: Humanities, 1986. 192–222.

Sohi, Harinder. "Ruth Jhabvala's Passage to India." *Panjab University Research Bulletin* 16.1 (April 1985): 3–15.

Sucher, Laurie. *The Fiction of Ruth Prawer Jhabvala: The Politics of Passion.* London: Macmillan, 1989.

Summerfield, H. "Holy Women and Unholy Men: Ruth Prawer Jhabvala Confronts the Non-Rational." *Ariel* 17.3 (July 1986): 85–101.

Williams, Haydn Moore. "Mad Seekers, Doomed Lovers, and Cemeteries in India: On R. P. Jhabvala's *Heat and Dust* and *A New Dominion.*" *New Literature Review* 15 (1988): 11–20.

———. "Reactions to Entrapment in 'Backward Places': V. S. Naipaul's *Miguel Street* and Ruth Prawer Jhabvala's *A Backward Place.*" *A Sense of Place in the New Literatures in English.* Ed. Peggy Nightingale. St. Lucia: U of Queensland P, 1986. 68–74.

5
Anita Brookner: On Reaching for the Sun

Kate Fullbrook

Since her turn to fiction in 1981, the annual appearance of a novel by Anita Brookner has attracted a mixed response. Highly praised as an exquisite stylist in the mainstream English line of women writers concerned with bourgeois manners and morals which runs from Jane Austen through Virginia Woolf and on to Barbara Pym (with whom Brookner's name is often coupled) and to Brookner's own favorites, Rosamond Lehmann and Elizabeth Taylor, her work also provokes exasperation among critics for its limited range, its miniaturism, and its ambivalence. Compared with equal frequency to classic French fiction and to popular romance, Brookner's novels occupy recognizable ground on the terrain of English fiction.[1] Polite, quietly comic, simultaneously ambitious and modest, Brookner's accounts of respectable, disappointed lives (usually disappointed *women's* lives) constitute meditations on some of the central ideological premises of the modern period; on the way, these premises are translated into ordinary experiences of failure and loss.

In her engagement with the ideology of the modern, Brookner takes the long view, with a perspective that locates itself in the Enlightenment and in the hopes attendant on the triumph of the bourgeoisie in the subsequent romantic period, with its mingled dreams of individual liberty, of the formation of the heroic self, and of the rejection of religious notions in favor of the promise of strictly secular fulfillment. The question repeatedly addressed in Brookner's fiction is whether the state of personal and cultural exhaustion experienced by the great majority of her characters inevitably follows from great eighteenth-century shifts in the cultural formation of European thought. The romantic vision of the heroic life persists in the shaping of the intimate hopes of the privileged individuals who are, in terms of their material well-being and that of their social class as a whole, the clear beneficiaries of these shifts, despite the historical events that have eroded the initial optimism of the romantic project. In Brookner's fiction this failure is signaled less by the general social cataclysms of war and political oppression (though these dark undertones are present in her fiction) than by the necessary persistence of stoic ideas of duty, self-sacrifice, and the limiting of personal desire which carry a moral weight that overbalances the enticement of both romantic promise and romantic despair.

Brookner's work is tightly focused on the nexus of issues which this interrogation suggests. That it should be so is not surprising, given the progress of her intellectual career. Born in London in 1928 (until 1985 she gave 1938 as the year of her birth), the only child of Jewish parents of Polish origin, Anita Brookner studied history at King's College, University of London, and then art history at the Courtauld Institute of Art, where, based on her work on Greuze in Paris, she earned her doctorate. Highly successful as an academic art historian, Brookner taught first at the University of Reading from 1959 to 1964 before taking up a post as lecturer, and in 1977 as reader at the Courtauld, the leading British center for the training of art historians, which she held until her retirement in 1988, securing a reputation as a kind and exhilarating teacher ("Anita Brookner" 13).[2] She served as the first woman Slade Professor of Art at Cambridge from 1967 to 1968, and is a Fellow of New Hall in Cambridge and King's College in London.

Equally distinguished as an art historian and as a novelist, Brookner has not lacked high public acclaim. Her fourth novel, *Hotel du Lac,* received the 1984 Booker Prize, the most prestigious award in contemporary British fiction; she was awarded the CBE (Commander, Order of the British Empire) in 1990. Despite the overwhelming nature of the official recognition afforded Brookner, in her interviews she has spoken often of her sense of her own marginality in English society, given her parents' non-English origins and her early life as a scholarly and dutiful daughter who looked after her parents. "Mine," Brookner notes, "was a dreary Victorian story: I nursed my parents till they died" (Kenyon, *Women Writers* 12).[3] She describes her own life precisely in the terms of unearned privilege and enervated longing which saturate the atmosphere of her fiction, and has always emphasized the at least partially autobiographical impulse that led her to writing fiction as an act of personal unburdening. Her first novel was, she states unequivocally, "an exercise in self-analysis," written "in a moment of sadness and desperation." "Writing," she has remarked with the notable melancholy that touches all her fiction, "has freed me from the despair of living" (Guppy 150, 151).

The modesty and politeness of Brookner's interviews (which, like many interviews with writers, are both strikingly revelatory and decidedly self-protective) tend to occlude both her high ambition and high achievement. Her career has been distinguished, enormously productive, and multifaceted. And it has been a writer's life. Brookner translated books on Utrillo, the Fauves, and Gauguin in the early 1960s. She has worked extensively as a journalist and reviewer. Her first four books established her as an authority on the romantic period in French painting. *Watteau* (1968), *The Genius of the Future: Studies in French Art Criticism: Diderot, Stendhal, Baudelaire, Zola, the Brothers Goncourt, Huysmans* (1971), *Greuze: The Rise and Fall of an Eighteenth-Century Phenomenon* (1972), and *Jacques-Louis David* (1980) are as much excursions into the history of ideas as commentaries on painters and paintings. Eminently readable, Brookner's art history is marked both by a narrative drive unusual in the discipline and by a continuing preoccupation with the development of the philosophical underpinnings of modernity, especially as evidenced by the two figures whom Brookner most clearly and consistently admires: the philosopher Diderot and the painter Jacques-Louis David. In interviews, Brookner has insisted on the discontinuity between her art history and her fiction. In response to John Haffenden's question regarding the connections between the two, she noted that "The awful thing is that I see no connection at all. It's a sort of schizophrenic activity as far as I'm concerned" (65).

Despite her disclaimers, the continuities that run through Brookner's different kinds of writing are pronounced. All her writing is notably shaped by her work as a historian of ideas. And her continuing and central concern is with variants of the romantic legacy, from the ways it structures ideas of love to the ever-present temptation of Nietzschean nihilism. For Brookner, romanticism is not an exhausted movement of the past, but the framework on which the contemporary world is pinioned. After agreeing, in an interview with Shusha Guppy, that existentialism is the sole philosophy she can endorse, Brookner goes on to explain what she means by noting that existentialism is a romantic creed:

> Freedom in existentialist terms breeds anxiety, and you have to accept that anxiety as the price to pay. I think choice is a luxury most people can't afford. I mean when you make a break for freedom you don't necessarily find company on the way, you find loneliness. . . . Romanticism doesn't make sense unless you realize that it grew out of the French Revolution in which human behavior sank to such terrible depths that it became obvious no supernatural power, if it existed, could possibly countenance it. For the first time Europeans felt that God was dead. Since then we have had Hitler, Stalin, Pol Pot, whose activities make the French Revolution seem like a picnic. (154)

The Enlightenment, founded on a faith in reason as the guiding principle for a new "Republic of Virtue," was blasted by the Revolution, after which, argues Brookner, "people realized that Reason could not change anything, that man is moved not by Reason but by darker forces" (154). And if this meant that the idea of evil without limits entered the secular European mind, it also opened the way to "inventive, creative, autobiographical behavior" (155). In the same interview Brookner signals her agreement with Isaiah Berlin's statement that "all the problems of our age can be traced back to Romanticism" (156).

The problems that most concern Brookner in her fiction are those that circle around the debris of the failures of both reason and romantic promise and their impact on that most romantic of figures, the solitary individual who longs for heroic fulfillment of the self. To understand precisely the nature of Brookner's interest in this area, consideration of her work as an art historian is instructive. In both *The Genius of the Future* and *Greuze*, Brookner outlines the origins of modern romanticism in the divide that opened in the eighteenth century between the English and French interpretations of Locke. The key work here is Locke's *Essay Concerning Human Understanding* with its emphasis on the absence of innate ideas, its insistence on the generation of knowledge as "the outcome of a dual process of sensation and reflection," and its location of all human knowledge in the experience guaranteed by the senses and translated into reason (*Greuze* 3–4). Given the additional argument that, for Locke, divine revelation is unavailable to human beings (with the exception of strictly personal intimations of the divine will), human morality and the pursuit of happiness must be governed by the dictates of reason. What the eighteenth-century British empiricists made of this doctrine tends toward the altogether practical and pragmatic habits of thought that still characterize English culture.

The French interpretation of Locke moved in entirely other directions. Brookner charts the key elements of the French reading of Locke which develop into a full-blooded revolutionary doctrine. Locke's "apparent destruction of Christian first principles is . . . the removal of pessimism." A "new emphasis on this world, a positive approach to man and his place in society," develops in response to the abandoning of religious foundations. In addition, "there emerges a conception of man as the sole guardian of his powers and moral instinct, and of his faculties as instruments for experiment." This radical jettisoning of faith in various kinds of authority resulted in the creation of a fevered, if optimistic, "moral climate which placed the supreme emphasis on personal experience of violent but self-congratulatory emotion, consciousness of evil being tempered and if possible overcome by the observation of a few principles, accessible to all, and finally a belief in the power of natural goodness" (*Greuze* 4, 5). The rise of the cult of *sensibilité*, the elevation of the man (and woman) of feeling to the highest point of cultural regard, has its origins in this spectacular ideological shift. The partial failure of the French Revolution—if it circuitously signaled the triumph of the bourgeoisie as the crucial power base in the modern period—also represented the fall from innocence for the French inheritors of Locke and their ideas. After the events of the 1790s and the rise and then collapse of the Napoleonic imperial adventure, the romantic reaction represented an extreme revision of the optimistic principles of the age of rationalism. In her book on Jacques-Louis David, painter-in-chief of both the revolutionary and Napoleonic periods in France, Brookner enumerates the key characteristics of the romantic reaction to the eclipse of the rationalist project in France. "Difficult as it is," notes Brookner, "to find a definition of Romanticism," certain of its elements and obsessions find general agreement from all quarters. Romanticism tends to engage with "the catastrophes wrought by loss of religious faith," to evidence a typical concern for melancholy events, "to live, existentially, in a metaphysical vacuum which negates all certainties," to display "geographical curiosity" and a taste for exoticism of setting and the insertion of the self into the elsewhere, the unknown. Romantic artists tend to interrogate the possibilities of their media. Crucially, the romantic author concentrates "on knowing himself and charting his own emotional progress," and, in all these things, the most fundamental principle, the "metaphysical heart" of romanticism, "is quite simply consciousness of a sense of loss," of defeat, of "the disappearance of the collective hope" that leads to the characteristic state of romantic despair, the state which is "the negation of all purpose" (*Jacques-Louis David* 172). The perceived failure of the project of enlightenment, which begins with Locke, dictates the outlines of the romanticism which, in its fullest nineteenth-century expression, produces, in turn, both the hedonism and nihilism of Nietzsche.

Brookner's saturation in this particular version of the development of the European history of ideas deeply informs her writing on eighteenth- and nineteenth-century painting; and her obvious concern with the impact of this history on the cultural formations of the self in the late twentieth century provides the continuum of often shifting positions with regard to identity, morality, and desire occupied by her fictional characters. It is Brookner's intense concentration on the kinds of residue left by the various stages of the breakdown of the Enlightenment project on the personal and domestic circumstances of her protagonists which gives her novels their consistent, quietly despairing, airless atmosphere, and their equally consistent air of the impossibility of the resolution between the poles of perceived possibility which tend to be labeled "love" and "freedom" by characters who, just as persistently, cannot find a satisfying resolution to their discordant needs. Enticed alternately by a sentimental paradigm of eternal love which finds its expression in a tender family harmony as unreal as those depicted in the highly popular genre paintings of Greuze, by high romantic dreams of sexual passion which transport the self to its fullest emotional pitch, and by bouts of Nietzschean temptation which push them to visions of the sheer exercise of the power of self and will in the pursuit of their desire, Brookner's characters carry the marks of modern cultural history within the muffled circumstances of the prosperous English upper middle class to which they belong. Typically, nothing much happens in a Brookner novel, and this perceived passivity causes a good deal of uneasiness both in readers who rightly

locate her in the realist tradition which has always, more or less consciously, undertaken to examine the same issues, but which has done so
through a concentration on action, and in readers who, also correctly, locate her in the women's popular romance tradition but avoiding the reassurance of the possibility of satisfaction, one of the choice attractions
of the genre.

In her interviews, Brookner clearly outlines her conscious lineage as
a writer of fiction. To answer John Haffenden's question about which
nineteenth-century writers she regards as "touchstones of truly great
writing," she lists Dickens (a writer she usually mentions with a supple-
mentary account of her Polish father's regard for Dickens as a guide to
English life), Henry James ("for moral scruple"), Trollope ("for decent
feelings"), Stendhal, Flaubert, and Zola (for "scrutiny" and "indignation"). Jane Austen (a writer with whom Brookner is often compared)
leaves her uneasy: Brookner feels that Austen leaves out too much, that
she "forfeited passion for wit" (68–69). Among recent women writers she
points to Fay Weldon (most interestingly, Brookner does so immediately
after making typically disparaging remarks regarding contemporary
feminism, which Brookner mischievously tends to caricature in terms of
"man-hating"),[4] Rosmond Lehmann, Elizabeth Taylor, Edith Temple-
ton, Mavis Grant, and Edith de Born (71). In her interview with Shusha
Guppy she adds Balzac and Proust to her list, as well as Edith Wharton
(she edited a collection of Wharton's stories, which appeared in 1988–89),
Storm Jameson, and Jean Rhys, and enthusiastically notes her pleasure
in the writing of Philip Roth. To Olga Kenyon she marks her position
most clearly. After earlier agreeing with a remark about the French influence on her fiction, she tellingly answers Kenyon's question "may I ask
you what you think of novelists like Henry James?": "He wars in my
mind for supremacy with Dickens. If you wish *scrutiny*, then it has to be
James—and the French. But if you want indignation, then it's Dickens"
(*Women Writers* 24).[5] Brookner's repeated use of the words of "scrutiny"
and "indignation" encapsulates succinctly her views of the chief purposes
of fiction. These views locate her squarely within the mainstream development of the novel. A highly self-conscious writer, Brookner has, from
the first, located her fiction precisely within the traditions of analysis,
scrutiny, and indignation which her remarks suggest.

Brookner's novels vary in the manner and degree to which they enact
the critique of the romantic legacy in the late twentieth century. I want

to turn here to look closely at two texts that illustrate the techniques and key concerns of her fiction: *Hotel du Lac* (1984), her most popular novel, which serves as the culminating work of the first phase of her fiction, and *A Private View* (1994), her most recent production, which evidences clearly the general outlines of her recurrent interests.

Edith Hope, the central figure in *Hotel du Lac,* provides a good example of Brookner's typical protagonist. A middle-aged, middle-class woman who lives by slightly outmoded but achingly respectable social conventions, Edith has been packed off by a friend to a dull but proper Swiss resort out of season to do a kind of secular penance for the committing a personally atypical act of impropriety. Her "sin"—her "crime" on which she is meant to reflect during her month of comfortable (if rather faded) social exile—is that, at the last moment, she shied away from marrying kind, lonely Geoffrey Long, a man of "mouse-like seemliness" (129) for whom Edith has no sexual feeling and whom she left standing (in a last-minute refusal of marriage without passion) at the Registry Office on the day set for their wedding. The precise nature of Edith's "unfortunate lapse" (8) remains unclear until late in the novel, though her obsession with her lover, her friend's husband, David, is signaled early in her jaunty, bantering letters to him, which form a significant portion of the text. Edith, a professor's daughter whose mother despised her husband for his dullness, makes her living writing women's romance fiction and uses the excruciatingly appropriate pseudonym of "Vanessa Wilde" (significantly, Edith, who looks like Virginia Woolf in the novel, is given the task of trying to come to terms with contemporary sexual decadence). In this role, Edith sees herself as caught in a "daily task of fantasy and obfuscation" (50), purveying to women, as she explains to her agent, "the old myths . . . that they are going to be discovered, looking their best, behind closed doors, just when they thought that all was lost, by a man who has battled across continents, abandoning whatever he may have had in his intray, to reclaim them" (27). In an often cited passage, Edith then observes that she writes to "the most potent myth of all," that of the tortoise and the hare, in which "the tortoise wins every time." She immediately notes that "This is a lie, of course. . . . In real life, of course, it is the hare who wins. Every time. Look around you. And in any case it is my contention that Aesop was writing for the tortoise market. Axiomatically." Edith says she writes for "the virtuous," not for "those multi-orgasmic girls with the executive briefcases" (27–28).

Despite her intelligence, Edith knows that she herself is of the tortoise kind, a woman who leads a life of silence, solitude, and discretion, marked by opportunities lost and made bearable only by her passion for her evasive lover, who cares a great deal less for her than she for him. Offered another chance at a marriage of convenience at the Hotel du Lac, by the suave, Mephistophelean Mr. Neville, Edith almost takes it, only to turn away (again at the last moment after having learned of his sexual cynicism) to flee back to London and the fairly indifferent arms of her supposedly Byronic David.

Like all of Brookner's fiction, *Hotel du Lac* focuses on disappointment and the failure of life to match the paradigms imposed on it. Much of the novel concentrates, generally, on failure of vision and, particularly, Edith's inability to make sense of the events and people around her. Images of indeterminacy and obscurity, represented by the grayness and mist of the air, sky, and water surrounding the hotel, suffuse the text. The hotel seems to exist almost exclusively for the reception of "cast-off or abandoned" women: the infertile, the aged, the somehow impaired—all of whom, nevertheless, concern themselves with fulfilling the needs of men who are simply not there (92). Despite her supposed powers of observation as a writer of fiction, Edith initially reads each of the guests incorrectly, correct vision returning only with the rare moments of the lifting of the mist in the novel. In this obscured environment, Edith almost accepts the Nietzschean bargain offered to her by Neville: "Whatever they told you about unselfishness being good and wickedness being bad was entirely inaccurate. It is a lesson for serfs and it leads to resignation. And my policy, you may be surprised to hear, will ensure you any number of friends. People feel at home with low moral standards. It is scruples that put them off" (96). As Edith swerves from a union with this man and the position he represents—the ultimate nihilist stage of the romantic tradition which Brookner clearly sees as overwhelmingly operative in contemporary society (many of the characters who serve as foils for her protagonists are of Neville's Nietzschean breed)—back to her own romance of loyalty to her extremity of feeling for her lover, Brookner completes the circle of damaging romantic positions she has traced on the shores of Rousseau's lake.

Distinguishing between writers of formulaic romance novels, who, notes Brookner, "seem to be writing about a different species," and romantic writers "who are characterized by absolute longing—perhaps for something that is not there and cannot be there," Brookner puts Edith Hope into the latter category: as such, Hope "is not a twentieth-century heroine, she belongs to the nineteenth century" (Guppy 161). Brookner further clarifies her orientation to the residue of romanticism in her telling remarks to Olga Kenyon about her heroines' exasperatingly limited choices. Bluntly, Brookner glosses her characters: "They are stupid—if they weren't they'd have more options. But the choice is never unlimited, that's the twentieth-century mistake, whereas the nineteenth century was more realistic. You can do this *or* that, not an unlimited number of things" (*Women Writers* 21).[6] Brookner is interested (like Edith Wharton, like Henry James) in the moral imagination governing the choice of the beloved. It is precisely the paucity of choice disguised by a variety of romantic ideological excrescences which hampers all the female characters in *Hotel du Lac,* despite the faith in one version of these principles which sustains Hope in the end.

Like the lecturers Dr. Ruth Weiss in *A Start in Life* (1981) (published as *The Debut* in the United States) and Kitty Maule in *Providence* (1982), and the librarian Frances Hinton in *Look at Me* (1983), Edith Hope exemplifies Brookner's rewriting of a classic type in English fiction: the lonely, bourgeois spinster (the dense patternings of literary allusions are never casual in Brookner's fiction and in *Hotel du Lac*—for instance, Brookner pointedly mentions Mrs. Gaskell's *Cranford*).[7] Brookner is interested in stripping back the social organism to the singular. The heroines in her early fiction (whose strong autobiographical impulse has often been noted by critics and by Brookner herself) are all such solitaries—siblingless children and orphans, unpartnered in any way but oblivious to want by virtue of modest if solid inherited wealth and by professional posts. Brookner, like Henry James, wishes to probe and portray these privileged creatures' consciousnesses when material needs are satisfied and yet any secure and honest link with other individuals is missing. (These characters, not simply middle class but properly bourgeois, tend to be backed not only by salaries but by capital. Their posts, in fact, are often a material irrelevance, undertaken more for their ability to fill time than for necessary financial support). Like the nineteenth-century novelists she admires, Brookner pays a good deal of attention to the material circumstances of her characters. These often iconographically loaded accounts of their food, their houses, their clothing, and their grooming (in all these things substantial but never adventurous, and, in all things, orderly) are carefully detailed and used to set up a dichotomy of experience in lives that are externally prosperous, if dull and overly careful, and internal lives in which the proprieties fracture at moments of wild longing for, on one hand, the completion of the domestic idyll with a spouse and children, and, on the other, the glamour of heroic sexual passion.

The atmosphere of disappointment and well-bred stoicism which rules in Brookner's fiction as her most typically observed response to the failure of romantic promise leads to nothing so much as exasperation in some readers. For Adam Mars-Jones, for example, reviewing *Hotel du Lac* for the *New York Review*, Brookner's novel "approximates to masochism." After noting that, on the evidence offered by Brookner, "the passive-aggressive heroines seem back in fashion," he comments that "the limpness of its heroine . . . has a positively bracing effect" and finishes by pointing to the pathology of the entire conception, finally judging *Hotel du Lac* as "divided between narcissism and self-mortification, between wallowing and astringency" (17, 19). Tiresome as Mars-Jones finds this configuration, it is precisely Brookner's point that this recognizable late-twentieth-century condition is part of the debilitation of a culture that has not yet found a way to replace the romantic paradigms by which it still orders its dreams.

As much as Dickens, Brookner is a London novelist; her particular patch is the part of London's West End which respectably, if unexcitingly, borders Hyde Park to the north. If she moves out from this location, she travels to dreary but respectable suburbs or to the anonymously public London of the National Gallery and the Royal Academy, of the busy shopping areas. To the chill and gray of London and her Londoners, she contrasts the sun and warmth of southern Europe. Paris, equally favored as a location for her fiction, Brookner treats as a borderline case: at times the antithesis of London in its glitter and promise, at times its partner as another dreary city of the north. The Riviera serves as the geographical foil to the northern bleakness. Brookner's characters long for the sun and for the Mediterranean culture that produced the paintings often serving as catalytic icons for their self-analysis. Within this field of European reference, Brookner deploys the classic Western myths of the garden and the fall from innocence, the dichotomy between

Christian and pagan values, lives of repression and sterility as opposed to lives of honesty and fecundity.

In the novels that followed *Hotel du Lac*, Brookner not only extended her cast of characters (although, male or female, young or old, they persist in their identifying marks of sedate despair and the wreckage of romantic dreams) but continued to examine the romantic mythology of place in Europe. *Family and Friends* (1985) opens with an epigraph from Goethe's *Werther* and concerns the fortunes of the members of a London family of German origin who, in their individual ways, enact the mythology of place as they scatter from the Riviera to Hollywood. *A Misalliance* (1986) traces the suffering of a woman whose husband has left her for the clichéd younger woman, and her musing on the rival claims of Christian and pagan worldviews prompted most forcefully by the Titian's *Bacchus and Ariadne* in London's National Gallery. *A Friend from England* (1987) ends in Venice and with a heroic adventure into love, which contrasts painfully with the smart, contemporary heartlessness of the London woman from whose viewpoint the story is told. *Latecomers* (1988), one of Brookner's most impressive novels, employs much of Europe's recent history as well as its imaginary past as its central figures, men who, as boys sent to England from Germany to escape the Holocaust in which their Jewish families perished, search for identities partially lost to them. *Lewis Percy* (1989), like many of Brookner's novels, explores the death of the possibility of heroism, while the recent novels *Brief Lives* (1990), *A Closed Eye* (1991), *Fraud* (1992), and *A Family Romance* (1993) all offer extensions and variations on the themes of loss, mistaken interpretation, and the failure of romantic promise.

The recent novel, *A Private View* (1994), works the characteristic Brookner ground. In it George Bland, just retired and grieving for the death of the friend with whom he was to travel the world in the total adventure that was to be his reward for a hardworking but timid life, is tempted to commit the folly of marrying a young woman, Katy Gibb, who appears from nowhere in his block of flats and who simultaneously incarnates New Age credulousness and the hucksterish entrepreneurial con artistry of recent years. George's reaction is to turn his back on his lifetime of propriety and annex Katy, give her the money she wants, and, in return, possess a creature who, whatever her moral and intellectual shoddiness, is full of the life that George feels he has never had. George speculates on playing a teasing game of loser wins, with the predatory Katy serving as a captive Albertine to his Marcel, an Albertine who is to be paraded as a sign of the power of his will in a nomadic life of power and placelessness. As George tries to come to terms with his aging, with time, and with the mortality that overtook his friend, his sadness and grief push him toward an overwhelming craving for the fulfillment of the ego before death overtakes him too. Brookner portrays all this in terms of access to an extreme emotional landscape which George had not known was his makeup. George realizes how he would relish physically damaging Katy: "For a brief moment he was afforded a glimpse into the heart of hedonism, something ancient, pagan, selfish. He saw it as movement, headlong rush, carelessness, the true expression of the essential ego. . . . Few were brave enough to accommodate it, although to taste it was addictive, Dionysian. . . . To live like that would be to know true freedom" (108–9). Freedom, the defiance of time, the reaching for the sun all subside as George's "new Nietzschean consciousness" (167) wavers and then falls away, leaving him in his safe but depleted existence of quiet English solitude and ordinariness, the manner of life that is his true spiritual home. This typical Brookner figure, following so many others, abandons a dream of spectacular romantic heroism (of the emotions, of the will, of absolute freedom, of the titanic self) and subsides into the everyday decency and disappointment that is figured as the general lot of even the successful and the privileged. This is the characteristic Brookner conclusion, one that invites the revisionary view of stoicism as the real heroism of the anti-romantic fabric of life.

Anita Brookner recently has remarked that she is working on her final novel. She believes that she has run out of ideas and has been cited in the *Observer* as saying "Sometimes I feel a fraud: I've written a book a year, and although I've enjoyed the process, I don't know if my readers have. I'm conscious of my failures." She says that she would welcome ideas, but meanwhile "I'd rather live with the realities and one is that I can't write anymore" ("Grapevine" 21). It may indeed be the case that Brookner's combination of the autobiographical impulse and the need to examine the legacy of failed romanticism has run itself into the ground. But then, most significant novelists have one tale they are driven to tell repeatedly. The Brookner tale will not be exhausted any sooner than the power of the romantic myths which she so surgically dissects.

Notes

1. For the best account of Brookner's relation to French fiction see Skinner, *The Fictions of Anita Brookner*. On the relationship with the tradition of women's popular romance see Kenyon, *Women Novelists Today*.

2. "Anita Brookner: Novelist with a Double Life" also contains fascinating information on Brookner's being used as a cat's paw by Sir Anthony Blunt, the director of the Courtauld and the spy who was at the center of the notorious *Spycatcher* case.

3. See also Haffenden, *Novelists in Interview* 61. One of Brookner's most telling subjects is that of the drain of aged parents on their children and the tensions between love, duty, and the wish for freedom this usually entails for both parties.

4. It is useful, I think, to look at precisely what Brookner has to say about contemporary feminism:

> As for feminism, I think it is good for women to earn their living and thereby control their own destinies to some extent. They pay a heavy price for independence though. I marvel at the energy of women who combine husbands, children, and a profession. Anyone who thinks she will fulfill herself in that way can't be realistic. The self-fulfilled woman is far from reality—it is a sort of Shavian fantasy that you can be a complete woman. Besides, a complete woman is probably not a very admirable creature. She is manipulative, uses other people to get her own way, and works within whatever system she is in. The *ideal* woman, on the other hand, is quite different; she lives according to a set of principles and is somehow very rare and always has been. As for the radical feminism of today, the rejection of the male, I find it absurd. It leads to sterility. They say it is a reasoned alternative, but an alternative to what? To continuity? (Guppy 161–62)

This response would take a great deal of analysis to disentangle. However, it is, I think, helpful to note in passing that in her refusal to be appropriated by the feminist movement, Brookner joins a most distinguished group of women writers. Both Katherine Mansfield and Gertrude Stein come to mind as members of this group in the early part of the century; Margaret Atwood's similar refusal recently is also noteworthy. This tendency, it seems to me, is both understandable in terms of the need for women writers of fiction to secure their independence *as* writers, and deserves much more attention by feminist critics as we, equally legitimately, analyze their work.

5. Brookner also remarks to Shusha Guppy, "Henry James seems to me to have all the moral conscience that everybody should have. He writes basically about scruples, and his hesitations are so valid that they are the secular equivalent of religious obligations" (158–59).

6. Brookner readily acquiesces to the statement that her central topic is love: "What else is there? Everything else is merely literature" (Kenyon, *Women Writers* 15); and, again: "What else is there? All the rest is mere literature!" (Guppy 169).

7. Although it is not directly concerned with Brookner's work, Laura Doan's *Old Maids to Radical Spinsters* is a useful compendium of ideas regarding this subject.

SELECTED WORKS BY ANITA BROOKNER

Altered States. New York: Random House, 1997.

Brief Lives. London: Jonathan Cape, 1990.

A Closed Eye. New York: Random House, 1991.

Falling Slowly: A Novel. New York: Random House, 1999.

Family and Friends. London: Jonathan Cape, 1985.

A Family Romance. London: Jonathan Cape, 1993.

Fraud. London: Jonathan Cape, 1992.

A Friend from England. London: Jonathan Cape, 1987.

The Genius of the Future: Studies in French Art Criticism: Diderot, Stendhal, Baudelaire, Zola, the Brothers Goncourt, Huysmans. London: Phaidon Press, 1971.

Greuze: The Rise and Fall of an Eighteenth-Century Phenomenon. London: Paul Elek, 1972.

Hotel du Lac. London: Jonathan Cape, 1984.

Incidents in the Rue Laugier. New York: Random House, 1996.

Jacques-Louis David. London: Chatto & Windus, 1980.

Jacques-Louis David: A Personal Interpretation (lecture). London: Oxford UP, 1984.

Latecomers. London: Jonathan Cape, 1988.

Lewis Percy. London: Jonathan Cape, 1989.

Look at Me. London: Jonathan Cape, 1983.

A Misalliance. London: Jonathan Cape, 1986.

A Private View. London: Jonathan Cape, 1994.

Providence. London: Jonathan Cape, 1982.

A Start in Life. London: Jonathan Cape, 1981.

The Stories of Edith Wharton. Ed. Anita Brookner. 2 vols. London: Simon and Schuster, 1988–89.

Visitors: A Novel. New York: Random House, 1998.

Watteau. London: Hamlyn, 1968.

Selected Works about Anita Brookner

"Anita Brookner: Novelist with a Double Life." *Observer* 7 Aug. 1988: 13.

Burchfield, Robert. "Two Kinds of English? Jeffrey Archer and Anita Brookner." *The State of the Language.* Ed. Christopher Ricks and Leonard Michaels. London: Faber and Faber, 1990. 356–66.

Charles, Gerda. "Anita Brookner." *Contemporary Novelists.* Ed. D. L. Kirkpatrick. 4th ed. London: St. James Press, 1986. 142–43.

Doan, Laura L., ed. *Old Maids to Radical Spinsters: Unmarried Women in the Twentieth-Century Novel.* Urbana: U of Illinois P, 1991.

Fisher-Wirth, Ann. "Hunger of Art: The Novels of Anita Brookner." *Twentieth Century Literature: A Scholarly and Critical Journal* 41.1 (Spring 1995): 1–15.

Giltrow, Janet. "Ironies of Politeness in Anita Brookner's *Hotel du Lac.*" *Ambiguous Discourse: Feminist Narratology and British Women Writers.* Ed. Kathy Mezei. Chapel Hill: U of North Carolina P, 1996. 215–37.

"Grapevine." *Observer Review* 17 July 1994: 21.

Grover, Jan Zita. "Small Expectations." *Women's Review of Books* July 1994: 38–40.

Guppy, Shusha. Interview with Anita Brookner in *Paris Review* Fall 1987: 147–69.

Haffenden, John. *Novelists in Interview.* London: Methuen, 1985.

Hosmer, Robert E., Jr. "Anita Brookner." *An Encyclopedia of British Women Writers.* Ed. Paul Schlueter and June Schlueter. London: St James Press, 1988. 62–64.

Kenyon, Olga. *Women Novelists Today: A Survey of English Writing in the Seventies and Eighties.* Brighton: Harvester, 1988.

———. *Women Writers Talk: Interviews with Ten Women Writers.* Oxford: Lennard Books, 1989.

Kurz, Helga. "The Impossibility of Female Friendship: A Study of Anita Brookner's Female Characters." *Arbeiten-aus-Anglistik-und-Amerikanistik* 12.1 (1990): 13–25.

Mars-Jones, Adam. "Women Beware Women." *New York Times Review of Books* 31 Jan. 1985: 17–19.

Pykett, Lyn. "Anita Brookner." *Contemporary Novelists.* Ed. Lesley Henderson and Noelle Watson. 5th ed. London: St. James Press, 1991. 147–48.

Ryan, Bryan, ed. "Anita Brookner." *Major Twentieth-Century Authors.* Vol. 1. London: Gale, 1991. 395–401.

Skinner, John. *The Fictions of Anita Brookner: Illusions of Romance.* London: Macmillan, 1992.

Tyler, Anne. "A Solitary Life Is Still Worth Living." *New York Times Book Review* 3 Feb. 1985: 1, 33.

6

"Witness to Their Vanishing": Elaine Feinstein's Fictions of Jewish Continuity

Phyllis Lassner

> How are we Jewish, and what brings us together in this
> most puritan of protestant centres? Are the others
> talking to God, or do they remember filial duties, or
> are they puzzled themselves at the nature of being
> displaced?
>
> ELAINE FEINSTEIN, "New Year"

For American readers, contemporary English literature often appears as continuous with its past and only marginally touched by change. And yet if its class and sex wars are still inflected with old school ties, more exotic customs and memories dot the literary landscape of postcolonial England. As the colonized claim their own ascendancy, they challenge the myth and ethos of a unified island-nation. For some English writers, this invasion coincides with a recognition of their own differences. Elaine Feinstein—poet, novelist, short-story writer, biographer of Bessie Smith and Marina Tsvetayeva, and radio and television playwright—connects English literary tradition to the dislocations of immigrant experience. Like her writing, Feinstein's literary identity is shaped by unsettling but revelatory travels in time and space. Rather than blending her Leicester childhood, Cambridge education, and Russian-Jewish heritage, she expresses their tense relations through her characters' sense of exile.[1] No matter how settled in their Englishness, they remain subject to memories of a historic identity that destabilize the self, memories that materialize as imagined odysseys to medieval Europe or real ones that recall war-torn Europe or involve them in a tumultuous Middle East.

For Feinstein, born in 1930 in Bootle, Lancashire, the granddaughter of Russian Jews who escaped the pogroms, the contemporary scene begins with exile "in the mist of invisible English power";[2] it then stalls at the Holocaust, encircled by haunting memories and questions about being a Jew in a postmodern age.[3] Feinstein's women embody these memories and questions, and much of her fiction focuses on their struggle to distinguish themselves as women residing in a collective and patriarchal historic consciousness. As their Jewish identity emerges, however, and then becomes a determining pressure, whatever Englishness or other identity they claim must itself be relocated, and this mutation redefines their sense of being a woman. So in her poem "Song of Power," the narrator becomes conscious of being a Jewish woman by "the baiting children in my / son's class who / say I am a witch," an identity whose "strangeness" she invokes as a powerful legacy, "a fire" the Jews' "children may learn to bear at last and not burn in" (53). In Feinstein's 1992 novel, *Loving Brecht,* the German-born, assimilated Frieda Bloom is shaped by her "almost earliest memory" of an English nanny identifying her as other—"Like an animal or an African" (3). Later, when Frieda's Jewishness becomes a dangerous identity, she links her abuse to "the two parts of myself"—Jew and woman (37). Among those postcolonial writers responsible for the emerging redefinition of Englishness, Feinstein offers the perspective of those whose historic identity resides in the tension between choosing and resisting marginalization.

A pivotal example is Feinstein's short story "The Grateful Dead." Anna, enjoying her first pregnancy, barely acknowledges her Jewish identity, but discovers that the open-ended future embodied in her unborn child is frighteningly determined by the omnipresence of the tragic Jewish past. Her husband, Michael, "would have liked her to accept the fact of her own Jewishness. But the history frightened her. She wanted to be free of all that knowledge of what people could do to people" (113). Anna embodies a tension between the English realist tradition of individual self-discovery and her collective historic identity. This tension not only defies realist conventions of representation, but suggests a reality from which even nonrealist conventions provide no escape. Michael, by contrast, finds refuge from the pall of Jewish history by identifying with his father's books: "as secret and silent as the tombstones of their two dead fathers lying in the same Jewish cemetery" (113). Throughout Feinstein's writing, such books contrast with the experience of her female characters. Figured as both the tomes and tombs of a patriarchal legacy of Jewish identity and destiny, these learned texts seek unified explanations for the cycle of persecution and destruction that marks Jewish identity and history, but their opposing methods deconstruct them all. As Anna's embodied knowledge demonstrates, the separation of rationalist from mystical wisdom proves as much an illusion as the hope that disaster can be predicted or explained.

In Feinstein's fiction and poetry, rationalist and mystical discourses undercut each other's truth claims. The title "The Grateful Dead" refers to a subtext in the form of knowledge that derives as much from history as it does from myth. Anna's Polish refugee maid narrates her husband's experiences of World War II as both the history of the Holocaust and its folk wisdom, a combination producing archetypes that challenge both Anna's individuality and her collective Jewish identity. The focus of the story is that Mrs. Kowalska's husband found and reburied an old Jewish merchant who had hanged himself in fear of the Nazis. The legend of "The Grateful Dead" is that he wanders between two worlds, responsible for any good that comes to his rescuer but claiming half: "Not to take. If you offer half, he is satisfied and can rest" (117). Despite this proviso and a move to England, Mrs. Kowalska reports that her husband went mad waiting for the Jew's return. The story transforms Anna. Upon hearing it, she finds "a voice she did not know she could muster . . . you shall *not* have my son. Your dead will do nothing to me, nothing. And I'll tell you why. They are *my* dead. You didn't recognize that, did you? Harm? They would rise in their millions to defend me" (118). Identifying with those millions of Jewish dead, she collapses and prematurely gives birth to a healthy girl. When Michael tells her that Mrs. Kowalska has disappeared, Anna sees the birth of her daughter as a victory over both belief and history. Part of the story's achievement is its palpable expression of Anna's fear and its narrative conveyance of that fear to the reader. Anna's response signals an ambiguous and therefore elusive and uncanny designation of the origins of her fear, identifying the threatening nature of both the Kowalskas and the dead Jew. The story thus resonates with mythic and historic forces and, in showing them to be beyond rational understanding and therefore uncontrollable, works against Anna's sense of victory. As bearer of the tale of Jewish victimization and omnipresence, the Polish woman becomes both tortured and torturer. The tale and the teller thus intertwine the legendary and historic relationship between Poles and Jews that ended, after a thousand years of uneasy symbiosis, in the death camps Hitler had built in Poland. For Anna, marginally identified Jew, the Holocaust invades her individually defined selfhood and pulls her into the collective Jewish past which she can no longer resist. On the one hand, this sense of Jewishness reviving irresistibly in the wake of the dead makes it fearful, but on the other, giving birth to a new generation of Jewish womanhood offers the possibility of a revisionary triumph. Anna's imaginative identification with Mrs. Kowalska's tale conflates valences of material, mystical, and historic testaments to reality, and thus adds a new genre of commentary to the tomes of the patriarchs, one that only a woman has offered.

It is not only through women's experience that Feinstein offers a revisionary commentary on Jewish identity and continuity. Her narrative relationship between folktale and realist story questions and revises readers' expectations that history is truth. Coincident with conventions of dream logic, the folktale gives expression to fantasy, desire, and fear, and thus becomes, for Feinstein, the appropriate genre to suggest the collective psychological costs of Jewish history and identity through Anna's individual and spontaneous transformation. In this frame, Feinstein subordinates the story's realist elements to the folktale's explanatory power, suggesting that Jewish history and identity cannot be explained solely by external material realities or protocols of empirical logic. Whatever characters may learn from recounting and analyzing historical events remains vexed by the need and fear of finding the narrative of Jewish history predictive. Although set in the past in this story, the Holocaust remains a haunting presence in the folktale, both for its teller and for Anna. Just as the Jewish merchant will not stay buried, so the event that caused his death will not be laid to rest. The memory of the Holocaust converges with fears of its repetition which cannot be allayed by the daylight safety of assimilated British Jews like Michael and Anna. And yet Feinstein does not completely subsume the rationalist element of the story: by insisting that a dark and terrible event must be kept alive as incontestable fact, the story embeds historical and social realities and prevents its folk wisdom from becoming gothicized or romanticized, and therefore undermined as truth.

Feinstein's first novel established women's consciousness as conduit among psychological, social, and historic realities.[4] Its title, *The Circle* (1970), reflects "the circle of [a woman's] own thought, listening" to her inner life and connecting it to irreconcilable tensions in her marriage (*Circle* 10). So, too, the woman narrator of the poem "Marriage" observes that "We have taken our shape from the / damage we do one another" (57). All Feinstein's writing negotiates an abyss between the desires of men and women which is never resolved. At best, beginning with *The Circle* and continuing into her most recent fiction, such as *Loving Brecht* (1992), a bemused if resigned understanding of their differences allows them to live with and without each other in a state of tense coexistence that later mirrors the relationship of her Jewish characters in a gentile world. In her second novel, *The Amberstone Exit* (1972), Feinstein dramatizes such tension as a young woman's developing self-consciousness, the shape of which alternates between her dreams and waking search for selfhood.[5] The narrative, compressed into an Oedipal ronde conflating sexual and parental desires, disruptively situates the young woman's story of self-discovery in a patriarchal plot of continuity.

No character in this novel is identified as Jewish, but certain narrative pressures evince concerns that Feinstein would later articulate as Jewish. Even as the Oedipal plot foregrounds a family romance, its structure extends to suggest tribal relations, enacting a sense of internalized, understood if unarticulated rules of allegiance to an identity outside individual family relations. It is as though the pressures of continuity and family ties signal a powerfully determining plot based on the nagging consciousness of a collective identity. Feinstein's 1974 novel, *The Crystal Garden* (published in Britain as *The Glass Alembic*), extends her exploration of material and emotional realities as subject of a debate between the rationalist consciousness of a scientist and a plot shaped by the interplay of coincidence and design. Matthew, living in Basel, compares himself to Paracelsus, "founder of biochemistry," but also "Sorcerer, wonder-healer," and finds himself apprehensive "of forces and patterns at work which were not precisely those of cause and effect" (20). The novel challenges essentialist divisions of male and female consciousness by mocking Matthew's hold on rationalism both through its plot and in the character of his wife, Brigid, whom he dismisses as irrational until events complicate their dif-

ferences. As in *The Amberstone Exit,* these complications take the form
of a sexual ronde, used here to argue that if order or design exists in human relationships it is based on irrational fleeting desires affecting both
men and women. The women take these eruptions as a matter of course,
while the men assign to them the metaphysical questions that legitimize
desire but obscure its origins and fulfillment.

In *The Crystal Garden,* Feinstein deploys a gendered critique of rationalism with social icons of the seventies, including psychedelic highs and
lows, but she also implicates it in a historical context that takes it beyond local culture. The European setting has far-reaching consequences
for Feinstein's future writing. Early in the novel this impact inheres in
an analogy drawn by Matthew's friend Ladislaw, who wishes to demonstrate that the attribution of cause is undermined by circumstances that
appear guided by chance or coincidence. Ladislaw recalls the way a plot
to kill Hitler failed, despite its having been engineered by a clockmaker
whose "mechanism worked perfectly" (40). Despite his precise calibra-
tion of the explosive device, "for some reason" Hitler and his entourage
left early (40). Through this combination of chance and human whim
the narrator foregrounds the subject of World War II, and its presence echoes throughout the rest of the novel. The narrator attributes
Matthew's easy dismissal of Ladislaw's analogy to his having "suffered little in the war" compared to "what horrors Ladislaw had moved
through, from city to city; to the next language; the next tenuous hold"
(40). As a result of this comparison, the narrator leads readers to conclude that the emotional exile of the novel's English characters highlights the suffering of those who survived the war in central and eastern
Europe. This comparison thus establishes Matthew's scientific mindset
as a luxury he can well afford, especially because his safety and security
have encouraged the use of rationalist principles to make "sense of this
side of the grave" (52). The novel's ending, which dismisses the idea of
"some kind of resolution" (52), confirms a lesson the European Ladislaw
offers in response to his English friend, that "it doesn't *make* sense" (176).
In Feinstein's fictive analysis, "the mess" of human desire and destruction
prevails over attempts to construct abstract "patterns" of causality (111).[6]
The extension of this lesson from English bedroom to European death
camp and exile revises English domestic comedy by historicizing it, setting the stage for Feinstein's articulation of her English characters' "otherness."

The protagonists of *Children of the Rose* (1975) are Jewish refugees whose attempts to build English lives are foiled by haunting memories of the European past. By overtly identifying her characters in this way, Feinstein uses her interrogation of marriage to dramatize a man's and a woman's conflicting self-consciousness. In Feinstein's elaboration of the intractable marital impasse explored in *The Circle* and the marriages dramatized in *The Crystal Garden,* Lalka's estrangement from Mendez clearly stems from their different responses to their Jewish pasts. In her detachment, Lalka protects herself from being violated by Mendez and the past, for in wanting "her memories," he would appropriate her history, but "there was nothing there but death. And silence" (61).[7] Ironically, her silence reiterates the past helplessness of the Jews while saving her from it. The narrative alternates between their silent impasses and reflections on the past, each serving as commentary on the other. As the past, the present, and the characters' historical consciousnesses become reflexive texts, the emotional locus of the novel becomes the painful recognition that Jewishness is not one moment or event, but continuity— always "*still* news" (61).

Mendez makes this last point in response to Lee, a young non-Jewish woman who represents his desire to escape the cyclical history of Jewish persecution. Because Jewish continuity depends on Jewish motherhood, having a child with Lee would break the cycle. But the novel's intertwined relationships reveal that such escape is impossible. Hence, Lee's dalliance with Mendez proves deadly, inspired by her reaction to the Jews her mother hid from the Nazis in their chateau. Her rejection of "the real pain" of Jewish history, marked by her confession that she betrayed their hiding place, only demonstrates its reality (61). Her efforts to erase the Jews' presence ensures it just as Mendez's purchase and renovation of the chateau foils his attempt to escape the Jewish past, for his desire takes him to a place haunted by ghosts of Jewish history. Moreover, Mendez's desire to escape that history leads him to misread it and parallels his false assumption that Lee is carrying his child. Of course, even if she were, such a pregnancy could in no sense be "a victory" over hatred for the Jews (95). Lee's revulsion would only repeat the history of exposing and persecuting those who were partially Jewish or totally assimilated. As in "The Grateful Dead," the gentile woman embodies "the loveliness of a haunted child, who probably already smelt in his own flesh the sick pallor of the people she had feared and resented" (93).

Feinstein does not present the problem of Jewish identity, history, and continuity as a dichotomy of self and other or victim and external forces of oppression. Instead, she situates part of the novel's reflexive structure in the Jews' construction of their history, as figured in the books Mendez inherited from his father. Both in their material reality and elusive meanings, these books are testaments to the endlessly contested sites and significances of Jewish continuity. Lining the walls of the chateau's ballroom, the books imagistically absorb and inscribe the ambiguities of events that transpired there, for in this ballroom Lee's mother distracted the Nazis by dancing with them, fueling Lee's hatred. Such diametrically opposed responses to the Jews read like a gloss on the Jewish sages and seers who inscribed Mendez's books with foretellings of the Holocaust but who offer no explanation except "macabre evasion" (93), another form of silence.

Lalka's responses to Jewish history work reflexively in relation to Mendez's, mirroring their personal incompatibility but exposing their incontrovertible bond. Despite her resistance to remembrance, Lalka travels to her ancestral home in Kraków and visits a Jewish cemetery where she is horrified by the sight of a rose which she imagines grows from the blood of the dead. It is this vision that connects her to Mendez, for he imagines the meek inheriting the earth, buried in it not as a regenerative force but as a reminder that Jewish identity is indelible: "if people want to hate, they will hate the poor Jews because they are dirty; and the beautiful because they are rich" (139). The shock of seeing both the rose and a reminder of her childhood home drives Lalka into a state of semiconsciousness, a kind of mental stasis that protects her from external violation but locks her into a replay of the silenced past. As though carrying the burden of Jewish history, Mendez brings her to his chateau, where he cares for her like the child he can never have. Free now of their incompatibility, their relationship teaches the reverse of his rationale for desiring to have a child, which he had articulated as "not for continuity [but] The opposite: to teach *someone, somehow* to be free of it all. Everything that destroyed Lalka and me. To escape" (184). Instead, the novel reveals the Jewish past not only as continuous, but as fusing both its dead and its heirs.

The dramatic replay of this past becomes the centerpiece of Feinstein's 1976 novel, *The Ecstasy of Dr. Miriam Garner*. Here again, the agent for reviving the past is a woman whose drugged consciousness transports her to her Jewish mother's ancestral past in Spain. What her imagination recovers, however, belies the truth her academic research asserts, exposing it as static, locked into the rationalist, progressivist discourse of the present. In the time warp of returning to medieval Toledo, the emerging historical truth is the price women pay for a civilization's claim to a golden age. In the trajectory from the modern age to the medieval, regardless of changing cultures and ideologies, the violation of women persists. Women are subjugated to men's messianic aspirations, whether political or scientific. Thus Miriam is sexually manipulated by Ramon, a would-be savior in Toledo, and mind-raped in contemporary Cambridge by Stavros, a former lover who rapes another woman and drugs her to test the apocalyptic calculations on which his scientific interests rest.

Intertwined with this self-reflexive plotting is the story of Miriam's parents' marriage, the divisions of which reenact the tarnished conclusion to the Jewish experience in medieval Spain. Garner reports that his wife, Esther, of an old Jewish Toledo family, frightened him because of her unrelenting belief in the history of Jews as "an unhappy persistent people. Such a centuries-enduring memory" (126). Like Mendez in *Children of the Rose,* Garner wants his child to grow up "free of that. . . . After all, what good did it ever bring any of them?" (126). Reminiscent of the Inquisition that drove the Spanish Jews into exile or into becoming Marranos who concealed their religious observances, Garner hides Esther's Jewish identity. Miriam's mental trip restores her Jewish lineage and implicitly represents a historicizing challenge to her father's pragmatism and Stavros's messianic science. Evolving somewhere between these two, in her long poem "The Celebrants," Feinstein portrays historical consciousness as a transmutation of human matter through myth and science that is experienced by Dionysiac women and immigrants, "nomads, wilderness people, having no / house of their own" (*Celebrants* 18).

In *The Shadow Master* (1978), Feinstein satirizes full-blown messianism as a solution to reclaiming Jewish history and rebuilding Jewish identity.[8] Prevailing fears of Middle Eastern terrorism provide ample opportunities to imagine a resurgence of messianic fever combining with political and capitalist forces, the ends of which are anything but spiritual in nature. Central agents in this comedy are two sisters, Anastasia, a cynical former Communist living in Istanbul, with deep ties to their eastern European origins and international business, and Lilian, a believing astrologer living in London, using her powers of persuasion to manipulate international money markets. More seriously, Lilian's role is also a function of "her childhood incapacity to move about their parents' home except as a shadow. In such a glitter she had to draw back, and hide. To invent for herself another way of knowing the world," one which by implication is inaccessible to the men in her life (125). Interweaving the medieval Jewish past and present highlights Lilian's strategy to achieve self-definition as a replay of the Marranos in its secrecy. As part of a continuum from Nell in *The Circle* to Lalka in *Children of the Rose* and to Miriam in *The Ecstasy of Dr. Miriam Garner,* the struggles of woman and Jew coalesce in their retreat from real time and space into an imagined sphere which redefines their inherited story. Although they meet only on the plane of narrative, the stories of Lilian and Anastasia question the personal and political mission of Vee, a self-styled, born-again Shabbatai Zvi, whose messianic claims extend the sense of patriarchal determination from past to future. At the end, however, the narrator's voice joins forces with Lilian's to provide an open ending in which a woman will enjoy agency, her ability to act outside the loop of a patriarchal messianism that produces only chaos and despair.

Feinstein's 1982 novel, *The Survivors,* explores women's agency as a problem central to the destabilizing effects of two European Jewish families acculturating to England. While the pressures of Jewish continuity shape both men and women, Feinstein shows that women pay more for choosing to save themselves through transformation. Feinstein designs their assigned roles as Jewish Angels of the Hearth to mediate between the benefits and costs of a history of marginalization. To leave the hearth and minister unto others, like one woman who becomes a nurse during World War I, denies continuity with the European experience, especially as she will reject its ritual observances which mark the choice to remain a distinct people. Feinstein thus links both becoming English and women's agency to Jewish codes of self-determination: to be a Jew inscribes an identity that remains separate even as it crosses boundaries of individuality, time, and space. When World War I breaks out and the German sphere becomes the enemy, Jewish identity becomes inexorably problematic: "We are Europe . . . perhaps the whole Jewish people, riven and divided by this war like no one else. We *are* Europe, eating and destroying itself" (86). The price Jewish women pay for choosing their own separateness is to be "riven and divided" within and between themselves and the world of the English. Hence, Diana, the first woman in both families to attend Cambridge, found she could not fit in because she clung "to bits and pieces of Yiddish. . . . The question of loyalty was poignant. . . . So many had died in mud and fire for being Jewish. To give up seemed a gross betrayal" (287).

The Border (1984) returns to a European scene to dramatize the question of loyalty to Jewish history and continuity against the backdrop of the World War II. Divided into different characters' narratives, the novel itself is "riven" by competing perspectives, and so foregrounds the textuality of Jewish history, "the content of the form."[9] The frame tale concerns Saul, a young historian who visits his grandmother, Inge, in Australia to exploit her memories of escaping from Vienna to Lisbon for his research on Walter Benjamin. Instead of satisfying his search for "facts," the diaries and letters she offers him add up to "stories [that] can be told many different ways" (83). We never learn how the historian uses this material, and so, like him, construct our own interpretations, the central issue of which will be loyalty, since interpretation requires fidelity to a text. This meaning of loyalty also reflects that of a particular history: of a people identified with their book. The interactive process of characters' memories in earlier novels is elided here to privilege the reader instead of the narrator. Feinstein's emphases on textuality and rhetorical strategy challenge us to struggle with the questions formerly given to her characters and thus transfer to readers the moral responsibility for bearing witness to the history that identifies Feinstein's writing.

Such responsibility, however, contains its own difficulties, for the rewards of reading private diaries and letters, with its suggestion of voyeurism, complicates any moral lesson. We are, after all, being offered history as a very personal story of obsessive passion and attachment, self-pitying narcissism, and private despair. Inge, who serves as archivist and repository of historical memory, connects the political and the personal, but her perspective cannot be universalized, questioning, as it does, any totalizing view of Jewish survival in World War II. Complicating her gendered analysis of rationalism, Feinstein creates Inge as a scientist whose analysis of the historic roots of the Nazi threat turns out to be no more explanatory than the ahistorical, deeply personalized sense of persecution felt by her poet-husband, Hans. Inge's ability to survive, moreover, while it springs from the ease with which she distances herself with "relentless logic," only highlights the existential question of individual purpose in a nihilistic void and the postmodern issue of surviving as a destabilized self in a decentered text (*Border* 19). The inseparability of historical and emotional logic are signaled by the author in a note which explains that the fictional presence of Walter Benjamin represents debates "about the weight of mysticism and Marxism" (19). His suicide in reality and in this fiction embodies not only the fusion of history and his belief in it as a determining force, but also the failure to reconcile individual purpose with the effects of Nazi dehumanization.

Inge's survival, alone and alienated from family and work in Australia, "enclosed" in her "piece of Central Europe," offers reconciliation in destabilization (*Border* 11). At the end of her narrative, which coincides with the end of the Jewish Day of Atonement, she proposes a toast "To the forgiveness of all our infidelities" (108). Her fleeting reunion with her grandson reconciles the "unequal duel" between rationalist and imaginative visions, and between hope for Jewish survival and continuity and the history and visions of Jewish destruction (107).[10] Asking forgiveness on this day constitutes a ritual act that, replicated over historical time and across individual purpose, performs a stabilizing function that unites individual and collective consciousness.[11] Thus Inge's toast also reconciles her with Hans's vision, which he articulates immediately afterwards in the poem that closes the novel. As though in response, he invokes a "mission" to perpetuate his history as both indelible and ephemeral, where "only ghosts remain / to know that we exist" (111). The decentered content here is once again stabilized by the form. The imaginative and historic textuality of his poem resonates with the rituals of "sing[ing] old prayers . . . at whatever cost" (112, 113).[12]

Feinstein's 1988 novel, *Mother's Girl*, explores the "whole" but "riven and divided" modern Jew as a confrontation between two half sisters and their competing constructions of Leo, a divided and divisive Jewish father. The older sister, Halina, has shared her father's European heritage, while Lucy is the American daughter doubly separated from him, for she lacks both the European experience and a Jewish mother. A dominant force in both their lives, Leo also controls access to the story of Halina's mother, Tilde, who disappeared at the end of World War II. As in *The Ecstasy of Dr. Miriam Garner*, the mother's hold on Jewish identity is scorned by her husband, but instead of deconstructing a golden age to explain the psychology of Jewish identity, this novel reconstructs a dark age to question the viability and positioning of Jewish identity. Feinstein's replay of an Oedipal rivalry for the father's affections does not foreground a single family; instead, the divided family represents individuality subsumed within a collective struggle for survival. Thus Halina and Lucy compete for individual and collective claims to suffering and oppression. When Lucy argues that her hospitalization for mental illness was an experience equal to the concentration camps, and Halina rejects the comparison, Lucy reminds her that "You don't have any more claim on all that than I do" (125).

Ironically, the primacy of collective history is affirmed by the mother's particular story; it begins with Halina's memory of Tilde's self-centered career as a singer, but is transformed into the collective by reports of her work with Jewish socialists hiding Jews. Its enigmatic ending with her disappearance into the Soviet Union after the war, combined with Leo's silence about her, suggests the story of the Holocaust and its problem of representability.[13] Feinstein genders this problem and links it to that of Jewish continuity by giving Halina the responsibility of rescuing her mother's story from oblivion. The story's emergence then raises questions about the burdens of Jewish identity and history for Jewish women. Since women are prescribed by Jewish law to pass on Jewish identity, they must also, in Feinstein's writing, embody Jewish history and endure the burdens of Jewish continuity, neither of which inscribes a story of Jewish women's self-determination. Just as Tilde sent Halina to England to save her from oppression and death, so Halina ponders the legacy of their story for her son: "I mustn't give you my pain to carry . . . it will damage you . . . perhaps that damage is part of the human inheritance and the only terrible burden is to have no inheritance at all" (158). By revealing the Jewish past through women's consciousness and indeterminate endings, Feinstein invokes Jewish history to challenge its status as a received and determining text.

In Feinstein's most recent novels, *All You Need* (1989) and *Loving Brecht* (1992), women who hardly know they are Jewish journey back and forth between a history of persecution and the burden of continuity because they embody Jewish identity as mothers.[14] Even childless women like Lalka and Miriam Garner carry the weight of their identity in their consciousness, which not only makes them witnesses to Jewish history and its burdens but also gives them the testamentary power of revision. Thus the sisters in *Mother's Girl* complete the story of modern Jewish history by rediscovering the mother at its center. For these women Jewish continuity means departing from a male-centered tradition and its domestic center of practice. By featuring the women's consciousness as a conduit to the Jewish past and by confronting it with the intransigence of its patriarchal texts, Feinstein reveals that the power men associate with Jewish continuity allows them to rationalize and dismiss the knowledge that women gain through their struggle against belief in predictive or rationalist arguments. By revealing the Jewish past through women's consciousness, she questions the extent to which patriarchal knowledge as inscribed in sacred Jewish texts constitutes the whole story. And because she leaves her women with indeterminate endings, Feinstein suggests that the discourse of Jewish history and continuity remains an ongoing process of revision and discovery.

NOTES

The quote "Witness to Their Vanishing" is from "Fellow-travelling," a poem in *The Magic Apple Tree* (London: Hutchinson, 1971).

1. Mary Lynn Broe and Angela Ingram's anthology, *Women Writing in Exile* (Chapel Hill: U of North Carolina P, 1989), shows the critical acumen women develop in voluntary and involuntary exile as conditions of race, gender, class, and culture. Feinstein's women combine these categories and develop critical faculties both consciously and unconsciously.

2. Elaine Feinstein, "Exile," *Some Unease and Angels: Selected Poems* 21.

3. My use of the term *postmodern* is indebted to Hayden White's assertion that making meaning of history is necessary, but as its meaning is constructed in language, history is inseparable from literature. See *The Content of the Form: Narrative Discourse and Historical Representation* (Baltimore: Johns Hopkins UP, 1987). In *Zakhor: Jewish History and Jewish Memory* (Seattle: U of Washington P, 1982), Yosef Hayim Yerushalmi shows how Jews from ancient to modern times respond to the biblical injunction to remember so as not to forget their historical past, "in which the great and critical moments of Israel's history were fulfilled. Far from attempting a flight from history, biblical religion [is] saturated by it and is inconceivable apart from it" (9). Feinstein's fictions combine questions about this imperative with those in medieval Jewish chronicles which assimilate contemporary events to the idea that "Persecution and suffering are, after all, the result of the condition of being in exile, and exile itself is the bitter fruit of ancient sins" (Yerushalmi 36).

4. Clive Jordan saw the heroine as being "real," but not "unique or interesting enough to merit attention," not being "in tune with *any* natural order"

(217). The anonymous reviewer for the *Times Literary Supplement* found the novel's tone "weary, unforced and sharply accurate" in its depiction of the heroine as "a victim not of the acrimony of others but of their indifference" ("Round and Round" 941).

5. Peter Buckman, like other reviewers, notes Feinstein's poetic "musical prose," which here finds "rhythm" in her theme "of the instructive and destructive power of sex" (168). The *Times Literary Supplement* noted the heroine's lust "after her father's opposite" ("Cad's Cradle" 935).

6. Reviews of *The Crystal Garden* focused on the characters' psychological development and thus took Feinstein to task for "thrusting" them, "stiff and unreal," into the most "dramatic situations imaginable"; *New Yorker* 3 June 1974: 109.

7. Victoria Glendinning noted that "this is a serious and intense novel on a serious and intense topic," but "longs for" the relief of a "few jokes at the gates of hell" and the presence of the "hard and frivolous" "goy" characters (489). Susannah Clapp observes the Mendezes's marital discord as related to their being "in the grip of a flashback or nightmare" ("Ghost Hunt" 445).

8. Susannah Clapp sees this novel marking a welcome departure for Feinstein because her characters "are allowed to stray from intensity into humour and waywardness" ("Letter Day" 751). Sarah Wintle sees the novel connecting "the search for identity . . . not only with being a woman but also with being a Jew" (666).

9. Feinstein's fictions dramatize an uneasy tension that Hayden White describes as follows: "the historical narrative, [measured] against the chronicle, reveals to us a world that is putatively finished, done with, over, and yet not dissolved, not falling apart" (21). Her novels create historical narratives that are unfinished, dissolving boundaries between cause and effect; even the past is unfinished. She raises questions of how to represent sites of moral responsibility instead of answering "the demand for closure in the historical story [which] is a demand . . . for moral meaning, a demand that sequences of real events be assessed as to their significance as elements of a moral drama" (21).

10. Tim Dooley finds that the novel justifies its "pessimism" because it offers the hope "of healing . . . divisions . . . between men and women, and between logical and intuitive modes of thought . . . with shared suffering" (632). Angela McRobbie notes that the presence of Walter Benjamin coincides with the subject of *The Border,* which "is one which continues to haunt, influence and fascinate a generation of post-war socialists, more interested in culture than in theory and more drawn by doubt and uncertainty than by cold, Eastern-bloc Marxism"

(24). James Lasdun found the novel perplexing because he feels it relies on the reader's "share of historical consciousness to supply the hidden shapes beneath" (51). Stephen Bann finds that Feinstein "has not constructed a mystery which lends itself to being solved" (18).

11. In his discussion of medieval Jewish historiography, Yerushalmi avers that "whatever memories were unleashed by the commemorative rituals and liturgies were surely not a matter of intellection, but of evocation and identification" (44). Again, Feinstein's women combine these.

12. Feinstein's review of Simon Weisenthal's memoir of tracking down Nazi war criminals validates his efforts on behalf of "that guilt of the survivor so well described by Primo Levi" ("Lest We Forget" 34).

13. The weight of the Holocaust's significance is borne out by ongoing debates about the moral issues concerning its representation. For a sampling of these debates, see Saul Friedlander, ed., *Probing the Limits of Representation: Nazism and the Final Solution* (Cambridge: Harvard UP, 1992).

14. Feinstein's consciousness of Jewish identity and continuity is framed within the history and experience of modern British Jewry and their experiences of social and economic pressures to assimilate. For recent discussions, see Todd M. Endelman, *Radical Assimilation in English Jewish History: 1656–1945* (Bloomington: Indiana UP, 1990), and Geoffrey Alderman, *Modern British Jewry* (Oxford: Clarendon, 1992).

Selected Works by Elaine Feinstein

"All Writers Are Outcast." *New Statesman* 26 Feb. 1982: 22–23.
All You Need. New York: Viking, 1989.
The Amberstone Exit. London: Hutchinson, 1972.
The Border. New York: St. Martin's, 1984.
Breath. Television script, 1975.
The Celebrants and Other Poems. London: Hutchinson, 1973.
Children of the Rose. London: Hutchinson, 1975.
The Circle. 1970. London: Penguin, 1973.
City Music: Poems. London: Hutchinson, 1990.
The Crystal Garden. New York: Dutton, 1974.
The Ecstasy of Dr. Miriam Garner. London: Hutchinson, 1976.
"Exile." *Some Unease and Angels: Selected Poems.* London: Hutchinson, 1977.
"The Grateful Dead." *The Silent Areas: Short Stories.* London: Hutchinson, 1980.

Introduction. Storm Jamison, *Company Parade*. Harmondsworth, England: Penguin (Virago), 1985.

Lawrence and The Women: The Intimate Life of D. H. Lawrence. New York: HarperCollins, 1993.

"Lest We Forget." Rev. of *Justice Not Vengeance*, by Simon Weisenthal. *New Statesman* 11 Oct. 1989: 34–35.

Loving Brecht. London: Hutchinson, 1992.

Lunch. Television script, 1981.

The Magic Apple Tree. London: Hutchinson, 1971.

Marina Tsvetayeva. London: Penguin, 1989.

"Marriage." *The Magic Apple Tree*. London: Hutchinson, 1971.

Mother's Girl. New York: Dutton, 1988.

"New Year." *Badlands: Poems*. London: Hutchinson, 1986.

Rev. of *Possession*, by A. S. Byatt. *New Statesman* 16 Mar. 1990: 38.

Selected Poems of Marina Tsvetayeva. London: Hutchinson, 1987.

The Shadow Master. London: Hutchinson, 1978.

The Silent Areas: Short Stories. London: Hutchinson, 1980.

"Song of Power." *The Magic Apple Tree*. London: Hutchinson, 1971.

The Survivors. London: Hutchinson, 1982.

SELECTED WORKS ABOUT ELAINE FEINSTEIN

Bann, Stephen. Rev. of *The Border. London Review of Books* 5 July 1984: 18.

Buckman, Peter. "Summer Uplift." *New Statesman* 4 Aug. 1972: 168.

"Cad's Cradle." Rev. of *The Amberstone Exit. Times Literary Supplement* 11 Aug. 1972: 935.

Clapp, Susannah. "Ghost Hunt." *Times Literary Supplement* 25 Apr. 1975: 445.

———. "Letter Day." *New Statesman* 4 June 1976: 751.

Conradi, Peter. "Elaine Feinstein." *Dictionary of Literary Biography*. Vol. 194. Ed. Merritt Moseley. Detroit: Gale Research, 1998. 292–97.

Cunningham, Valentine. "Women Who Look Like Witches." *Listener* 21 June 1973: 837.

Dooley, Tim. "Mystical and Material." *Times Literary Supplement* 6 Aug. 1984: 632.

Gerrard, Nicci. "More Than Just Making Do." Rev. of *All You Need. New Statesman* 15 Sept. 1989: 34.

Glendinning, Victoria. "In the Swim." *New Statesman* 11 Apr. 1975: 489.

Jordan, Clive. Rev. of *The Circle*. *New Statesman* 21 Aug. 1970: 216–17.

Lasdun, James. "Books and Writers." *Encounter* Oct. 1984: 51.

McRobbie, Angela. "Cross Winds." *New Statesman* 8 June 1984: 24.

Rev. of *The Crystal Garden*. *New Yorker* 3 June 1974: 109.

"Round and Round." Rev. of *The Circle*. *Times Literary Supplement* 28 Aug. 1970: 941.

Warner, Eric, Hermione Lee, and Fran Kermode. "Elaine Feinstein." *Virginia Woolf: A Centenary Perspective*. Ed. Eric Warner. New York: St. Martin's, 1984. 146–65.

Wintle, Sarah. "A New Jerusalem." *Times Literary Supplement* 4 June 1976: 666.

7

"Women Like Us Must Learn to Stick Together": Lesbians in the Novels of Fay Weldon

Patricia Juliana Smith

Over the past two decades, Fay Weldon has produced a prodigious number of novels of British social manners and mores in the wake of the "Swinging Sixties." A veritable postmodern Jane Austen, Weldon chronicles the disintegration of the patriarchy and middle-class respectability with acerbic wit and gleeful malice. Prosperous and successful heads of households abandon beleaguered wives for the beds—or cots or sleeping bags—of adolescent paramours, while discarded women, bereft of financial support and ill-prepared for any role in life save those of wife or mistress, must of necessity redefine and re-create their lives and seek alternatives as the structures of institutional heterosexuality crumble. With remarkable frequency, Weldon places lesbians—or the abstract concept of lesbianism—in the midst of her narratives' sexual chaos. While never central figures, Weldon's lesbian characters invariably play crucial and provocative roles, providing her put-upon heterosexual protagonists with foils, role models, experimental sexual encounters, or objects upon which to focus their all-pervading anxieties. And while lesbianism does not necessarily provide solutions to the heroines' dilemmas, it indicates the existence of modes of sexual, social, or even economic viability other than institutional heterosexuality—which, in Weldon's representations, never seems overly felicitous—as well as modes of interaction between women other than shrewish rivalry. At the same time, Weldon refuses to fall into the trap of well-intentioned but artistically self-limiting "political correctness." Her narrative landscapes offer no "safe sea of women," and her imperfect lesbian characters are far from the now-stereotypical noble, sensitive, artistic, intelligent, and long-suffering paragons of Sapphic virtue favored by some earlier lesbian novelists and critics who, along with some feminist critics, have found Weldon's ironic vision at the very least problematic.[1]

In this essay, I will avoid such pitfalls of "irony failure" while exploring the subversive significance of Weldon's representations of lesbians. I intend to demonstrate that ironic wit does not detract from but rather augments the subversive nature of Weldon's art; and that by subjecting her lesbian characters to the same exacting analysis and rigorous criticism as she does their heterosexual counterparts, she is, in fact, not only transforming them into complex and fully human members of society, but also implying the common interests of and bonds between post-patriarchal heterosexual women and their lesbian sisters. Although lesbians or the abstract concept of lesbianism appears in nearly all of Weldon's novels, I am focusing on those in *Remember Me* (1976), *Words of Advice* (1978), and *The Life and Loves of a She-Devil* (1983). Each of these novels, written during Weldon's acutely feminist "middle period," features a lesbian who, while not at the center of the text, significantly affects the narrative structure and the textual meaning of female sexuality.[2] This literary representation mirrors the social position of lesbians, who are obviously not at the center of society's heterosexual "plot" but who nevertheless play a significant role in altering and indeed undermining the shape and meaning of that plot.

A tangled web of rivalry, infidelity, paternity, and maternity engulfing the lives of three heterosexual women forms the central structure of Weldon's postmodern gothic parody *Remember Me*. Renee, a lesbian divorcée fallen upon hard times, plays a pivotal role in the denouement and provides insight into the perceptions of (and anxieties about) lesbian sexuality that are held by many heterosexual women. Positioned, for the most part, outside of the vicious intrigues that inform the lives of Madeleine Katkin, Margot Bailey, and Lily Katkin, Renee's primary function in the narrative is that of a foil to each of the three protagonists. Weldon creates a conspicuous contrast between Renee and Madeleine, the embittered former wife of architect Jarvis Katkin, who has replaced her with the glamorous, materialistic, and considerably younger Lily. Madeleine, as a result, sinks from middle-class comfort and respectability to life on the dole with her awkward and unsocialized fourteen-year-old daughter, Hilary. Her only friend in her reduced state is Renee, a fellow rejected wife and welfare mother. Unlike Madeleine, however, Renee has not succumbed to self-hatred and self-neglect; indeed, she has found a saving alternative. The "fresh," lovely, and "long-legged" Renee has

> renounced men. Renee has her girl friends instead, from whom, physically and emotionally, she extracts comfort, company and solace. From time to time Renee kindly offers the same to Madeleine, in the shape of a warm and companionable bed, but Madeleine is too conscious of her own raggedy body and troubled mind to be able to offer herself on such simple terms. Although, as Renee complains, she seems perfectly able to offer herself to any passing man. (56)

Not only does Weldon juxtapose the attractive, healthy, and sexually vibrant Renee with the woebegone Madeleine, but she also reverses conventional expectations of the relative happiness and sanity of lesbians. Characteristics stereotypically ascribed to lesbians, such as social and psychological degeneration, lack of physical charm, and lack of sexual self-determination, are notably absent in Renee while evident in Madeleine, who, "without a man around . . . scarcely seems to exist" (56). Moreover, because she understands and appreciates the value of community between women, Renee provides a contrast to Madeleine's successor, the grasping and manipulative Lily. Simultaneously, with her uninhibited and unproblematic expression of sexuality, she is the antithesis of the bland and repressed Margot, whose identity is based on her position as the doctor's wife and Jarvis's part-time secretary, and who, for the sake of maintaining her hard-won middle-class respectability, buries any trace of erotic desire remaining in her body or spirit beneath her Marks and Spencer wardrobe and the burden of outward propriety. Accordingly, through most of the novel Renee simply stands as a reminder that the functions and the fates of her three heterosexual sisters are neither essential nor inevitable.

This is not to say that Renee's travails are any less painful or significant than those of the other women. Because of lack of "proper accommodation" in her basement flat, Renee has lost custody of her two small daughters to her former husband, who can afford to provide the children with "a succession of au-pair girls, with whom he sleeps if he can" (150). Renee nonetheless suspects, probably correctly, that her housing situation is not the central issue in her custody dispute; her acknowledged sexual preference has, in the eyes of the judiciary, rendered her former spouse a better example of sexual decorum for her children than she. Additionally, although her lesbianism provides her with a more pleasurable sex life than her previous state afforded her, it does not necessarily follow that the emotional quality of her liaisons has improved. Indeed, her ongoing affair with Bonnie, a married eighteen-year-old, places her in direct competition with a man, re-creating and reinscribing her previous battles with the male domination and institutional heterosexuality. Yet despite Renee's travails and the personal traits that distinguish her from the other women, Weldon does not allow Renee to disintegrate into the stereotype of the long-suffering and noble lesbian martyr. Flawless characters cannot exist—much less survive—in Weldon's chaotic and ironic universe, and Renee is no exception. In her weaker moments she exhibits an inclination toward childlike emotionality, particularly in interacting with older women; she also evinces a propensity for self-pity and a belief in romantic love which, in Weldon's view, is undoubtedly a character flaw. In Renee's case, however, her dissociation from institutional heterosexuality and its subjugation of women renders her romantic notions merely a foolish rather than a fatal flaw.

Through a series of macabre and fantastic events, Renee becomes a catalyst in the resolution of a complex and humorously grotesque plot. Madeleine, driving home from a sexual assignation with her Dial-a-Date, is killed—wearing Renee's best silk shirt—when her aged automobile disintegrates on the motorway. The dying Madeleine realizes that Hilary will be doomed to the custody of Jarvis, her inattentive father, and Lily, her insensitive and greedy stepmother. Filled with more concern for her daughter than she exhibited in life, Madeleine's spirit takes possession of Margot's body in order to set matters to right. One of the newly possessed Margot's first acts is to supervise the disposal of Madeleine's meager effects so as to prevent them from falling into Lily's avaricious hands. While in Madeleine's old flat, Margot/Madeleine—for at this point she is two women in one—encounters Renee. Like any true gothic heroine facing a loss of "virtue," Margot/Madeleine faints, only to awaken in the arms—and the bed—of Renee: "Or rather, Margot reclines on an ethnic bed of Ethiopian splendor, for there are no chairs in the room" (205). Aware that she should be preparing her children's tea rather than drinking wine and relaxing in Renee's embrace, Margot gives in to tears.

Ostensibly distraught over Madeleine's sorry life and gruesome death, Margot expresses a desire to remain in Renee's room; and Renee, who recognizes the "presence" of Madeleine in Margot, makes sexual overtures.[3] Yet Margot, although tantalized by such erotic attention and such a prospect, is simultaneously terrified by the possibility of its fulfillment. In contrast to the battle of opposites to which she has been accustomed all her adult life, she understands the comforting and serene attraction of the "union of like to like" but senses the danger in sexual pleasure between "woman and woman." Society has taught her well the lessons of fearing the "forbidden." To succumb to the lesbian love that beckons her will, she fears, introduce a relationship "so dangerous, so monstrous that the very sun might hide its face in horror and the light of the world go out" (207).

Margot/Madeleine's "homophobia," that is to say, a *literal* fear of lesbianism, is founded on shame—shame directed toward her own body, her own sexuality, and her own capacity for sensual pleasure. Because lesbianism is a "union of like to like," it requires a reciprocity that neither Madeleine nor Margot has known in their respective histories of heterosex requiring only passivity and cooperation rather than pleasure or even active response. Consequently, Margot, echoing Madeleine before her, is ashamed, in the presence of the lovely and sensuous Renee, of her "fat and flabby" body, the manifestation of years of sexual apathy.

Margot/Madeleine therefore balks. Renee, stung by this rejection, cries, thereby eliciting the older woman's maternal instincts. Inspired perhaps as much by quasi-maternal guilt and the need to pacify an aggrieved child as by forbidden desire, Margot/Madeleine passively consents to Renee's seduction—in a manner that reflects her conditioned sexual response. Yet lesbian lovemaking is far different from anything Margot has heretofore experienced and much more intense—indeed, too intense. Appalled at her powerful "upsurge" and sense of gratification in response to sexual pleasure (210), Margot leaves, resolving never to return; yet an afternoon "in the arms of a lesbian lady" (226) emboldens her—and Madeleine's spirit within her—to new feats of daring. She sets forth to confront Jarvis with the dual purpose of demanding custody of

Hilary and avenging Madeleine. She accomplishes the latter—and consequently the former—by recounting for her erstwhile employer his drunken seduction of her some fifteen years before, a heretofore unspeakable recollection for the "respectable" Margot. She confronts her husband, Phillip, as well, angrily charging him with years of emotional, spiritual, and even physical neglect, repression, and abuse, all of which he had heretofore deemed his husbandly prerogative. He is suitably chastised and agrees to take Hilary into his home. Subsequently, order—of an entirely new sort—is restored, or more correctly, created. Hilary finds a new family, and Margot resigns from Jarvis's employ; thus Madeleine's spirit is appeased, if not necessarily departed.

Although Margot's foray into lesbianism is experimental and brief, it nonetheless has long-lasting ramifications. Aside from enabling her to strike out—successfully—at the two men who had held economic, psychological, and sexual power over her, her afternoon with Renee also teaches Margot two very significant lessons. The first is love of her own body. When she reminds Jarvis of his long-past infidelity to Madeleine, she strips naked to assist his recollection. For once, she feels no shame in displaying her body to herself or another; rather, she experiences pride: "Margot, in truth has pretty breasts, plump, firm and white. Renee admired them, and Margot now has a better opinion of them" (218). Although Freud and Lacan would posit that the "narcissism" of lesbian mirroring (which, in their paradigms, almost inevitably becomes intertwined with mother-daughter bonds) stands in opposition to the "normal" female tendency to altruism, the opposite is in fact evident here.[4] For Margot, the validating gaze of the other woman not only leads to a sense of bodily self-worth heretofore unknown, but also to a sense of female community, the second item of wisdom Renee imparts to her.

Contrastively, when Margot laments the "struggle" that characterized Madeleine's life, a life possibly lived in vain, Renee retorts that Madeleine's fate was a matter of choice, failed responsibility, and, ironically, a heterosexist lack of altruism: "She'd only ever get angry for herself. She didn't see she had a duty to get angry on everyone else's behalf. She had no sense of sisterhood. It diminished her as a person" (206). Through Madeleine's "possession," however, Margot metaphysically acquires this "sense of sisterhood" and the ability to get angry on another woman's behalf. She actualizes this "spirit" of community in a more tangible form, however, through her adoption of Hilary, an act that results in Margot's epiphany that a complicated maternal—and paternal—community, which has existed all along, has found unity under her care. While observing her now-extended family at the dinner table, she realizes that Laurence, her eldest son, is not the child of her husband, Phillip, but rather the product of her illicit tryst with Jarvis—and that Hilary is in fact her husband's child, conceived when Madeleine, enraged at having witnessed this betrayal, sought comfort from Phillip, who was looking for the missing Margot on the same long-ago night. By acknowledging the "grief, and loss, and the damage done to me by time, and other people, and events—and the damage that I did," Margot realizes with a previously unknown happiness that she now embodies female community: "I am Margot and Madeleine in one, and always was. She was my sister, after all" (247). Thus, while Margot does not "become" a lesbian through her encounter with another woman, she attains both a sense of common purpose with her lesbian sister and an accepting understanding of their difference. At the funeral, the two women acknowledge each other: "Renee is there with her friend Bonnie. . . . Renee smiles at Margot, and Margot smiles back. Each to her own taste" (242).

Two generations of lesbians, one "confirmed" and the other closeted and, perhaps, not "really" lesbian at all, appear in a sequence of interpolated stories that inform and intersect with the main plot of Weldon's elaborately structured postmodern fairy tale *Words of Advice* (originally published in Great Britain under the title *Little Sisters*).[5] At the novel's center is Gemma, a would-be princess turned witch, confined to a wheelchair and missing the ring finger of her left hand, old and isolated at the age of thirty. Rejected by her "prince"—who was gay, as it turns out—and disappointed by the vision of romantic love that governed her view of the world, Gemma has married a "frog," the aging, unattractive, unlovable, but fabulously wealthy Hamish. Surrounded by vulgar if expensive ostentation, Gemma, a latter-day, high-tech Miss Havisham, constructs and consequently justifies her life through the medium of a fairy tale which she narrates compulsively and, apparently, revises constantly. Her literally captive audience is another would-be princess, Elsa, the teenaged mistress of middle-aged antique dealer Victor, who is Gemma's houseguest while her paramour appraises Hamish's vintage furniture. Gemma hatches a bizarre and megalomaniacal scheme, replete with unarticulated homoerotic desire, for Elsa to bear "her" child— that is, the child she cannot herself conceive—through the agency of her semipotent husband. To accomplish this end, Gemma must lure Elsa away from Victor, and therefore does all that is within her power to coerce the younger woman. She attempts to seduce Elsa through the narration of her cautionary tale qua autobiography, a story of love, intrigue, and murder set in the trendy decadence and ephemerality of Carnaby Street at the height of the 1960s "Mod" culture.

Through her narrative we discover that long before Gemma arrived in "swinging" London, the impoverished teenager had been a mother's helper in a rural village to one Mrs. Hemsley, a Anglican vicar's widow with five daughters. The Reverend Mr. Hemsley, disappointed at having sired five female offspring but not a single male heir, dropped dead from a heart attack the day after the birth of Alice, his youngest child. Born into such confusion, Alice becomes "singular" among the Hemsley girls, a status signified by her being the only child in the family whose given name does not begin with the letter "H." Marked by such an unfortunate heritage, Alice understands that her sex is somehow undesirable, and therefore aspires to fulfill her late father's wishes by acquiring "maleness" and, ultimately, taking his place in the family: "Little Alice, pulling on trousers instead of a skirt, saying, 'That's what Daddy wants. I saw it in a dream.' Little Alice with a daddy never seen in the flesh but known in the spirit" (89–90).

Alice, to whom Gemma was particularly close, enters the present-day narrative as the invalid's physiotherapist. As she rides up to Gemma's palace of bad taste on her motorcycle, Hamish spots her with dismay, and describes her to Victor as "some dyke friend of Gemma's" (106). The initial view of Alice, in juxtaposition to the pathological decadence of Gemma and the mindlessly naive sexual dependency of Elsa, would seem a refreshing one of health, vitality, and heroic courage:

> Alice Hemsley, bold and beautiful, in black trousers and white shirt, tall, tanned, handsome and hook-nosed, swaggers in, hands on hips. Her hair is black, short and curly, and her cheeks full and pink beneath their bronze. Her voice booms huskily. Her bosom is high and full; the eye searches it out in the attempt to define male or female, and finding it, is both surprised and gratified. (123)

Gemma greets Alice passionately, and Elsa, whose feelings about Gemma are at best ambivalent, finds herself "unaccountably jealous" (123). In Elsa's presence, Alice proceeds to supervise Gemma's "physical therapy," clinging suggestively to her patient as she goes through the motions of exercise in the pool. Gemma, once Alice's caretaker, now plays the role of the child while Alice patiently scolds her for her "naughtiness" on a variety of scores, particularly her habitual self-fictionalizing. But while Alice appears, both in form and manner, to be mature, strong, and in control, Weldon soon shatters this illusion.

During the evening following Alice's arrival, Elsa consents to "procreate" with Hamish; Gemma, meanwhile, wheels herself into Victor's room so that he might "bring [her] to life" (147). While Gemma and Victor are in medias res, Alice, whom Victor first mistakes for Hamish, knocks on the door, pleading pathetically with Gemma to stop her "disgusting" behavior. Gemma, who has regained the upper hand over her caretaker, taunts the importunate Alice: "Come inside and see what we're doing . . . I know that's what you want. You have to find out how normal people behave, poor thing" (150). Stung by Gemma's ridicule, Alice retreats to Elsa's room—from which Hamish has just departed—and begs to be let in. Alice's motivations for this visit are ambiguous. Ostensibly, she wants to warn Elsa of Gemma's cruelty and duplicity; she also appears, at least subconsciously, to take some pleasure in playing the spoiler, informing Elsa of Victor's treachery. But Elsa, who in her just-completed liaison with Hamish has, for the first time in her life, comprehended the possibility of being a sexual subject instead of sexual object, sees only one reason for Alice's intrusion; once Alice scales the wall and climbs through the fourth-floor window of her room, Elsa initiates sexual contact:

> Elsa draws Alice in [to bed] beside her. It is the nearest, for a long time, than she has lain next to a contemporary in age; she is surprised to remember the difference between stretching naked next to a young person, and next to one who is old. . . . Elsa kisses young Alice . . . she covers Alice with her body, lets her hands comfort and penetrate Alice as if it were her own body she thus cajoled. Alice . . . cries out and calms, and smiles in the cold light. (163)

Weldon here reverses completely the expectations she has previously created. Not only is Elsa, who has heretofore seemed helplessly and heedlessly heterosexual, the sexual aggressor rather than the apparently "dykeish" Alice, but she is no stranger to this mode of sexual expression:

"Thus Elsa did with her schoolfriends on many an educational and recreational school journey to the Swiss Alps, the Italian Riviera and the Austrian Tyrol, until the exchange rate made such journeys difficult" (163). We may assume that the "exchange rate" that ultimately creates difficulty is that of heterosexuality as much as it is that of the European Common Market.

Simultaneously, Alice is revealed to be other than what she seems. Although she apparently receives physical pleasure from her sexual encounter with Elsa, no sooner has the *jouissance* faded than she announces, "I'm not a lesbian . . . I have trouble with my hormones." She significantly adds, "I am as normal as the next person—just unhappier." Elsa, who has equated Alice's appearance of independence and *machisma* with lesbianism, is amazed: "You seemed so sure of yourself this morning" (163). Alice attempts to convince the somnolescent Elsa to run away with her and escape the "evil" Gemma, but her plan comes to naught when Gemma wheels herself into the room. Gemma inquires suggestively, "Which of you kept the other warm, I wonder?" Alice again falls short of expectation, pointing an accusing finger at Elsa, "displaying cowardice and conceding defeat all at once" (165). Enraged at this abjection, Gemma orders Alice to jump naked from the window and disdainfully throws her clothing after her.[6] The sobbing Alice roars off on her motorbike, never to be seen again in this tale.

Although Gemma is quite evidently psychotic, as Alice departs she conveys a bit of the skewed if legendary wisdom of the mad through a highly ambiguous comment she makes to Elsa: "I am afraid [Alice] has some kind of genetic deficiency and is sexually ambivalent. Her mother is a confirmed lesbian. There is a lot of it about. It is nature's answer to the population problem. I can't bear anything unnatural myself. Can you?" (166). Although far from a "natural woman" herself, Gemma curiously has no quarrel with "confirmed" lesbians, whom she finds part of nature's plan. Yet it is clear that she "can't bear" Alice, whom she deems, with some unwitting accuracy, "unnatural." Alice not only denies being lesbian (and all the responsibility the identity entails) while preferring to find comfort in the essentialist argument of "hormone problems," but she also denies, in effect, being female. As such, Alice is an "unnatural" representation of the stereotypical expectations of homosexual "inversion"; she is, moreover, Freud's theory of the "female Oedipal complex" come to life.[7] Having internalized her father's fatal disappointment in her gender, she not only experiences guilt but rejects her biological sex; under these conditions, she is both obsessed with women and ultimately rejects identifying with or loving them. Her Oedipal anxieties are further aggravated by being displaced from the position she enjoyed when, her older sisters grown, she had her mother all to herself, and thus could occupy her father's role. Mrs. Hemsley, however, finds relatively late in life a fulfillment and prosperity unavailable to her earlier, as Weldon reveals in the *other* lesbian story within the novel.

In the unfolding of Gemma's history, Weldon tells the story of the lecherous village dentist who, to humiliate his flat-chested wife who assists him, drops amalgam down the cleavage of the voluptuous teenaged Gemma while administering a filling—for the sole purpose of retrieving it in his wife's presence. When he subsequently dies, Mrs. Hemsley "move[s] in with the dentist's wife, at first for company and later for comfort as well" (133). Having discovered lesbianism and having freed herself from any semblance of her past repression, the dentist's widow "qualified as a dentist, and took over her deceased husband's practice, extracting his old fillings with a shocked and ultraprofessional frown" (133). With this substantial increase of income, the women are able to enjoy independence and prosperity, and are joined by an influx of "lady couples of a certain income and age" who have retired and bought homes in the community (133). As a result of this population shift, the once economically depressed and culturally retrograde village is transformed into a beautifully renovated and booming community with new businesses, such as upscale delicatessens featuring gourmet foods, to meet the demands of its more cultivated and civilized residents.

Through this striking contrast between openly lesbian mother and neurotically dysfunctional daughter, Weldon suggests that for women to model their identity or to shape their life around *any* masculinist pattern spells disaster—whether economic, moral, psychological, or sexual. Furthermore, she indicates, albeit ironically through the observations of Gemma, that while those who conduct themselves with an open, honest, and healthy attitude toward their own lesbianism are rewarded with personal felicity and, ultimately, respect and acknowledgment from others, those who conceal or deny their sexuality to themselves or others are inevitably miserable, and leave themselves prey to the scorn and psychological blackmail of others.

For Ruth Patchett, the eponymous protagonist of *The Life and Loves of a She-Devil,* brief excursions into lesbianism are not so much a matter of desire and love between women as they are highly pragmatic ploys, the means to an end in her obsessive quest to avenge herself against the institutional heterosexuality from which she has been forcibly ejected. Indeed, "it [is] from . . . the need to be on the safe side" (US 119, UK 117), the need to ensure financial support for her project of revenge, that Ruth assumes a place in Nurse Hopkins's bed.[8] The grotesquely awkward and unattractive Ruth is discarded by her husband, Bobbo, as he pursues Mary Fisher, a writer of popular romance fictions abounding in glamour, fame, and—above all else—wealth. Left without any resources save her own considerable psychic energy, Ruth torches her suburban home and dispatches her children to their errant father and his mistress, then sets forth on a ruthless campaign of destroying the institutions that had heretofore oppressed her. To accomplish one phase of her design, she adopts the improbably romantic alias "Vesta Rose," acquires a position as a nurse's aide in the home in which Pearl Fisher, Mary's mother, is a resident, and in the process restores the elderly woman to normal mental functions—and facilitates her return home—by substituting vitamins for her tranquilizers. Thus the discarded mother is enabled to torment her daughter once again. Fired for her efforts, Ruth sets out on a new venture in her unholy pilgrim's progress, this time in search of Mrs. Fisher's former caretaker, "a certain Nurse Hopkins, . . . who'd come into a fortune," after which "she'd gone to work in a hospital for the criminally insane . . . where she'd look no different from anyone else" (US 91, UK 90). Knowing firsthand the vulnerabilities peculiar to the physically undesirable, Ruth finds the potential benefits of a relationship with an unattractive woman in possession of "several hundred thousand dollars" (US 114, UK 112) most attractive; thus she traces Nurse Hopkins to Lucas Hill Hospital, where she accepts a job few others would desire and becomes, in rapid succession, Nurse Hopkins's friend, roommate, and lover.

"Four feet eleven inches high and weigh[ing] two hundred pounds," Nurse Hopkins, in spite of her fortune, works gladly in the abject confines of the psychiatric hospital, finding "security and regularity . . . among people more peculiar than she" (US 113–14, UK 111–12). If examined only on the surface, the representation of this lesbian character might seem a mere retroping of the stereotypical invert too ugly or abject to attract erotic attention from men. Weldon's complex and sophisticated narrative structure, however, belies this assumption; while Ruth's designs on Nurse Hopkins are clearly exploitative, the relationship between the two women provides a thorough and beneficial transformation for Nurse Hopkins—as well as prosperity and success for both characters. As a result of "much cuddling, kissing, and sexual experimentation between the two women," physical changes manifest themselves quickly: "Sexual activity seemed to have a tonic effect on Nurse Hopkins: her menstrual cycle became regular, her eyes brightened, she lost weight, divested herself of many layers of sweaters, and moved briskly about the hospital" (US 120, UK 118). Nurse Hopkins's discovery of lesbianism also precipitates a psychological sea change; the former self-styled "freak" gains self-confidence and a profoundly lesbian feminist sense of sisterhood. She cheerfully proclaims that "Women like us . . . must learn to stick together," adding that "People think because you're not the same . . . as other people you're not interested in sex, but it isn't so" (US 119–20, UK 117–18). Subsequently, as a result of her metamorphosis—as well as ample prodding from Ruth—Nurse Hopkins, who once found comfort from an unsympathetic world in the abject ethos of a psychiatric prison, discovers that her professional life is boring.

Nurse Hopkins places her trust, her future, and, above all else, her fortune in Ruth's hands, and the two women venture forth into the business world, inaugurating the Vesta Rose Employment Agency. Through this enterprise they revitalize and recycle women who, discarded from the traditional roles of wife and mother and deprived all of self-esteem, would otherwise be completely unemployable. In a matter of a few months, the two send forth an army of "Vesta Roses" into the working world and, through assisting and supporting their fellow women, reap profits that multiply Nurse Hopkins's initial investment many times over; thus, as in the case of the dentist's widow and Mrs. Hemsley in *Words of Advice*, a quasi-Calvinistic system of material reward serves as a secular justification for the virtues of lesbianism. Echoing the proclamation of the biblical Ruth to Naomi, Nurse Hopkins declares her undying love for another, very different Ruth: "Wherever you go . . . I will follow. I have never been so happy in my life" (US 122, UK 120).[9] In this atmosphere of female-female love and feminist solidarity, Nurse Hopkins even becomes a mother; she adopts the autistic child of a client who had heretofore been unable to pursue a long-sought and ultimately successful singing career. Yet, like most things edenic, this bliss is short-lived.

Benefits of the liaison for both women are obvious, and they do not,

interestingly, at any time incur social persecution or the moral disappro-
bation of any other character. Ruth's undying need for revenge, however,
far surpasses any desire for or recognition of either nurturing love or
erotic pleasure. She deploys her "Vesta Roses" to infiltrate, sabotage,
and ultimately destroy her estranged husband's flourishing business and,
having accomplished this phase of her long-term plan, leaves Nurse
Hopkins. Despite the calculated callousness of Ruth's actions, not only
in her departure but in instigating the affair in the first place, the relationship is, ironically, beyond a doubt the most fortuitous event ever to
occur in Nurse Hopkins's life. Ruth leaves her "the Vesta Rose Agency to
run and [a] little boy to love." With a consideration that she shows none
of her subsequent, heterosexual lovers, she consoles Nurse Hopkins, reminding her that she is—as a result of their encounter—a fabulously
wealthy woman, exhorting her to look toward the future positively and
self-confidently, and advising her that a double "legacy" of enterprise and
motherhood will keep her "too busy to grieve for me much" (US 131, UK
128). Weldon provides a brief glimpse of Nurse Hopkins much later in
the novel. More successful than ever, she blithely tells Ruth, "I've missed
you so, but I've been too busy to notice." With much admiration and
more than a touch of irony, Ruth responds, "Spoken like a man" (US 208,
UK 206).

After this leave-taking, Nurse Hopkins (and, in the American editions of *The Life and Loves of a She-Devil*, lesbianism) disappears from
the narrative. Ruth returns to the realm of heterosexuality in order to
advance her schemes, becoming first the mistress of a pathologically sadistic judge and subsequently the lover of a masochistic Roman Catholic
priest before undergoing the long and painful series of cosmetic surgeries
necessary to render her in the image and likeness of her nemesis Mary
Fisher. But not, in British editions, before a journey to Lesbian Nation.[10]

After parting company with Father Ferguson, whom she dispatches
not only to convert Mary Fisher but to provide her with sexual compan-
ionship in the wake of Bobbo's incarceration, Ruth joins a "separatist
feminist" commune whose members have broken all ties with men and
who live off the land (UK only 119). Engaging in manual labor and sharing the high-fiber diet of "the Wimmin," Ruth sheds most of her excess weight and improves her physical endurance; yet this sojourn is
merely a means to an end—to prepare herself for the rigors of surgical
re-creation—for the She-Devil has no real love of women nor any desire

to stay in a world lacking in "glitter at the edges" (UK only 119). But while Weldon makes clear that Ruth's dealings with the separatists are intrinsically devious and exploitative, she does not, in turn, represent the denizens of the commune as Ruth's innocent victims; nor does her irony spare the self-righteousness and hypocrisy almost inevitably inherent in extremism. While they assert that appearance makes no difference, Ruth notes that "look-ism" is hardly absent from communal romantic interactions and that "here," the same "as anywhere," people fall in and out of love, causing enough tears and suffering to go around—although the most attractive suffer less than their unattractive friends (UK only 200, 204). And although they eschew worldly goods and patriachal values, the separatists are quick to charge Ruth "$27 for her laundry and [confiscate] her few small belongings, including alarm clock and leather gardening gloves" when she announces her departure (UK only 209, 210). Thus Ruth reaps the consequences of individual dissent from the communal whole; these recipients of social intolerance have not themselves acquired the virtue they found lacking in "the giddy mainstream of the world": "The Wimmin did not take easily to those who disagreed with them: they made them honorary un-women" (200).[11] But if "the Wimmin" would attempt to distinguish themselves completely from women like Ruth—and vice versa—the binary opposition that would apparently ensue becomes, in effect, a mirror. Their mutual animosity arises from the unarticulated recognition of one's own worst flaws in another, in this case self-deception in matters of romantic ideologies and self-worth. Indeed, all parties concerned in the episode evince the grandiose illusions that result from the internalization of social marginalization and devaluation; and while the "solutions" they set upon may be creative, none of them are particularly constructive or even tenable.

Significantly, Ruth's departure from lesbianism with Nurse Hopkins coincides with a basic change in her characterization. Through the first half of the novel, the physically unattractive and powerless Ruth's desire for revenge is understandable and sympathetic; indeed, she has nothing to lose and much to gain by playing havoc with Bobbo, who personifies all negative patriarchal qualities. Her personal and professional success through feminism and lesbianism would seem to allegorize the adage that "living well is the best revenge." Her renunciation of her life with Nurse Hopkins, then, is ultimately a destructive and even self-destructive move, particularly in the light of her desire to transform herself into her own enemy, Mary Fisher, the embodiment of female heterosexual self-enslavement through the fiction of romantic love.[12]

In the end, Ruth acquires not only the physical form but also the estate and the men of her now-deceased nemesis. With Mary Fisher dead and the errant Bobbo broken in spirit and completely enthralled, Ruth emerges as the victor, albeit a pyrrhic one, in the heterosexual power struggle. While lesbianism no longer plays a role in her own "life and loves," it reemerges nonetheless—in the person of Ruth's daughter. Abandoned by Ruth and subsequently neglected by Bobbo and Mary Fisher, Nicola witnesses the worst that heterosexuality, institutional or otherwise, has to offer; and, having inherited her mother's presurgical physical appearance, her only potential role in the plot of romantic love is that of victim. Left to her own devices, then, she rejects the relentlessly infelicitous role models offered by her "mother-figures." Ruth, long estranged from her children, observes her daughter surreptitiously and, as a result of her newfound social and economic power, scornfully: "Nicola lives in the village with the science teacher from her school: one Lucy Barker. Nicola loves only women." She adds with disdain, "She will never make a she-devil" (US 230, UK 229). Ironically, Ruth fails to see that Nicola, having found an alternative to the travails of institutional heterosexuality, has no need to be a "she-devil."

In speaking of her aspirations for and discontents with the women's movement, Weldon has explained the telos of her fictions: "I want to lead people to consider and explore ideas that aren't very popular, which many people would rather not think about. But if anybody's to get anywhere, they had better think about it" ("Me and My Shadows" 164). Certainly lesbianism falls into the category of ideas "many people would rather not think about"; indeed, if Weldon were a lesbian novelist writing for a predominantly lesbian audience, her representations of lesbians as women who are, by and large, better off than their heterosexual counterparts might be dismissed as heterophobic propaganda. But in these novels written for mass audiences—which, we may assume, are for the most part heterosexual—Weldon quite evidently requires heterosexual women to think about lesbianism "if they are to get anywhere."

Yet, because, as Elizabeth Bowen once observed, "humor is being satisfied you are right, irony, being satisfied that they should think you wrong,"[13] it is perhaps inevitable that some—indeed, some of those who are most in need of Weldon's message—will fail to see the point of her ironic humor. Harriet Blodgett observes that Renee, in *Remember Me,* "is portrayed more sympathetically than is Weldon's wont with lesbians" (755); but this assessment not only begs the question of how "sympathetic" Weldon tends to be with her heterosexual characters, but also that of what it means to treat a lesbian character "sympathetically." As a lesbian and a critic, I would argue that treating with uncritical idealism any character who, for better or worse, stands as a "representative" member of a marginalized group is, potentially, as pernicious as mindlessly demonizing her. The assumed prohibition against supposedly negative representation has, I believe, far too often resulted in images of lesbians as permanent victims who are not—and cannot be—held responsible for their own actions. Thus, the blandly "positive" images that ensue have the effect of not only infantilizing the lesbian character (and, by extension, all lesbians) but rendering her as a *type* rather than an *individual*. Weldon, contrastively, by subjecting her lesbian characters to the same critical and ironic scrutiny as her heterosexual protagonists, creates lesbian figures who are mixed bags of strengths and weaknesses and, moreover, distinct in personality from one another. Thus, by treating them as she does other women, she humanizes and, to the extent that it is at all possible, "normalizes" the lesbian.

Lesbian critic Paulina Palmer expresses concern that "the assimilation of lesbian feminist themes into women's fiction in general," by Weldon and such authors as Margaret Atwood and Angela Carter, will obviate lesbian fiction "as a specific mode."[14] Yet this anxiety presumes, perhaps contradictorily, not only that lesbianism *can* be fully assimilated into present-day social discourse but also that the differences between lesbians and heterosexual women are greater than their shared concerns. I would suggest instead that Weldon, with her ironic and irreverent portraits of all sorts of women and her deconstruction of their gender-based self-justifications, exhorts us to look at ourselves, individually and collectively, if we are eventually to "get anywhere," and that "women like us"—regardless of sexual orientation—"must learn to stick together."

NOTES

1. See, for example, Paulina Palmer, *Contemporary Women's Fiction: Narrative Practice and Feminist Theory* (Jackson: UP of Mississippi, 1989), 37–38, 73–75, 99, 101–2; Paulina Palmer, "Contemporary Lesbian Feminist Fiction: Texts

for Everywoman," *Plotting Change: Contemporary Women's Fiction*, ed. Linda Anderson (London: Edward Arnold, 1990), 59–62; and Harriet Blodgett, "Fay Weldon," *Dictionary of Literary Biography*, vol. 14, ed. Jay L. Halio (Detroit: Gale, 1983), 754–56 passim. The best and by and large unflinching feminist critiques of Weldon's novels are those by Olga Kenyon, *Women Novelists Today: A Survey of English Writing in the Seventies and Eighties* (New York: St. Martin's, 1988), 104–28; and Regina Barreca, *Untamed and Unabashed: Essays on Women and Humor in British Literature* (Detroit: Wayne State UP, 1994), 147–61; yet these, like the commendable analyses by Margaret Crosland, *Beyond the Lighthouse: English Women Novelists in the Twentieth Century* (New York: Taplinger, 1981), 204–10; Lorna Sage, *Women in the House of Fiction: Post-War Women Novelists* (New York: Routledge, 1992), 153–60; and Patricia Waugh, *Feminine Fictions: Revisiting the Postmodern* (New York: Routledge, 1989), 189–96, generally avoid any discussion of Weldon's lesbian characters and subtexts. The phrase "safe sea of women" alludes to Bonnie Zimmerman's exhaustive study of 1970s and 1980s lesbian feminist fictions, *The Safe Sea of Women: Lesbian Fiction, 1969–1989* (Boston: Beacon, 1990), the title of which is, in turn, derived from June Arnold's novel *Sister Gin* (Plainfield, VT: Daughter's, 1973), 92; in both cases, the reference is to the ideal of a lesbian utopia. Conversely, in Weldon's texts, utopias, lesbian or otherwise, function by and large as fantasies for the self-deluded, as acutely demonstrated in her more recent novel *Darcy's Utopia*.

2. Lesbianism plays a significant role in two of Weldon's other novels, *Female Friends* and *The Heart of the Country*. The former has provoked the ire of certain lesbian feminist critics for its representation of lesbianism as an aspect of male fantasy. In one episode, Oliver, the tyrannical and sadistic husband of the protagonist Chloe, manipulates a sexual liaison between his wife and Françoise, the young French au pair with whom he is having an affair, for the purposes of accusing Chloe of lesbianism and for his own voyeuristic enjoyment. Significantly, Oliver calls a halt to the arrangement in medias res when he is confronted by the disturbing thought that the two women might derive pleasure from each other, exclusive of him. While this scene has caused considerable consternation to some critics who have seen it as a representation of "lesbianism from a phallocentric perspective" (Palmer, "Contemporary Lesbian Fiction" 60), such ready denunciations overlook the textual evidence that neither woman is, in fact, a lesbian nor does she identify herself as such. (Thus, I am not including the novel in this discussion of lesbian *characters*.) More importantly, such condemnations effectively elide the *real* problem that Weldon is obliquely addressing: that the literary and visual representation of female homoerotic desire and

activity is almost inevitably encumbered associatively by a long history of woman-on-woman scenarios in male-authored pornography, an issue that has received little straightforward discussion among lesbian or feminist critics until recently. (See, e.g., Colleen Llamas, "The Postmodern Lesbian Position: *On Our Backs," The Lesbian Postmodern,* ed. Laura Doan (New York: Columbia UP, 1994), 85–103, for a thoughtful discussion of this and related issues.) In the case of *The Heart of the Country,* a highly complex erotic dynamic is at work between the two female protagonists, a narrative situation that would perforce suffer from oversimplification in an essay of this scope. I am examining the female homoeroticism of this novel in a book-length manuscript, now in progress, on lesbian panic as a narrative strategy in twentieth-century British women's fictions.

3. In her discussion of the "ghosted" or "apparitional" lesbian, Terry Castle, *The Apparitional Lesbian: Female Homosexuality and Modern Culture* (New York: Columbia UP, 1993), writes that "to try to write the literary history of lesbianism is to confront, from the start, something ghostly: an impalpability, a misting over, an evaporation, or 'whiting out' of possibility" (28), and suggests that lesbianism has often been rendered obliquely in literature through the metaphorical or literal "ghosting" of the lesbian character. The attempted consummation of unrealized possibilities between Renee and Madeleine through the medium of the "possessed" body of Margot is, I would suggest, an extreme example of this narrative phenomenon.

4. See Sigmund Freud, "On Narcissism: An Introduction," *Standard Edition of the Complete Psychological Writings of Sigmund Freud,* vol. 14 (London: Hogarth, 1953–74), 73–102; and Jacques Lacan, and the école freudienne, *Feminine Sexuality,* ed. Juliet Mitchell and Jacqueline Rose, trans. Jacqueline Rose (New York: Norton, 1982), 61–73, 99–136. For a feminist rebuttal, see Luce Irigaray, *The Speculum of the Other Woman,* trans. Gillian C. Gill (Ithaca: Cornell UP, 1985), 112–29.

5. The fairy tale Weldon "updates" in *Words of Advice* is the traditional English tale commonly known as "Mr. Fox" or "The Robber Bridegroom." (As such, it invites subtextual comparison with Margaret Atwood's novel *The Robber Bride* [New York: Doubleday, 1993]). For the fairy-tale antecedent of *Words of Advice,* see Angela Carter, ed., *The Old Wives' Fairy Tale Book* (New York: Pantheon, 1990), 8–10; on the tale's contemporary function as urban myth, see Jan Harold Brunvand, *The Baby Train and Other Lusty Urban Legends* (New York: Norton, 1993), 24. See also Nancy A. Walker, *Feminist Alternatives: Irony and Fantasy in the Contemporary Novel by Women* (Jackson: UP of Mississippi, 1990), 101–4.

6. In her jump from the window, Alice complains that she has scratched her eye on a bramble. Although, considering the lesbianism of Alice's mother, this might suggest an Oedipal transference and subsequent "blinding," Alice's defenestration, preceded by her climb to the room in which Elsa is "imprisoned" by Gemma, more closely resembles the fairy tale "Rapunzel," to which Weldon alludes earlier in the text (8, 10). On lesbian retropings of "Rapunzel," see Ellen Cronan Rose, "Through the Looking Glass: When Women Tell Fairy Tales," *The Voyage In: Fictions of Female Development*, ed. Elizabeth Abel, Marianne Hirsch, and Elizabeth Langland (Hanover, NH: UP of New England, 1983), 209–27, 215–19.

7. See Sigmund Freud, *Women and Analysis*, ed. Jean Strouse (New York: Grossman, 1974), 24, 42–43, 77–92.

8. A number of incidents in the original British edition of *The Life and Loves of a She-Devil* (UK: London: Coronet, 1984; US: New York: Pantheon, 1983), including a lengthy episode in which Ruth becomes a resident of a lesbian separatist commune, are missing from American editions. For the sake of continuity and clarity, I am citing both American ("US") and British ("UK") editions to indicate those passages that appear in both, as well as indicating those absent from absent from American editions ("UK only"). Although there have been several editions of the novel published in the respective countries, the textual differences are peculiar to the nation of publication rather than the given publisher. Hence, as far as I am able to determine, the same "original" text appears in all British editions, while all American editions are "bowdlerized." In both cases, pagination varies according to publisher.

9. See Ruth 1:16 (KJV): "And Ruth said, Entreat me not to leave thee, or to return from following after thee: for whither thou goest, I will go; and where thou lodgest, I will lodge."

10. "Lesbian Nation" refers in general to the movement of lesbian separatism, often communitarian and replete with a newly created female, goddess-based mythology, that flourished in the 1970s and early 1980s. The name is derived from Jill Johnston's eponymous political manifesto, *Lesbian Nation* (New York: Simon and Schuster, 1973). On this movement, see Johnston, also Zimmerman (121–26) and Lillian Faderman, *Odd Girls and Twilight Lovers: A History of Lesbian Life in Twentieth-Century America* (New York: Columbia UP, 1991), 215–45.

11. Paulina Palmer, although generally positioning herself contra Weldon, particularly on lesbian issues, acknowledges the accuracy of this representation: "Her perceptive analysis of the mixed flaws and advantages of the lesbian femi-

nist farming commune . . . is very similar to the representations of lesbian feminist community to be found in lesbian novels" ("Contemporary Lesbian Fiction" 61).

12. Interestingly, while *She-Devil*, Susan Seidelman's 1989 film version of Weldon's novel, completely elides the sexual aspect of the relationship between Ruth and Nurse Hopkins (called "Nurse Hooper" in the film), it also omits both Ruth's subsequent and pernicious heterosexual liaisons and her surgical re-creation. Thus, while the film oversimplifies the moral, social, ethical, and psychological complexities Weldon poses by avoiding them, it also preserves audience sympathy for Ruth and presents her "romantic friendship" with "Nurse Hooper" as a positive and ongoing situation. Moreover, Mary Fisher does not die but, disillusioned by her affair with "Bob," rejects romantic love and popular romance fiction, becoming, rather like Fay Weldon, an acclaimed postmodern novelist.

13. Qtd. in Barreca 109.

14. Palmer, "Contemporary Lesbian Fiction" 62.

Selected Works by Fay Weldon

Affliction. London: HarperCollins, 1993.

Angel, All Innocence, and Other Stories. London: Bloomsbury Publishing, 1995.

Big Girls Don't Cry. New York: Atlantic Monthly Press, 1997.

Big Women. London: Flamingo, 1997.

The Cloning of Joanna May. London: Flamingo, 1993.

Darcy's Utopia. New York: Viking, 1991.

Down Among the Women. London: Heinemann, 1971.

The Fat Woman's Joke. London: Panther, 1969.

Female Friends. Chicago: Academy Chicago, 1988.

Growing Rich. London: HarperCollins, 1992.

The Heart of the Country. New York: Viking, 1988.

A Hard Time to Be a Father. New York: Bloomsbury Publishing, 1999.

The Hearts and Lives of Men. London: Flamingo, 1992.

Leader of The Band. New York: Penguin, 1990.

The Life and Loves of a She-Devil. 1983. London: Coronet, 1984.

Life Force. London: Flamingo, 1993.

Little Sisters. London: Sceptre, 1993.

"Me and My Shadows." *On Gender and Writing.* Ed. Michelene Wandor. London: Pandora, 1983. 15–27.

Moon over Minneapolis: Or Why She Couldn't Say. New York: Penguin, 1999.

New Year's Eve. Holybourne, Alton, Hampshire: Clarion Publishing, 1996.

Nobody Likes Me! London: Bodley Head, 1997.

Praxis: A Novel. New York: Penguin, 1990.

The President's Child. Sevenoaks, Sussex, UK: Sceptre, 1993.

Polaris and Other Stories. New York: Penguin, 1989.

Puffball. New York: Penguin, 1990.

Rebecca West. New York: Viking Penguin, 1985.

Remember Me. New York: Random House, 1976.

The Rules of Life. London: Vintage, 1992.

Sacred Cows. London: Chatto & Windus, 1989.

Splitting: A Novel. New York: Atlantic Monthly Press, 1996.

"Towards a Humorous View of the Universe." *Women's Studies: An Interdisciplinary Journal* 15.1–3 (Winter–Spring 1988): 309–11.

Trouble. New York: Penguin, 1994.

Watching Me, Watching You. 1981. Sevenoaks, Sussex, UK: Sceptre, 1993.

Wicked Women: A Collection of Short Stories. London: Flamingo, 1996.

Words of Advice. New York: Ballantine, 1978.

Worst Fears. A Novel. New York: Atlantic Monthly Press, 1996.

Selected Works about Fay Weldon

Alexander, Robyn. "A Question of Style: Preliminary Notes on Theory and Four Fay Weldon Novels." *Interaction.* Ed. Loes Nas and Lesley Marx. Cape Town: U of Cape Town and Dept. of English, U of Western Cape, 1994.

Bird, Liz, and Jo Eliot. "*The Life and Loves of a She-Devil.*" *British Television Drama in the 1980s.* Ed. George W. Brandt. Cambridge: Cambridge UP, 1993. 214–33.

Blodgett, Harriet. "Fay Weldon." *Dictionary of Literary Biography.* Vol. 14. Ed. Jay L. Halio. Detroit: Gale, 1983. 750–59.

Ford, Betsy. "Belladonna Speaks: Fay Weldon's Waste Land Revision in *The Cloning of Joanna May.*" *West Virginia Philological Papers* 38. Morgantown, WV, 1992. 322–33.

Gholson, Craig. "Fay Weldon." *BOMB* 30 (Winter 1990): 45–47.

Marshall, Denise. "Dear Reader: Intercepting Romance and Transforming Acculturation in Woolf and Weldon." *Virginia Woolf Miscellanies: Proceedings of the First Annual Conference on Virginia Woolf.* Ed. Mark Hussey and Vara Neverow-Turk. New York: Pace UP, 1992. 123–24.

Mergenthal, Sylvia. "'Seeing Is Believing': The Rhetoric of Looking in Angela Carter's *Nights at the Circus* and Fay Weldon's *Life and Loves of a She-Devil*." *GRAAT: Publication des Groupes de Recherches Anglo-Américaines de l'Université François Rabelais de T, Tours, France* 11 (1993): 105–17.

Smith, Patricia Juliana. "Weldon's *Life and Loves of a She-Devil*." *Explicator* 51.4 (Summer 1993): 255–57.

Wilde, Alan. "'Bold, But Not Too Bold': Fay Weldon and the Limits of Post-structuralist Criticism." *Contemporary Literature* 29.3 (Fall 1988): 403–19.

Young, Pauline. "Selling the Emperor's New Clothes: Fay Weldon as Contemporary Folklorist." *Folklore in Use* 2.1 (1994): 103–13.

8

Crossing Boundaries: The Female Artist and the Sacred Word in A. S. Byatt's Possession

Deborah Denenholz Morse

The British writer A. S. Byatt has vaulted into literary prominence with the publication of her Booker Prize–winning novel, *Possession*. In the wake of *Possession*, all of Byatt's six works of fiction have been republished. Despite her relative obscurity in America until recently, Byatt has for quite some time been a distinguished writer and critic in England, renowned not only as a novelist but also as a scholar. Her work on Iris Murdoch—*Degrees of Freedom* (1965) and *Iris Murdoch* (1976)—is her best-known literary criticism. Byatt has also written the recently reprinted *Unruly Times: Wordsworth and Coleridge in Their Time* (1970; reprinted by the Hogarth Press in 1989). Her many essays and reviews of nineteenth- and twentieth-century English and American literature and culture range from writings on George Eliot, Robert Browning, and Willa Cather to Van Gogh, Elizabeth Bowen, and Toni Morrison.

Born Antonia Susan Drabble (her younger sister is the noted critic and writer Margaret Drabble)[1] in Sheffield on August 24, 1936, Byatt read English at Newnham College, Cambridge and received her B.A. with first-class honors; the first draft of her debut novel, *The Shadow of the Sun* (1964), was actually written between 1954 and 1957, during her undergraduate years. Byatt was a graduate student at Bryn Mawr College in 1957–58 and at Somerville College, Oxford, in 1958–59, and a lecturer in literature at the Central School of Art and Design from 1965 to 1969. She then taught English and American literature at University College, London, from 1972 to 1983. Byatt was made a Fellow of the Royal Society of Literature in 1983, and has been a judge on several literary prize panels, including the Booker, Hawthornden, Betty Trask, and David Higham.

Byatt's own work is richly allusive, demonstrating an encyclopedic knowledge of both English and American literature. *The Shadow of the Sun,* the story of Henry Severell, a brilliant visionary novelist, and his adoring daughter Anna, is meant, as Byatt tells us in her 1991 introduction, to invoke writers from Raleigh to Coleridge to D. H. Lawrence, writers who have dwelt upon the artist's fierce, illuminating vision. *The Game* (1967), the story of two brilliant sisters' inability to escape their girlhood obsessions, suggests the Brontës' famous "web of childhood" from Charlotte's poem "Retrospection," quoted in one of the novel's two epigraphs.[2] *The Virgin in the Garden* (1978), the first novel in a projected quartet, invokes Tudor history and Shakespearean drama, with literary allusions on every page ranging from *King Lear* and *The Faerie Queene* to Charles Kingsley's *Water-Babies,* Thomas Hughes's *Tom Brown's School-Days,* and T. S. Eliot's essays. *The Virgin in the Garden* and its sequel, *Still-Life* (1985), can be interpreted as semi-autobiographical, with the bright, artistic heroine, Frederica, as a persona for Byatt herself. In these novels, Byatt focuses on artistic creativity, not only Frederica's, but also that of the fictional dramatist Alexander Wedderburn, of Shakespeare, and, in *Still-Life,* of Vincent Van Gogh, about whom Alexander is writing a play. *Angels and Insects* (1992), the two interlocking novellas "Morpho Eugenia" and "The Conjugial Angel," are set in the High Victorian period and demonstrate a rich and complex knowledge of the scientific and spiritual debates in that period, which issued in part from the evolutionary theories of Darwin, debates engaged by the hallmark poem of the age, Tennyson's *In Memoriam.* The novellas also demonstrate a feminist and politically radical view of the limitations of Victorian social class and gender distinctions; in each text, a woman creates her own freedom through her vision, art, and love.

Possession (1990) is the story of two modern literary scholars, Roland Michell and Maud Bailey, who meet and fall in love while discovering the secret love of two Victorian poets, Randolph Henry Ash and Christabel LaMotte. Byatt's emphasis on couples a century apart in which both partners are writers points to her feminist reinscription of the romantic vision of the poet.[3] In Byatt's tale, both women, Christabel and Maud, must struggle to maintain their identities as artists. The interpenetration of the two narratives and the two pairs of lovers is central to the novel's concern with liminality and thresholds, with crossing boundaries, illegitimacy, and metamorphosis, modes of expressing the recognition of visionary truth in the work of both male and female artists.

Possession's great theme is the truth of the poet's imagination and the power of words to create poetry that transcends the boundaries between word and thing. For Byatt the Word is not simply words upon a page but, as it was for the romantic poet-prophets, a mode of embodying the sacred. The canonized English romantic poets were all male, but Byatt creates a Victorian poet, Christabel LaMotte, who is their literary descendant, and an inspired literary critic, Maud Bailey, who is both her biological great-great-great-granddaughter and heir to her sacred vision. At the end of the story, both Maud and her beloved Roland comprehend the significance of "the words that named things, the language of poetry" (513).[4] Through the words of the poet, we can once again inherit the Garden—we are all in possession of paradise.

Roland's words express Byatt's own fear that, as Michael Westlake states in his thoughtful article on her novel *Still Life*, "recent post-structuralist ideas, emphasising only the 'untrustworthiness' of language, undermine the social and logical possibility of truth" (33). In Byatt's book of essays, *Passions of the Mind* (1991), the necessary, difficult relationship between words and things is a reiterated concern. A typical statement of her beliefs forms the conclusion to "Accurate Letters: Ford Madox Ford," in which she approves Wallace Stevens's statement that "the accuracy of accurate letters is an accuracy with respect to the structure of reality." Byatt interprets Stevens's pronouncement: "Sceptically, but firmly, Stevens believed that words and things were necessarily related. . . . In our time, when we too often see language as a system singing to itself, conducting us and closing us from the world it tells to us . . . it is necessary . . . to have a Ford . . . to distinguish what Iris Murdoch called 'the hard idea of truth' from 'the great lie'" (*Passions* 108).

In *Still Life* Byatt insists that "the hard idea of truth" can only be found through language. In *Possession* she goes further and affirms the significance of language by inscribing it as sacred truth, as the romantic avenue into paradise, a reimagined Eden. Byatt asserts the sacred primacy of the Word in multiple ways. Literary allusions are crucial to the novel's larger meanings, embodying as well the permeability of the border between past and present, between fiction and reality, between legend and history. The complete title of Byatt's work is *Possession: A Romance.* In the book's first epigraph, she cites Nathaniel Hawthorne's definition of the romance genre as distinct from the novel; for example, in romance, using language to mingle past and elusive present, one approaches "the truth of the human heart" (preface to *The House of the Seven Gables*).

As if to illustrate Hawthorne's definition of romance, Byatt endows the present-day lovers, Roland and Maud, with names redolent of literary history and text. Roland Michell's name evokes not only Charlemagne's legendary hero, celebrated in the eleventh-century *Chanson de Roland,* but Browning's mysterious quester Childe Roland—himself a figure in Edgar's Song in *King Lear:* "Child Rowland to the dark tower came; / His word was still / 'Fie, foh, and fum! / I smell the blood of a British man.'" One thinks too of Roland de Vaux in Coleridge's *Christabel,* a literary Roland who provides a connection to Christabel LaMotte. Maud Bailey's first name inevitably recalls Tennyson's beautiful poem ("Come into the garden, Maud") as well as W. B. Yeats's adored Maud Gonne, who—like Byatt's Maud Bailey—had the beauty of a classic Greek goddess, was a rebel, and became the poet's muse. In Byatt's rewriting, Maud herself is writer as well as muse, and Roland the poet/quester is muse as well.

Byatt insists that we possess our literary heritage in order to touch the sacred Word through our imagination. To this end, literary allusion suffuses the novel. Byatt names her Victorian lovers Christabel LaMotte and Randolph Henry Ash with literary history in mind. Christabel LaMotte is named by her folklorist father after the Christabel in Coleridge's eerie poem, and her character, poetry, and letters recall not only those of Elizabeth Barrett Browning but also Emily Dickinson, Christina Rossetti, and even Emily Brontë. Christabel is painted by her friend and possible lover, the artist Blanche Glover, as "Christabel Before Sir Leoline"; the painting hangs above the mantel of their home. Coleridge's Christabel is a kind of Christ figure who is to be sacrificed to the lamia (serpent-woman) Geraldine, a figure akin to Blanche Glover, to be pitied as well as feared; Christabel LaMotte is associated through her name and through her own epic poem's Melusina, a serpent-woman, with both of Coleridge's poetic characters. An additional connection exists, as Danny Karlin[5] points out, in the German romantic poet and novelist Friedrich, Baron de la Motte Fouque's fairy tale "Undine," about the water sprite who kills her faithless lover with a kiss. Undine is a fictional relation of Christabel LaMotte's Melusina, who is a fish or serpent from the waist down; she forsakes her husband for betraying his promise not to look upon her in her private bath. All of these allusions suggest the power and possible danger of female art, and the necessity of female solitude for independent creativity.[6]

The Victorian poet Randolph Henry Ash in his turn is very much like Robert Browning,[7] whose dramatic monologue "Mr. Sludge, 'the Medium'" is the second epigraph of the novel, following Hawthorne's statement about romance. While Browning's Mr. Sludge is a fake, exploiter of the bereaved who ache for evidence of the supernatural, Ash is a voice of poetic truth, of visionary access to the divine.[8] Ash is one of the great poets of the age, a writer of dramatic monologues who falls in love with Christabel LaMotte through her words and his own, through a passionate exchange of letters like that through which Browning and Elizabeth Barrett fell in love. Like those real-life literary lovers, the fictional Ash and LaMotte run off together; their elopement, however, unlike that of the Brownings, is only for a brief few weeks rather than a lifetime, for Ash is already married. Ash's name adds substance to *Possession*'s theme of the sacred Word, of the biblical Creation and Apocalypse, of the visioned New Eden of the poet. The poet defines his name in both its aspects—as burned cinders or as the ash tree—in his poetry and in his letters. Christabel writes to Ash, citing his own apocalyptic image in his poem *Ragnarok,* a retelling of the Norse twilight of the gods.[9] In a letter to his godchild Sophia, Ash states: "my namesake, the mighty Ash . . . is a common and magical tree[10] . . . rooted in the underworld and touching Heaven" (106).[11] Ash's name suggests beginnings and endings, death and rebirth, time and eternity.

Ash's reference in his letter to Tennyson's poem "The Gardener's Daughter" ("More black than ashbuds in the front of March") exemplifies Byatt's romance world: all characters and events, however minor, mesh with literary history. Perhaps Byatt thinks of the great art that both Ash and Christabel produce after their passionate interlude of love, rewriting Tennyson's poem so that both lover and beloved, man and woman, are artists, both muses.[12]

Not only the pairs of lovers, but all important characters in the novel have literarily significant names. The embattled scholar Beatrice Nest, who is editing the journal of R. H. Ash's wife, Ellen, is reviled by feminists for admiring the women married to great men; her very Victorian-sounding book is called *Helpmeets*, a title that evokes myriad Victorian Angels-in-the-House depicted in countless novels and paintings. Beatrice, like her precursor in Dante's *Divine Comedy*, has spiritual beauty, a beauty that is unrecognized except by Roland and Maud. Both Beatrice's nurturing capacity (suggested in her name) and the fine instincts of her nature—kindness, generosity, honesty—are crucial to the novel's comic ending.

The sexual predator and postmodern critical theorist Fergus Wolff, termed "devourer" (554) by Roland Michell, is named not only for his predatory sexual nature but also, ironically, for the Irish king Fergus, the dreaming king of Irish legend and Yeats's famous poem[13]; Fergus Wolff, in contrast to his namesake, learns nothing of the poet's truth, of the passion for the sacred Word, of naming, of love.[14] The study of literature for him is mere gamesmanship, the pursuit of fame and glittering prizes, including the bodies of beautiful women like Maud Bailey. This cavalier attitude toward his rights of possession characterizes his relation to Maud at a Paris conference on "Gender and the Autonomous Text," where, she remembers with repugnance, he lured her into his bed with pronouncements on their mutual intelligence and her incomparable beauty. Fergus lectures and argues about sexuality in terms of psychoanalytic and feminist theory—his paper is on "The Potent Castrato: The Phallogocentric Structuration of Balzac's Hermaphroditic Hero/ines"—but he never comprehends romantic love. Roland Michell, in contrast, is "an old-fashioned textual critic" (56), Byatt's true literary quester—and true lover as well.[15]

The title of the book, *Possession*, takes on nasty implications with Fergus Wolff. He is what one of Byatt's literary precursors, the British writer Elizabeth Coles Taylor (1912–75), would have termed a "monstrous egoist."[16] James's vision in *A Portrait of a Lady* of Gilbert Osmond, who obsessively acquires beautiful objets d'art—including Isabel Archer—is a near-perfect analogue to Byatt's imagined Fergus Wolff, with his ambition to collect prizes, despite the cost to others. Inadvertently, Wolff's machinations only facilitate the communal revelation at the end of the novel, during which all of the novel's important characters except him participate in the illumination of Ash's and LaMotte's love, and the discovery of their child.[17] Byatt does not allow him to appropriate the legacy of the fertile imaginations and bodies of the Victorian poets.

The other villain of Byatt's novel, the American Mortimer Cropper, a collector of a different kind, evokes Gilbert Osmond's cold aesthetic sensibility even more clearly. Cropper, a wealthy Ash scholar and curator of the New Mexico Stant Collection of Ash manuscripts and memorabilia, is a kind of vampire figure who lives his life vicariously through the great poet, yet never comprehends—as Roland and Maud will—the truth of the poet's soul. Ironically, Cropper's ancestor, Priscilla Penn Cropper, from whom he inherited his wealth, was a true, if misguided, seeker after truth whose life intersected with both LaMotte's and Ash's and whose name (Penn) suggests both the writer's implement and a connection to Quaker spirituality (William Penn). Mortimer Cropper's names both sound like death—the French word "mort," the Great Reaper who crops with his scythe; it is his own acquisitive soul that is dying, suffocating in the temperature-controlled glass museum that holds Ash artifacts but not the essence of Ash's art, the imaginative vision.

Lines from poetry, the names of poems and novels, and literary figures and their muses are invoked in crucial scenes to enrich the sense of the presentness of the past, the liminal space between the literary worlds of yesterday, the modern figures in Byatt's fiction, and the mind of the contemporary novelist herself. The romantics in particular are prominently invoked—Coleridge, Wordsworth, Keats, Byron, and Shelley—both because they would have been read by the High Victorians Ash and LaMotte and, more significantly, because their emphasis on the prophetic insights of the poet's imagination is ever in Byatt's mind, from her 1970 book on Coleridge and Wordsworth to her recent introduction to *The Shadow of the Sun*, in which she states that "the one person I was sure I loved and admired at the time was Coleridge" (x). In one instance of this literary allusiveness, Christabel LaMotte tries to explain the peaceful domesticities of life with Blanche Glover, and cites, in her letter to Ash, Wordsworth's line from "Tintern Abbey" about the "little, nameless, unremembered, acts / Of kindness and of love" that have characterized life at Bethany House, where LaMotte lives with Blanche.

Blanche Glover and Christabel LaMotte meet at a Ruskin lecture that emphasizes the handicrafts movement, a lecture that precipitates their experiment in spinster living. Ironically, it is Blanche Glover, Christabel's sister artist, who is drawn to her death when she is separated from Christabel, perhaps a comment on the necessity of female identification and community for women's art to flourish. Blanche's despairing suicide by drowning is consciously performed in imitation of Mary Wollstonecraft's attempted suicide (instigated by Gilbert Imlay's abandonment); from the radical feminist Wollstonecraft, whom Blanche admires, she learns that she must sew stones in her pockets in order to sink.

The two pairs of lovers, the Victorian poets and the modern literary scholars, meet in romantic Yorkshire, in Brontë country, a fact that recalls the tragic passion of Catherine and Heathcliff and the more fortunate love of Jane Eyre and Rochester. Christabel's cousin Sabine de Kercoz, herself an aspiring writer, actually compares Christabel's passion to that of the "powerful" Jane Eyre (365). More particularly, the lovers meet at Whitby, the site of Elizabeth Gaskell's *Sylvia's Lovers,* a tragedy of thwarted love which promises yet to be made right in the New Eden that Sylvia prophesies at the novel's close. Byatt's narrator recalls Gaskell's novel when she introduces Maud and Roland's excursion to search for evidences of the poets' love affair (263), perhaps thinking of that ill-fated love, and of the daughter born to Sylvia and her doomed husband, Philip, a daughter who does find love and freedom, as Christabel's descendant Maud Bailey will.

In order to amplify her theme, Byatt imbues even small details with literary significance. Toward the end of the novel, as the mystery of the Victorian lovers is about to be discovered, four of the novel's twentieth-century characters visit the law offices of Densher and Winterbourne, names evoking two central Jamesian figures, Merton Densher in *The Wings of the Dove* and Winterbourne in *Daisy Miller,* both of whom are implicated in the deaths of spiritually superior women, the invalid American Milly Theale in *Wings* and the innocent American Daisy.[18] The idea of moral dilemma is underscored as the questers for the lovers' secret lives close in on the truth—and on the grave of Ash and his wife. Perhaps Byatt means to suggest the loss of American innocence in the contemporary American Mortimer Cropper as well.

There are two scenes in particular that close *Possession* in which the literary allusiveness of the novel crests. In the first scene, the letter that

Christabel LaMotte writes thirty years after the end of her love affair with Ash is read before an assemblage of scholars and lawyers who have become involved in their story through Maud and Roland's quest. The scene resembles the end of a Shakespearean comedy, a parallel that the lawyer Euan MacIntyre points out in an earlier gathering of these same questers at Beatrice Nest's home in Arthurian-sounding Mortlake (524). Digging up the poet's grave, they find the box that might hold the answer to their questions about Ash and LaMotte.[19] The male pajamas worn by women and the wearing of others' clothing again deliberately challenges limits of gender and identity and underscores the theme of liminality and the crossing of boundaries.

When the box is opened, the very specimen container that Randolph Ash used in Yorkshire on his trip with Christabel LaMotte is revealed. The "specimens" that are removed from the box—the factual evidence of that adventure—are, first, the oiled silk bag that contains a blue envelope with a braid of pale hair in it, and the hair bracelet adorned with two joined hands worked into a sliver clasp that Ellen Ash has made of her hair and her husband's in the months he is dying, emblem of the enduring bond that drew him back to her. A second oiled silk bag contains the love letters between Ellen and Randolph Ash before they were married and an unopened envelope from Christabel to the dying poet, sent under cover to Ellen and never delivered, which is unsealed to reveal not only her heartbreaking missive but also the photograph of her daughter, May.

Christabel's letter itself invokes the literary genre of "Romance" (543) to describe her flight to Brittany secretly to bear her illegitimate child, and the manner in which she colluded with her married sister Sophie to raise the baby daughter as her own. "This is in some sort my Testament" (544), she writes to Ash, and although her confession of love and loneliness is unread by him, her great-great-great-granddaughter Maud—who loves Christabel's poetry and looks like her ancestress, white and green and pale-haired—will hear the poet's words and remember. For Maud it will be possible to be a writer herself and to live with a male poet, an impossibility for her Victorian ancestor Christabel, who could protect her child, her art, and her self only by turning to her sister. Christabel must resist even the benign male dominion of Ash to create either child or poem; sadly, in order to provide her daughter with shelter and respectability, she must be a spinster aunt rather than a fallen woman who is a mother. Byatt's conflation of these roles for Victorian womanhood again blurs the boundaries between "kinds" of women, identifying the strength of female community and sisterhood.

Christabel writes that "in calm of mind all passion spent," she is reading Milton's *Samson Agonistes,* that great poem of suffering and regeneration. She likens herself to the "villatic fowl" of Milton's epic and Ash to the "dragon," asking: "Shall we survive and rise from our ashes? Like Milton's Phoenix?" (546). The reader remembers that when Ash is first in love with her, he calls Christabel his "Phoenix," promising to renounce everything for her (217). Again boundaries are crossed: between the Melusina legend, Christabel's poem, and her life; between Christabel in Coleridge's poem, victim/savior of the lamia Geraldine, the mermaid/fairy Melusina, Christabel LaMotte the teller of Melusina's tale, and Milton's dragon, identified with the poet R. H. Ash; between the legend of the Phoenix, Milton's Phoenix, and the possibility that from Randolph Ash's and Christabel LaMotte's love will rise an enduring art as well as a living legacy in their descendants through May. May's son Walter bears affinities with Coleridge's Ancient Mariner, who receives the poetic blessing of "snakes" (546).[20]

In the final scene of the novel, in which Randolph Ash meets his eight-year-old daughter, May, the literary allusiveness in the novel richly defines Ash's and LaMotte's literary inheritance—and ours. They meet in an edenic setting, where Ash names Christabel the "Belle Dame Sans Merci," again invoking Keats's mysterious ballad poem. In this last encounter of the novel, the first and only meeting of the poet and his daughter, the poet also crowns May as the child of a beautiful fairy, alluding to the supernatural femme fatale of Keats's poem, and identifying May with Ash's own Christabel, as well as with Christabel's fairy Melusina.[21] At the beginning of their relationship, Ash has envisioned Christabel as "Elizabeth," "Virgin Huntress," and "implacable Artemis" (201). Literary, mythic, and historical figures of Woman as solitary, as siren, as huntress become fused with Ash's and Christabel's literary creations and with their daughter. Male and female creativity—both artistic and biological—is acknowledged. Ash seems to have come to a difficult recognition that he can possess neither Christabel nor her daughter, both of whom remain desired but unattainable, self-possessed.

Ash's comprehension of loss—his own and Christabel's—is expressed in his choice of *Paradise Lost* as his text, and of the story of Ceres' sorrow over her daughter Proserpina in particular. He recites lines from *Paradise*

Lost to May, asking if she knows "that fair field / Of Enna, where Proserpina, gathering flowers, / Herself a fairer flower, by gloomy Dis / Was gathered, which cost Ceres all that pain / To seek her through the world?"[22] May replies that Christabel, whom she mistakenly believes is her aunt, tells her "poems like that. But I don't like poetry" (554). May's response tells of the poets' connection through words, as Ash's return to Milton's poetry recalls Christabel's letter invoking Milton's Phoenix, a document read earlier by the reader of *Possession* but not written until many years after this scene between father and daughter. Even though they have not spoken to each other for many years, the two poets' minds and souls are aligned, in sympathy through Milton's poetry. May is identified in her father's mind with Proserpina, goddess of springtime, and she is an inspiration for Ash's *The Garden of Proserpina,* his own great poem of regeneration and rebirth, his *Paradise Regained.* Yet Byatt perhaps intends the reader to understand more even than Ash comprehends in the identification of May with Proserpina: the separation of mother and daughter leads to a kind of death of female creativity in May, who rejects the art Christabel creates in unrequited desire and sorrow.

Byatt's commitment to the significance of female-created art is demonstrated by her reinscription of Milton's *Lycidas.* Ash again invokes Milton when he at last asks May to tell her mother that he is going to "fresh fields and pastures new," echoing the final lines of Milton's pastoral elegy. Through this allusion Ash identifies himself with Milton, and in a sense identifies Milton's mourning for the dead poet Lycidas with Ash's grief for the living poet Christabel. The parallel to Milton's pastoral elegy is reinforced by the flower-filled crown that Ash weaves for his pleased daughter, a crown like the one she will wear in her wedding, to be recorded in the photograph that will be sent to Ash by Christabel as he is dying, but which he will never see. In exchange for the crown, the child May allows him to cut a long lock from her golden hair. May braids this hair for him, and he carries the plait in his watch, a cherished memento of generation and eternal love encompassed in time. The plait is discovered by Ellen Ash after his death. Ellen thinks that the fair hair is Christabel's, and buries it with Randolph in his specimen box, to be discovered a century later by May's great-great-granddaughter, the fair-haired Maud Bailey.

In a story that tells of the quest to know, to ferret out a secret, one of the great themes is the limit to our knowledge on this earth, the imperfection which is the state of the fallen world. And yet, as Ash himself writes to Christabel, they cannot deny their human desire to know and to understand. Two of the letters Christabel sent to Ash are burned, and the knowledge they contained is lost. No one except the reader and Byatt knows what Randolph and Ellen Ash kept secret: their marriage was unconsummated because of her frigidity and his compassion. After the poignant letter from Christabel to the dying Ash is read before the group, Beatrice Nest and the others sorrow to think that Ash never knew his child lived. The reader learns in the epilogue that Ash did in fact meet May, in the scene in which she gives him the braided hair. Ellen Ash thinks it is Christabel LaMotte's hair, and those who find the specimen box that Ellen buried also think that the hair is Christabel's. No one will ever know that it is not, except the author and reader of *Possession*. And even Christabel did not know that her great love was aware that he fathered a living child, and that he met that child. The last sentence of the book tells us that in response to Ash's message of love for the "Belle Dame Sans Merci," May's delivery of Ash's words is interrupted: she meets her brothers, breaks her crown, and forgets to deliver the message (555). Life is not resolved, but instead is filled with ellipses and broken sentences, messages undelivered. Art too can be unresolved, as Christabel laments of Coleridge's poem of Christabel, "which teases so," because we can never know the outcome (193). But both life and art require the faith that one day there will be completion, the sacred unity the poet—Coleridge, Christabel LaMotte, R. H. Ash, Roland Michell, Maud Bailey, perhaps the child Walter—can imagine.

The emphasis on the protean nature of life and the idea of metamorphosis is a related concern in *Possession*, another expression of the novel's focus on boundary crossings and liminality. The poetry of both R. H. Ash and Christabel LaMotte is riveted on metamorphosis as the liberated state of the imagination. Byatt portrays thought as ever-changing, and consciousness is portrayed in the novel as fluid, often embodied in the interpenetration of memory and consciousness, of the narrator's description of present actions and thought and of writing from the past, often letters or journals. In one instance of this narrative mode, Ellen Ash's memory, the reading of Ash's unearthed letters, and her own present thoughts collide with each other. Ellen finds an unposted letter written by her deceased husband to Christabel that discloses his agony over the fate of their child. After burning the letter, Ellen thinks of her own erotic history, remembering the beauty of her youth; she then locks all her precious mementos in the japanned specimen box that will be buried with Ash, the box that will be found by the modern questers, whom she anticipates with dread and relief. Ellen reads one of Ash's early love letters to her—written long before her father permitted the unorthodox poet to marry her—a letter in which the ardor of his love is beautifully inscribed. In the light of this romantic letter, so full of love and longing, Ellen recalls the disaster of her honeymoon.

Ellen is a victim of patriarchy, both through her own father, who so adamantly opposed Ash, the heretical poet, as suitor for his beautiful daughter, and through the literary conventions that make Ash desire her as inaccessible princess in a fortress that must be stormed. Ellen's frigidity is the legacy of her father's authority and her dutifulness as his daughter; had she eloped with Ash like Christabel—had she dared to rebel—she might have lived a richer and more fertile life. Ellen might have felt that she truly possessed her husband, instead of thinking that his true wife is Christabel. Perhaps Ellen's inability to write is the mark of her passivity and lack of creative force, the force that is so powerfully possessed by the fallen woman/poet Christabel. Perhaps Byatt intends us to read Ellen's history as metamorphic, interpenetrating with Christabel's and with Christabel's daughter's, a happier, freer daughter and wife.

The most prominent element in *Possession* is water: female, translucent, dissolving, mirroring, drowning, sacralizing, Protean. Maud and Roland have their first erotic moment, fittingly, outside the bathroom at Seal Court, amid images of dampness and steam. Maud's own bathroom, decorated with watery-green glass, looks like an undersea fairy cave. The green that is associated always with Christabel—and with Melusina—is also Maud's color. It is an ocean color, the color of sea serpents, mermaids, and sirens. The snake in Ash's Garden of Proserpina is green. Green is the color of the rain-soaked ribbon that the feminist critic Leonora puts on Christabel's grave; of the first volume of Christabel's poems; of the shining pair of laced boots that Christabel wears to her rendezvous with Ash at Whitby; of the jade ring that belonged to Christabel's great-aunt Sophie de Kercoz (Sabine's great-grandmother), which Christabel wears as a wedding-ring at Whitby, along with Ash's mother's plain gold band, engraved with daisies; of Maud's green turban—held together with Christabel's jet mermaid pin bought at Whitby during the

Victorian lovers' holiday and passed down through the generations to Maud, who is, appropriately, drawn by its antique beauty and oddity.

The romantic idea of Nature imbued with the divine (natural supernaturalism) and in sympathy with human nature is often imagined in the novel through water: Christabel and Ash embrace for the first time in the moment of "madness" in "watery sunshine" at Richmond Park; they make love passionately for the first time beside the sea in Whitby, an encounter described in watery metaphor by Ash. He compares her to Proteus, the male sea god. Byatt could intend Ash's view of Christabel as the male Proteus to serve as a critique of Ash's imagination or to illustrate his recognition of a truth, a further interpenetration of elusive female- and male-constructed myth.

The Victorian lovers' favorite place at Whitby is also the place the modern literary scholars gravitate toward, reincarnating the poets' love. Randolph Ash thinks about how he and Christabel had gone to Boggle Hole because the name appealed to them and the day was one of sunshine and blue sky. Maud and Roland are similarly attracted to Boggle Hole because of its strange and funny name. They too have a romantic, paradisal day on which to fall in love by the sea, a day of "blue and gold good weather" (291). Maud and Roland walk through flowering lanes of white and pink dog roses, in a kind of wild Garden. There is a sense that not only are the two scholars living again the lives of the Victorian poets, but that they are immersed in an edenic moment, almost in one of Wordsworth's "spots of time," when the present connects to the past and to eternity, and a unity inheres in all things.

In Christabel's first letter to Ash, before falling in love with him, she writes about her imaginative self, her need for solitude to write her poetry—and of the danger to those who thwart the making of her web. She is the "Spider in the centre of her shining Web" opposed to Ellen Ash's "Princess in a thicket" (97), the artist opposed to the male construction of the passive female to be rescued and won. Much later, when threatened by the passion between herself and Ash, Christabel writes to him again, clarifying her desperate need for enclosure within herself and within Bethany House, that place of female artistic community. Indeed one of the major subjects in *Possession* is the issue of female artistic identity. The need for enclosure and privacy in order to create as one's own self is a vexed desire in the novel for both Christabel and Maud.

The book's repeated tales of women in towers—Rapunzel, the Lady of Shalott, Dahud—echo the two central female writers' artistic dilemma.

Finally, Christabel admits, "I am out—I am out of my Tower and my Wits" (215) as she invites Ash into Bethany Cottage for the first time. Despite their longing to possess the women they love, Ash and Roland ultimately respect the intense need for privacy in the woman writer. On the train to Whitby, Ash recalls Christabel's imagination and mystery, her solitariness, and her most private self. However, many years later, when Ash knows that his child is well and happy, he is able to leave Christabel in her "fortress" at the marine-named Seal Court, although he will write to her for the rest of his life, and will read John Donne and remember his true love's "eyes, lips, and hands" even as he is dying.

Roland gains Maud's love by willing her freedom and respecting her privacy. Maud thinks of her past relationship with Fergus as "a huge, un-made, stained and rumpled bed . . . dust and ashes" (63). In contrast, Maud and Roland spend idyllic days in Brittany lying side by side peace-fully, neither moving nor speaking. Significantly, their love is nurtured in a womblike bed in the country where the poets' child developed and was born. Both Roland and Ash desire the free expansion of the female self, the rising up of her powerful, unconstricted beauty. In the scene in which Roland and Maud confess their love to each other, the Victorian poets' unresolved issues of privacy and artistic identity promise to be less thwarting to the modern-day lovers. Maud speaks first:

> "People treat you as a kind of *possession* if you have a certain sort of good looks . . . I keep my defences up because I must go on *do-ing my work*. I know how she [Christabel] felt about . . . [h]er self-possession, her autonomy. . . . I write about liminality. Thresholds. Bastions. Fortresses." . . .
>
> "I have my own solitude."
>
> "I know. You—you would never—blur the edges messily—"
>
> "Superimpose—"
>
> "No, that's why I—"
>
> "Feel safe with me—"
>
> "Oh no. Oh no. I love you. I think I'd rather I didn't."
>
> "I love you," said Roland. . . . "In the worst way. All the things we—we grew up not believing in. Total obsession, night and day."
> (550)

True love, in Byatt's world, is still possible. Roland's words are meant to echo R. H. Ash's confession of love to Christabel, his fervent avowal in the letter he writes to her after their first passionate embrace in the stormy park.

The interpenetration of the two love stories that is so evident in this passage—as if the literary scholars are reliving the Victorian poets' lives—is nowhere more eerily evoked in the novel than at Seal Court, when Maud is led by what seems like memory of a former self to the dolls' bed where Christabel hid the poets' letters. The dolls, symbolic images of conventional Victorian womanhood, in fact disguise a very unconventional Victorian female artist and the record of her adulterous liaison. Maud recites Christabel's poem about the dolls like an "incantation" (92) in a sacred ritual, and then explains that the poem clarifies her situation. At the novel's close, the modern-day lovers Roland and Maud make love at last, re-creating the sexuality of Eden as they relive the illicit passion of the Victorian poets, liberated and unashamed, as Roland literally takes possession of her and she cries out in "triumph" and delight (551). All of the mythic eternal cycles told of in narrative and poetry and alluded to in *Possession* are evoked in the final image of the novel, the morning after Maud and Roland's paradisal lovemaking: Ash's retelling of the Norse saga in *Ragnarok* and his poem upon the Greek myth of the seasons, *The Garden of Proserpina;* the rising up of Milton's Phoenix and the fall, expulsion, and promise of return in *Paradise Lost;* the Arthurian myth in Tennyson's *Idylls,* with its sensual conflation of life, death, and hope.

The poet of regeneration and rebirth, and of love and the transforming, metamorphosing imagination, is Roland Michell. He experiences the sacred beauty of words, their transfiguring and incantatory power, and he begins to write poetry. What Roland has learned through the poetry of Christabel and Ash—and through their love and his own for Maud—is that both love and the Word are sacred and One: "the tree, the woman, the water, the grass, the snake and the golden apples" (551).[23]

The words of the poet embody divine revelation. Byatt's crucial reinterpretation of Wordsworth's literary manifesto in the preface to *Lyrical Ballads* ("what is meant by the word Poet? . . . He is a man . . . who rejoices more than other men in the spirit of life that is in him") is the inclusion of the woman artist in the Garden, the necessity of Christabel LaMotte's poetic vision as "the life of things" and of Maud Bailey's brilliant insights as literary critic symbolizing her role as Christabel's reincarnation, her modern artistic descendant. Byatt reinscribes Tennyson's "Come into the garden, Maud" as the inclusion of Woman not only as beloved by the artist, but as herself writer, herself creator of the Garden.[24]

The struggle to portray artistic consciousness has been an obsession for A. S. Byatt. Her early valediction of Coleridge coincided with her own writing of *The Shadow of the Sun*, in which the daughter, Anna Severell, fails to possess the artistic vision of her brilliant father, Henry. Byatt tells us in her recent introduction to the text that "Henry Severell is partly simply my secret self . . . someone who saw everything too bright, too fierce, too much, like Van Gogh's cornfields. . . . This vision of too much makes the visionary want to write—in my case—or paint, or compose, or dance or sing" (ix). Byatt goes on in this passage to tell us that when she was an undergraduate at Cambridge she was also obsessed by the story of Cassandra, the Trojan princess who "was loved by the sun god, also Lord of the Muses, and wouldn't give in to him, so couldn't speak, or not [so as] to be believed by anyone. Female visionaries are poor mad exploited sibyls and pythonesses. Male ones are prophets and poets. Or so I thought" (ix). *Possession* can be viewed as the culmination of Byatt's fascination with artistic vision from Shakespeare to Iris Murdoch. More particularly, it embodies Coleridge's description in *Biographia Literaria* of the imagination as "androgynous," a quality of mind Virginia Woolf claims for the female as well as for the male writer in *A Room of One's Own*.[25] Coleridge stated famously in *Biographia Literaria* that art is a "mediatress between, and reconciler of, nature and man" (ch. xiv). In *Possession*, A. S. Byatt shows us that through the poet's words— the words of male and female artists—we are in true possession of our sacred lives.

Notes

I wish to acknowledge Robert E. Hosmer's bibliography in *Contemporary British Women Writers: Texts and Strategies*. The bibliography was extremely helpful to me.

1. In her *New York Times Magazine* article of 26 May 1991, Mira Stout discusses Byatt and Drabble as "vigorous rivals since childhood" (15). See Giuliana Giobbi's fascinating "Sisters Beware of Sisters: Sisterhood as a Literary Motif in Jane Austen, A. S. Byatt, and I. Bossi Fedrigotti" for an analysis of this ob-

sessive theme in Byatt's *The Game*. Giobbi suggests that "accepting Austen's heritage, Byatt expresses women's moral struggles and imposes a female aesthetic" (246); and "by means of focusing her attention on the sibling relationship, the woman writer can explore the relation of self to other, illustrate the possibility of a divided self, or see the reason for a psychic split" (254).

2. The second epigraph to *The Game* is Coleridge's famous statement in the *Biographia Literaria* that "The principle of the imagination resembles the emblem of the serpent, by which the ancients typified wisdom and the universe, with undulating folds, for ever varying and for ever flowing into itself—circular, and without beginning or end."

3. After I had completed this essay, I read Louise Yelin's provocative article on *Possession*, "Cultural Cartography: A. S. Byatt's *Possession* and the Politics of Victorian Studies." Yelin states, in agreement with my argument: "*Possession* reworks one of the commonplaces of Victorian literature, the critique of Romantic excesses, rewriting it as a critique of Romantic androcentrism: Byatt's Ash departs from such Romantic precursors as Wordsworth, Coleridge, and Byron in not regarding female exotics simply or even mainly as the matter of poetry" (38). However, her criticism of Byatt's "repressions" of Victorian cultural cartography "mystifies" me, to use Yelin's own terminology. She states that Byatt "represses . . . the best that has been thought and said by women as well as men in a material ensemble in which knowledge and power are always in contention" (41). Yet Byatt, as I argue, deliberately critiques sexist literary paradigms, including the male romantic—and Victorian—artist figures, and recalls female literary history from Austen through the Brontës, Dickinson, Gaskell, Rossetti, George Eliot, and Woolf. Byatt's recent deconstruction of the Victorian heroicizing of A. H. Hallam (and Tennyson himself) in "The Conjugial Angel" (*Angels and Insects*) illustrates anew that she is quite aware of what Yelin terms "the conscription of culture in an imperial cartography that is anything but disinterested" (40). Byatt does refuse, as Jane Campbell recognizes in "The Hunger of the Imagination in A. S. Byatt's *The Game*," to "make feminism by itself the subject of a novel . . . she makes her own distinctions within the continuing language of the world in which both sexes inhabit" (161).

4. All quotations from Byatt's *Possession* are from the 1990 Random House edition.

5. Danny Karlin, "Prolonging Her Absence."

6. The surname "LaMotte" (de terre) means "lump of earth" in French, which might call forth an image of Eve in the Garden, of R. H. Ash's Creation poem "Ash to Embla," in which Christabel LaMotte is the prototype for

"Embla." LaMotte perhaps visually suggests the masculine "word" ("le mot") and evokes the consummate writer Flaubert's dictum about "le mot juste," a pronouncement that precedes Wallace Stevens's ruminations about the relation of words to things and the structure of reality. Christabel LaMotte's names resonate with the sacred Word that both creates and saves us. Professor Jack Willis of the College of William and Mary also suggests that "La Motte" is slang for "mound of Venus," thus suggesting the fallen woman aspect of Christabel's character.

7. Richard Jenkyns states in his review, "Disinterring Buried Lives," that "Ash bears some general resemblance to Browning, though one detects elements of Arnold, Morris, perhaps Carlyle too" (214). Anita Brookner states—wrongly, I think—that Ash "is a cross between Browning and Mr. Casaubon: his verses put one in mind of the Bishop ordering his tomb in St. Praxed's Church" (35). Louise Yelin credits Rachel Brownstein for "suggesting the part played by Meredith in the depiction of Ash" (38).

8. In "The Conjugial Angel" (*Angels and Insects*), Byatt creates a female medium who is authentic; she is the heroine of the novella, rewarded in the end with the return of her beloved, long-lost sailor husband.

9. See the *New Larousse Encyclopedia of Mythology*, ed. Robert Graves (London: Hamlyn Publishing Group Ltd., 1968), for a good summary of the Teutonic myths.

10. The ash tree that is the other meaning of his name is evoked in old legends as a tree that has the power to keep away serpents. In this text so imbued with the doubleness of serpent-women and the serpent in the Garden, this reading of Ash's name is redolent of meanings. Another meaning of the ash tree is suggested in "Le Fresne" ("The Ash Tree") in Marie de France's medieval *Lais*, in which an ash tree hides an abandoned daughter who is later reconciled to her mother and married to a king, although she herself may be barren. In Byatt's text, in which Christabel LaMotte gives her illegitimate child by R. H. Ash to her sister, and in which the frigidity of Ellen Ash is presented to the world as barrenness, Marie de France's story resonates. I am indebted to Professor Monica Potkay at the College of William and Mary for directing me to these sources.

11. The "mighty Ash" the poet writes of is the world tree Yggdrasil. After the final battle of the gods, which the old Icelandic bards called ragna rok ("the fatal destiny, the end of the gods"), the ancestors of a future race of men would emerge from the wood of Yggdrasil, where they were sheltered during the universal conflagration that yet could not consume the "mighty Ash." The great

Victorian moralist and biographer Thomas Carlyle writes of the Tree Yggdrasil in *Heroes, Hero-Worship, and the Heroic in History* in the third lecture, "The Hero as Poet." The context of Carlyle's discussion is Shakespeare and the Elizabethan era. I am indebted to Professor Terry Meyers at the College of William and Mary for reminding me of Carlyle's discussion. The poet's surname also evokes the art of another eminent Victorian, Dickens, in particular his meditations on dust and ash in *Our Mutual Friend*, a Victorian novel concerned—as is Byatt's work—with the sacred immanent in the world and the Word.

12. For background on Tennyson's poem, see editor Christopher Ricks's notes in *The Poems of Tennyson* (London: Longmans, Green, 1969), 507. The poem alludes to Tennyson's love for his friend Arthur Hallam (the narrator's for the poem's lover Eustace) and to Hallam's for Emily Tennyson (Eustace's for Juliet), and Tennyson's difficulties in courting Rosa Baring (Rose, the gardener's daughter) are also suggested. In the poem, the narrator and Eustace visit the garden to see Rose: "Not wholly in the busy world, nor quite / Beyond it, blooms the garden that I love" (ll. 33–34).

13. For the stories of Fergus, see Lady Gregory's *Cuchulain of Muirthemne* in *A Treasury of Irish Myth, Legend, and Folklore: Fairy and Folk Tales of the Irish Peasantry*, ed. W. B. Yeats (New York: Crown Books, 1986).

14. Another perspective on Fergus Woolf is offered in Mira Stout's article, where Byatt is quoted as saying, "For the Victorians, everything was part of one thing: science, religion, philosophy, economics, politics, women, fiction, poetry. They didn't compartmentalize—they thought BIG. Ruskin went out and learned geology, and archaeology, then the history of painting, then mythology, and then he thought out, and he thought out. Now, if you get a literary theorist, they only talk to other literary theorists about literary theory. Nothing causes them to look out!" (14)

15. If Byatt's consideration of the meanings of names in *Possession* extends to R. H. Ash's first names, one might note that "Randolph," a nineteenth-century name deriving from the Old English *Randwulf* from *rand* (shield) + *wulf* (wolf), suggests that Randolph Ash's poetic legacy is protection from the devouring egoism of Fergus Wolff—or that Randolph Ash without the influence of Christabel LaMotte would have had some kinship to Fergus Wolff. "Henry" is from the Old German *Haimirich*, meaning "protector of an estate," from *haimi* (home) + *ric* (ruler) or (protector). In any event, the names are suggestive, given Byatt's attentiveness to nomenclature.

16. Cf. "Flesh," from *The Devastating Boys*. One thinks of Casaubon in Eliot's *Middlemarch* or Willoughby Patterne in Meredith's *The Egoist* as less in-

telligent embodiments of this violator of others' souls, the first tragic, the other comic.

17. Danny Karlin points out that "the theme of the lost literary legacy invokes *The Aspern Papers;* James might be cited again in relation to the book's punning deployment of 'possession' as a term of material, erotic and demonic significance, an association that also reminds you of Dickens; indeed, the Dickens of *Bleak House* (family romance, Gothic quest, detective thriller) displaces the moral arbiter George Eliot as chief Victorian precursor" (17).

18. "Winterbourne" evokes too that other famous nineteenth-century literary character, Hardy's hero of Nature, Giles Winterbourne in *The Woodlanders,* who dies tragically while sacrificing himself for his beloved, in contrast to James's Densher and Winterbourne. The thought of Hardy's rustic protagonist perhaps underscores the tragedy of the poets' frustrated love.

19. I disagree with the assessments of critics who react unsympathetically to Leonora Stern. Ann Hulbert, for example, focuses on Byatt's characterization of Leonora Stern's feminist criticism and Mortimer Cropper's dry biography as a "merciless satire" of "two of the cruder varieties of literary analysis" (58). "Leonora" is of course a form of "Helen," meaning "light," and might be used ironically both in terms of the connotations of "light"—true enlightenment, knowledge—and with reference to the Helen of Greek mythology. However, Leonora is treated sympathetically—certainly much more kindly than Mortimer Cropper. If her lesbian feminist criticism is parodied by Byatt as somewhat reductive, the American scholar is portrayed as intelligent, flamboyant, and a bit larger than life. She is generous and honest, and a distinctly better human being than Cropper.

20. In Coleridge's poem, the Ancient Mariner is doomed to a kind of purgatory for shooting the albatross; after he sees the sea snakes and "blessed them unawares," he is himself blessed, and the albatross falls from his neck into the sea.

21. Ash is also Raimondin of Lusignan, the knight who is enamored of Melusina in Christabel's poem, begun as the poets start to fall in love through their letters: "And his face took the brightness of her glance / As dusty heather takes the tumbling rays / Of the sun's countenance and shines them back. / Now was he hers, if she should ask of him / Body or soul, he would have offered all. / And seeing this, at last, the Fairy smiled" (322–23).

22. Tennyson also retold the myth of Proserpina in his poem "Demeter and Persephone (in Enna)" (1889), a dramatic monologue in which the narrative is derived from the Homeric *Hymn to Demeter* (Walter Houghton and Richard

Stange, *Victorian Poetry and Poetics* [Boston: Houghton-Mifflin, 1968], 160). In Tennyson's poem, Demeter speaks, addressing her daughter from the Vale of Enna, where Persephone was originally abducted.

23. Ann Hulbert writes of this scene: "The escape from criticism into creative writing, as Byatt tells it, occasions a kind of conversion in one's attitude toward the word" (55). I read Hulbert's short but illuminating 1993 essay about sixteen months after writing the first draft of this article, and I find her argument tallies at points with my own.

24. In Juliet Dusinberre's rigorous "Forms of Reality in A. S. Byatt's *The Virgin in the Garden*," she argues against my analysis of Byatt's world redeemed by art. Dusinberre states that Byatt "heeds Murdoch's warning against consolation, refusing to take refuge in the idea of life ordered into art. Her novel demands whether any form can define reality, or whether the real is a dark chaos which even the Word—and the Christian Logos is part of Byatt's reference—cannot record or control. The irreducible reality may be the unimaginable formlessness of human suffering" (58). One might argue that Byatt subtitles *Possession* "a romance" for this very reason. However, the entire thrust of my argument works against Dusinberre's statement, although one could view Byatt's works as a continuum, with *Possession* a response to the moral and aesthetic dilemmas posed in *The Virgin in the Garden*. I also wonder if Byatt's seeming change in aesthetic view is not linked to biography. The death of her son, killed at age eleven by a drunk driver, reinforced a dark view of life "partly influenced by the bleak Norse myths of her childhood and the grim Yorkshire coal fields" (15), as Mira Stout comments in her interview with the author, "What Possessed A. S. Byatt?" *The Virgin in the Garden* is dedicated to Charles, Byatt's son. *Possession*, written many years later, might express Byatt's recognition that "she has only lately been able to see again properly, after a sort of blind grief" (15).

25. See Virginia Woolf, *A Room of One's Own* (New York: Harcourt, Brace, Jovanovich, 1957), 102–3.

Selected Works by A. S. Byatt

"After the Myth, the Real." Rev. of *The Van Gogh File: A Journey of Discovery*, by Ken Wilkie; *Young Vincent: The Story of Van Gogh's Years in England*, by Martin Bailey; *The Love of Many Things: A Life of Vincent Van Gogh*, by David Sweetmen; and *Vincent Van Gogh: Christianity versus Nature*, by Tsukasa Koderal. *Times Literary Supplement* 29 June–5 July 1990: 683–84.

"Amatory Acts." Rev. of *The Chatto Book of Love Poetry*, ed. John Fuller, and *The*

Collins Book of Love Poetry, ed. Amanda McCardiel. *Times Literary Supplement* 31 Aug.–6 Sept. 1990: 913.

Angels and Insects: Two Novellas. 1993. New York: Vintage, 1994.

Babel Tower. New York: Random House, 1996.

"Beginning in Craft and Ending in Mystery." Rev. of *The Penguin Book of Short Stories,* ed. Malcolm Bradbury; *The Oxford Book of Short Stories,* ed. V. S. Pritchett; *The Dragon's Head,* by W. Somerset Maugham, Saki, and others; *The Green Man Revisited,* by Roger Sharrock; *The Killing Bottle,* ed. Dan Davin; and *Charmed Lives,* ed. T. S. Dorsch. *Times Literary Supplement* 13 May 1988: 527.

Degrees of Freedom: The Novels of Iris Murdoch. New York: Barnes and Noble, 1965.

"Dickens and His Demons." Rev. of *Dickens,* by Peter Ackroyd. *Washington Post Book World* 10 Feb. 1991: 1–2.

The Djinn in the Nightingale's Eye: Five Fairy Stories. New York: Random House, 1994.

Elementals: Stories of Fire and Ice. New York: Random House, 1998.

The Game. 1967. New York: Vintage, 1992.

"The Hue and Cry of Love." *New York Times* 11 Feb. 1991: A19.

Imagining Characters: Conversations About Women Writers: Jane Austen, Charlotte Brontë, George Eliot, Willa Cather, Iris Murdoch, and Toni Morrison. New York: Vintage Books, 1996.

"Impressions in Their Rendering." *London Times Literary Supplement* 13 Feb. 1981: 171–72.

"Insights Ad Nauseum." *London Times Literary Supplement* 14 Nov. 1986: 1274.

Introduction. *Death Comes for the Archbishop.* By Willa Cather. London: Virago, 1989.

Introduction. *Enormous Changes at the Last Minute.* By Grace Paley. London: Virago, 1979.

Introduction. *The History of England from the Reign of Henry the 4th to the Death of Charles the 1st.* By Jane Austen. Chapel Hill, NC: Algonquin Books of Chapel Hill, 1993.

Introduction. *The House in Paris.* By Elizabeth Bowen. London: Penguin, 1976.

Introduction. *The Little Disturbances of Man.* By Grace Paley. London: Virago, 1980.

Introduction. *A Lost Lady.* By Willa Cather. London: Virago, 1980.

Introduction. *The Mill on the Floss.* By George Eliot. London: Penguin, 1979.

Introduction. *My Antonia.* By Willa Cather. London: Virago, 1980.

Introduction. *The Song of the Lark.* By Willa Cather. London: Virago, 1989.

Iris Murdoch. London: Longman, 1976.

"Marginal Lives." Rev. of *An Academic Question,* by Barbara Pym. *Times Literary Supplement* 8 Aug. 1986: 862.

The Matisse Stories. New York: Random House, 1993.

"Obscenity and the Arts." *Times Literary Supplement* 12–18 Feb. 1988: 159.

"The Obsession with Amorphous Mankind." *Encounter* Sept. 1966: 63–69.

"'The Omnipotence of Thought': Frazer, Freud, and Post-Modernist Fiction." *Sir James Frazer and the Literary Imagination: Essays in Affinity and Influence.* Ed. Robert Frasher. New York: St. Martin's, 1990. 270–308.

Passions of the Mind: Selected Writings. London: Chatto & Windus, 1991.

"People in Paper Houses: Attitudes to 'Realism' and 'Experiment' in English Postwar Fiction." *The Contemporary English Novel.* Ed. Malcolm Bradbury. London: Edward Arnold, 1979. 270–308.

Possession: A Romance. 1990. New York: Vintage, 1991.

"Reading, Writing, Studying: Some Questions about Changing Conditions for Writers and Readers. *Critical Quarterly* 35.4 (Winter 1993): 3–7.

The Shadow of a Sun. 1964. Rpt. as *The Shadow of the Sun.* New York: Harcourt Brace and World, 1991.

Still Life. 1985. New York: Collier Books, 1991.

Sugar and Other Stories. 1987. New York: Vintage, 1992.

"The Trouble with the Interesting Reader." Rev. of *Romanticism, Writing, and Sexual Difference: Essays on "The Prelude,"* by Mary Jacobus. *Times Literary Supplement* 23–29 Mar. 1990: 310.

Unruly Times: Wordsworth and Coleridge in Their Time. 1970. London: Hogarth Press, 1989.

The Virgin in the Garden. 1978. New York: Vintage 1992.

"Wallace Stevens: Criticism, Repetition, and Creativity." *Journal of American Studies* 12 (1978): 369–75.

"Worldly Wise." Rev. of *The Realists,* by C. P. Snow. *New Statesman* 3 Nov. 1978: 586–87.

Selected Works about A. S. Byatt

Bernikow, Louise. "The Illusion of Allusions." Rev. of *The Virgin in the Garden.* *Ms.* June 1979: 36–38.

Bradbury, Malcolm. "On from Murdoch." Rev. of *The Game. Encounter* July 1968: 72–74.

Bronfen, Elisabeth. "Romancing Difference, Courting Coherence: A. S. Byatt's *Possession* as Postmodern Moral Fiction." *Why Literature Matters: Theories and Function of Literature.* Ed. Ruger Ahrens and Laurenz Volmann. Heidelberg, Germany: Anglistische-Forschungen, 1996. 117–34.

Brookner, Anita. "Eminent Victorians and Others." *Spectator* 3 Mar. 1990: 35.

Campbell, Jane. "The Hunger of the Imagination in A. S. Byatt's *The Game.*" *Critique: Studies in Modern Fiction* 29.3 (Spring 1988): 147–62.

Cosslett, Tess. "Childbirth from the Woman's Point of View in British Women's Fiction: Enid Bagnold's *The Squire* and A. S. Byatt's *Still Life.*" *Tulsa Studies in Women's Literature* 8.2 (Fall 1989): 263–86.

Creighton, Joanne V. "Sisterly Symbiosis: Margaret Drabble's *The Waterfall* and A. S. Byatt's *The Game.*" *Mosaic* 20.1 (Winter 1987): 15–29.

Cunningham, Valentine. "The Greedy Reader." Rev. of *Passions of the Mind: Selected Writings. Times Literary Supplement* 16 Aug. 1991: 6.

Cushman, Keith. Rev. of *Sugar and Other Stories. Studies in Short Fiction* 25.1 (Winter 1988): 80–81.

Dinnage, Rosemary. "England in the 50's." Rev. of *The Virgin in the Garden. New York Times Book Review* 1 Apr. 1979: 20.

Duchene, Anne. "Ravening Time." Rev. of *Sugar and Other Stories. Times Literary Supplement* 10 Apr. 1987: 395.

Durant, Sabine. "Shavings and Splinters." Rev. of *Sugar and Other Stories. New Statesman* 15 May 1987: 30.

Dusinberre, Juliet A. "A. S. Byatt." *Women Writers Talking.* Ed. Janet Todd. New York: Holmes and Meier, 1983. 181–95.

——. "Forms of Reality in A. S. Byatt's *The Virgin in the Garden.*" *Critique: Studies in Modern Fiction* 24.1 (Fall 1982): 55–62.

Feinstein, Elaine. "Eloquent Victorians." Rev. of *Possession: A Romance. New Statesman and Society* 16 Mar. 1990: 38.

Giobbi, Giuliana. "Sisters Beware of Sisters: Sisterhood as a Literary Motif in Jane Austen, A. S. Byatt, and I. Bossi Fedrigotti." *European Studies* 22 (1992): 241–58.

Hargreaves, T. Rev. of *Sugar and Other Stories. Hermanthena* 142 (1987): 77–78.

Hulbert, Ann. "The Great Ventriloquist: A. S. Byatt's *Possession: A Romance.*" *Contemporary British Women Writers: Texts and Strategies.* Ed. Robert Hosmer. New York: St. Martin's, 1993. 55–65.

Irwin, Michael. "Growing Up in 1953." Rev. of *The Virgin in the Garden. Times Literary Supplement* 3 Nov. 1978: 1277.

Jenkyns, Richard. "Disinterring Buried Lives." Rev. of *Possession: A Romance. Times Literary Supplement* 2 Mar. 1990: 213–14.

Johnson, Diane. "The Best of Times." Rev. of *Possession: A Romance. New York Review of Books* 28 Mar. 1991: 35–36.

Karlin, Danny, "Prolonging Her Absence." Rev. of *Possession: A Romance. London Review of Books* 8 Mar. 1990: 17–18.

Kenyon, Olga, ed. *Women Novelists Today: A Survey of English Writing in the Seventies and Eighties.* New York: St. Martin's, 1988. 51–84.

King, Francis. "Grand Scale." Rev. of *The Virgin in the Garden. Spectator* 2 Dec. 1978: 26–27.

Lewis, Peter. "The Truth and Nothing Like the Truth: History and Fiction." *Strand Magazine* 27 (Spring 1986): 38–44.

Lewis, Roger. "Larger Than Life." Rev. of *Still Life. New Statesman* 28 June 1985: 29.

Mars-Jones, Adam. "Doubts about the Monument." Rev. of *Still Life. Times Literary Supplement* 28 June 1985: 720.

Merkin, Daphne. "Writers and Writing: The Art of Living." Rev. of *The Virgin in the Garden. New Leader* 23 Apr. 1979: 16.

Murdoch, Iris. "Force Fields." Rev. of *The Virgin in the Garden. New Statesman* 3 Nov. 1978: 586.

Musil, Caryn McTighe. "A. S. Byatt." *Dictionary of Literary Biography.* Vol. 14. Detroit: Gale, 1983. 194–205.

Parini, Jay. "Unearthing the Secret Lover." Rev. of *Possession: A Romance. New York Times* 21 Oct. 1990: 9–11.

Paulin, Tom. "When the Ghost Begins to Quicken." Rev. of *The Virgin in the Garden. Encounter* May 1979: 72–77.

Rifkind, Donna. "Victorians' Secrets." Rev. of *Possession: A Romance. New Criterion* Feb. 1991: 77–80.

Rothstein, Mervyn. "Best Seller Breaks Rules on Crossing the Atlantic." Rev. of *Possession: A Romance. New York Times* 31 Jan. 1991: C17, C22.

Schumann, Kuno. "English Culture and the Contemporary Novel." *Anglistentag 1981: Vortrage.* Ed. Jorg Hasler. Frankfurt am Main: Lang, 1983. 111–27.

Schwartz, Lynne Sharon. "At Home with the Supernatural." Rev. of *Sugar and Other Stories. New York Times Book Review* 19 July 1987: 5.

Showalter, Elaine. "Slick Chick." Rev. of *Passions of the Mind: Selected Writings. London Review of Books* 11 July 1991: 6.

Smith, Anne. "Sifting the Ash." Rev. of *Possession: A Romance. Listener* 1 Mar. 1990: 29.

Spufford, Francis. "The Mantle of Jehovah." Rev. of *Sugar and Other Stories. London Review of Books* 25 June 1987: 22–23.

Stout, Mira. "What Possessed A. S. Byatt?" Rev. of *Possession: A Romance. New York Times Magazine* 26 May 1991: 13–15, 24–25.

Todd, Richard. "The Retrieval of Unheard Voices in British Postmodernist Fiction: A. S. Byatt and Marina Warner." *Liminal Postmodernisms: The Postmodern, the (Post-)Colonial, and the (Post-)Feminist.* Ed. Theo D'haen and Hans Bertens. Amsterdam: Rodopi, 1994. 99–114.

Webb, Caroline. "History through Metaphor: Woolf's *Orlando* and Byatt's *Possession: A Romance.*" *Virginia Woolf: Emerging Perspectives.* Ed. Mark Hussey and Vara Neverow. New York: Pace UP, 1994. 182–88.

West, Paul. "Sensations of Being Alive." Rev. of *Still Life. New York Times Book Review* 24 Nov. 1985: 15.

Westlake, Michael. "The Hard Idea of Truth." Rev. of *Still Life. PN Review.* 15.4 (1989): 33–37.

Yelin, Louise. "Cultural Cartography: A. S. Byatt's *Possession* and the Politics of Victorian Studies." *Victorian Newsletter* 81 (Spring 1992): 38–41.

9

Emma Tennant: The Secret
Lives of Girls

Marilyn C. Wesley

GHOST STORIES

In a review article that appeared in the *Village Voice*, Gary Indiana places Tennant's fiction in the context of American metafiction by citing Gore Vidal's definition of the "hyper-novel or the novel elevated to the square or the cube." "This kind of book" Indiana explains, "ranges across several species of literature, lays waste to seamless narrative, and piles on improbabilities with surreal abandon" (14). Indiana cites *Hotel de Dream*, Tennant's 1973 work *The Crack*, and *Two Women of London*, written in 1989, as evidence for his ascription. In these works and *The Color of Rain* (1963), her first novel, as well as the 1986 *Adventures of Robina*, Tennant does create characters who, in Indiana's apt phrasing, "inhabit the space between verisimilitude and farce, vehicles for ideas colliding on a narrative expressway loop" (14).[1] But Tennant also writes another kind of novel, the subject of this study. Frequently avant-garde in style, Tennant's best novels achieve something more: a radically politicized but touchingly intimate portrayal of the psychological predicament of the young woman.

Tennant's simplest story serves to establish some preliminary points about the special forms of her work. In *The Ghost Child*, a children's book written in 1983, Melly wishes that her yearly vacation with her grandparents could be as exciting as the holidays planned by her sixth-form classmates, and it is. On the first evening of her visit Melly meets Rick, a boy of about her own age, who tells her he is her grandfather's brother. They do cartwheels on the dew-covered lawn, and Rick shows her the treasures of his boyhood, among them a silver trophy for champion diving. Melly says that she wishes she could learn to dive, and Rick promises to teach her the following evening; but the next morning Rick's room has disappeared, and Melly's grandparents tell her that since his death as a young man in World War II he has returned to his childhood home once a year on his birthday. Melly feels sad to lose her new friend, and disappointed that Rick will be unable to teach her to dive, as he promised. That evening, however, she is delighted to discover that the dewy lawn has been converted into a wonderful pool. Although Rick fails to appear, his voice leads her through the intricate steps of all sorts of dives, and he awards her his silver loving cup for her accomplishments. A violent storm marks Melly's return to London, but when she glances out the window she discovers that the noise and flashes she had mistaken for thunder and lightening are really a wartime firestorm. At the center of this mysterious tumult stands Melly's grown-up Uncle Rick, who can only return to London in the form of a young soldier he took there.

When a writer introduces a ghost into a story, she immediately signals that the narrative can no longer be considered simply mimetic. Ghosts are not so much supernatural, or subnormal, as they are the sign of participation in the genre of imaginative literature that is their only genuine source: it is, after all, not ghosts that invent stories, but stories that introduce ghosts, define them, and tell what tales can be told about them. The ghost story is inevitably, then, a story about other stories. All of Emma Tennant's fiction constitutes an elaborate ghost story in this sense; no matter how ordinary her characters, how commonplace the setting, how routine the action, like Melly's vacation they are haunted by the influential ghosts of other stories. Melly's holiday is shaped by its ghosts, and so is Tennant's fiction. Melly's story is about the possibilities inherent in that shaping, and so is Tennant's.

In *Hotel de Dream* (1976), for example, not so much novel as tour de force, the inhabitants of a run-down London boardinghouse dream the stories that make their empty lives supportable. Mr. Poynton dreams a city in which he would be king, Jeanette Scranton a society of Amazons that will take her into their midst. Miss Briggs dreams she assumes the queen's role. Cecelia Houghton dreams Melinda and Johnny, the lovers who thread their way through the tired plots of her three-decker magnum opus. And while Mrs. Routledge, the proprietor of the Westringham, dreams bourgeois success, Cridge, her comic-gothic minion, dreams tabloid revenge. Not surprisingly, these compensatory dreams, drawn from the mass dreamwork of the fictions of popular culture rather than the individual creativity of the tenants, muddle together to overwhelm the insubstantial reality of the individuals and even the nation.

Postmodern fiction, metafiction, surfiction, anti-fiction—like the creations of the occupants of the *hotel de dream*—make us aware of their own fictivity. But I shall argue for a slightly different category for Tennant's special use of the ghosts of culture. Again Melly's story functions to specify the separate kinds of ghosts that represent separate kinds of contemporary fiction. Thomas Pynchon, Donald Barthelme, Robert Coover, Raymond Federman, and many others are haunted by the grown-up ghost of Uncle Rick. Fully determined by a consciousness of terrifying political events, they understand that modes of perception shape such events, and they mount an imaginative firestorm against the fictive modes of that shaping. Mundane institutions, the museum we mistakenly call reality, children's stories, the events of history—the ostensible subjects of these authors—are emptied out, purged of effect, revealed as illusory.[2] American postmodern fiction of the 1970s fashions a kind of hyperactive, pop-up version of *Hamlet*. Claudius and Polonius are murdered, as expected, but before the play is over even the creaking ghost on the battlements must be hauled out by his ropes and pulleys and laid to rest.

Tennant's works, however, as in the child's story above, demonstrate a special regard for her protagonists, a certain kind of engaged attention, not quite pity, but a long way from farce, that has been largely exorcised from more typical postmodern fiction. And, like Melly, Tennant is partial to her ghosts. Although Tenant is no less politically conscious than the American postmodernists, her fiction, nevertheless, generally retains something of the effect of young Rick on Melly's holiday. Recognizing the existence of the ghosts is a first step to learning the lessons they have to teach.

That teaching characteristically provides insight into the experience of young women. When Tennant selected material for the anthology culled from *Bananas,* the periodical of experimental literature she edits, she included Martin Seymour-Smith's survey of the European forerunners of contemporary modernist fiction, suggestive, perhaps, of her own influences. In contrast to the attack on the modes of meaning characteristic of the American school, Seymour-Smith endorses "expressionistic" writing that "uses images, or other imaginative devices to express the inner processes, or even the inner reality of situations."[3] In the work he describes, as in Tennant's, "the *real,* the inner, state of a certain aspect of modern life" takes the form of "a hallucinated vision, full of meaningful phenomenological detail" (101). Such works as *The Half-Mother* (1983), *The House of Hospitalities* (1987), *Wild Nights* (1979), *Alice Fell* (1980), and *Queen of Stones* (1982) use the "ghosts" of other stories for the expressionistic rendering of the secret lives of girls.

The Hallucinated Vision

> Challenge any such problem with any intelligence, and you immediately see how full it is of substance; the wonder being all the while, as we look at the world, how absolutely, how inordinately, the Isabel Archers, and even much smaller fry, insist on mattering.[4]

If one can move beyond Henry James's patronizing attitude toward his female subjects, the preface to the New York edition of *Portrait of a Lady* contains suggestions on writing fiction about girls which qualify him as the presiding ghost in all Tennant's fiction addressed to the concerns of young women: because "It was naturally of the essence that the young woman should be herself complex," James's advice to writers is to "press least hard . . . on the consciousness of your heroine's satellites, especially the male; make it an interest contributive only to the greater one" (11).

Imagine Henry James writing for Harlequin! That is something of the effect of *The Half-Mother.* The protagonist is one of those "smaller fry" James notes who so "insist on mattering." The story is the girl's gothic voyage of discovery, but rather than setting out to a distant land and being rescued by a handsome stranger from the obscure threat symbolizing her own family history, as is typical of the present-day gothic form, Tennant's heroine explores an idealized version of the enigmatic family itself. Tennant's focus is the "complex" nature of a young woman, and her prose, like James's, documents the subtle waverings of consciousness as the heroine tries to decipher the most basic of riddles.

The ghosts of *The Half-Mother* include Mrs. Radcliffe, the founding mother of the traditional gothic; Emily and Charlotte Brontë, who contribute a focus on the nuanced decorum of the passionate outsider; and the popular formula of the contemporary gothic novel, which inserts a naive young woman into a sinister house: "In the typical Gothic plot, the heroine comes to a mysterious house, perhaps as a young bride, perhaps in another capacity and either starts to mistrust her husband or else finds herself in love with a mysterious man who appears to be some kind of criminal. . . . Often, but not always, the man is proven innocent by the end of the novel, and the real culprit is discovered and punished."[5]

While significantly altering the second half of the formula, Tennant makes use of the conventions of the portentous house ("Suitable for the Man in the Iron Mask" [124]) and the ethereal girl ("silly as a heroine in a romantic novel" [64]). Her name is Minnie: like the prefix, the name means not counting for much, means less impressive than the luxury model. In the novel she returns to the fascinating house that holds the secret of her identity. More than a setting, the house in Tennant's fiction represents the quintessential female space, especially as girls experience it in childhood. Tennant equates the house with the mother figure in the novel, who is equally "difficult to describe" (12): "one can only look up with awe at Cliff Hold. Not that it's so big—it's more the effrontery of the building so far out on the rock. . . . And the other thing about the house: it's as far along the cliffs as you can go. From Moura's bedroom window . . . you can see grey waves—and no hills on the other side of the bay—they've been left far behind in a race for the open sea" (11). Minnie's description of the house, the place of Moura, the ideal mother, as a dramatic and desperate place of last resort rather than a comfortable and domestic space, underlies the tensions of the novel.

Following the murder of Hugo Pierce, Moura's husband and Minnie's ideal father, Minnie, after a ten-year absence, has ostensibly returned to Cliff Hold in the capacity of the poor relative/companion to comfort Moura, and be comforted by Moura. The apparent mystery in the novel is the cause of Hugo's brutal death, but the real mystery is the one surrounding Minnie's rejection by Philip Pierce, the son of Moura and Hugo, and Minnie's resultant estrangement from the "perfect family" in whose company she spent the significant moments of her childhood.

Despite the enigma of Hugo's death, the story centers on Minnie's engulfing love and vindictive hate of Moura. Instead of writing the father-daughter story of the typical gothic novel, Tennant has altered the form to treat the buried relation of mother and daughter.

In the manner of the typical gothic and like the pre-Oedipal feminine union described by psychologists, both good and evil doubles dominate *The Half-Mother*. Hugo Pierce is both the ideal father ("Hugo made me love him when I realized, thanks to his apparently effortless attentions, that to be a child was not necessarily to be boring" [231]) and the heroic male ("Hugo the Communist, the brilliant needler of the Establishment, already then a praised novelist, 'a man like an eighteenth-century man' . . . like someone born before the birth of self-consciousness, anxiety, and doubt" [211]). But he is also the vain philanderer who gets himself killed because of a degrading lovers' triangle in which he is not even really a lover. Worse, Minnie initially believes that the hypocritical Hugo, holding out for a wealthier match, has prevented her marriage to Philip.

If Tennant doubles the father, she at least quadruples the central figure of the mother. There are the two good mothers: Moura, a Lady Bountiful of culture and compassion, and Lily, Moura's cook, to whom Minnie turns for reassurance and comfort. And there are several bad mothers: Minnie's petty and abandoning natural mother, and Moura's dead mother, an Irish witch with the power of the evil eye that Moura herself may also possess. Finally, there is the bad mother Minnie cannot consciously acknowledge: Moura, the deceitful, the rejecting mother whom Minnie comes to believe has caused Philip to spurn her.

At first, we see only Minnie's conscious persona, the docile and admiring outsider, her nose pressed to the glass of family happiness. But, finally, we recognize a darker double, the unconscious self murderously angry with the family that failed to love her as she fantasized: "Who's Minnie?" the brother of Philip asks when he learns that she has returned to Cliff Hold for his father's funeral (69).

But even more important than the duplication of plots or characters is Tennant's doubling of setting. For everyone but Minnie, Hugo's murder can be explained by the turbulence of Irish political life: the third member of his inauspicious triangle serves, unfortunately, as an assassin in the IRA. For Minnie, however, the funeral becomes an unacknowledged opportunity to recapture the past. Evidently, she secretly hopes that the occasion of family grief will reunite her with the lost Philip, but the reunion that does occur is both more subtle and more dangerous.

"What happens," Minnie asks "if you walk into your own memory?" (46), a project symbolized by an antique tapestry which she imagines tells her own story:

> In my room is a tapestry. . . . It is tall and dark and green, and in a forest where there are people riding on horses with long thin legs, there are also a dying fox, gored by hounds, a rabbit in a cross-stitching of snowdrops and winter aconites, and a young woman gathering sticks. On the horses are a distinguished elderly man, a father, a seigneur—a woman in a white coif that looks as it sails on her head like a white bird; and several young men in green jerkins and pointed hats. They are going towards the edge of the wood: the light in the thinning trees shows that. Only the girl gathering sticks will be left behind in the forest. Her hair is black, the woofs of her face are ruddy. None of the hunting party, on their steeds with absurdly narrow and elongated haunches, turns to look back at her. (98)

As she writes her story, Minnie imagines that she walks into the tapestry and participates in its tragic events. Minnie, of course, assumes the role of the vulnerable peasant girl abandoned by the high-born family to the dangerous onset of night in the dark forest of fairy tales, but she also operates as the classic unreliable narrator suffering from inexplicable accidents, headaches, auras, and vague episodes of mental disturbance that provide the bridge from the sordid twentieth-century murder mystery to the stuff of folk story and Scottish balladry—the revenge narrative woven into her interpretation of the tapestry.

In an ironic reversal of the standard gothic denouement, the mother—not the father-substitute—appears to be the guilty villain, but circumstances fail to exonerate her or effect a happy ending. In Tennant's version, like the gothic she bases it on, the real culprits are discovered and punished. By the end of the novel Minnie has not only projected her own desire for revenge onto Moura, but she has avenged her unconscious self against the mother who she believes has disappointed her. While her conscious persona imagines that as an agent of the wronged family she kills the slayer of Hugo, the unconscious and enraged Minnie murders

Philip, her own lost love and heir apparent of Hugo Pierce's mastery, thus avenging herself on both the man who cast her aside and the mother who clearly preferred her absent son to her would-be daughter.

The impressive country houses in Tennant's fiction also represent class privilege, a privilege from which Minnie, struggling along as a children's tutor, is clearly excluded. In *The House of Hospitalities* another outsider, fourteen-year-old Jenny Carter, is invited for the weekend by her schoolmate Amy Lovescombe to the prestigious country estate of the Lovescombe family. The enigma of this house inheres not in the demonic rage of the mother-daughter bond but in the demonic anger surrounding class privilege. The manor itself fills Jenny with awe and confusion. She enters it with a sense of welcome relief from unattractive reality: "all I knew, after the drab months of a London summer, still threadbare after the war, was that I wanted magic" (9). But she also senses that despite her attraction, the "glamour" the place casts over her is somehow inimical (108).

Tennant expresses the secrets of the compelling attraction and repulsion of the Lovescombe world through the ghosts of Japanese court literature and children's fairy tale. Lovegrove Manor is presided over by the absent spirit of Amy's dead grandmother, who apparently loved children. The legacy of such affection appears not only in the form of family legend but in the childish whimsicality of concrete objects Amy's grandmother has created: the ornate Oriental gardens of the estate and an extraordinary tree house cum miniature medieval village called "The Far House in the Woods." Jenny's encounters with these two structures suggest the special dangers the Lovescombes represent.

Although Jenny associates British wealth with the stray pieces of Chinese porcelain her aunt sells at her Portobello stall,[6] she is unprepared for the extraordinary display of half-moon bridges and paper houses of the elaborate Japanese gardens of Lovegrove. Acquainted with Lady Murasaki's depictions of the court life of ancient Japan, she equates the gardens with the romance of the world of the Shining Prince of *The Tale of Genji:* "it was too near my dream of the Chinese bowl, too near to the court where whispers and wooden ox-carts carrying the whispering women to each other's screened houses made a rustle from dawn until nightfall; too near that world where poems dropped like courtiers' colored silks in the sadness of loss, of leaves falling" (32).

This evocation of tenth-century Japan suggests the extraordinary artistic achievement of an imperial society in the Heian dynasty devoted to the cultivation of beauty, but it also must suggest to anyone acquainted with the period the extraordinary insularity and self-absorption of the participants of imperial court life. Ivan Morris estimates that the population of Japan during this period was about five million, but only one percent lived in the capital and less than one-tenth of that number participated in the noble life of the court. Preferment of rank and position was obtained almost exclusively through the politics of family connection, and courtiers, although highly educated within the bounds of their own cultural preoccupations, were generally oblivious to the world of people, nations, ideas, and commerce beyond the confines of their capital.[7]

By alluding to the difference between privileged and unprivileged classes, the Oriental exotica suggest the special situation of Britain in 1953: the postwar world of reality occupied by Jenny and her Aunt Babs in a commercial section of London and "pockets" (60) of prewar aristocratic entitlement "willfully unaware of the realities of post-war life." This second zone of inherited title and wealth, like Murasaki's court, is the location of culture, even beauty, but also of blatant immorality: "It seemed that in surroundings like Lovegrove, any behavior could be tolerated, because none of it made the slightest difference. The surroundings, and their dead progenitors, were all" (74). This abstract point manifests itself to young Jenny, when on the evening of her arrival at the estate, she glimpses a startling apparition in the Japanese garden: a "ball of twigs" that "grew" into "a pale column as it came closer" (36), a sight that turns into the pubis of a naked woman involved in a flagrant act of adultery with Amy's father.

The juxtaposition of decadence and whimsical beauty becomes even more apparent during Jenny's visit to the children's playhouse the next day. If the Japanese garden represents an escape to the historical past, the children's house appeals to a longing for the psychic past. Jenny says that she saw in Amy's eyes "the longing for the wood, the house her grandmother had built like some kind of refuge against the grown-up world" (116). The little "house in the woods" evokes "memories of infancy, when animals speak and witches lurk in the corners of the house" (129). It is a "fantasy of permanent immaturity" (130) inhabited, however, by a grotesque Peter Pan who demonstrates the problem of such appeal. Fifty-five-year-old "Uncle Si," in the elaborate makeup of a movie siren and the flowing robes of a cinematic Lawrence of Arabia, is the tutelary spirit of this encounter. His appearance and childishness teach Jenny that there is no such thing as innocence revisited, only cloying imitation like that pathetically shammed by Hollywood.

Writing thirty years later, Jenny recognizes the creations of Lady Azeby, the grandmother of Lovegrove Manor, as "games of power and love" (128), which for Jenny had been a seductive mixture because of her attraction to the beauty of the past represented by the estate and the personal appeal of Amy and her handsome older brother Ludo. Tennant structures the story as a Bluebeard narrative (58, 121) in which Jenny unlocks room after room until she discovers the ultimate depravity, an incestuous union between Amy and her brother. In addition to Murasaki and the fairy-tale world of Cinderella (96, 98), Sleeping Beauty (51), and Beauty and the Beast (143), the work invokes the literary ghost of Thomas Hardy (30) to suggest the failure of the past as a model for the present. But the sexual immorality of the Lovescombe world is only an emblem for the social dissolution and economic inequality they also represent, and which the adult Jenny has come to understand. In the penultimate chapter of *The House of Hospitality* she observes: "That money was the very pigment that ran through the pictures at Lovegrove, the cement of the fairytale construction, was undoubtedly true. I daresay, too, that my own preoccupation with Ludo had made me more foolish than usual when it came to the realities of life" (181).

THE REALITIES OF LIFE

The realities encountered by the young women of Tennant's texts are those of feminine psychology, as in *The Half-Mother,* and the inequalities of modern society, as in *The House of Hospitalities.* The house as a space of the drama of childhood attraction and repulsion is central to two other treatments of these concerns. *Wild Nights* draws upon psychological experience, while *Alice Fell* concerns social situation. As Gary Indiana notes, *Wild Nights* is inspired by Bruno Schultz's *The Street of Crocodiles,* but it retains from the original only the mood of "the child's magical perception of the everyday world" (14). A fanciful rendition of a young girl's particularized and imaginative consciousness, it mythologizes the reactions of the inhabitants of her home and even of the house itself to yearly visits by family members. This passage epitomizes the mood and technique of the whole:

> The window of my father's study was square, and a bright red since he had turned on the light. Round it the rest of the house was un-recognizable. The walls and turrets—all of them unoccupied—of the mock castle his grandfather had built seemed to hang in folds, uncertain, waiting for the new season, for the advent of Aunt Zita. The evening wind puffed a few leaves from the rowan tree by the door, but they went out of sight before they reached the ground. Other windows of rooms long empty shone in their own way, by reflecting the new moon, and ghosts began to get ready for Aunt Zita in these dusty rooms full of dead flies. After she had eaten the ordinary food with my mother and father, she would go up and be with them. I had seen her on a window sill, with the moon shin-ing straight in on her. When I couldn't sleep, I heard their skirts rustling on the floor above. (10)

It is not incidental that the witchcraft attributed by the child to the aunt, evoked through the ghosts and the blood-color of the window, the de-tails of the rowan tree and the moon—frequently associated with the female supernatural—effects a matriarchal transformation of the patri-archal castle, "the stone guns and flying buttresses of mid-nineteenth-century capitalism" (11). In fact, the foremost effect in Tennant's diverse stories of young women is an implicit insistence on the power of the feminine perspective of these stories.

If the title *Wild Nights* summons Emily Dickinson's spirit as inspira-tion for the fey vision of the small world of the family, in *Alice Fell* Virginia Woolf seems to animate the vision of the particularities of fam-ily life as set against the larger world. I was reminded in reading this work of the "Time Passes" section of *To the Lighthouse,* in which the small moments and details of life in a country house—the children's pro-jected visit to the lighthouse, the maternal solicitude about the mundane details of daily life—are suddenly reimagined in terms of the impinging forces of time and politics: "What people had shed and left—a pair of shoes, a shooting cap, some faded skirts and coats in wardrobes—those alone kept the human shape and the emptiness indicated how once they were filled and animated; how once hands were busy with hooks and buttons; how once the looking-glass had held a face; had held a world hollowed out in which a figure turned, a hand flashed, the door opened, in came children rushing and tumbling; and went out again."[8]

In Tennant's novel a child is born into the microcosm of life in an old man's house in which her parents are employed as servants. His masculine presence dominates this country house. Even as events occur in the maternal household within the old man's house, the elegiac tone of their presentation suggests the overpowering reality of his unspecified but omnipresent influence. This representative passage, which concludes the novel on the occasion of Alice's wedding, has, I believe, in subject and tone, more than passing reference to Woolf's impressionistic novel and the theme of inevitable loss in the passage just quoted:

> In the window, Alice's life played in the stabbing colors of blind sight. She saw summers in the Old Man's house, and William and her mother, and clumps of forget-me-nots in long rushes by the river, in the blue flashes of comet's tails dancing into her eyes. White summer grass ribboned the black sky. And she saw the winter month, ruby streets where she would be drawn to live at the time the ground by the river was as hard and grey as stone. And she turned to Ella. There was nothing to say. Ella pulled at hooks and eyes with cake-y fingers. They both knew with the ending of summer, that Alice would soon be gone. At the sequin-fall of the wedding dress she would step out of the ring and go. Then, Mrs. Paxton and William must set out to search the forest for her—and Alice would never be there, in the artificial clearing, in the red earth hole her mother had first looked down so anxiously, for signs of her fall. (124)

The tension in *Alice Fell* is not simply between reality and childhood imagination; as in the Lewis Carroll story that inspires the title, the world of imagination also hints at unexpressed meanings in the world of reality. The overall effect of Tennant's fiction is to suggest that the feminine zone of mythic childhood must finally "fall" into the masculine province of social and economic power. Nevertheless, though differing in content, the similarly evocative presentations of *Wild Nights* and *Alice Fell* argue for a special richness and significance in both the internal and external experience of young women.

As a fitting conclusion to this discussion of the twin poles of psychology and social situation in the secret lives of girls in Emma Tennant's fiction, we follow a group of young women out of the mythological house of memory into the greater world of the struggle for social power. In *The Queen of Stones,* a novel that echoes William Golding's *Lord of the Flies,* the protagonists are literally forced away from their childhood houses into the wild zone of adult freedom and responsibility. As in *The Bad Sister, The Adventures of Robina,* and *Black Marina,* Tennant frames the tale ironically with an editor's preface and other forms of public documentation. But the authority of the documentary reference is undercut by the deeper and richer detail of the reconstruction of the children's narrative. *The Queen of Stones,* then, provides the mythic and social depth of the experience of girls that adult accounts leave out, even while the girls are engaged in their initiation into adult concerns.[9] The plot recounts the journey of a group of girls, ranging in age from six to thirteen years, who have accompanied the "Walks Lady" on a benign excursion, only to be enveloped by a thick, white fog. As a result, they wander the English coast unsupervised for a weekend in October 1981. During their journey, like Golding's characters, they must create social forms to provide leadership, secure their safety, and mediate their disputes.

The central form emerging from the needs of the group and the psychological realities of its leaders is a reenactment of the struggle for power between two historic leaders known to every British schoolgirl, the deadly competition between Queen Elizabeth and Mary Queen of Scots. By the time the children return to the civilization in which their central myth originated, they have attempted to resolve their social and psychic tensions by beheading one of their number.

Of all Emma Tennant's works, *The Queen of Stones* most directly reveals its philosophic sources. A Marxian interpretation of classed reality is evident in the choice of victim for the reenacted execution. It is not the royal Mary figure who loses her head, but a scapegoat notable for her exclusion from the wealth and privilege of the girls' leaders. Freudian psychology, inserted as a report from a psychoanalyst and quotations from Freud himself, provides a basis for understanding the feminine sexual predicament that produces such violent resolution as Oedipal competition for the affection of the father. And in this novel, as in all the others, the stories that are our collective heritage provide an outline for the situations that may be comprehended in contemporary experience.

Rather than deconstructing the novel in the vein of the American postmodernists to whom she has been compared, Tennant insists that the narratives of culture are deeply influential in defining the elements we weave into the equally storylike version of our own experience. With wit and style, with subtlety and intelligence, she employs the ghosts of culture to explore the feminine preoccupations with memory, identity, family, and space. Finally, the fact that *The Queen of Stones* recasts a boys' book into a girls' adventure reiterates the feminist project evident throughout Emma Tennant's oeuvre: girls, too, have secret lives worthy of fiction.

Notes

1. Indiana does suggest that the "hypernovel" should not be conflated with 1970s postmodernism, "if only because the latter term presumes an a priori concern with theory" more than with "the world" (14) toward which Tennant's interest in feminism and Marxism inclines her. But in his analytic comments on specific works, Indiana favors the jokes and usurpations that effect the conflation he warns against.

2. The best discussions of the tenets of American postmodernism appear in *Surfiction: Fiction Now and Tomorrow,* ed. Raymond Federman (Chicago: Swallow Press, 1975). On the issue of the need to destroy previous forms, Jerome Klinkowitz quotes Kurt Vonnegut, Jr.: "in *Breakfast of Champions* he ponders the abominable behavior of his countrymen and concludes that 'They were doing their best to live like people invented in story books. This was the reason people shot each other so often: It was a convenient literary device for ending short stories and books'" (165–66). Implicit in this tongue-in-cheek observation is the connection between patterns of traditional fiction and the destructiveness of modern culture. While "postmodernism" is a blanket term that covers many aspects of contemporary writing, I am arguing that destruction and renovation of forms is seen as a necessary moral measure.

3. Martin Seymour-Smith, *Bananas,* ed. Emma Tennant (London: Quartet Books, 1977), 97.

4. Henry James, *The Portrait of a Lady,* ed. Robert D. Bamberg (New York: Norton, 1975), 7.

5. Tania Modleski, *Loving with a Vengeance: Mass-Produced Fantasies for Women* (Hamden, CT: Archon, 1982), 59.

6. For Jenny, Oriental porcelain signifies the romance of a privileged standard and style of living: "I wanted to see everything I imagined to lie in the name

Lovesgrove; and to my childish mind this was a great bowl, Chinese porcelain probably (for Aunt Babs had pointed one out to me in the V & A and said the rich eighteenth-century English had liked to order their designs made up for them in China), a great bowl, exquisitely drawn all round with the scenes from the Lovescombe lives: birds in dovecotes, riding, fields of barley and of rye—everything" (22).

7. Ivan Morris, *The World of the Shining Prince: Court Life in Ancient Japan* (New York: Knopf, 1972). See especially chapter 3, "Politics and Society," 79, 66.

8. Virginia Woolf, *To the Lighthouse* (New York: Harcourt, 1955), 194.

9. It is significant with regard to the theme of female initiation that the events in the text are preludes to the protagonist's first menstruation.

SELECTED WORKS BY EMMA TENNANT

The Adventures of Robina: By Herself. New York: Persea Books, 1986.

Alice Fell. London: Jonathan Cape, 1980.

The Bad Sister. 1971. New York: Coward, McCann & Geoghegan, 1978.

Black Marina. Boston: Faber and Faber, 1985.

The Color of Rain. 1963. London: Faber and Faber, 1988.

Emma in Love: Jane Austen's Emma Continued. London: Fourth Estate Classic House, 1999.

The Ghost Child. London: Heinemann, 1983.

The Half-Mother. Boston: Little, Brown, 1983.

Hotel de Dream. London: Picador, 1976.

The House of Hospitalities. London: Viking, 1987.

Pemberley or Pride and Prejudice Continued. New York: St. Martins Press, 1993.

The Queen of Stones. London: Jonathan Cape, 1982.

Rag Rugs of England and America. London: Walker, 1992.

Strangers: A Family Romance. New York: New Directions, 1999.

The Time of the Crack. London: Jonathan Cape, 1973.

Wild Nights. New York: Harcourt, Brace, Jovanovich, 1979.

SELECTED WORKS ABOUT EMMA TENNANT

Anderson, Carol. "Listening to the Women Talk." *The Scottish Novel since the Seventies: New Visions, Old Dreams.* Ed. Gavin Wallace and Randall Stevenson. Edinburgh: Edinburgh UP, 1993. 170–86.

Birat, Kathie. "Feminist Principles and Fictional Strategies: Otherness as a Narrative Strategy in *Sisters and Strangers* by Emma Tennant and *Orlando* by Virginia Woolf." *L'Altérité dans la litterature et la culture du monde anglophone.* Le Mans: University du Maine, 1993. 36–45.

Connor, Steven. "Rewriting Wrong: On the Ethics of Literary Reversion." *Liminal Postmodernisms: The Postmodern, the (Post-)Colonial, and the (Post-) Feminist.* Ed. Theo D'haen and Hans Bertens. Amsterdam: Rodopi, 1994. 79–97.

Indiana, Gary. "Novel^2: Emma Tennant's Higher Powers." *Voice Literary Supplement* May 1991: 14–16.

Roe, Sue. "Women Talking about Writing." *Women's Writing: A Challenge to Theory.* Ed. Moira Monteith. New York: St. Martin's, 1986. 117–53.

Widdowson, Peter. "Newstories: Fiction, History, and the Modern World." *Critical Survey* 7.1 (1995): 3–17.

10

Margaret Drabble: Chronicler, Moralist, Artist

Mary Rose Sullivan

For almost thirty years, Margaret Drabble has been recognized as one of the most accomplished novelists of her generation. Ever since her first book, *A Summer Bird-Cage* (1963), written when she was only twenty-three, was hailed for its wit and perceptiveness, each successive novel has been eagerly greeted, both by women who felt they had found a spokes-woman for their concerns and expectations and by a wider audience who found in her a chronicler of modern consciousness, a George Eliot of contemporary Britain.[1] Still, even as the chorus of praise continued to swell—for her narrative power, her brilliantly rendered portraits of ordi-nary domestic life, her increasingly wide-ranging explorations of cultural and social currents—a persistent undertone of disappointment, or per-haps bafflement, sounded from the critics. Feminists, who wanted to re-gard her as one of their own, were dismayed by an increasingly ambiva-lent attitude toward women's issues in Drabble's 1970s novels and her virtual abandonment of the feminist cause by the 1980s. At the same time, admirers of her technical skills were discomfited by her narrative idiosyncrasies: heavy reliance on coincidence, inconclusive endings, and authorial commentary disruptive to the finely wrought illusion of reality. Drabble's response to these complaints is forthright: she writes not to provide a blueprint for women's lives but to explore her own experiences,

experiences that confirm her sense that our freedom to choose is limited and that the curious workings of fate, or coincidence, are inescapable. Moreover, she herself is too much in process, and life too "continuous," to allow for definitive endings in her fiction.[2] Her most recent works, however, particularly the trilogy written between 1987 and 1992, indicate that Drabble feels prepared to take a more reflective and judgmental view of the social scene she has so long chronicled, and to explore more self-consciously her relationship as artist to her subject matter and audience.[3]

Fate seems to have played a part in making Margaret Drabble a writer. Born in 1939 in the Brontë country of Yorkshire, into a family that she says resembled the Brontës in size and constitution, she was the second of three girls who, with their younger brother, played childhood games of making up stories. Her mother was an English teacher, her father a barrister who wrote novels, and her older sister became a critic and novelist under the name A. S. Byatt. To these influences of environment and heredity, Drabble would add the strong sense of service inculcated at The Mount, a Quaker preparatory school, and her study of literature at Cambridge University.[4] Immediately on graduation in 1960 she married fellow student Clive Swift and with him joined the Royal Shakespeare Company until, sidelined by pregnancy, she turned to writing. *A Summer Bird-Cage*, written strictly for "fun," proved an immediate success, as did *The Garrick Year* (1964) and *The Millstone* (1965).

After bringing out a volume on Wordsworth in 1966, Drabble produced two novels in quick succession: *Jerusalem the Golden* (1967), recounting a young woman's attempt to escape provincial life, and *The Waterfall* (1969), a technically ambitious and compelling description of a woman's sexual awakening. By 1972, separated from her husband (whom she would divorce in 1975) and supporting her three young children, Drabble had added to her list of publications a play, three screenplays, ten short stories, and scores of book reviews and magazine articles.[5] With her sixth novel, *The Needle's Eye* (1972), she expanded her motherhood theme to include a child custody battle between husband and wife. Broadening the canvas even further, she made the protagonist of *The Realms of Gold* (1975) an anthropologist who successfully balances career and motherhood even as her travels take her as far afield as Africa, and in *The Ice Age* (1977) she featured a male protagonist who moves from speculating in London financial markets to bankruptcy and imprisonment in the Balkans. With *The Middle Ground* (1980) Drabble returned to a narrower and more domestic focus, describing the uncertain progress of a professional woman negotiating the middle years of life.

At this point Drabble addressed her own professional uncertainties by taking an extended sabbatical from novel-writing to turn back to literary studies. She had already produced, in the interstices of creative work, a biography of Arnold Bennett (1974) and had edited a collection of essays on Thomas Hardy (1976). Now she cast a wider literary-historical net by undertaking, single-handedly, the first major revision of the classic *Oxford Companion to English Literature.*[6] Far from being diminished by the hiatus, Drabble's narrative drive and inventiveness were more robust than ever when she resumed novel-writing with *The Radiant Way* (1987). Its large cast of characters and intertwining story lines were then carried over into a sequel, *A Natural Curiosity* (1989), and finally into a third volume, *The Gates of Ivory* (1992)—the whole constituting a panoramic view of British social life in the 1980s. The trilogy ends with the death of a main character, attaining the kind of closure Drabble had heretofore resisted, and marks a new confidence in her own vision: she was joining the ranks of those novelists, such as Hardy and Zola, who "can end a novel with a death" (Brans 225).

Drabble had predicted such an evolution in her writing. "I can actually conceive of the possibility of writing an ending when I'm older, when I've had more experience of the turns" (Brans 225), she had said, and at the age of fifty, after three decades of engagement—socially, intellectually, artistically—in the currents of change sweeping late-twentieth-century Britain, she seemed ready to take a more retrospective view of experience. Hers is a unique vantage point, not limited to the ivory tower. Besides her literary-historical studies, she has interviewed celebrities (ranging from Doris Lessing to Jane Fonda) and written general-interest magazine articles (running the gamut from the how-to's of child-rearing to the sexual revolution). She has taught adult education courses, lectured at home and abroad for the British Council, chaired the National Book League, and joined fund-raising drives for worthy causes, for all of which services she was awarded the CBE (Commander, Order of the British Empire) in 1980. Obviously Drabble believes that "one ought to say yes to almost everything," from a sense of duty and as a challenge to oneself and, not incidentally, as a good way "of seeing people" who make up her subject matter (Brans 220).

Drabble's saying "yes" has extended to discussing her work, even work in progress. In dozens of encounters with critics and journalists over the course of her career, she has spoken candidly about such topics as her work habits (she writes quickly, with little revising), autobiographical elements in her books (almost everything that occurs in her novels has happened to her or to someone she knows), and her philosophy of art (art is moral as well as aesthetic, being intimately connected with our judgments of life). She has not hesitated to identify real-life sources for characters and incidents in her books or to admit to parallels between herself and her protagonists.[7] She acknowledges that for many readers, particularly women, the appeal of her writing lies not in largeness of scope but in skillful rendering of apparently insignificant details of daily life, the "little movements of the spirit in its daily routine" and the "inner dramas of ordinary events"[8] that she so admires in Arnold Bennett's novels. Fellow novelist Margaret Atwood characterizes the Drabble terrain as the most mundane aspects of domesticity. A woman tries on a new makeup, and "the way the stuff comes out of the bottle," Atwood says, "what it looks like as it lies in a blob in her hand, how it goes on, and what she thinks about it: each is done in loving detail, and you think *That's it. She's got it right*" (65). Drabble herself has said that the apparently trivial incident she describes acts as a kind of passport into the reader's consciousness—something, for instance, as "silly" as "the difficulty of folding fitted sheets into proper squares" (Brans 237).

Ironically enough, this very skill—for rendering ordinary events with precision—has led some feminist critics to charge Drabble with a lack of seriousness. Elizabeth Fox-Genovese, for one, sees Drabble's attentiveness to social shifts as trendy cultural awareness, a readiness to spot straws in the wind, so to speak, instead of spinning those straws into philosophical gold. Joanne Creighton acknowledges Drabble's search for a "moral and humanistic center" beneath her domestic concerns but concludes that she "has yet to find the right voice" for narratives of social realism (*Margaret Drabble* 16). These critics, and others who share their reservations about the ends to which Drabble has put her formidable skills, are concerned mainly with the work of her first two decades, through *The Middle Ground* of 1980. The novels since then, however, a departure in tone and theme, unite Drabble's characteristically witty social criticism with a brooding consideration of the direction of modern civilization. The ambitious scheme of the 1987–1992 trilogy allows

Drabble to consider more comprehensively those issues of moral choice discernible, in nascent form, from her earliest works. From the vantage point of her most recent work, *The Gates of Ivory*, we can look back and see how consistently her work expresses the conviction that life lays certain inescapable conditions on each of us who aspires to be fully human. One must first come to terms with the past; second, reach out beyond the self to connect with another; and last, respond to larger social and communal needs.

Indeed, each of Drabble's novels works in some way as a criticism of life, an illustration of what happens when we fail to observe these three requirements. Even such a jeu d'esprit as *A Summer Bird-Cage* revolves on the issue of distinguishing between what is fated and what freely chosen. The novel's title—from John Webster's observation that the birds outside the cage long to be within as much as the birds within long for freedom[9]—expresses the reality that Sarah Bennett, with her "shiny, useless new degree" (7) from Oxford will have to learn to accept. Asked what she would like to do with her life, Sarah says, only half-jokingly, that she would like to write a novel like Amis's *Lucky Jim*—a ruefully comic coming-of-age tale of lowered expectations and deflated hopes. In the end, she opts for marriage, despite its riskiness, and accepts that, however unfairly life's gifts are distributed, one is required to make the most of them.

This theme—of the need for choice, compromise, and commitment—is more explicit in the motherhood novels that follow. In *The Garrick Year*, Emma Evans is forced to spend a year on tour with her husband's acting company, children in tow, and resentment at the required sacrifices—of income, sleep, and friends—leads her to indulge in a brief love affair. Unlike her friend who succumbs to despair by drowning himself, Emma makes an uneasy accommodation with circumstances, declaring that "You will not find me at the bottom of any river. I have grown into the earth, I am terrestrial" (219). Similarly, in *The Millstone*, Rosamund Stacey reluctantly recognizes that the demands of motherhood invest her more fully in humanity. Thrust from the ivory tower of graduate student life when a single sexual encounter leaves her pregnant, Rosamund's decision to bear the child changes her whole stance toward life: she gives up being "nice," fights to be with her hospitalized child, acknowledges her dependence on others' help. Her connectedness is grudging: she will share neither the burdens nor the pleasures of parenthood with the baby's father, clinging to the notion of determinism ("There's nothing I can do about my nature, is there?" [172]). But her accommodating of herself to another's needs exemplifies Drabble's conviction that only in acknowledging kinship can we find ourselves.

In *Jerusalem the Golden* the constraints of heredity and environment weigh heavily and maternal bonds are constricting, but even here Drabble suggests the dangers in denying natural attachments. Clara Maugham determines to escape her dominating mother's provinciality for the "golden" life of the Denham family, which epitomizes for her "some truly terrestrial paradise, where beautiful people in beautiful houses spoke of beautiful things" (39). Although we sympathize with Clara's bedazzlement with the Denhams—like Charles Ryder's with the Bridesheads—and with her Gatsby-like aspirations to remake herself, Drabble will not let us overlook the ruthlessness involved in such self-realization, and her use, for the first time, of a third-person rather than first-person narrator seems to reflect the intent to distance us from the protagonist.

The Waterfall, technically more complex than anything Drabble had yet attempted, in alternating first- and third-person narration and extensively using Freudian symbols, adopts what seems to be a more ambiguous moral stance. The sometime narrator Jane Gray is pregnant and separated from her husband until rescued from her Sleeping Beauty state by her cousin Lucy's husband and, after her child's birth, swept up into a passionate affair. Her fantasizing and her sense of guilt undercut the reliability of her narration ("Lies, lies, it's all lies" [84], she exclaims at one point of her own narration), leaving the reader to sort out the truth and resolve the oppositions still in force at story's end. In our last view of her, Jane is enmeshed in a triangle with a lover and his wife but tentatively putting her house in order and writing poetry again. The ambiguity of her situation is conveyed in the book's title: "waterfall" refers both to the magnificent natural phenomenon emblematic of her powerful sexual awakening and to the elaborate card trick her lover occasionally manages to perform successfully. It thus represents opposing values in Jane's love affair—the natural and sublime, the artificial and mundane—and forces the reader to render the moral judgments on the affair that Jane cannot or will not articulate.[10]

With *The Needle's Eye,* the need for considered moral choices becomes the overt theme. The title's biblical warning (that "it is easier for a camel" to pass through a needle's eye "than for a rich man to enter" the kingdom of heaven [Mark 10:25]) motivates Rose Vassiliou to give away her fortune, marry a penniless Greek, and ally herself with the working class. When she finds herself pitted against her husband in a child custody suit, it is also a religious motive that sends her back—against her natural instincts—to her husband, thereby ensuring justice to him, peace for the children. This ending, uncharacteristically clear-cut for Drabble, left many readers dissatisfied, and Drabble herself has expressed some reservations about it.[11] However, if she fails here to reconcile conflicting moral demands of others and the self, she effectively dramatizes the seriousness of the struggle. The novel is replete with images borrowed from a favorite work of her Quaker school days, John Bunyan's *Pilgrim's Progress*.[12]

The title of Drabble's next novel, *The Realms of Gold*, comes not from Scripture but from a Keats sonnet,[13] signaling a very different fate for its heroine. At thirty-five, Frances Wingate is an internationally known archaeologist, a highly competent mother of four, and lucky in love—clearly at home in those golden realms of which earlier Drabble heroines could only dream. Feminist critics hailed Frances as the contemporary role model they had been awaiting from Drabble (although some complained of her being paired with a lover who is insufficiently matched to such a high-powered woman). Strong-willed, disciplined, resilient even when deserted by her lover and assailed by depression, Frances refuses to let herself be, like her cousin Janet, extinguished by a man or, like her nephew Stephen, overcome by the world's wrongs. Discarding the family weaknesses and making the most of the family strengths, she asserts herself personally and professionally with a success unusual for a Drabble protagonist.

To this celebration of female power, *The Ice Age* stands in sharp contrast. Anthony Keating's realms are anything but golden: we first see him, a minor literary talent who has ridden high on the London real estate boom, discovering a dead bird on his country estate where he recuperates from a heart attack and awaits bankruptcy. We last see him as a prisoner in an obscure Balkan country where, inspired by the sight of a bird on the barbed wire, he is writing a treatise on Boethius's *Consolation of Philosophy*. Drabble provides us with a dreary spectacle of the greed, ugliness, and dislocation wrought in the 1970s in the name of progress.

Her two epigraphs to the novel ironically juxtapose Milton's stirring vision of England in *Areopagitica* ("Methinks I see in my mind a noble and puissant Nation rousing herself") against Wordsworth's lament in "London, 1802" that England, now a land of "selfish men," needs another such visionary as Milton. If Anthony Keating's end, finding consolation in philosophy, offers a grain of hope for the country's future, Drabble unexpectedly offers none at all for his lover, Alison Murray, who sacrificed both her acting career and her love for him to care for her handicapped child. The novel's last lines are uncompromisingly bleak about her fate: "Alison can neither live nor die. Alison has Molly. . . . Britain will recover, but not Alison Murray" (320). Drabble is showing that even maternal love can have its darker side and, when as all-consuming as Alison's, can be blind to other claims of the heart.

The Middle Ground is less pessimistic about England's social climate but more so about the situation of women in general. Drabble expresses her discomfort at the radicalization of the feminist movement through the novel's protagonist, Kate Armstrong, whose circumstances at the end of the 1970s parallel Drabble's own. At forty, Kate is a liberal writer and commentator on cultural trends who feels increasingly pressured by women's special-interest groups. She resists herding ("Shapeless diversity, what was wrong with that?" [213]), but can find no satisfactory direction on her own. Divorced, disillusioned with sexual liaisons, deprived of her maternal role—by her children's leaving home and by an aborted pregnancy—Kate is immured on the middle ground, between an outgrown past and an unclear future. She and her friends form a cohort of "forty-year-old women, as strange a social phenomenon in our time as the new aged, and with as few guidelines for behavior" (73–74). Not for them a clarifying journey back to their beginnings such as Frances Wingate's: a visit to her old school—to film a documentary about "Women at the Crossroads"—leaves Kate appalled at the girls' limited prospects and the meagerness of her own family ties. Drabble ends nevertheless on a note of muted optimism, with Kate preparing to throw a huge, all-purpose party. The decor features, in place of cut flowers (like those of Mrs. Dalloway, to whom Drabble draws some sly parallels), an ungainly bay tree that, with care, may outlive her—proof of her openness to the future. Questioned about why the novel ends with the protagonist caught in a "stereotypically feminine" kind of indecision (about what dress to wear), Drabble explained that it characterizes Kate as someone

more concerned with others than herself (the guests' roles taking prece-
dence over her own) and, further, as a woman whose "personality hasn't
crystallized, hasn't settled" (Brans 220–21). Although "connectedness"
serves the woman less dependably in this uncharted middle passage, she
can somehow muddle through, for a future "waits, unseen, and she will
meet it, it will meet her" (*Middle Ground* 257).

What met Margaret Drabble at this critical juncture in her career was
the editing of the *Oxford Companion to English Literature,* a monumental
task that gave her the chance to read widely in novels and to reflect about
a writer's goals in creating fictional worlds.[14] Her reflections brought her
back, reinvigorated, to novel-writing with *The Radiant Way,* the first of
three ambitiously conceived and interconnected novels. Taken together,
the trilogy covers the entire span of the 1980s. Drabble had often referred
in one novel to a character from one of her earlier works; now she carries
a large cast of characters from book to book. Earlier novels had taken
characters far afield on occasion—Frances Wingate to an African conference, for instance; here much of the action takes place in such unfamiliar locales as Thailand and Cambodia. The expanded time frame and
setting allow Drabble to show characters in the process of change against
a background of historical as well as social movements. And she finds a
means of expanding and deepening her enduring concern about the need
to forge personal and communal bonds by focusing her wide-ranging
narrative on the intersecting lives of three women whose sustaining
friendship exemplifies the power of human connectedness. Drabble sees
passionate relationships, whether sexual or maternal, as too biologically
imperious and volatile to survive; friendship, on the other hand, with its
less unremitting demands, can more comfortably accommodate change
and growth.[15]

Drabble's three protagonists are middle-aged professional women
who have maintained their close ties for a quarter of a century. Drawn
together initially by their outsider status at university, they have since
taken different routes. Intellectual Liz Headleand is a London psychotherapist, briskly competent, twice married, and now the focal point of
an extended network that includes spouse, children, stepchildren, patients, and colleagues. Moral Alix Bowen, widowed and now comfortably remarried, subordinates her career to her teacher-husband's and
does part-time counseling. Aesthetic Esther Breuer, single and emotionally wary, is an art historian and lives mainly abroad. We meet them first

in *The Radiant Way*, the title of which refers to their childhood primer and which takes on ironic overtones in the light of the women's mood as they enter into the turbulent 1980s. Liz's husband wants a divorce, and her mother's final illness uncovers a family scandal; Alix's husband loses his job in government cutbacks, and her favorite student is brutally murdered; Esther's longtime love, an Italian art professor, declines into madness and death. Their individual crises intersect: Liz's sister marries into Alix's family; her mother's secret is connected with the man now courting Esther; Esther lives in the same apartment house as the killer of Alix's student. Musing on these linkages, Alix considers the possibility that "such interlockings were part of a vaster network, that there was a pattern, if only one could discern it" (*A Natural Curiosity* 76), expressing Drabble's increasingly strong conviction that what we call coincidence is part of a significant though indiscernible design governing our lives. She pushes the idea here to the extreme as Liz comes face-to-face, through sheerest "chance," with a previously unknown half sister. This kind of Dickensian plot twist, startling in a contemporary setting, functions as it did for Victorians: to remind us that we are all in a very real sense "related" to each other as members of the human family.

Earnest Alix acts on this insight (that "we cannot exist independently for we are nothing but signs, conjunctions, aggregations" [*A Natural Curiosity* 76]) by trying to help Paul Whitmore, her student's killer. Drabble continues Paul's story in *A Natural Curiosity*, allowing herself to revisit another of her favorite theories: the necessity of settling vast accounts if we are to move on into the future. The "curiosity" in this second volume's title refers to the human instinct to solve mysteries. "I want to know," says Liz, of the pathology of Paul, of her family, of human nature in general, "*what really happened*" (75). Her friend Stephen Cox calls this urge to know a "fatal" curiosity (172), and for him it proves just that, drawing him to death in a far-off jungle in a futile effort to understand the failed revolution there. But "natural" curiosity, an openness to understanding human nature, can be life-affirming ("Curiosity has kept her alive, Liz thinks" [22]) when it moves beyond egoism and illusion. So it is with Alix, who forages like a "detective" (26) in psychology, mythology, and literature for clues to explain Paul's deviancy and humankind's taste for death.

In the third volume of the trilogy, *The Gates of Ivory*, curiosity and a sense of responsibility send Liz Headleand halfway around the world to find the missing Stephen Cox. With her only clue, a mysterious package from the Far East containing some manuscript pages and a piece of human bone, Liz journeys as far as the Cambodian border and finds no trace of Stephen other than his passport, passed on to her by a British television crew. Manuscript and bone remain teasing mysteries, but the passport proves, in the economy of Drabble's design, to signify much: the only proof of his death, as it was in his travels proof of his existence, it also tangibly represents his connection to others. Unmarried, estranged from family, Stephen had listed his friend Liz Headland on the document as next of kin. And Liz, in need of greater leverage in her quest, had changed her own passport to read "Mrs. S. Cox." Thus they together establish for the record, so to speak, that however platonic their bond, it constituted a relationship demanding recognition.

Stephen Cox is a familiar Drabble figure: the female protagonist's male ally who—like Simon Camish in *The Needle's Eye* and Hugo Mainwaring in *The Middle Ground*—is essentially solitary, physically or emotionally maimed, but capable of forging a strong friendship with a woman. As their passports link Stephen and Liz, so do physical weaknesses (an injured ankle, a jungle illness) and shared alliances (his literary executor, Hattie Osborne, and his Thai intermediary, Miss Porntip, both aid Liz's search). Differences of a deeper kind, however, account for his perishing and her surviving their similar journeys. Stephen is a romantic, Liz a realist. He goes to Kampuchea hoping, despite the evidence, to find that Pol Pot's utopian scheme for a new order might still be realized. In his quixotic quest for a place "where the water runs uphill" (105), he chooses dreams from the gates of ivory which, as Drabble's epigraph reminds us, are false dreams. Liz, by contrast, reaches out only to dreams that come through the gates of horn, dreams that "speak plainly of what could be and will be."[16] In learning to let old secrets remain hidden, she takes a leaf from the book of Stephen's other two friends—film actress Hattie, one-time barmaid, and entrepreneur Porntip, onetime peasant—both of whom have jettisoned their old selves and are living to the hilt in the present.

These two assertively self-made women are among the most vividly realized characters in the Drabble canon, and they demonstrate that she has lost none of her celebrated ability to render, in convincing detail, the varying realities of contemporary feminine experience. But Drabble is clearly concerned to do something more in *The Gates of Ivory:* to find a new method of relating the novel to history. She alludes to the idea in the novel's opening line: "This is a novel—if novel it be—about Good Time and Bad Time" (3). Good Time is the West's experience of the 1980s, and Bad Time is the East's—more particularly Cambodia's, on the killing fields of the Khmer Rouge. To convey the idea that the boundary line between the telling of her story and the telling of history is in actuality a permeable one, Drabble adopts a shifting stance as narrator. Sometimes the narrator's voice is that of a detached observer recording in semi-documentary style various firsthand accounts by real-life figures, such as journalist William Shawcross and photographer Sean Flynn (a citing of authorities that Drabble takes to extraordinary lengths by appending to *The Gates of Ivory* a bibliography of nonfiction readings on the Vietnamese-Cambodian conflict).[17] Sometimes the narrator, as if conceding the impossibility of distinguishing fact from rumor, merely recites a litany of conflicting reports ("Pol Pot is in Beijing with Prince Sihanouk. Pol Pot has gone mad. Pol Pot is dead" [130]). Sometimes the narrator limits claims of omniscience to the fate of fictional characters only, telling us, for example, that the imperiled Stephen Cox "will not die for a while yet" (123). And sometimes the narrator questions the very process of fiction-making: "Why impose the story line of individual fate upon a story which is at least in part to do with numbers? A queasiness, a moral scruple overcomes the writer at the prospect of selecting individuals from the mass of history" (138).

Drabble, of course, knows full well why she as storyteller must focus on the individual amid the mass—the artist's task, and prerogative, being to transcend the contingent experience and create, out of one individual's story, a universal experience. What concerns her is finding the proper mode of storytelling to do justice to the "anguish of the particular" (*Gates of Ivory* 138) amid a sea of suffering. That mode must not allow readers the catharsis of tragedy; it must be instead "the most disjunctive, the most disruptive, the most uneasy and in-competent of forms" (138), if it is to convey the chaos and futility of the scene. Hence, Drabble's abrupt changes of narrative tone—now omniscient, now skeptical or perplexed—and hence, too, her uncharacteristically muted depiction of characters in the Cambodian setting. Mme Akrun seeking a lost son, Stephen Cox seeking a lost revolution—these hauntingly shadowy figures seem always receding into the jungle darkness. By forgoing her novelistic strengths—intimacy of tone, convincingly realistic detail—

Drabble suggests the remoteness and unfathomability of Southeast Asia's killing fields, a "sunlit darkness" (3) into which the novelist can penetrate only a little further than the historian.

These stylistic experiments in *The Gates of Ivory* have more to do with Drabble's sense of moral responsibility for depicting the contemporary world in all its complexity than with an interest in new fictional modes. She never repeated the linguistic and narrative experiments of her most self-consciously "literary" novel, *The Waterfall*, despite that work's continuing interest to critics, and apparently still holds to her oft-quoted statement that she is content to write the traditionally told story: "I'd rather be at the end of a dying tradition which I admire than at the beginning of a tradition which I deplore" (qtd. in Bergonzi 204). Critics who suspect that inside the Drabble novel of social realism is a postmodernist text struggling to get out[18] are perhaps misled by her unorthodox habit of interrupting her narrative to address the reader directly about her novelistic strategies—wondering which fate she should visit on a character, or challenging the reader to come up with a better solution than hers. The most notorious example is her pert comment in *The Realms of Gold*, following her disposal of Frances Wingate to a man who is no match for her: "So there you are," she says. "Invent a more suitable ending if you can" (356). Her challenge to readers is even more direct in *A Natural Curiosity;* after describing Shirley Harper's surprising reaction to her husband's suicide (a wild Parisian fling with a stranger), she asks: "What do *you* think will happen to her? Do *you* think our end is known in our beginning, that we are predetermined?" (252). To objections that such intrusions break the narrative spell, she argues that "Everybody knows the writer is there—why shouldn't he say so? It seems very artificial, in a way very pretentious, to pretend that there is no writer."[19] Her recent use of the tactic, however, goes beyond reminding us that "the writer is there" to remind us that the *reader* is there as well. Of Shirley Harper's behavior she writes: "If you are [one of those who objects to the turn her life has taken] you might reflect that it might be your task, not mine or hers, to offer her a satisfactory resolution" (*A Natural Curiosity* 254). How can we read this odd calling-to-account except as an emphatic restatement of her belief that the gift of imagination, that capacity to conceive of and realize alternate choices in life, lies in each of us—the forces of fate and chance notwithstanding?

All the Drabble heroines ultimately survive and triumph by the strength of their creative imagination. Even Liz, the brisk realist, experiences the sensation of a world conforming to her will. Awaiting her party guests, she feels a sense of "preternatural power," anticipating—like a novelist spinning her plot—that "Soon their possible presences would become real presences, and here, under this roof, at her command, patterns would form and dissolve and form again, dramas would be enacted. . . . The dance would be to her tune" (*Radiant Way* 10). Rose Vassiliou says of the home she has made for herself: "I carved it out, I created it by faith, I believed in it, and then very slowly, it began to exist" (*Needle's Eye* 42). Frances Wingate says of her archaeological discovery: "I imagine a city, and it exists. If I hadn't imagined it, it wouldn't have existed" (*Realms of Gold* 34). Miss Porntip envisions a "New Plot" to replace the "one story for woman in Thailand" (*Gates of Ivory* 79), and she lives it. Clearly, Drabble's invitation to readers to be co-creative with her in the fiction-making process—to put ourselves not only in Shirley Harper's place but in Margaret Drabble's place as well—is evidence of her faith in the potential of the creative imagination, willed and disciplined, to shape our lives and world. It evidences also her openness to reflect on her means and ends as an artist and her commitment to the idea that "writing novels is a very serious thing to do."[20]

The experience of taking an extended break from novel-writing and then devoting several years to one long work (as we may characterize the trilogy) was obviously a salutary one for Drabble.[21] The opportunity for reflection and the adoption of a format allowing for tracing characters' development over time and against a historical backdrop helped her reformulate some basic assumptions about life and art. To see her recent protagonists reconsidering long-held positions and weighing new options is to see Drabble herself evolving as woman and writer. Steady Alix, disillusioned in her liberal principles, considers having an affair but instead nurses her husband through a critical illness and contents herself with helping the murderer Paul rather than explaining his deviance. Emotionally wary Esther tries living with a woman in Italy after her lover's death but returns to England and a comfortably conventional marriage. Self-assured Liz, tempered by her Cambodian odyssey and a brush with death, gives up demanding to know "*what really happened*" in other places and times and focuses on nurturing present relationships. The changes are gradual, sometimes unexpected, but in Drabble's hand all are convincing, with each character seemingly freed to proceed at her own pace in her own direction. Without conceding her belief in coincidence-as-design, Drabble has obviously qualified her view that fate (in the form of heredity or environment or chance) shapes character; the power to reimagine oneself is a stronger force than fate. And, while still insisting on the need to put right the past, she defines the process more liberally: we can cut ourselves off from roots if they fail to nourish; simply laying to rest the past, whether it be good or evil, may be enough. On the other two foundation blocks of her moral philosophy, the need for forming personal attachments and caring communities, Drabble stands firm. Liz's failed but healing search for Stephen Cox, and the memorial service to which she gathers, from near and far, those who cared for him, together serve as a comprehensive symbol in *The Gates of Ivory* of the bonds that make us fully alive, fully human.

Margaret Drabble's preeminence as a chronicler of contemporary life has been widely acknowledged; her roles as moralist and artist are becoming increasingly appreciated as her canon grows and its aesthetic strategies come into ever clearer focus. A. S. Byatt's assessment of George Eliot seems to have particular application to Drabble. Eliot, said Byatt, described the way it felt to be a woman, "and did it better than most writers, too—because it was not all she did: she made a world, in which intellect and passion, day-to-day cares and movements of whole societies cohere and disintegrate. She offered us scope, not certainties."[22] The progression of Drabble's work, it is now clear, has been toward that same goal. She has expressed the hope of growing old like her fellow novelist Doris Lessing, who, in her sixties, is still changing and "moving on." She also admitted to the dream of someday writing "the great novel" (Clifford 19). Readers who have followed her career over three decades will feel some confidence that hers are no vain hopes from the gates of ivory but rather dreams from the gates of horn that "speak plainly of what could be and will be."

NOTES

1. See, e.g., Phyllis Rose's review of *The Middle Ground* in the *New York Times Book Review*, in which she calls the novel "a kind of superior reporting." Penelope Lively, in "New Novels," *Encounter* 55 (November 1980): 61–62, expresses a widely held view that Drabble's "precise landscape" will be a "godsend" to future social historians.

2. See, e.g., her remarks in an interview with Barbara Milton, "Margaret Drabble: The Art of Fiction LXX," on fate and free will, and with Jo Brans, "Margaret Drabble: Beasts of the People," in *Listen to the Voices* 215–42, on process and "continuous" life. For an extended analysis of her view of fate, through *The Ice Age*, see John Hannay, *The Intertextuality of Fate*.

3. A comprehensive view of Drabble's philosophy in the novels up to *The Middle Ground* can be found in Mary Hurley Moran, *Margaret Drabble: Existing within Structures*. Moran paraphrases Drabble's moral position, which is expanded but not fundamentally changed in the later books, as holding that "We are all part of a long inheritance, a human community in which we must play our proper part" (15).

4. On a scholarship at Newnham College, she read English literature under F. R. Leavis, whose theory of the moral tradition of the English novel strongly influenced her (see "Margaret Drabble" in Firchow 104–21). Drabble says that Leavis's "exceedingly high standards" were intimidating to students with creative aspirations and drove her from literature to acting. See "Margaret Drabble" in *Current Biography* 42 (1981): 22–25. Even while active in undergraduate dramatic productions, however, she graduated with double honors in English.

5. For a listing of Drabble's short stories, literary criticism, and edited texts, see "Works by Margaret Drabble" below. For her book reviews and general-interest articles, see Packer 9–50. The short stories are discussed by Jane Campbell in "Becoming Terrestrial." In the 1960s she wrote two screenplays, a television play, and a stage drama which, when produced, taught her only, Drabble says, that she "can't write plays" (Brans 220).

6. Only minor revisions had ever been made to Sir Paul Harvey's 1932 edition before Drabble's revision. Her work on it has been highly praised (except for the decision to omit an entry on herself). In 1987 she edited, with Jenny Stringer, *The Concise Oxford Companion to English Literature*.

7. She has revealed, e.g., that Mrs. Maugham, the difficult mother in *Jerusalem the Golden*, is based on her own grandmother and that the bouts of depression suffered by Frances Wingate in *The Realms of Gold* come from observation of her mother's similar symptoms. See Milton 56 and Sadler 187 n. 6. On her writing habits and philosophy, see Firchow (104–21) and Joanne V. Creighton, "An Interview with Margaret Drabble."

8. The phrases are from Drabble's *Arnold Bennett: A Biography*. She tries to capture "our small daily lives" as Bennett did, but "colored by the social climate in which we live" (Brans 230).

9. John Webster, *The White Devil*, I.ii.42–45.

10. For a close reading of the novel's unresolved ambiguities, see Joanne V. Creighton, "Reading Margaret Drabble's *The Waterfall.*"

11. Drabble has admitted that had she not still been involved in her own troubled marriage, she might not have reconciled Rose and her husband (see the Hardin interview). Her dissatisfaction with Rose's ending might account for bringing her back, almost twenty years later, for a brief appearance as an embittered middle-aged mother in *The Gates of Ivory*. Drabble, however, makes a habit of reintroducing characters, often in bit parts, in subsequent novels.

12. For Drabble's comments on Bunyan's influence, see "Margaret Drabble," *Current Biography* 42 (1981): 22–25.

13. "On First Looking into Chapman's Homer" (1816).

14. In a newspaper article Drabble described her interest in the obscure women novelists of an earlier age, and wondered if there is "anything representative, necessary in their odd destinies." See Margaret Drabble, "Publish."

15. While writing *The Radiant Way*, Drabble discussed her feelings about such relationships: the sense of "very close understanding" in an erotic relationship is "usually transient," because male-female bonds are "more tense" than female-female bonds. Of women's friendships she feels that "when they have survived a decade or two they can survive almost anything" (Brans 228–29).

16. Epigraph to *The Gates of Ivory*, from Homer's *Odyssey*, IX, ll. 560–65.

17. In an interesting parallel, Drabble's sister A. S. Byatt added a list of nonfiction readings to her latest work of fiction, *Angels and Insects* (New York: Random House, 1992), even though, as she notes, "a work of fiction doesn't need a bibliography" (339).

18. See, e.g., Daphne Merkin, "Constructed Expectations," *New Leader* 22 Sept. 1980: 12–13. Drabble herself distrusts "self-reflecting" fictions that fail to reflect the outside world; see her "Mimesis." Among critics who have found elements of postmodernism in her novels are Joanne Creighton, who, in "The Reader and Post-Modern Fiction," reads authorial intrusions and ambiguities as an invitation to the reader to join in constructing the text, and Michael F. Harper, who points out in "Margaret Drabble and the Resurrection of the English Novel" that, while not a poststructuralist in the sense of a Thomas Pynchon, Drabble goes far beyond the Victorian tradition to examine limitations of modernism, knowledge, and language. Eleanor Honig Skoller finds in Drabble's novels, especially the later ones, "a parody of plot and genre that is a repudiation of high modernist artists" (22). Contemporary novelists with whom Drabble

feels a kinship are Angus Wilson, Saul Bellow, and Doris Lessing. See, e.g., Brans and Creighton interviews.

19. Creighton, "An Interview With Margaret Drabble" 18.

20. Quoted in "Ambassadress of Literary London," *Observer* 19 Apr. 1987: 7.

21. She had agreed to edit the *Oxford Companion* after feeling a "block" during the writing of *The Middle Ground* (see Clifford 19). The novel was not generally well received; critics found the depiction of the protagonist's stasis and fragmentation unsatisfyingly shapeless. See, e.g., Jean Strouse, who calls it "an exhausted book about exhaustion." Drabble herself called it a "mistake," but a book she "had to" write (see Forster). For further evidence that this period was crucial in Drabble's career, see her son's comments, in the *Observer* "Ambassadress" article (cited in previous note), that she was experiencing "tremendous doubts" about political beliefs she had long held. The early 1980s were years of profound changes in her private life as well: the death of her parents, her children's move into adulthood, and marriage to the writer Michael Holroyd.

22. A. S. Byatt, *Passions of the Mind* (New York: Random House, 1992), 67.

SELECTED WORKS BY MARGARET DRABBLE

Angus Wilson: A Biography. New York: St. Martin's, 1996.

"Angus Wilson: Cruel-Kind Enemy of False Sentiment and Self-Delusion." *New York Times Book Review* 29 Jan. 1995: 3, 17, 18.

Arnold Bennett: A Biography. 1974. New York: G. K. Hall, 1986.

"The Author Comments" [on *The Needle's Eye*]. *Dutch Quarterly Review of Anglo-American Letters* 5.1 (1975): 35–38.

Bird of Paradise. Screenplay. 1969.

"A Book I Love: Margaret Drabble on the Novels of Angus Wilson." *Mademoiselle* Aug. 1975: 94, 106.

The Concise Oxford Companion to English Literature. Ed. with Jenny Stringer. London: Oxford UP, 1987.

"Crossing the Alps." *Penguin Modern Stories 3.* Ed. Judith Burnley. Harmondsworth: Penguin, 1969. 63–85. Rpt. in *Mademoiselle* Feb. 1971: 154–55, 193–98.

"A Day in the Life of a Smiling Woman." *Cosmopolitan* Oct. 1973: 224, 252–57. Rpt. in *In the Looking Glass: Twenty-One Modern Short Stories by Women.* Ed. Nancy Dean and Myra Stark. New York: Putnam, 1977. 143–65.

"The Dying Year." *Harper's* July 1987: 59–69.

"Faithful Lovers." *Saturday Evening Post* 6 Apr. 1968: 62, 64–65.

Foreword. *Jane Austen's Beginnings: The Juvenilia and Lady Susan.* Ed. J. David Grey. Ann Arbor: University Microfilms International Research Press, 1989. xxii.

For Queen and Country: Britain in the Victorian Age. 1978. New York: Seabury Press, 1979.

The Garrick Year. 1964. New York: Morrow, 1965.

The Gates of Ivory. New York: Viking, 1992.

The Genius of Thomas Hardy. Ed. with introduction. New York: Knopf, 1976.

"The Gifts of War." *Women and Fiction: Short Stories by and about Women.* Ed. Susan Cahill. New York: New American Library, 1975. 33–47.

"Hardy and the Natural World." *The Genius of Thomas Hardy.* Ed. Margaret Drabble. New York: Knopf, 1976. 162–69.

"Hassan's Tower." *Winter's Tales 12.* Ed. A.D. Maclean. Los Angeles: Sylvester and Orphanos, 1980. 149–68.

"Homework." *Cosmopolitan* [England] Nov. 1975: 192, 194, 196, 198. Rpt. in *Ontario Review* 7 (1977–78): 7–13.

The Ice Age. 1977. New York: Warner, 1983.

Lady Susan; The Watsons; and Sanditon. By Jane Austen. Ed. by Margaret Drabble. Harmondsworth: Penguin, 1974.

Introduction. *Wuthering Heights.* By Emily Brontë. Ed. P. Henderson. New York: Dutton, 1978. v–xxii.

Isadora. With Melvyn Bragg and Clive Exton. Screenplay. 1969.

Jerusalem the Golden. 1967. New York: Plume, 1987.

Laura. Produced by Granada Television. 1964.

"Les Liaisons Dangereuses." *Punch* 28 Oct. 1964: 646–48.

London Consequences. Ed. with B. S. Johnson. London: Greater London Arts Association, 1972.

"Margaret Drabble on Virginia Woolf." *Harper's Bazaar and Queen* Sept. 1972: 90–91, 128. Rpt. as "How Not to Be Afraid of Virginia Woolf." *Ms.* Nov. 1972: 68–70, 72, 121.

The Middle Ground. 1980. New York: Bantam, 1982.

The Millstone. New York: New American Library, 1965. Harmondsworth: Penguin, 1968. Rpt. as *Thank You All Very Much.* New York: New American Library, 1969. Rpt. as casebook with introduction by Drabble. London: Longman, 1970.

"Mimesis: The Representation of Reality in the Post-War British Novel." *Mosaic* 20 (Winter 1987): 1–14.

"Money as a Subject for the Novelist." *Times Literary Supplement* 24 July 1969: 792–93.

A Natural Curiosity. New York: Viking Penguin, 1989.

The Needle's Eye. 1972. New York: Popular Library 1977.

New Stories 1. Ed. with Charles Osborne. London: Arts Council, 1976.

"'No Idle Rentier': Angus Wilson and the Nourished Literary Imagination." *Studies in the Literary Imagination* 13 (Spring 1980): 119–29.

The Oxford Companion to English Literature. 5th ed. Oxford: Oxford UP, 1998.

"Pamela Hansford Johnson." *Sunday Times* (London) 21 June 1981: 42.

"Publish—And If You're a Woman You'll Be Damned." *Guardian* 12 July 1982: 8.

"A Pyrrhic Victory." *Nova* July 1968: 80, 84, 86.

The Radiant Way. New York: Knopf, 1987.

The Realms of Gold. 1975. Harmondsworth: Penguin, 1977.

"The Reunion." *Winter's Tales 14.* Ed. Kevin Crossley-Holland. New York: St. Martin's, 1968. 149–68.

Stratford Revisited: A Legacy of the Sixties. Shipston-on-Stour, Warwickshire: Celandine Press, 1989.

"A Success Story." *Spare Rib* [London] 2 (1972): 26–27, 33. Rpt. in *Fine Lines: The Best of Ms. Fiction.* Ed. Ruth Sullivan. New York: Scribner's, 1982. 259–71.

A Summer Bird-Cage. 1963. Harmondsworth: Penguin, 1967.

A Touch of Love. [Screenplay of *The Millstone.*] 1969.

The Tradition of Women's Fiction: Lectures in Japan. Tokyo: Oxford UP, 1982.

Twentieth Century Classics. London: Book Trust, The British Council, 1986.

Virginia Woolf: A Personal Debt. N.p.: Aloe Editions, 1973.

"A Voyage to Cythera." *Mademoiselle* Dec. 1967: 98–99, 148–50.

The Waterfall. 1969. New York: Fawcett, 1977.

The Witch of Exmoor. New York: Harcourt Brace and Co., 1996.

"A Woman Writer." *Books* 11 (Spring 1973): 4–6. Rpt. in *On Gender and Writing.* Ed. Micheline Wandor. London and Boston: Pandora Press, 1983. 156–59.

"Women Novelists." *Books* 375 (1968): 87–89.

Wordsworth. 1966. New York: Arco, 1969.

Wordsworth's Butter Knife: An Essay. 1966. Northampton, MA: Catawba Press, 1980.

"The Writer as Recluse: The Theme of Solitude in the Works of the Brontës." *Brontë Society Transactions* 16.4 (1974): 259–69.

A Writer's Britain: Landscape in Literature. New York: Knopf, 1979.

Writers in Conversation: Mary Gordon and Margaret Drabble. Video recording. London: ICA, 1986.

Selected Works about Margaret Drabble

Atwood, Margaret. "Margaret Drabble: The Magic of the Ordinary." *Ms.* Nov. 1987: 62, 65.

Beards, Virginia K. "Margaret Drabble: Novels of a Cautious Feminist." *Critique: Studies in Modern Fiction* 15 (1973): 3–47.

Bergonzi, Bernard. *The Situation of the Novel.* London: Macmillan, 1970.

Bokat, Nicole Suzanne. *The Novels of Margaret Drabble: "This Freudian Family Nexus."* New York: Peter Lang, 1998.

Brans, Jo. *Listen to the Voices: Conversations with Contemporary Writers.* Dallas: Southern Methodist UP, 1988.

Campbell, Jane. "Becoming Terrestrial: The Short Stories of Margaret Drabble." *Critique* 25.1 (1983): 25–44.

Clifford, Judy. "A Substance of Entertainment." *Times* (London) 27 Apr. 1987: 19.

Creighton, Joanne V. "An Interview with Margaret Drabble." *Golden Realms.* Ed. Dorey Schmidt and Jan Seale. Edinburg, TX: Pan American UP, 1982. 18–31.

———. *Margaret Drabble.* London: Methuen, 1985.

———. "The Reader and Post-Modern Fiction." *College Literature* 9.3 (Fall 1982): 216–30.

———. "Reading Margaret Drabble's *The Waterfall*." *Critical Essays on Margaret Drabble.* Ed. Ellen Cronan Rose. Boston: G. K. Hall, 1985. 106–18.

Firchow, Peter E., ed. *The Writer's Place: Interviews on the Literary Situation in Contemporary Britain.* Minneapolis: U of Minnesota P, 1974. 104–21.

Forster, Margaret. "What Makes Margaret Drabble Run and Run." *Guardian* 28 Feb. 1981: 9.

Fox-Genovese, Elizabeth. "The Ambiguities of Female Identity: A Reading of the Novels of Margaret Drabble." *Partisan Review* 46.2 (1979): 234–48.

Hannay, John. *The Intertextuality of Fate: A Study of Margaret Drabble.* Columbia: U of Missouri P, 1986.

———. "Margaret Drabble: An Interview." *Twentieth Century Literature* 33 (Summer 1987): 129–49.

Hardin, Nancy S. "An Interview with Margaret Drabble." *Contemporary Literature* 14 (Summer 1973): 273–95. Rpt. in *Interviews with Contemporary Writers.* Second series, 1972–82. Ed. L. S. Dembo. Madison: U of Wisconsin P, 1974. 89–111.

Harper, Michael F. "Margaret Drabble and the Resurrection of the English

Novel." *Contemporary Literature* 23.2 (Spring 1982): 145–68. Rpt. in *Critical Essays on Margaret Drabble.* Ed. Ellen Cronan Rose. Boston: G. K. Hall, 1985. 52–73.

Libby, Marion Vlastos. "Fate and Feminism in the Novels of Margaret Drabble." *Contemporary Literature* 16 (1975): 17–92.

Milton, Barbara. "Margaret Drabble: The Art of Fiction LXX." *Paris Review* 20 (Fall–Winter 1978): 40–65.

Moran, Mary Hurley. *Margaret Drabble: Existing within Structures.* Carbondale: Southern Illinois UP, 1983.

Myer, Valerie Grosvenor. *Margaret Drabble: A Reader's Guide.* New York: St. Martin's, 1991.

———. *Margaret Drabble: Puritanism and Permissiveness.* New York: Barnes and Noble, 1974.

Packer, Joan Garrett. *Margaret Drabble: An Annotated Bibliography.* New York: Garland, 1988.

Parker, Gillian, and Janet Todd. "Margaret Drabble." *Women Writers Talking.* Ed. Janet Todd. New York: Holmes and Meier, 1983. 160–78.

Poland, Nancy. "There Must Be a Lot of People Like Me." *Midwest Quarterly* 16 (Apr. 1975): 25–67.

Preussner, Dee. "Talking with Margaret Drabble." *Modern Fiction Studies* 25 (1979–80): 563–77.

Rose, Ellen Cronan, ed. *Critical Essays on Margaret Drabble.* Boston: G. K. Hall, 1985.

———. *The Novels of Margaret Drabble: Equivocal Figures.* Totowa, NJ: Barnes and Noble, 1980.

Rose, Phyllis. "Our Chronicler of Britain." Rev. of *The Middle Ground. New York Times Book Review* 7 Sept. 1980: 32–33.

Rozencwajg, Iris. "Interview with Margaret Drabble." *Women's Studies* 6 (1979): 33–47.

Sadler, Lynn Veach. *Margaret Drabble.* Boston: Twayne, 1986.

Schmidt, Dorey, ed. *Margaret Drabble: Golden Realms.* Edinburg, TX: Pan American UP, 1982.

Skoller, Eleanor Honig. *The In-Between of Writing: Experience and Experiment in Drabble, Duras, and Arendt.* Ann Arbor: U of Michigan P, 1993.

Strouse, Jean. "Modern Muddles." *Newsweek* 6 Oct. 1980: 95.

11

To Pose or Not to Pose: The Interplay of Object and Subject in the Works of Angela Carter

Dee Goertz

Vampires and sleeping beauties, winged trapeze artists and puppets, werewolves and showgirls—the female characters of Angela Carter's exuberant fiction assume a variety of roles, some from the conventions of realistic fiction but most from fairy tale and fantasy. By using magical realism with a feminist edge, she makes up for the rarity of the female perspective in initiation myths and quests for self-discovery. She portrays young women (and, in some cases, mature women) threading their way through their own awakening sexual desires, male desires, male threats, and self-knowledge. The way is filled with beauty and terror, danger and freedom. In story after story, one of the main obstacles that Carter's female characters confront is their treatment as objects, as things for men to look at, manipulate, and possess. Her protagonists learn that being an object of desire is dangerous, leading not only to a diminishing of the self, but sometimes to physical annihilation.

Carter discusses this issue on a theoretical level in her long essay on the Marquis de Sade, *The Sadeian Woman,* in which she says of his much abused character, Justine: "To be the *object* of desire is to be defined in the passive case. . . . To exist in the passive case is to die in the passive case—that is, to be killed" (77). In her fiction, Carter treats this theme in all its complexity. She acknowledges the pleasure as well as the danger of being desired, of being thought beautiful. She condemns neither women for wanting to be desired nor men for desiring them. However, as her protagonists examine their roles as objects, they learn more about themselves and discover ways to counter their objectification. At times they reverse the gaze and become the subject; at others they take control of their image and use it for their own ends. Looking at Carter's works chronologically, we can see that her treatment of this theme evolves through her female characters' increasing skill in overcoming the liability of their objectification by the male gaze.

Her second novel, *The Magic Toyshop* (1967), is probably one of the most delightful and disturbing coming-of-age stories ever written. It follows fifteen-year-old Melanie's perilous journey toward sexual awakening in which she discovers the reality of woman's position in an often hostile male-dominated world. Carter explores the way Melanie forms her self-image as a sexually mature woman: she relies at first on the role models of her mother and the images of women she sees in art and literature. These all lead her to picture herself as an object of desire—a pleasing enough fantasy when she playacts alone in her room, but a role that leaves her vulnerable in the real world. By alluding to a multitude of myths and fairy tales, including the stories of Leda, Sleeping Beauty, and Bluebeard (stories that Carter uses again and again in her fiction), Carter demonstrates the ways girls have as models women who are objectified and sexually passive.

When Melanie first begins to discover her sexuality, she fantasizes about herself as an object of desire. Early in the novel, she imagines herself as a painter's model:

> She . . . posed in attitudes, holding things. . . . A la Toulouse-Lautrec, she dragged her hair sluttishly across her face and sat down in a chair with her legs apart and a bowl of water and a towel at her feet. She always felt particularly wicked when she posed for Lautrec. . . .
>
> . . . she contrived a pale, smug Cranach Venus with a bit of net curtain wound round her head and at her throat the necklace of cultured pearls they gave her when she was confirmed. (5–6)

Her model for adulthood is formed by the images of adult women in paintings: static images of women existing only because they were looked at by men. Carter's tone here is comic/lyrical, but later she will use similar images to show the darker side of Melanie's fantasy.

Melanie also imagines herself as a present to be opened by her future husband: "she used the net curtain as raw material for a series of nightgowns suitable for her wedding night. . . . She gift-wrapped herself for a phantom bridegroom" (6). This metaphor of bride-as-gift-object grows when Melanie sneaks into her absent parents' bedroom one night to gaze at their wedding portrait: her mother's elaborate dress is as elegant a bridal gift-wrapping as any fifteen-year-old could imagine: "an epiphany of clothing . . . a pyrotechnic display of satin and lace" (14). What more powerful role model of adult womanhood could a girl have than the image of her mother on the threshold of her sexual life? But again, Melanie's lesson on adulthood comes from a static image of a woman existing only to be looked at by men.

Melanie cannot resist trying on the gown, and this role-playing begins a highly complex and symbolic scene in the novel. Although the gown makes her feel beautiful, it becomes a trap; the veil of tulle is particularly confining: "She unfolded acres of tulle, enough for an entire Gothic Parnassus of Cranach Venuses to wind around their heads. Melanie was trapped, a mackerel in a net; the veil blew up around her, blinding her eyes and filling her nostrils" (18). She manages better with the gown, but after she accidentally locks herself outside in the garden, the gown hampers her climb up the apple tree to return to her room. She removes it, but the gown is shredded and bloodstained. Obviously, the scene has many symbolic dimensions: wearing her wedding dress signifies Melanie's attempt to replace her mother; her bloodying of the dress, sexual maturity both through menstruation and loss of virginity; the climb up the apple tree, her loss of innocence. For my purposes, however, the experience with the wedding dress is most important because it develops the theme of women's objectification: Melanie's vision of herself as woman lies in herself as gift-wrapped package presented to the groom. Her playacting in the dress, even though it makes her feel beautiful and womanly, ultimately demonstrates that her objectification usurps her freedom.

Melanie becomes especially vulnerable when her parents' accidental deaths force her to live with her tyrannical Uncle Philip and his cowed family in a seedy London suburb. There her seemingly harmless fantasies are echoed in her uncle's humiliation of her: he decides she will be Leda in his puppet show of the myth of Leda's rape/seduction by Zeus-as-swan. Uncle Philip's objectification of Melanie works on several levels: not only is she the victim (object) in a mock rape, but since her costar is a puppet, she is reduced to the status of a puppet. Moreover, this dramatization is all part of a show, watched by the reluctant Aunt Margaret and the rest of the family.

The costume Uncle Philip designs for her echoes both the wedding dress and her improvised role-playing as artist's model. Melanie herself makes the connection as her aunt starts measuring her for the Leda costume: "Melanie would be a nymph crowned with daisies again; [Uncle Philip] saw her as once she had seen herself. In spite of everything, she was flattered" (135). Indeed, dressing up for the role of Leda takes her back to the ecstatic days of self-discovery in the first pages of the novel. For the first time since moving to Uncle Philip's, Melanie observes "with interest" her developing body: through the diaphanous material, her breasts "seemed to have grown and the nipples to have got rather darker" (135). But her joy at her sexual maturing contrasts painfully to Uncle Philip's crude reaction: "I wanted my Leda to be a little girl. Your tits are too big" (136). By intruding into Melanie's secret world of pubescent musings, he violates her almost as seriously as he will later do with the swan. Melanie now discovers the difference between dressing herself for an imaginary Toulouse-Lautrec or "phantom bridegroom" and dressing herself for a real Uncle Philip: he sees her quite differently from the way she sees herself.

The objectification of herself which previously brought her pleasure has become a source of humiliation and danger. Melanie understands the danger more clearly as she considers her role as rape victim: "it was not precisely the swan of which she was afraid, but of giving herself to the swan" (154). This view echoes the discussion of rape in Carter's *Sadeian Woman:* "Somewhere in the fear of rape, is a more than physical terror of hurt and humiliation—a fear of psychic disintegration, of an essential dismemberment, a fear of a loss or disruption of the self" (60). By becoming an object of desire, Melanie has been made vulnerable to a complete loss of the self.

But *The Magic Toyshop* is not a tragedy, and Melanie suffers neither psychic disintegration, nor murder, nor a real rape. Nevertheless, the pantomime rape frightens her enough that she momentarily loses her sense of self. Afterwards, she has to "put Melanie back on like a coat, slowly" (159). The phrasing echoes a line in Yeats's "Leda and the Swan": "Did she put on his knowledge with his power . . . ?" Melanie, however, "puts on" the knowledge not of the swan but of herself—a somewhat changed version of herself. Although Carter gives her no conscious epiphany, Melanie's behavior implies that she has rejected her fantasy of being gift-wrapped for the phantom groom. She has moved out of the passive case into the active. She gives away to Aunt Margaret her best dress from her pre-London life, as well as the confirmation pearls that had formed part of her costumes as Cranach's Venus and Uncle Philip's Leda, thereby divesting herself of her ornaments from the days of self-objectification. No longer the "young and inexperienced and dependent" (80) girl who entered Uncle Philip's house, Melanie now feels "young and tough and brave" (179). She has grown away from her dependency on the relics she once thought essential for a mature woman, and in the process becomes better able to determine her own life's course.

In her collection of short stories based on familiar European fairy tales, *The Bloody Chamber* (1979), Carter returns to this theme of the objectification of women and examines it in a variety of settings. In three stories in particular—"The Bloody Chamber," "The Tiger's Bride," and "The Company of Wolves"—Carter uses the motif of undressing to portray the power relations between men and women: who is looking (the dominant/subject position) and who is being looked at (the submissive/object position). Although the women in these stories live in a culture where the male claims the right to objectify them through his gaze, they learn ways to overcome this oppression.

"The Bloody Chamber" reworks the story of Bluebeard and his fated wives. Like Melanie in *The Magic Toyshop*, the unnamed protagonist/narrator of this story finds herself under the power of a tyrant who treats her like an object; however, unlike Melanie, this character has sold herself to the tyrant through marriage and knows it. She understands early on that she has been seduced by her husband's wealth, has been "bought with a handful of coloured stones and the pelts of dead beasts" (18), but she still embraces her lot in the first half of the story.

The narrator expresses her husband's power over her in terms of his gaze: "I saw him watching me in the gilded mirrors with the assessing eye of a connoisseur inspecting horseflesh, or even of a housewife in the market, inspecting cuts on the slab. I'd never seen, or else had never acknowledged, that regard of his before, the sheer carnal avarice of it; and it was strangely magnified by the monocle lodged in his left eye" (11). This description makes explicit the relationship between his position as observer of her and his attitude toward her as a piece of meat. But even as it objectifies her, his gaze also becomes the means for initiating her self-discovery: "I saw myself, suddenly, as he saw me. . . . And, for the first time in my innocent and confined life, I sensed in myself a potentiality for corruption that took my breath away" (11). Carter creates a similar exchange a few pages later (20) to emphasize the narrator's dawning understanding of her own complicity in her husband's domination of her. By seeing herself through his eyes, even as object, she becomes subject by turning her inward eye on herself.

In another scene, Carter shows the sexual as well as economic nature of the husband's domination: the narrator describes his removal of her clothing after their wedding as "a formal disrobing of the bride, a ritual from the brothel," and connects it with images from his collection of pornography: "the child with her sticklike limbs, naked but for her button boots . . . and the old, monocled lecher who examined her, limb by limb. He in his London tailoring; she, bare as a lamb chop. Most pornographic of all confrontations. And so my purchaser unwrapped his bargain. And, as at the opera, when I had first seen my flesh in his eyes, I was aghast to feel myself stirring" (15). Although the narrator realizes with horror that she is aroused by her own objectification, she does not reject her status until she discovers the extreme result of this objectification: the corpses of her husband's previous wives in the "bloody chamber." (Thus, curiosity, instead of the moral failing of the original fairy tale, becomes in Carter's story the means of discovering an important truth: that allowing oneself to become an object can be annihilating.) Significantly, at the end of the story, the narrator chooses as a lover a blind man incapable of imposing his gaze on her—although she says, "I know he sees me clearly with his heart" (41).

Although both Melanie of *The Magic Toyshop* and the narrator of "The Bloody Chamber" learn the dangers of objectification, they remain largely passive, the latter to the point of mounting the beheading block while waiting for her heroic mother to save her from Bluebeard. The remaining characters discussed in this essay, however, take much more active roles in choosing their fates, manipulating their images, and reversing or even erasing the subject/object paradigm of male-female relationships. In "The Tiger's Bride" and "The Company of Wolves" the protagonists' self-determinism counterpoints "The Bloody Chamber" narrator's passivity through parallel scenes of undressing. Whereas in "The Bloody Chamber" the narrator is undressed and gazed upon by her husband, the characters in the former stories initiate their own undressing and insist that the antagonist males undress, too.

In "The Tiger's Bride," one of the two reworkings of "Beauty and the Beast" in the collection, the narrator's father loses her in a card game to the Beast. Fully aware of her status as object to be bartered in a male economy, she bitterly resents it. When she discovers that the Beast wants only to look at her naked, she laughs in his face and, in tones that mock the obscenity of his request, makes a counteroffer, to expose herself only from the waist down (59): even though the tiger keeps her prisoner, she refuses to give in to his demand. Only after the tiger removes his clothes (his human disguise) for her does she freely undress for him, after which she feels "at liberty for the first time in my life" (64). Even though the narrative is "inherently voyeuristic," Carter has turned the power structure around, as Sylvia Bryant notes (448). Not only does the protagonist refuse to become the object of the gaze until she obtains the status of the subject, but she also narrates her own story: "the terms of looking . . . are significantly altered," as Bryant asserts, because the narrator is now both subject and object (448).

Likewise, in "The Company of Wolves," Carter's version of "Little Red Riding Hood," the protagonist is in mortal danger of becoming the most vulnerable kind of object—the werewolf's dinner—when she takes action by removing her clothes and throwing them in the fire. This defiant gesture perhaps defies only her own fear at first, yet results in a positive outcome. Like the narrator in "The Tiger's Bride," she laughs when the wolf proposes to eat her: "she knew she was nobody's meat. She laughed at him full in the face, she ripped off his shirt for him and flung it into the fire, in the fiery wake of her own discarded clothing" (118). By undressing the wolf, she puts herself in the dominant position, that of the subject of the gaze. Moreover, by burning their clothes, she determines their mutual fate, since that action makes them werewolves forever. In both stories, the protagonists choose to undress on their own terms. Avis Lewallan, though, argues that the "choice is already prescribed" since the characters exist in a male-dominated world in which the rule is to "fuck or be fucked" (149). To the contrary, I believe that the protagonists create an option outside this paradigm, for at the end of both stories their actions lead to amicable equality between female and male, human and animal. By trading sides of the subject/object paradigm, the characters erase it.

In her last two novels, *Nights at the Circus* (1985) and *Wise Children* (1991), Carter significantly makes her protagonists "showgirls"—a winged trapeze artist ("Is she fact or is she fiction?") and identical twin vaudeville dancers, respectively. Of all professions (excepting modeling), that of showgirl most relentlessly places the woman in the vulnerable position of being looked at. Carter seems to have deliberately chosen this profession for her characters in order to explore their options for overcoming this liability. Although of all her characters these protagonists are in the most danger of being marginalized as objects, Carter depicts them triumphing through self-discovery and sheer force of will.

In the first chapter of *Nights at the Circus,* the winged protagonist, Fevvers, is an object not only to Walser, the main male character, but to the reader as well. Carter manipulates the point of view of the novel so that the reader learns to see Fevvers as a human being even as Walser does. In the first chapter, however, Carter compels the reader to look Fevvers from the outside and try to solve the mystery, "Is she fact or is she fiction?" As a woman who supposedly has wings, she is either a freak or a con artist, to us as well as to Walser who interviews her. Since she is by profession a spectacle, we are distanced from her and feel allied to the observer Walser: Fevvers is the Other. The narrative tone, moreover, conveys awe for Fevvers's larger-than-life persona, pronouncing her the "democratically elected divinity of the imminent century [it is 1899]" (12), and thus treats her more like symbol than woman. We find that almost everyone Fevvers comes in contact with gives her a role to play. The madame who helps raise her dresses her as first Cupid and then Winged Victory to amuse the customers; the proprietress of a "museum of woman monsters" poses her as the Angel of Death; a crackpot who buys her intending to kill her and absorb her life-giving essence sees her as the goddess Flora. Moreover, Fevvers promotes herself as an object, the Bird in the Gilded Cage. Creating wonder in her audience builds her ego, and it is good for business.

For the reader, Fevvers evolves from object to subject (as much as a fictional character can be subject, in the sense that we identify with her) because of shifts in the narrative point of view. As mentioned, the limited omniscient narration of the first section views her as a mystery. In chapter two of the first section, however, Fevvers begins to tell her story to Walser. Although she speaks within the third-person narration, she is in control of her own image as her story of her past creates it, and hearing her voice lessens for us the distance created by the perspective. In sections two and three, she shares the focus of the narration with Walser as, now a clown in the circus he joins to follow Fevvers, he begins a journey of self-discovery. In section three, however, the point of view shifts back and forth from third-person to first-person with Fevvers as narrator. Without announcing the shift through quotation marks, Carter begins the third part with Fevvers's voice: "How do they live, here? How do they cope with it? Or aren't I the right one to pop the question, I'm basically out of sympathy with landscape, I get the shivers on Hampstead bloody Heath" (197). This personal, particularized human reaction to the Siberian landscape helps us to identify with Fevvers rather than view her voyeuristically.

As the shift in point of view moves her from object to subject in the reader's perception, so the events of the novel teach Fevvers more about her status as object and ways to free herself from it. Early on, her comments about her job as a living statue at a brothel show her awareness of the dangers of objectification, but she also acknowledges that this is her fate and she must learn to cope with it: "I existed only as an object in men's eyes after the night-time knocking on the door began. Such was my apprenticeship for life, since is it not to the mercies of the eyes of others that we commit ourselves on our voyage through the world? . . . I waited . . . although I could not have told you for what it was I waited. Except, I assure you, I did *not* await the kiss of a magic prince, sir! With my two eyes, I nightly saw how such a kiss would seal me up in my *appearance* forever!" (39).

On three occasions in the novel, in increasingly subtle ways, men attempt to seal Fevvers up in her appearance. Carter uses these crises as organizing and structuring devices, pointedly situating each near the end of one of the three sections of the novel. Near the end of section one, she tells Walser about the first attempt. A rich lunatic buys her to sacrifice her in a ritual of his own invention that he thinks will make him immortal. He "apostrophizes" her as "manifestation of Arioriph, Venus, Achamatoth, Sophia" (81). Clearly, he desires her not as a human being but as a hodgepodge of the symbols he tries to impose on her. Her greed for the treasures he offers her allows her to be kidnapped. When she sees he is about to stab her, she escapes from this obvious danger by attacking with her own sword and flying away. Her courage and quick action save her; this heroine rescues herself.

However, she has not quite learned her lesson about the connection between men paying money for her and their treatment of her as an object, and so she falls into another trap, lured by a Grand Duke in St. Petersburg who tempts her with gifts of diamond jewelry. Although Lizzie, her wily companion/mother figure, senses danger in Fevvers's visit to the Grand Duke, Fevvers herself does not fear him until she notices that his hall lacks windows through which she can fly to freedom. He then breaks the sword that had protected her in her previous danger. She finally recognizes the Duke's plans for her when he offers her a tiny jeweled egg containing a gold cage in which he intends to keep her, making real her theme song, "Only a bird in a gilded cage." He will use her own stage image to trap her. In one of the more surreal moments in the novel, Fevvers chooses instead an egg containing a toy train, which somehow turns into the real Trans-Siberian Express, allowing her to escape. After this scare, she repudiates her greed by throwing away the diamond jewelry he gave her. She has also learned to repudiate the dangerous image of the caged bird she created for herself.

Fevvers's near miss and her growing attraction to Walser precipitate a bout of depression and introspection in section three. Lizzie forces her to examine her identity, accusing her of becoming "more and more like [her] own publicity" (198). Lizzie reminds her that she must seize her freedom to create her own autonomous identity and refuse to be the object that her profession demands her to be: "You never existed before. . . . You haven't any history and there are no expectations of you except the ones you yourself create" (198). Since Fevvers is associated with the New Woman of the twentieth-century, Lizzie's message may be intended for all of us about to usher in another century and its even Newer Women.

In this last section of the novel, Fevvers must negotiate the most subtle danger of all, that of "throwing herself away," as Lizzie puts it, in marriage, allowing the kiss of the magic prince to trap her in her appearance. Will her love for Walser be the same kind of trap as her greed? At the end of the novel, her and Walser's journeys to self-discovery converge, and she hopes that he remains malleable enough for her to shape or objectify: "I'll make him into the New Man . . . fitting mate for the New

Woman" (281). As it turns out, neither can pin down or objectify the other, although the potential for doing so lies on both sides. During this critical moment, however, as they readjust their views of each other, Carter illustrates Fevvers's complex relationship to the gaze. First, she resists becoming either object or symbol to Walser and the tribal shaman who is his tutor: "She felt her outlines waver; she felt herself trapped forever in the reflection in Walser's eyes. For one moment, just one moment, Fevvers suffered the worst crisis of her life: 'Am I fact? or am I fiction? Am I what I know I am? Or am I what he thinks I am?'" (290). Prompted by Lizzie, she spreads her wings, one broken and both molting (her trip to Siberia has "diminished" her), and astonishes her viewers. She fits neither the categories created for her by the shaman and his temporarily befuddled pupil, nor those symbols partly imposed on her and partly self-invented earlier in the novel. She has escaped the confinement of the objectifying gaze.

At this point, however, Carter pushes her examination of the gaze one step further. Although Fevvers fears losing her human identity by being "trapped in the reflection in Walser's eyes," she invites and revels in the gaze of the tribespeople in the hut: "the eyes that told her who she was" (290). The difference between these two gazes, the one that diminishes and the one that "refreshes," is not immediately apparent. Perhaps the villagers' gaze, filled with "wonder," "astonishment," and "awe," does not categorize Fevvers, but, since it is more generalized, restores rather than diminishes her self-esteem.

As Walser fails to objectify Fevvers, so her plan for reshaping him fizzles out when she realizes that he has already "reconstructed" himself after losing his memory when their circus train wrecked. Moreover, the now-awakened but still partly amnesiac reporter no longer attempts to confine her as he fires new questions at her: "What is your name? Have you a soul? Can you love?" She approves of this new interest in her humanity rather than her symbolic value.

Until now, Lizzie's earlier question remains unresolved: will the obligatory happy ending—marriage—require Fevvers to "give" herself to Walser? The "Envoi" gives an answer. As Walser orally reconstructs his identity, including a reference to "my wife, Mrs. Sophie Walser" (294), he abruptly stops, saying "Oh!"—presumably in response to Fevvers's sexual advances. When he resumes talking, he avoids using the "married" name for her. Also, he is surprised to learn that, contrary to her insistence earlier in the novel, she is not a virgin. Fevvers has successfully controlled her image not only in Walser's eyes but also in ours. She feels so pleased with having fooled him that she lets rip a gargantuan "spiralling tornado" of laughter that magically creates laughter all over the world. Far from giving herself away, Fevvers has grown larger in her union with Walser, as shown by this cosmic laughter in the grandest of all happy endings.

Rory Turner has explored Fevvers's ability to be object of wonder without losing her humanity, and asserts that "she is full-blown symbol but she is also a living, changing, thinking person" (42): "She is a double symbol, one breaking out of the other. First, she is a frozen, virginal queen of ambiguity and wonder, a fetishized commodity in male fantasy without any room for her swarming subjectivity. Beyond that, she is gro-tesque [in the Bakhtinian sense], uncontained and uncontainable, a sym-bol that defies placement in any structure except finally the newborn anti-structure of freely given love" (48). By the end of the novel, for both Walser and the reader, Fevvers is more than just something to look at. Along the way, she also learns about herself as object.

Perhaps Carter felt that she made her fullest statement about the sub-ject/object paradigm in *Nights at the Circus,* for the theme is muted in her last novel, *Wise Children,* even though the twin protagonists' careers as showgirls would seem to call for a more foregrounded treatment of it. However, compared to the previous works examined in this essay, *Wise Children* contains fewer passages about objectification. Carter does add a few new twists to the theme in this novel, though. Dora Chance, the narrator, and her twin, Nora, take more active control in their careers than does Fevvers. Fevvers emphasizes the portions of her life when she posed as a living statue. Moreover, she never fully uses or feels unre-strained pleasure in her miraculous wings. Ironically, she must conceal her powers to maintain her essential mystery, "Is she fact or is she fic-tion?" Her wings are a burden. On the other hand, Dora makes a firm distinction between passive posing on stage and the more active roles she and her sister perform. She bemoans the nudie shows at the "fag end of vaudeville" (59) that caused her profession to decline: "There was a law that said, a girl could show her all provided she didn't move, not twitch a muscle, stir an inch—just stand there, starkers, letting herself be looked at. . . . We always kept our gee-strings and our panties on, mind. Never stripped. We'd still sing, we'd still dance" (165). The activity of singing and dancing is of central importance to the Chance sisters; they display their art, not their bodies, and their art gives them pleasure in their lives: the last sentence of the novel, which is also a refrain throughout, is "What a joy it is to dance and sing!" Even though their profession requires them to be looked at, they maintain their subject-ness as active creators of art rather than objects.

Carter does not posit a world where women are free from the male gaze and their own objectifications of themselves, but rather worlds where women learn to deal with this inevitability. Awareness of the dangers is the first step, as she shows in *The Magic Toyshop* and "The Bloody Chamber." Reversing the paradigm by making the male the object is one possible recourse, as "The Tiger's Bride," "The Company of Wolves," and *Nights at the Circus* suggest. But in these three works, too, the sharing of the roles of subject and object by male and female makes a happier ending. And, finally, the best protection against becoming an object, as the Chance sisters illustrate, is living one's life as fully, actively, and autonomously as possible.

Selected Works by Angela Carter

"Ashputtle: Or, the Mother's Ghost." *Village Voice* 13 Mar. 1990: S22–23.

Black Venus. London: Hogarth Press, 1985.

The Bloody Chamber. New York: Harper & Row, 1979.

"Bloody Chamber." *Triquarterly* 47 (Winter 1980): 142–82.

Burning Your Boats: The Collected Short Stories. New York: Henry Holt & Company, 1996.

Come Unto These Yellow Sands. Newcastle upon Tyne: Bloodaxe, 1985.

"The Curse of Ancient Egypt." *New Statesman and Society* 1 Sept. 1989: 31–32.

"Dark Tower." *Triquarterly* 35 (Winter 1976): 45–46.

"Desperate Poignancy." *Atlas* 19 (Oct. 1970): 21–25.

"An Earthquake in My Family." *New York Times Book Review* 6 Apr. 1986: 7.

"The Encyclopedia of the Dead." *New York Times Book Review* 23 Apr. 1989: 14.

Expletives Deleted: Selected Writings. London: Chatto & Windus, 1992.

The Fairy Tales of Charles Perrault. Trans. Angela Carter and Martin Mare. London: Victor Gollancz, 1977.

Fireworks. 1974. Rev. ed. London: Chatto & Windus, 1987.

"Forty Means You Cry." *New York Times Book Review* 13 Aug. 1989: 3.

"Forty-Seventeen." *New York Times Book Review* 13 Aug. 1989: 3.

"Foxybaby." *New York Times Book Review* 24 Nov. 1985: 1.

Heroes and Villains. London: Heinemann, 1969.

Honeybuzzard. New York: Simon and Schuster, 1967.

The Infernal Desire Machines of Doctor Hoffman: A Novel. London: Rupert Hart-Davis, 1972.

Introduction. *Villette.* By Charlotte Brontë. London: Virago, 1990.

"Is Santa Claus Really St. Nicholas or Just Some Jolly, Beery Old Elf?" *New York Times Book Review* 7 Dec. 1986: 7.

The Magic Toyshop. London: Heinemann, 1967.

"A Magical Moment in Prague." *New York Times Book Review* 10 Feb. 1991: 1.

"Masochism for the Masses." *New Statesman* 3 June 1983: 8.

"The Miracle Game." *New York Times Book Review* 10 Feb. 1992: 1.

"Missing the Titanic, Drowning in the Bath." *New York Times Book Review* 6 Apr. 1986: 7.

"The Mummy: Or Ramses the Damned." *New Statesman and Society* 1 Sept. 1989: 31.

Nights at the Circus. New York: Viking, 1985.

"Notes from a Maternity Ward." *New Statesman* 16 Dec. 1983: 25.

Nothing Sacred: Selected Writings. London: Virago, 1982.

The Passion of New Eve. New York: Harcourt Brace Jovanovich, 1977.

"A Ribbon around a Bomb." *New Statesman and Society* 12 May 1989: 32–33.

"Rumors Come Too Often True." *New York Times Book Review* 23 Apr. 1989: 14.

The Sadeian Woman and the Ideology of Pornography. New York: Pantheon, 1978.

Several Perceptions. London: Heinemann, 1968.

Shadow Dance. London: Heinemann, 1966.

"Tokyo: Choreography of Protest." *Nation* 3 Nov. 1969: 476.

"Told and Re-told: Picture Books 2." *Times Literary Supplement* 29 Nov. 1985: 1360.

The Virago Book of Fairy Tales. Ed. Angela Carter. London: Virago, 1990.

Wayward Girls and Wicked Women: An Anthology of Stories. Ed. Angela Carter. London: Virago, 1986.

Wise Children. London: Chatto & Windus, 1991.

The Second Virago Book of Fairy Tales. Ed. Angela Carter. London: Virago, 1992.

SELECTED WORKS ABOUT ANGELA CARTER

Brown, Richard. "Postmodern Americas in the Fiction of Angela Carter." *Forked Tongues? Comparing Twentieth-Century British and American Literature.* Ed. Ann Massa and Alistair Stead. London: Longman, 1994. 92–110.

Bryant, Sylvia. "Reconstructing Oedipus through 'Beauty and the Beast.'" *Criticism: A Quarterly for Literature and the Arts* 31.4 (Fall 1989): 439–53.

Clark, Robert. "Angela Carter's Desire Machine." *Women's Studies: An Interdisciplinary Journal* 14.2 (1987): 147–61.

Duncker, Patricia. "Re-Imagining the Fairy Tales: Angela Carter's 'Bloody Chambers.'" *Literature and History: A Journal for the Humanities* 10.1 (Spring 1984): 3–14.

Goldsworthy, Kerryn. "Angela Carter." *Meanjin* 44.1 (March 1985): 4–13.

Haase, Donald P. "Is Seeing Believing? Proverbs and the Film Adaptation of a Fairy Tale." *Proverbium: Yearbook of International Proverb Scholarship* 7 (1990): 89–104.

Hanson, Clare. "Each Other: Images of Otherness in the Short Fiction of Doris Lessing, Jean Rhys, and Angela Carter." *Journal of the Short Story in English* 10 (Spring 1988): 67–82.

Kinmonth, Patrick. "'Step Into My Cauldron': A Chat with Angela Carter." *Vogue* Feb. 1985: 224.

Landon, Brooks. "Eve at the End of the World: Sexuality and Reversal of Expectations in Novels by Joanna Russ, Angela Carter, and Thomas Berger." *Erotic Universe: Sexuality and Fantastic Literature.* New York: St. Martin's, 1986. 61–74.

Lewallen, Avis. "Wayward Girls But Wicked Women? Female Sexuality in Angela Carter's 'The Bloody Chamber.'" *Perspectives on Pornography: Sexuality in Film and Literature.* Ed. Gary Day and Clive Bloom. New York: Greenwood, 1986. 144–58.

Lokke, Kari E. "Bluebeard and 'The Bloody Chamber': The Grotesque of Self-Parody and Self-Assertion." *Frontiers: A Journal of Women's Studies* 10.1 (1988): 7–12.

Mitgang, Herbert. "A Separate World in South London." *New York Times Book Review* 7 Sept. 1986: 129.

Moore, Steven. "Writers in Conversation: Kathy Acker, William Burroughs, Angela Carter, William Gaddis, et al." *Review of Contemporary Fiction* (Fall 1989): 230–31.

Palmer, Paulina. "From 'Coded Mannequin' to Bird Woman: Angela Carter's Magic Flight." *Women Reading Women's Writing.* Brighton, England: Harvester, 1987. 177–205.

Punter, David. "Angela Carter: Supersessions of the Masculine." *Critique: Studies in Modern Fiction* 25.4 (Summer 1984): 209–22.

———. "Essential Imaginings: The Novels of Angela Carter and Russell

Hoban." *The British and Irish Novel since 1960.* Ed. James Acheson. New York: St. Martin's, 1991. 142–158.

Review of Contemporary Fiction: Special Angela Carter Issue 14.3 (Fall 1994).

Rose, Ellen Cronan. "Through the Looking Glass: When Women Tell Fairy Tales." *The Voyage In: Fictions of Female Development.* Ed. Elizabeth Abel, Marianne Hirsch, and Elizabeth Langland. Hanover, NH: UP of New England for Dartmouth College, 1983. 209–27.

Schmidt, Ricarda. "The Journey of the Subject in Angela Carter's Fiction." *Textual Practice* 3.1 (Spring 1989): 56–75.

Smith, Amanda. "Angela Carter" [interview]. *Publishers Weekly* 4 Jan. 1985: 74–75.

Snitnow, Ann. "Conversation with a Necromancer." *Village Voice Literary Supplement* 75 (June 1989): 14, 15–16.

Turner, Rory P. B. "Subjects and Symbols: Transformations of Identity in *Nights at the Circus.*" *Folklore Forum* 20.1–2 (1987): 39–60.

Wilson, Robert Rawdon. "Angela Carter, In/Out/In the Post-Modern Nexus." *Past the Last Post: Theorizing Post-Colonialism and Post-Modernism.* Ed. Ian Adam and Helen Tiffin. Calgary: U of Calgary P, 1990. 109–23.

Wyatt, Jean. "The Violence of Gendering: Castration Images in Angela Carter's *The Magic Toyshop, The Passion of New Eve,* and 'Peter and the Wolf.'" *Women's Studies: An Interdisciplinary Journal* 25.6 (1996): 549–70.

12
During Mother's Absence: The Fiction of Michèle Roberts

Clare Hanson

Michèle Roberts is one of the most interesting and accomplished writers working in English. Her fiction is vivid, sensuous, and imaginative, its formal inventiveness matching the richness of her vision and insight. Roberts explores many of the key issues facing women today, but from the perspective of a woman half-English and half-French, split between nations and identities. She was born in 1949, the daughter of a French mother and an English father, and has published to date nine novels, two volumes of poetry, and a collection of short stories. Her first novel, *A Piece of the Night* (1978), was the first work of new fiction published by The Women's Press, and immediately established her as an original and powerful voice. In the novels that followed—*The Visitation* (1983), *The Wild Girl* (1984), *The Book of Mrs. Noah* (1987), *In the Red Kitchen* (1990)—Roberts explored women's identities and passions in complex fictions that suggestively weave together history, myth, and fiction. In 1992 her *Daughters of the House* was short-listed for the Booker Prize and won the W. H. Smith Literary Award. She also published the short story collection *During Mother's Absence* (1993) and the novels *Flesh and Blood* (1994), *Impossible Saints* (1998), and *Fair Exchange* (1999).

Roberts is one of a generation of British women writers profoundly affected by the second wave of feminism in the 1960s and 1970s. Like

Angela Carter, Roberts sees her writing identity as inseparably bound up with her feminism. In her essay "Questions and Answers" in Michelene Wandor's collection *On Gender and Writing* (1983), she writes that "accepting and questioning my femaleness is inseparable from accepting and questioning my drive to write" (63–64). In this essay she describes her alienation during adolescence from the view of femininity purveyed in the late 1950s and early 1960s, and its adverse effect on her early writing. Only when she discovered the women's liberation movement in 1970 was she able to write authentically, realizing that "I wasn't mad so much as confused and angry" (64). Feminism provided the terms through which identity could be tested, questioned, and challenged, but was itself questioning and fluid—hence the diversity of the fiction it inspired. So, although we can link such writers as Roberts and Carter through their involvement with feminism, considerable differences distinguish their separate works. One could, indeed, see Roberts as a kind of antithesis to Carter, a view which I pursue in this essay. Where Roberts differs from Carter is in her commitment to what she calls "the mother principle, the feminine principle" (65). Carter denies the existence of the feminine: for her the feminine is an invention, a dangerous invention, a social fiction palmed off on her as "the real thing." Roberts, on the other hand, emphasizes the ways in which "feminine" values have been suppressed in our culture. Just as women have, historically and physically, been oppressed in Western culture, so, she suggests, the qualities traditionally associated with them have been derogated and downgraded. Roberts does *not* insist on any essential link between feminine qualities and the female body, but she does suggest that the derogation of the feminine is profoundly damaging and destructive for our culture. In this respect her work has, as we might expect, affinities with French psychoanalytic feminism, although it is also nourished by the work of Freud, Klein, and Jung.

Roberts has memorably described her writing as driven by the quest for the lost mother. In 1983 she wrote:

When I began trying to analyse (because I was asked to) my need to write, several years ago, I came up with an explanation I tracked down as echoing aspects of the work of Sigmund Freud and Melanie Klein. I know that I write out of the experience of loss; the earliest experience of that is the loss of my mother. Loss is an emptiness filled with terrifying feelings: burning hate, sizzling despair, rage that tears you apart. I hated my mother (the fantasy image of her I constructed inside myself) for not always being there when I wanted her, or as much as I needed. She hadn't wanted twin daughters, but a son. ("Questions and Answers" 64)

As Roberts herself points out, her description of the origins of her writing echoes Melanie Klein's account of the child's need to internalize the mother as "good object" following the early separation between them. Klein describes the way in which the child's initial rage and aggression toward the (lost) mother must be channeled into the creation of a restorative and reparative image of her which can in turn form the basis of the image of the self. In one of her essays, Klein argues that this reparative process structures the entire oeuvre of the painter Ruth Kjar, and a similar dynamic operates in Roberts's fiction. However, this interpretation does not mean that her work should be seen as narrowly therapeutic. Indeed, one of the most important qualities of Roberts's fiction is its movement away from the subjective preoccupation with the mother which marks the work of many earlier twentieth-century writers, most notably Virginia Woolf. As Roberts herself explains in the essay quoted above, she sees the loss of the mother as having a cultural significance that goes far beyond the personal experience of loss. She writes: "I now see the loss as on a different, larger scale, and the reparation likewise. I still think that women, though embedded in the heart, factory and kitchen of culture, are treated as though we are peripheral to it; and many of us feel like exiles. Certainly my new (unfinished) novel tackles the theme of separation on this scale" (65).

This emphasis on the wider cultural context distinguishes Roberts's work and also links it with the work of French feminists such as Luce Irigaray. Irigaray contends that the whole of our culture in the West rests upon "the murder of the mother." For Irigaray, our philosophical systems depend on an unacknowledged foundation, the unsymbolized maternal-feminine. Women have no identity within the symbolic order: they exist in relation to it as its residue or its waste. As a result they live in what she calls a state of "*déréliction*," a term Margaret Whitford translates as meaning "abandoned by God."[1] This definition, I think, comes very close to what Roberts means when she says that women feel "like exiles." Roberts, raised as a Catholic, emphasizes in her writing the ways in which women are denied not only subject status but also spiritual identity within our culture. For Roberts, as for Irigaray, the loss of the mother, or as Roberts puts it, "the loss of any symbol of the power of the female" ("Questions and Answers" 65), is damaging not just politically, but also ethically and spiritually.

For Irigaray, the unsymbolized mother-daughter relationship constitutes the greatest threat to the symbolic order as we know it. To think this relation amounts to undermining the symbolic order, introducing as it does feminine identity and difference into the economy of the same. Indeed, the exploration of this pivotal relationship lies at the heart of Roberts's fiction, too. Paradoxically, however, Roberts's emphasis on articulating difference is linked to a drive to find unity, to heal the split between the masculine and the feminine in each of us. Both individually and collectively, she suggests, we must own the repressed/oppressed feminine if we are to achieve wholeness. It is perhaps relevant at this point to note again that Roberts is not only half-French and half-English, but also a twin: hence, perhaps, her constant preoccupation with fragmentation and wholeness, splitting and unity. She has written, "That *is* my myth: the quest for wholeness" ("Write, She Said" 233). It is also worth emphasizing at this point that although Roberts's work bears the traces of a rich mixture of influences and sources, it could never be seen either as derivative or as mechanically "applying" theory in fictional practice. To borrow a metaphor from her first novel, *A Piece of the Night,* one could say that she takes images and fragments from a range of sources and turns them into a rich and nourishing broth of her own—or witches' brew, perhaps.

A Piece of the Night is a sensuous and dazzling first novel in which Roberts conveys through metaphor and through the texture of her prose the troubled state of the central character, Julie. As a note at the beginning of the novel tells us, "julienne" is a French term for a mixture of vegetables for soup. In the novel this soup is fed to generations of the men in Julie's family, like a kind of domestic version of the body and blood of Christ, only this time the sacrificial body is feminine: "Monsieur Fanchot père called his wife soupe, or else he called soupe his wife, Julie was never sure which: la mère soupe, dabbing with his large white napkin at the traces of carrots, potatoes, onions clinging to his fat silky moustache" (36). The question which the novel brilliantly explores is whether woman can exist independently of her position as "la mère soupe"—or, in Irigaray's more abstract terms, can she have an identity in the symbolic order distinct from the nurturing function? Roberts has also said that this novel "asked and tried to answer the question: how can women love each other[?]" ("Questions and Answers" 67): in other words, the novel approaches the question of women's identity through the "key" of woman-to-woman relationships. The prototype for all woman-to-woman relationships is the mother-daughter relationship, which is central to this as to all Roberts's novels. The relationship between Julie and her mother, one of fluid intersubjectivity and utmost need, conforms with uncanny accuracy to Irigaray's account of the cultural situation of women as mothers and daughters. Irigaray argues that the fluidity of the relationship between mother and daughter is the symptom of their not being represented in the symbolic. Because neither is defined as individual subject but both occupy, actually or potentially, the "place of the mother," their relationship to each other cannot be properly articulated. Irigaray also argues, more generally, that because the child's relation to the mother is not adequately symbolized, he or she may suffer from an uncontrollable need for the mother, "what is known in analytic therapies as orality, infinite thirst, the desire to be gratified by her that we hear so much about."[2] Such an unsatisfactory and unsatisfying identification with the mother corresponds exactly to Julie's experience:

> Love is her duty: a mother gives and gives. I snatch at her fat breast, she winces. We glare at one another. Love is a battle now, between the two of us. I suck too eagerly, I choke on love and sweetness. Am I allowed to go at my own speed, am I allowed to suck to satiety? And why not? She feeds me when she, not I, decides I need it because she, like me, does not recognise that there are boundaries between us. (137)

Roberts links this memory seamlessly with Julie's experience of *dérélic-tion*, her sense of abandonment by a church which cannot stop her hunger or her need because it fails to recognize either her spiritual being or that of her mother:

> Neither of us, the ageing mother, the adolescent daughter, is much impressed with life for women after puberty. We concentrate instead on our eternal hopes. We swallow the Christ, who should be our sufficiency. We are two heretics who get up, sighing still with

hunger. . . . The priest reads the Fathers of the Church on the vo-
raciousness of women. (137)

In exploring the question "how can women love each other?" Roberts
uses in this novel what she calls the two "icons" of the nun and the lesbian, both being women without men. Roberts interweaves Julie's story
with the briefer and more muted story of Sister Veronica, an aging nun
in the convent where Julie has gone to school. Sister Veronica's life appears as one of "patient self-murder." In her youth she had traveled in
Asia, but felt rejected by the gods of Asia, who "exiled" her, denying her
a soul because she was a woman. After she takes the veil, the god of
the Catholic Church does the same, requiring of her nothing but patient
self-abnegation. This pattern reaches its logical conclusion when, feeling
ill, she chooses to "accelerate death" by lying out in the rain in the re-
motest part of the convent garden. Traditionally, the life of the nun has
been seen as offering some independence for women: by abjuring all relations with men, nuns gain a spiritual status denied to other women.
However, as Marina Warner has pointed out, this status is profoundly
problematic, founded as it is on denial of the female body and of female sexuality.[3] In *A Piece of the Night,* Roberts contrasts the path taken
by Sister Veronica with Julie's identification of herself as a lesbian and
her learning to celebrate the female body and female sexuality. Through
her love affair with Jenny, Julie rediscovers the life of the female body
which her husband has denied her, and through the mutuality of this
woman-to-woman relationship learns to "recognize" herself: "I want you
to mirror me, to bring me out of confusion and lack of self into recognition of self and acceptance of a pattern I share and shape, fusion that
is not drowning. While you are here, having chosen me, I know who I
am" (127).

However, this process of feminine self-discovery has its darker side,
and Roberts's exploration of this constitutes one of the most interesting
and radical aspects of her fiction. During her marriage, Julie reflects on
the fact that, whether by her own or by other women's definition, she
has no existence: "in men's consciousness she remains part of the natural
world, the perimeter to his centre . . . a repository for all he fears to be"
(68–69). For this reason, in the passage that gives the novel its title, she
thinks of herself in negative terms as "a piece of the night, broken off

from it, a lump, a fragment of dark" (84). However, in the second half of the novel, although Roberts emphasizes the positive possibilities opened up through Julie's relationships with Jenny, with her mother, and with her daughter, she does not simply jettison or erase all the negative or "dark" imagery earlier connected with the feminine. In Roberts's fiction, a positive feminine identity is possible, but this does not mean that the negative qualities associated with femininity can simply be denied or abandoned. Conventionally, femininity is linked with passivity, nature, and the body, as opposed to the "masculine" qualities or attributes of activity, culture, and spirit. For many feminists, the point of feminism is precisely to challenge these conventional identifications and to enable women to take up a "masculine" subject position. Roberts's fiction, however, insists on the need for both men and women to find a new, plural subjectivity. Within this subjectivity "masculine" and "feminine" would coexist. Such a multiplicity would ideally extend to wider cultural identities and meanings, so that the repressed "feminine" aspects of our culture might be restored and returned to it. Nature, the body, and even death would no longer be consigned to the unconscious: the repressed would be allowed to surface. As Roberts explains it in "Questions and Answers": "The repressed feminine principle struggles for birth. The female body, my knowledge of it, becomes part of my prose. . . . I'm back to Demeter and Persephone: what does Persephone's sojourn underground teach her, and what does she tell Demeter on her return?" (68).

Roberts's third novel, *The Wild Girl,* takes up this question, exploring the connections among the feminine, the unconscious, and death. Perhaps Roberts's most passionate and polemical work of fiction, *The Wild Girl* retells the story of Jesus through an invented "fifth gospel" of Mary Magdalene. A point of departure for the novel may have been the work done by feminist theologians on the distortion of Jesus' teaching by later Christians, but the novel is important less as part of a debate about history than as a powerful indictment of the disavowal of the feminine in Western religious thought. The novel tells the story of Mary's early life, her imagined love affair with Jesus, and her life with Jesus and the apostles. It imagines a relation of reciprocity between Mary and Jesus, each learning from the other. So, for example, Jesus is led to contest the misogyny of established religious systems after hearing Mary's anger over the priests' rejection of women. He is led to make the most explicit state-

ment anywhere in Roberts's fiction about the need for balance and harmony and the need to integrate masculine and feminine principles.
Speaking to Simon Peter, he says:

—So, Simon, be like Mary, for she is trying to join the male to the
female inside herself, and to break down the boundaries between
what is above and what is below, and what is inside and what is
outside, and to become whole. . . . You must do the same for yourself: first you must know what is male, and what is above, and what
is outside, and then you must learn from the woman how to join
her and become whole, as Mary is learning from me and I from her.
(61–62)

Jesus here reproduces the metaphors that structure Western religious
and philosophical thought. The feminine, seen as that which is "inside"
and "below," is thus linked with the unconscious and the body, while the
masculine, both "above" and "outside," is linked with the transcendent
spirit. Roberts seizes on the metaphorical structure which Irigaray has
also seen as subtending Western thought. In her analysis of Plato's allegory of the cave, Irigaray argues that Western philosophy is founded on
the following structural oppositions:

Between the "world outside" and the "world inside," between the
"world above" and the "world below." Between the light of the sky
and the fire of the earth. Between the gaze of the man who has left
the cave and that of the prisoner. Between truth and shadow, between truth and fantasy, between "truth" and whatever "veils" the
truth. . . . Between the intelligible and the sensible.[4]

The novel explores these issues further through Mary's dream-vision
of the creation of the world and Jesus' interpretation of it. Mary's dream
offers an alternative account of creation in which origins are dual: masculine and feminine, darkness and light are equally aspects of God.
However, Mary dreams that in time the feminine part of God, Sophia,
has a son who forgets that he was born of the duality of God, and believes that he has created himself. Sophia names him Ignorance, and his
children become "the adversaries of the fullness of God" (82). Jesus argues that Mary's dream is a warning about the consequences of ignoring
the wholeness of God:

Men have forgotten the feminine and the darkness, and praise only the masculine and the light. The children of Ignorance are the adversaries of God because they prevent the man and the woman from living out the fullness of God. The children of Ignorance perpetuate a false creation, a world in which one side of knowledge is stifled, in which barriers are set up between man and woman, body and soul, civilization and nature. (82)

Here Jesus voices Roberts's critique of a patriarchal symbolic order, which she sees as a "false creation" founded on oppression and repression. The issue of repression is particularly important for Roberts. She is, as we have seen, a feminist interested not merely in the achievement of equal rights but also in the ways in which, individually and collectively, we repress and disavow aspects of "the feminine" which are currently seen negatively but which in her view need to be re-valued and reviewed. One of the most powerful aspects of her fiction is its evocation of those aspects of the feminine which inspire horror—the body/matter, the unconscious (including the death drives), and death itself. Insofar as possible, death is written into *The Wild Girl*, through Mary Magdalene's experience after Jesus' crucifixion. In a vision, Mary travels to the place "of the lost Mother, of death, of the dark side of God" (115). In an imaginative tour de force, Roberts describes Mary's journey through the bitter waters of dissolution into a "fierce and chilling sea" (115). In this section, a kind of unraveling of the self takes place as we are taken "back" to the experience of what Julia Kristeva calls "abjection," that pre-Oedipal state in which we are unable to establish boundaries between the self and the other/mother: "I alternately bobbed and sank for what seemed like an endless stretch of time, with no division between night and day and neither sun nor moon to lighten the deep in which I kicked and tried to stay alive. . . . My life was not my own: I tossed up and down at the mercy of currents and winds and could not steer" (*Wild Girl* 115). The "unutterable wastes of black seas" (115) represent aspects of one's own or the maternal body from which one struggles to escape in the process of individuation: here Mary reverses the process, and yields to engulfment in matter. Yet at the limit point of the imagination, the point of death, Mary experiences a rebirth under the sign of Salome, who describes herself as "the ancient one. . . . She who has many names" (*DH* 95). Salome, the feminine principle, represents at this point the death which men fear and deny. Mary's rebirth under her tutelage does not necessarily imply a belief in personal immortality; rather, it points to what Roberts in the 1983 essay calls a "mystical" acceptance of the necessary relation between opposing principles: masculine and feminine, life and death. As she writes in "Questions and Answers": "We're all part of the nitrogen cycle, the dance of atoms. Life begins below ground; the plants push up their green tips after the long death of winter" (68).

The Wild Girl is preoccupied, then, with Roberts's "myth of wholeness," particularly the affirmation of the life of the body in the context of a religion that denies it. *Daughters of the House* (1992) takes up and applies further pressure to these themes. In this novel, the Christian myth of the fall from grace into sexuality and death (the fall from the spirit into the body) is replaced as a framing myth by another which derives from Lacanian psychoanalysis and which also structures French feminist theory. This is the myth of the fall from a pre-Oedipal fullness of being into a being-in-language characterized by fracture and separation (a fall from the body into the spirit, as it were). Roberts uses the Lacanian story as just that, a powerful and suggestive myth which she appropriates for her own creative ends: she is in no sense simply "following" French feminist doctrine. As in *The Wild Girl,* she also stresses the interdependence of aspects of being (such as body and soul) which are conventionally opposed to each other.

The title of the novel points to the inherent importance of the relation with the mother. The house is a metaphor for the body of the mother, and the project of the novel, metaphorically speaking, is to define the relationship of two daughters to a lost mother. (The two daughters are in fact cousins, and no single mother figure exists, but the metaphorical structure is clear.) The daughters, utterly opposed in temperament, appear to represent aspects of a split self. Léonie is the materialist, Thérèse the idealist, and the form and style of the novel reflects these differences, as Roberts herself has noted: "The story of a woman obsessed with material possessions *had* to be told as her inventory of the contents of her house; the story of the cousin she quarrelled with *had* to be a saint's autobiography that could quarrel with the version contained in the inventory" ("Postscript" 171). The novel is the story of a struggle over the meaning of the feminine, both inside and outside the Church. Reunited in middle life because of the reopening and violating of a grave, the cousins remember their early life together and the scenes and images that shaped their respective identities. The novel tracks back to the death of Thérèse's mother, Antoinette, which lies at the novel's center. It is after the loss of this mother that the two girls begin to have diametrically opposed, competing visions of the Virgin Mary. Léonie envisions a black and red Madonna—a virgin who is not a virgin but a woman with a sexual life. When she sees this woman, whose sexual, bodily, feminine identity is not denied but affirmed, Léonie is reminded of the earliest stage of union with the mother and of communication by rhythm and touch (the stage which Kristeva calls the semiotic):

> Something outside her, mysterious and huge, put out a kindly exploring hand and touched her. . . .
> . . . Then she remembered it. A language she once knew but had forgotten about, forgotten ever hearing, forgotten she could speak. Deeper than English or French; not foreign; her own. She had heard it spoken long ago. She heard it now, at first far off, thin gold, then close, warm. The secret language, the underground stream that forced through her like a river. (86)

Thérèse, however, sees her lady in the woods as a more abstractly conventional Virgin figure, and happily recites her familiar attributes: "She had on a long blue dress. Her hair, which was long and fair, was almost completely covered by her white veil. Her hands were clasped, and she carried a crystal rosary over one arm. Her feet were bare, and there was a golden rose resting on the toes of each one" (95).

As we move back through the folds of memory and time which structure the novel, we discover that in the place where the girls see their visions, there used to be a shrine with a statue of a goddess holding a bunch of corn, a kind of Bona Dea or fertility goddess, an ancient saint. In the past this was a powerful and magic place, where the villagers came to pray and also to dance at harvest festival time. However, the curé has put a stop to this practice, telling the villagers to pray not in the woods but in the church. The curé, the bishop, and the Church find Thérèse's version of the Virgin infinitely preferable to that of Léonie, for it conforms to religious rather than to pagan tradition. Léonie's goddess is black and red, linked both with strangeness and fertility, whereas Thérèse's goddess troubles none of the conventions surrounding the representation of the sexless Virgin. So while Léonie and Thérèse continue to struggle silently over the meaning of their red and blue visions, the Church accepts Thérèse's version and even builds a chapel to Our Lady according to her specification in place of the old shrine. Subsequently, Thérèse becomes a nun, denying the body in order to advance the spirit, while Léonie lives her life in accordance with her more worldly vision, celebrating the life of the body, marrying and having children.

Throughout the novel, the perspectives of Léonie and Thérèse are held in tension, and although the end of the novel brings surprises and reversals, this tension (or poise) is maintained as each cousin learns to accept the beliefs for which the other stands. At the end of the novel, Thérèse, who has been associated with the father, God, and suffering, dreams of the mother she has denied and whose house she has left. In her dream, she and her sisters from the convent put the dead mother's body back together again, restoring it and making it whole, preparing it for burial. Immediately afterwards, Thérèse goes down to the cellar where she discovers the statue that used to stand in the woods, now buried in a heap of sand "in the airless dark . . . shut up like a cry in a box, the weight of the house pressing on her." During the war her mother had hidden the statue, defying the priest and the Church to preserve it, acting for once in her life "in a way that allied her to the villagers not just to the big house" (162). In descending into the cellar (to the unconscious and hidden), Thérèse has rediscovered the buried or repressed feminine principle, the goddess with "a dark gold face." When she then goes to the church, which is decorated for the harvest festival, she rejects the image of the Virgin sold to her "ready-made" by the priests of her church: "Perfect, that Mother of God, that pure Virgin, a holy doll who never felt angry or sexy and never went away. The convent was the only place where Thérèse could preserve that image intact. Away from there it melted in the heat of her hands" (165–66). Thérèse comes to feel that in accepting the Church's view of women (as virginal or spiritually nonexistent), she has betrayed both her mother and the feminine part of herself. So in a final, transgressive gesture she sets fire to the church and herself, reuniting with the maternal principle in death: "Then, at last, after all these years, she saw her for the first time, that red and gold lady. . . . She was outlined in gold, she held out her hands to her daughter, to pull her in, to teach her the steps of the dance" (166).

While Thérèse is in the church, Léonie wakes from a dream that leaves her restless and troubled. She tries to calm herself by reciting a litany of her possessions, her household gods, but the formula does not work. Then, just as Thérèse is drawn to the cellar of the house, Léonie is drawn to the first floor, to her old bedroom that used to give her nightmares as a child. Something has been hidden in here too, a memory she has fought against all her adult life. Now the opening of the grave and Thérèse's return force Léonie to rediscover words, names, and identities that she has repressed: the names of the Jewish people who were shot in the war, and the identity of the priest (then the curé) who betrayed them to the Germans: "She twisted the handle of the door. She opened it. She paused in the doorway, then went in. The voices came from somewhere just ahead, the shadowy bit she couldn't see. She stepped forward, into the darkness, to find words" (172). At the close of the novel, as the would-be-saint Thérèse comes to recognize the importance of the mother, the body, and death, so Léonie comes to recognize the importance of the father, the spirit, and language. Without words (the symbolic order) Léonie would be unable to name past crimes, and would be exiled from time and history. The novel ends, then, by balancing the claims of the feminine and the masculine, or, in Kristeva's terms, the semiotic and the symbolic. The loss of the mother (who appears at the end of the novel in the guise of Rose, the surrogate mother of both cousins) is seen as a necessary loss or break, a *felix culpa*. Still, however, the novel suggests that the suppression of the feminine within the symbolic—the fact that the feminine is not represented in the symbolic—leads to a profound distortion of subjectivity and culture. How can the feminine be written into our culture? Roberts again takes up this question in her recent novel, the dense and poetic *Flesh and Blood*.

Flesh and Blood is a beautifully and intricately shaped novel, formed like a loop of pearls, moving out to the central jewel, the prose-poem section "Anon," and then back to its starting point. The novel snakes through time and weaves stories together. It opens with the story of Frederica, who thinks she has murdered her mother: Irigaray's "murder of the mother" is here literalized. This is a twentieth-century story, and Frederica's struggle with her mother is a representative one. As a child she loves her mother, who seems the embodiment of feminine glamour, looking like the soignée models in women's magazines. Her mother has converted to Catholicism, and Freddy tends to mix her up with the Virgin Mary, to the extent that when she decides to create a shrine to the Virgin, she decides that relics of her mother will substitute perfectly well for relics of the Virgin, whose bones have been taken up to heaven. Accordingly, she collects traces of the waste from her mother's body (wax from her ears, clippings from her toenails, hair from her hairbrush) and keeps them for her shrine. As Kristeva argues, this is the material of abjection, and Freddy's bizarre collection points to her difficulty over separating from the maternal body. As she grows older, Freddy begins to assert her difference first through her wish to be an artist, second through sexual independence. The mother has difficulty accepting Freddy's different and separate existence: the two seem locked in a struggle over female identity.

The next section moves back to the nineteenth century and tells the story of Felicité, whose name means "happiness" or "bliss." Felicité is given happiness despite the repression of female sexuality in nineteenth-century France. She falls in love with a painter, George, whom we discover to be a cross-dressing woman only much later in the novel. George takes Felicité into a house whose owners have left it, empty in the quiet afternoon. They go to the heart of the house, the main bedroom with a four-poster bed and a tall armoire, "like a small castle inside the heart of the house" (FB 109). The armoire acts as a linen cupboard, clean and sweet-smelling. As an uninvaded, private female space, the cupboard has special significance for Felicité because it is the only positive image she can connect with her impending marriage. This is a space Felicité cannot share with her fiancé, Albert, but she can share it with George, who makes love to her in the dreamlike privacy of the empty house. Later in the novel we may connect the sweetness of this experience with the fact that this is love between women. Violence follows, however, as Albert rapes Felicité to punish her for infidelity. Physical violence leads us into the next tale, which explores some of the more distressing aspects of women's experience in eighteenth-century France. In particular, this section focuses on the power of the Church in shaping, controlling, and distorting women's lives. The central figure, the wealthy Madame de Dureville, aspires to sainthood and, to that end, distances herself as much as possible from the life of the female body. She suffers rather than enjoys her husband's embraces, and when her daughter is born she attempts (successfully) to "mortify her natural desires and impulses," seeing her daughter very seldom and soon sending her away to school. Madame de Dureville further cultivates the life of the spirit by running a penitentiary where the mothers of illegitimate children (often those of her husband) can be brought to "the most abject state of wretchedness and sorrow that the heart of their preceptress could desire" (58). Appropriately enough, given her belief that female sexuality is wicked and degrading, Madame de Dureville marries her daughter to a follower of the Marquis de Sade, a torturer who shares this view of the sinfulness of women. So Roberts traces the connections between religious misogyny and secular sadism.

The Catholic Church comes under further scrutiny in the next section, which tells the story of a small group of nuns in sixteenth-century Italy. The nuns live in the small convent of Santa Salome, ruled over by the narrator's sister. The convent contains the relics of Santa Salome, midwife and patroness of wandering women, and a central figure also in *The Wild Girl.* The abbess's name, Bona, also suggests that this is a community of women dedicated to the feminine aspect of God. Inevitably, this community comes into conflict both with the local people and with the religious hierarchy. Rumors spread of "abominable rites" performed by the nuns, and of "lewd activities" among them. As a result, the Inquisition is called in and the story-fragment ends with the abbess under threat.

All the tales so far have tended toward violence and have ended with the heroine in some kind of predicament or danger. Collectively they portray a world of chance and danger, in which women are often physically at risk. However, in the next five sections of the novel, Roberts moves us outside time and history to a realm of the imagination which, through fantasy and dream, provides a seed of resistance and renewal enabling the novel's heroines to change the direction of their stories. In this "inner text" we enter the space of the feminine, transhistorical to the extent that it represents a psychological reality. Here Roberts explores and rewrites the key feminine drama of separation from the mother. In the section called "Rosa," Roberts takes us to a landscape of bitter cold and privation. The young girl Rosa (whose name, like "Bona" and "Felicité," forms part of a cluster of "feminine" names in the novel) tells the story of her mother's disappearance in the dead of winter. She simply vanishes, leaving her daughter bereft, tormented by need, physical hunger, and guilt. An angel appears to guide her to a dream landscape which figures both the lost maternal body and that pre-Oedipal stage in the girl's development which Freud describes as "grey with age and shadowy and almost impossible to revivify": "Our insight into this early, pre-Oedipus, phase in girls comes to us as a surprise, like the discovery, in another field, of the Minoan-Mycenaean civilization behind the civilization of Greece."[5]

Rosa's dream-country is fertile and well irrigated, "a great garden" full of fruit and flowers in which images of female creativity abound (the tumbledown bread oven, for example, "like a tiny mosque"). Among images of ease and plenty we are taken back to the origins of self in the bodily relation to the mother. A naked masseuse (with stretch marks on her stomach) traces on the body "love messages for your shut eyes to read": "mamabebe love you are here with you together us now over and over so non-stop mamabebe so wanting you born this love us so close skinskin talking heartbeat belonging with you allowed love home flesh my mamabebe our body singing to you so beautiful love listen mamabebe listen" (109). This lyrical evocation of a state of closeness to the mother seems to haunt the imagination of twentieth-century women writers. Other writers who have attempted to represent it include figures as diverse as Virginia Woolf and Toni Morrison. Does this preoccupation continue because, as Irigaray has claimed, in the early relation with the mother—before she is recognized as mother/other within the symbolic order—the germ of an authentic woman-to-woman relation may be found? Irigaray argues that new ways of speaking about relationships between women must be invented if pressure is to be put on the symbolic order that excludes them. A woman must be able to identify with her mother in a way that does not objectify her: "It is necessary for a woman to be able to speak her identity in words, in images and in symbols within this intersubjective relation with her mother, then with other women, in order to enter into a relation with men that is not destructive."[6] Such speech is, perhaps, what Roberts attempts in this section of *Flesh and Blood*, a generative section that signals and supports a change of direction in the text. So, as Rosa is guided back into time and history, the narrative begins to play with oppositions that had previously seemed ineradicable and binding: between masculine and feminine, virgin and whore, scholar and whore. We learn that these oppositions are not immutable, but simply "the way they do things out there" (116). This fact holds out a possibility of freedom and change which is built on as Rosa restores her dead mother to life. In this reversal of the story of Demeter and Persephone, it is the daughter who brings the mother back from the underworld, melting the ice of death with her own bodily fluid, her hot tears: "I kissed her. My lips burned and blistered on the casing of ice. I kissed her again and again, I sucked and bit her glass flesh, I threw my salt tears on to her, to make her cool surface start to melt, I drove my kisses at her, I hammered an iron spike of crying into that ice block and shivered it to splinters" (116). Here the daughter's tears are like the mother's milk, feeding and sustaining.

The next story yet again turns round the mother-daughter relation, as Bona's mother rescues her from the clutches of the Inquisition. Again the question of female identity is paramount. We learn of the rituals that Bona instituted as abbess, rituals in which the body of women, as opposed to the sacrificial body of Christ, formed the ground of worship. In question here, of course, is not the literal worship of the female body but rather the introduction of the (symbolic) female body into the iconography of religious discourse: "The Abbess bared her breast. She said: this is my body, which was broken and given for you, and this is my blood, which was shed for you. . . . Then each of the nuns came forward and kissed the Abbess's breast, and let her mouth rest there, as though she was an infant being nursed by her mother" (135). We then move to a story "about a beautiful maiden and her quest," revealed as another mother-daughter story in which one of the "magdalenes" treated so badly by Madame de Dureville searches for the daughter who has been taken from her. After many years, she finds not her own daughter but Eugenie, the daughter of Madame de Dureville, who has fallen on hard times and is kept as a freak in a cage at a fair. Marie-Jeanne joins her in her cage, to nurture her and heal the split between mother and daughter.

The split between the masculine and the feminine within the self is healed in the next chapter, which discloses the double life of George/Georgina, a late-nineteenth-century painter. She/he lives as a woman in England and as a man in France, joining the separate parts of herself: she made herself into a marriage. "She married two split parts of herself, drew them together and joined them, and she also let each one flourish individually" (156) Despite the stress on wholeness, the representation/creation of female identity/subjectivity remains at the heart of this section. In one of the most striking scenes of the novel, for example, George returns to Felicité as a heavily pregnant woman. Instead of rejecting this image of fecundity, Felicité receives her with the utmost kindness and insists on giving her the best linen from her own trousseau, a gift that recognizes the validity of the woman-to-woman relation between them. This theme continues in the last sections of the novel, in which we return to the twentieth century and to Freddy/Frederica, whose prayer for her daughter is also an elegy for her mother, and who draws on the past to create an image of female identity for the future. The novel offers itself, its own texture, as an optimistic answer to the questions that have haunted Roberts throughout her career: "I write novels to understand the wordless images, spin a story around them that will lay them, like ghosts. Also to answer questions: can mothers truly love daughters? Does a woman belong in this world and is she allowed to have a house of her own?" ("Postscript" 171).

NOTES

1. Margaret Whitford, *Luce Irigaray: Philosophy in the Feminine* (London: Routledge, 1991), 77.

2. Margaret Whitford, ed., *The Irigaray Reader* (Oxford: Blackwell, 1991), 40.

3. Marina Warner, *Alone of All Her Sex: Myth and the Cult of the Virgin Mary* (New York: Random House, 1983).

4. Luce Irigaray, *Speculum of the Other Woman*, trans. Gillian C. Gill (Ithaca: Cornell UP, 1985), 246–47.

5. The Pelican Freud Library, vol. 7 (London: Penguin Books Ltd., 1977, rpt. 1987), 372.

6. Irigaray, quoted in Whitford, *Luce Irigaray* 45.

SELECTED WORKS BY MICHÈLE ROBERTS

All the Selves I Was: New and Selected Poems. London: Virago, 1995.
The Book of Mrs. Noah. London: Methuen, 1987.
Daughters of the House. London: Virago, 1992.
During Mother's Absence. London: Virago, 1993.
Fair Exchange. London: Little, Brown, 1999.
Flesh and Blood. London: Virago, 1994.
Food, Sex & God: On Inspiration and Writing. London: Virago, 1998.
Impossible Saints: A Novel. Hopewell, NJ: Ecco Press, 1998.
In the Red Kitchen. London: Methuen, 1990.
Mind Readings: Writers' Journeys Through Mental States. London: Minerva, 1996.
The Mirror of the Mother. London: Methuen, 1986.
More Tales I Tell My Mother. London: Journeyman Press, 1987.

A Piece of the Night. London: Women's Press, 1978.

"Postscript." *The Semi-transparent Envelope: Women Writing—Feminism and Fiction.* Sue Roe, Susan Sellers, and Nicole Ward Jouve, with Michèle Roberts. London: Marion Boyars, 1994. 171–175.

Psyche and the Hurricane. London: Methuen, 1991.

"Questions and Answers." *On Gender and Writing.* Ed. Michelene Wandor. London: Pandora Press, 1983. 62–68.

Tales I Tell My Mother (fiction, with Zoe Fairbanks, Sara Maitlad, Valerie Miner and Michelene Wandor). London: Journeyman Press, 1978.

Touch Papers (poetry, with Judith Kazantziz and Michelene Wandor). London: Allison and Busby, 1982.

The Visitation. London: Women's Press, 1983.

The Wild Girl. London: Methuen, 1984.

"Write, She Said." *The Progress of Romance: The Politics of Popular Fiction.* Ed. Jean Radford. London: Routledge and Kegan Paul, 1986. 221–35.

SELECTED WORKS ABOUT MICHÈLE ROBERTS

Luckhurst, Roger. "'Impossible Mourning' in Toni Morrison's *Beloved* and Michèle Roberts's *Daughters of the House.*" *Critique: Studies in Contemporary Fiction* 37.4 (Summer 1996): 243–60.

Sceats, Sarah. "Eating the Evidence: Women, Power, and Food." *Image and Power: Women in Fiction in the Twentieth Century.* Ed. Sarah Sceats and Gail Cunningham. London: Longman, 1996. 117–27.

White, Rosemary. "Five Novels as History: The Life and Times of Michèle Roberts' Prose Fiction." *Bete Noire* 14–15 (1996): 144–57.

———. "Michèle Roberts" [interview]. *Bete Noire* 14–15 (1996): 125–40.

13
Navigating the Interior Journey: The Fiction of Jeanette Winterson

Jan Rosemergy

"I'm not looking for God, only for myself," says Jordan, foundling and world explorer, in *Sexing the Cherry* (115). Each of Jeanette Winterson's novels is a quest to know the self and the world. In the autobiographical *Oranges Are Not the Only Fruit*, a friend advises Winterson's fictional counterpart that one must know the world within as well as the world without: "'There's this world,' [Elsie] banged the wall graphically, 'and there's this world,' she thumped her chest. 'If you want to make sense of either, you have to take notice of both'" (32). In her fiction Winterson portrays the journey into the external world, where gender stereotypes and oppressive institutions of family and religion limit the self. Walls and pollution are recurring metaphors for these social forces that distort the self. She also portrays the interior journey, symbolized by water imagery, where imagination and passion free the self. For Winterson, the very act of creating fiction is a means of liberation. Thus she uses inventive fictional structures and interweaves autobiography, history, satire, myth, and fantasy to feed the spirit—"heart-food" (*Boating for Beginners* 66).

Like her fictional creation Jordan, Winterson is a "foundling," adopted and raised by an evangelical Christian couple in England's industrial Midlands. Her first novel, *Oranges Are Not the Only Fruit* (1985), is a fictional autobiography, by genre a storytelling directed at understanding the self. *Boating for Beginners* (1985) retells the biblical story of the Flood as a contemporary event, satirizing popular culture from religion to romance. Yet threading through the narrative is the story of Gloria, dominated by her mother, who is swimming to the surface of her life, coming to awareness. *The Passion* (1987) tells the stories of Henri, a French soldier serving Napoleon, and Villanelle, a Venetian gambler, who risk life for passion and freedom. The dark maze of Venice's canals operates as a metaphor of the quest that ultimately constitutes an interior journey to self-discovery. In *Sexing the Cherry* (1989), Dog-Woman discovers the corruption of self and soul symbolized by London during the Puritan Revolution, while her foundling son Jordan travels the world in search of the illusive dancer Fortunata, only to discover that the true voyage is an interior journey. Set within contemporary culture, *Written on the Body* (1993) is, literally and figuratively, an anatomical exploration of passion.[1]

The family, most particularly the mother, defines the child's present and future identity—unless the child challenges that definition. Winterson's characterizations of mothers reveal the possibilities of oppression or liberation in the parent-child relationship. In her fictional autobiography *Oranges*, Winterson as author/narrator tells of her adoption by a dominating, evangelical mother. This mother is an Abraham dedicating her long-awaited child, a female Isaac, to God: "She would get a child, train it, build it, dedicate it to the Lord" (10). She is a Zeus creating Venus: her daughter becomes "Her flesh now, sprung from her head. Her vision" (10). In a society where women are often powerless, her mother's strength of will and leadership in her church influence the narrator to aspire to being a "priest" (161), a position of authority in a patriarchal society. Later, when her mother and then her church discover the narrator's lesbianism, they condemn her for being herself. Thus this mother-daughter relationship is both liberating and oppressing.

The theme of maternal domination is continued in *Boating for Beginners*, where Mrs. Munde would determine her daughter Gloria's identity. The mother's name, Latin for "world," implies that as Mrs. Munde overpowers Gloria, so the world overpowers Gloria: "It never occurred to [Mrs. Munde] that Gloria had chosen to be nothing in order to avoid being her mother's something" (20). Mrs. Munde is so forceful that Gloria fears even to touch her, feeling "the way natives feel about looking into a camera: her soul might be transferred by accident" (23).

Both the *Oranges* narrator and Gloria discover that finding one's self requires breaking free of the parent's vision and fabricating one's own vision of the self. In *Oranges*, fairy tale, fantasy, and myth express the narrator's quest for identity. In a fairy tale woven into the story of the young narrator's indoctrination in the Church, a prince searches futilely for a perfect woman to marry. Years later, when he finds a woman who is perfect but not flawless, she refuses to marry him, explaining that his search for perfection is in truth a search for "balance, for harmony" (64), which "lies in the sphere of [his] own hands" (66). He chops off her head and continues his quest. This tale foreshadows the narrator's dilemma that she cannot be the perfect person her mother and her church expect; her true quest involves a search for inner harmony, and the outcome is in her own hands.

After the discovery of the narrator's first lesbian relationship, when her mother and church isolate her to cast out the devil, the narrator intuits that indeed a "demon" dwells within her—a demon who makes her unique. This orange demon, who recurs in Winterson's fiction as a metaphor for the liberating imagination, argues with the narrator, helping her decide what she wants. The narrator asks what will happen if she keeps the demon, who prophesies, "You'll have a difficult, different time" (109).

In *Oranges*, walls symbolize the constructs of family, religion, and society that constrain the self: "Walls protect and walls limit" (112), the narrator realizes. She must decide whether to risk destroying the walls in order to be herself. The narrator's conflict is symbolized in a dream, with her choices presented as a dialogue between herself and her alter ego, who warns that eventually she must choose the wall or herself, safety or freedom. When she asks if the cost of choosing herself is journeying through life unprotected, her alter ego advises her to "distinguish the chalk circle from the stone wall" (112). The walls represent the laws of religion, society, world; they offer safety, yet limit freedom to discover one's self. Even if one risks living in exile rather than in the walled city of society, the quester still has the protection of the chalk circle—an expansive world created by the liberating imagination.

The narrator's decision to choose freedom of self, even at the cost of exile from the world she has known, is enacted in the extended fantasy of Winnet; rhyming with Jeanette, her name suggests her role as the author/narrator's alter ego. The sorcerer who adopted and taught Winnet threatens to banish her for befriending a young man. To stay, she must relinquish her magic powers. The raven Abednego advises her that sorcerers cannot retrieve powers given, that instead she will learn to use her powers differently. Winnet sets out on a quest for a sacred city "where truth matters, [and] no one would betray her" (158). She follows a river to the sea, which she must dare to cross alone, without a guarantee of safety but with the confidence that what she searches for exists, providing she has the courage to seek it (159). The magic powers Winnet/Jeanette learns from the sorcerer/mother are the acts of the imagination, the stories that Jeanette-as-narrator and Winterson-as-author are inventing to destroy the constricting walls of family, religion, and society. On her quest, Winnet is protected by the chalk circle, an act of the mind and spirit. To make a magic circle with one's mind and imagination is to discover one's power, to change the self. The changes that her mother and the Church have attempted to force on her "mutilate" and are "evil" (141) because they fail to respect her individuality. They aim to expel her orange demon, her uniqueness that empowers her. By courageously keeping her demon, even at the cost of exile, the narrator discovers and frees herself.

Interwoven with the narrator's and Winnet's stories is the legend of Sir Perceval's quest for the Holy Grail. Perceval—solitary, near despair—symbolizes the narrator's exile and doubts about her quest. Alone at night, Perceval stares at his hands and contrasts them; one is "curious, sure and firm. . . . The other hand looked . . . stark, questioning, blank, uncomfortable" (173). Earlier in the novel, the prince's futile search for perfection taught the lesson that the true quest should be for a harmonious balance between one's inner and outer worlds. Here, near the novel's conclusion, the Perceval story adds the lesson that this harmony is attainable not by the perfect self but by the vulnerable self. Winterson's focus on Perceval's hands implies that the power of creating the self rests in each individual's hands. In the Winnet fantasy and in the Perceval myth, the quest is not completed; both end with the quester still searching, suggesting that the individual's quest for identity is likewise incomplete.

Like the *Oranges* narrator, Gloria in *Boating for Beginners* must discover a self outside the bounds of her mother's world. Gloria "lived at the bottom of a deep pool where her mother and the rest of the world were only seen as vague shadows on the surface. Now she was being forced into a graceless breaststroke to find out what everyone else was talking about" (18). The water imagery in this description of Gloria's awakening self indicates she is undergoing a kind of birth. Paradoxically, while her mother impedes Gloria's quest for self, she also offers Gloria the key to that quest by telling her a story of a traveler who wanders the world because he felt it held a secret (63). On his journey, he meets and helps first an old woman, then a young woman, and finally a middle-aged woman. He asks each if she knows the secret; the first two women reply enigmatically, but the third reveals the mystery: "The world is entirely circular and you will go round and round endlessly, never finding what you want, unless you have found what you really want inside yourself" (65). This tale conveys a central premise about the quest for self which Winterson's fiction so consistently dramatizes: although the quest involves an outward search leading to worldly knowledge, the quest ultimately requires an interior journey. Three women know this secret; together they suggest manifestations of the Great Goddess as crone, virgin, and mother—and it is the mother who reveals the key to the quest for self. Moreover, it is notable in this tale that Gloria's alter ego is male, since it anticipates the dual male and female narrators in Winterson's subsequent two novels, suggesting that the true self transcends gender.

While the mothers of *Oranges* and *Boating* define and limit their daughters, Dog-Woman, the mother of Jordan in *Sexing the Cherry*, liberates her child. Dog-Woman's size suggests that the domineering mothers who towered over their daughters in the earlier novels now have been transformed from figurative to literal giants. Dog-Woman is unmarried and childless until she finds a male child in the Thames. Unlike those other Winterson mothers, Dog-Woman consistently recognizes her child's identity and freedom. She names her son for a river, since rivers are not tied to anything; in birth a child flows out of the mother's natal waters and "runs free" (3–4). When Jordan is three years old, Dog-Woman takes him to meet a world explorer, an encounter that influences Jordan to explore the world physically and imaginatively, ultimately exploring himself. Despite her grief at losing Jordan as a companion, the independent Dog-Woman respects her son's independence.

Winterson's fiction reveals the multitude of ways that societally created gender roles destructively wall the self. In *Oranges* the Church interprets the narrator's lesbianism as a sign of the Church's error in "allowing women power" (133). In the eyes of her mother and the Church, "The devil had attacked me at my weakest point: my inability to realize the limitations of my sex" (134). Paradoxically, the mother in *Oranges* and Mrs. Munde in *Boating* find in their religion a freedom otherwise unavailable to women, even while they use religion in restrictive and destructive ways. Gloria understands that "When Mrs. Munde delivered herself into the everlasting hands of the Almighty she did so because her heart was too loud for this muffled world" (67). She lacks the self-confidence to question "her family, her marriage, her career prospects," all of which made her unhappy. Religion offers a kind of safety; it belongs to the walls that protect. Gloria says of her mother, "the mind gave way a little . . . but her heart is still loud; and to keep the roaring inside, however you do it, must be worth something" (67). Because of societal walls of gender roles, the creativity of these women has been misdirected, yet still the "heart" deserves respect.

The oppressive consequences of gender are most apparent in *The Passion,* set during the Napoleonic Wars. Structuring the novel in four sections, Winterson alternates the voices of Henri and Villanelle, the male and female narrators. These dual narrative voices suggest a "plural reality," since no single perspective—and, by implication, no single gender—can adequately convey truth. Disguise is a motif throughout the novel, and gender roles are one type of disguise. The novel presents gender roles fatalistically: "Soldiers and women. That's how the world is" (45). All other roles are transitory.

The devastating consequences of men's role as soldiers is epitomized on July 20, 1804, when Napoleon orders his army to rehearse an attack on England's navy by launching barges in the midst of a storm; two thousand men drown, and the next day just as many new recruits replace them (24–25). The insanity of purposeless deaths only intensifies when more men witlessly follow. Henri believes that the soldiers seek the passion of war so that they will feel more than a "lukewarm people," but instead of finding "burning summer in their bodies," they feel nothing but "lust and rage" (28).

This masculine rage is, in turn, directed against women. As Napoleon brutalizes his soldiers, so the soldiers brutalize women, trapped in their gender role of "meat" for men. The butcher, who supplies Napoleon's army with meat and horses, beats and rapes Villanelle and throws her a coin as he leaves; she comments that this is what she should have expected from a "meat man" (64). Napoleon orders women to sexually "serve" his soldiers: Henri meets one of these women "crawling home" in the frigid cold following an officers' party; she reports that after thirty-nine, she lost track of the men who had used her. "Christ lost consciousness at thirty-nine" (38), Henri recalls. Winterson unmasks the oppression of women and elevates their suffering by associating it with the lashings of Christ, whose suffering redeems humanity. This linking of women's oppression with Christlike suffering recurs in Villanelle's narrative when she loses a wager to a soldier and yields her body, stretching out her arms like Christ on the cross (70). Henri's friend Patrick, a defrocked priest, dares to suggest that even God raped the Virgin Mary (40). Yet despite their oppression, women endure (27).

Gender itself is a kind of mask. When Villanelle invites Henri to accompany her to Venice, the "city of disguises," he responds that he is already disguised by his uniform (100); his gender role as soldier is a masquerade, not his true identity. Cross-dressing in Venice, hiding one's gender, is a common game (54). Villanelle is dressed as a man when she meets her husband and again when she meets her lover, a married woman. When she debates revealing her gender to her lover, she suggests that her "breeches and boots self" is as genuine as her gartered self (66). Villanelle is the daughter of a Venetian boatman, a hereditary occupation (49). According to legend, the boatmen's wives follow a ritual so that their sons will be born with webbed feet, the secret sign of their identity. Villanelle's mother errs in the ritual, and Villanelle—a daughter—is born with webbed feet. Thus Villanelle has both male and female characteristics. Like the boatmen, her male counterparts, she can walk on water, yet this icon of her true identity is hidden from the world. Her female gender—outward appearance—restricts her; because she is a woman, she cannot be a gondolier (53). The narration of *The Passion* alternates between Henri and Villanelle, male and female voices not notably distinct, implying that gender masks the essential self.

The motif of disguise in *The Passion* carries into the setting, where Venice's maze of canals represents the maze one follows in the quest for self. Villanelle explores the waterways, discovering the "city within the city" that only a few know (53). The interior city symbolizes the interior self. When Henri, lost in Venice for five days, asks Villanelle for a map, she replies that it would be useless, that the city is alive and changing, that the "cities of the interior" are uncharted (114). This journey of the self, like Venice's canals, leads one in unpredictable ways; one must freely explore multiple paths. Henri recalls his boyhood face refracted into multiple images in his father's shaving mirror where he recognized the many possibilities for his future identity (26). Similarly, Villanelle saw her girlhood image refracted in the water of a Venetian canal (62). Ultimately, then, unconfined by a single identity, the self has many possibilities.

In *Sexing the Cherry,* her fourth novel, Winterson uses fairy tale, myth, and fantasy to undermine stereotypes of gender and sexual orientation and to empower the individual to change self and world. Jordan and Dog-Woman are the dual narrators in this novel whose focal setting is the physically and morally foul London of the Puritan Revolution. Their reincarnations, Nicholas Jordan and an unnamed woman, narrate the novel's concluding sections set amid the corruption, pollution, and inequality of contemporary society.

The theme of women's power over their own lives and identities appears collectively in the stories of the Twelve Dancing Princesses, a symbolic focal point in Jordan's quest. Earlier in his travels, he has seen a "woman whose face was a sea voyage" (15) he did not dare to attempt, a dancer so light she can magically descend a thin rope as she cuts and reknots it (16). Searching for her, he consults women who advise him to disguise himself as a female (27). Thus Jordan experiences the world as women do, thereby discovering, in Jordan's words, the "burdens of . . . gender" (28). Gender stereotypes limit both sexes. Both need wholeness; Jordan questions whether his quest was for a dancer or the "dancing part of [him]self" (39).

In the traditional fairy tale,[2] the twelve princesses are locked in their room each night by their father, yet each morning he finds their worn-out satin slippers. He promises that any man who can discover the mystery can marry the daughter of his choice—that is, the daughters are property at their father's disposal. After many suitors fail, Star Gazer, a gardener made invisible by a magic potion, discovers that the princesses dance away the night in a secret kingdom. He marries Princess Lina, the youngest, and her sisters marry princes. In this tale told from a male perspective, the princesses' power over their own lives is challenged by their father and their suitors. At last, the husband-to-be bests the women, concluding this cautionary tale of independent women tamed by love and marriage.

Winterson's transformation of this fairy tale explodes the myth that every woman is a princess rescued by marriage to a prince. In Winterson's tale each woman suffers in different ways but ultimately acts to rescue herself. The first princess tells Jordan that they all were "given in marriage" and lived happily every after—but not with their husbands (48). The first princess leaves her husband when she falls in love with a mermaid, with whom she now lives in the well. In a reversal of Browning's "My Last Duchess," the second princess has on the wall a portrait of her late husband "looking as though he were alive" (49). When her husband destroyed one of the religious relics she collected, she killed him. The third princess loved her husband, but he loved a boy; she kills them with a single arrow as they lie together (50). The husband of the fourth princess lusts after madwomen and, maddened himself with syphilis, dies in the snow; she wonders why he was not able to "turn his life" toward her (51). In a revision of another fairy tale, the fifth princess loves Rapunzel. A prince disguises himself in women's clothing and steals Rapunzel, blinding her princess lover. The sixth princess one night watches her husband, a hunter on horseback, leap a fence; his "flight" over the fence recalls to her a time when she, too, was "free to fly" unencumbered by the weight of land, house, and possessions. Leaving everything behind, she frees herself from her life as wife. Recalling her passionate love for her husband, the seventh princess reveals she had married a woman (54). When the outraged villagers assault their castle, she kills her lover to save her from persecution and flees. The eighth princess is married to a brutish glutton; she kills him with rat poison (55). The ninth princess is married to a falconer who chains her to him day and night: "I was his falcon" (57). One night she "flew off his wrist and tore his liver from his body," biting her chain in pieces. She marvels that her fierce attack surprised him: "As your lover describes you, so you are" (57). The tenth princess's husband was unfaithful but refused to leave, wanting to keep his possessions, which included her. She leaves, despite the unfairness and pain of losing what was her home as well (59). The eleventh princess is married to a man who spends his days alone, obsessed with solving the "problems of Creation." One night he asks that she kill him; she does, releasing his tortured spirit (60). Collectively, these eleven stories challenge the "happily ever after" marriage myth, for they clearly demonstrate that neither heterosexual nor homosexual love prevents suffering. Each woman has had the courage to free herself from oppression and heartbreak. Although they are women living together in community, each is an individual. They are not property, but rather own themselves. These are stories of women's survival, not as broken, wounded persons, but as whole, healed persons.

And the twelfth princess? The others say she, the youngest, about to be married to the prince who had discovered their secret, escaped from the altar as a bird escapes a trap (61). She was the "best dancer," able to change shapes as the others could not. She danced because she could not be false to herself: "She didn't burn in secret with a passion she could not express; she shone" (61). Her name is Fortunata, the fortunate one. Later, Jordan finds her on an island, where she teaches dance. Fortunata tells Jordan that for a long while she had lived her life waiting to be "rescued," hoping to "belong" to another. Then she had "learned to dance alone, for its own sake and for hers" (112). Thus this twelfth princess symbolizes freedom—freedom of movement (free even from gravity) and freedom of spirit, free to change identities, free to create the self. Jordan and Fortunata part, both continuing their individual quests to explore self and world. In the tales of the eleven princesses, attempts to own the beloved destroyed their relationships. By contrast, Jordan and Fortunata love one another enough to free the beloved to be his or her essential self.

Winterson's revision of the Artemis and Orion myth dramatizes women's liberation from oppression. The Greek myth has several variants, one in which Orion was killed because he challenged Artemis to throw the discus against him, another in which he was shot by Artemis because he tried to violate one of her maidens, and another in which he tries to violate Artemis, who brings forth from the ground a great scorpion that kills him.[3] In creating a variant in which Artemis kills Orion for raping her, Winterson transforms the myth into a paradigm not of women's victimization but of women's ability to overcome victimization.

In Winterson's version, Artemis has persuaded her father, Zeus, to give her a bow and arrows, a man's gear; a tunic, a man's dress; and an island "free from interference" (150), a man's prerogative. Artemis knows of the world's division of labor between "heroes" and "home-makers"; she chooses her solitary life not as a repudiation of her woman's role but to enjoy the "freedoms of the other side" (150). She considers traveling the world as heroes do. One night in the fire Artemis sees successive images of herself as child, woman, hunter, and queen (150). When she chooses one image, another escapes her. She realizes it would be futile to search the world when ultimately "she would have to confront herself" (150–51). Orion, that hunter-hero who travels the world, arrives "bellowing like a bad actor" with a reputation that "hung around him like bad breath" (151). He keeps her silent for hours as he tells his stories. But Artemis refuses to be silent; she talks to Orion about her love for the land and its constant alterations, of finding freedom without journeying (151). As she gets up to leave him, Orion rapes her—and falls asleep (151). Swiftly she avenges his attack, killing him with a scorpion (152). Yet the story is not ended, because this act has changed her: "She is not who she thought she was" (152). Burying Orion, she longs for a time free of violation (153). At last she realizes she is safe: "No safety without risk, and what you risk reveals what you value" (154).

Just as the independent princesses are a threat that men must control through marriage, so Artemis, living out her vocation as a solitary hunter, usurping a man's role, threatens the status quo—and thus she is punished by rape, the ultimate expression of male control. Yet in this Winterson revision, Artemis responds by killing Orion. The lessons seem complex. First, no matter where one travels, ultimately the self must be confronted. Second, one must avoid choosing a single image of the self, since that limits one's freedom. Finally, one must accept the risks of freedom, for freedom is necessary not to explore the world but to explore the self.

Winterson's theme of women's empowerment continues in the novel's final section in the fantasy of Dog-Woman's reincarnation, the nameless contemporary woman. Her narration opens, "I am a woman hallucinating. I imagine I am huge, raw, a giant" (138). She fantasizes that she travels the world filling up a bag with men, stopping first at the World Bank, next at the Pentagon, then snatching up world leaders. After "compulsory training in feminism and ecology" (139), the transformed men solve world hunger by redistributing surplus food in a "great human chain of what used to be power and is now co-operation" (139). Together women and men change the world, and on the "seventh day" they celebrate and "the peoples of the earth keep coming in waves and being fed and being clean and being well" (139). In this feminist Genesis, power is replaced by cooperation.

Dog-Woman and her reincarnation represent women with the strength to change self and world. Like Dog-Woman, literally a giant, her reincarnation realizes she is fat because she must be strong enough to combat the power the world wields against her. Her vast body symbolizes her vast rage (141) at this "hypocritical stinking world" (144). After she internalizes her power, she loses the weight but maintains this "alter ego who

was huge and powerful, a woman whose only morality was her own"
(142). She is a chemist, specializing in pollution research, because the
"earth is being murdered" (142). As Dog-Woman saw the "black" (11),
"boiling" (16) Thames and the Plague as symbols of corruption and so
set the Great Fire of London to purify society, her reincarnation sees the
mercury-polluted river by whose banks she lives as symbol of a world
corrupted by the military-industrial complex, and so she burns the mer-
cury factory.

Dog-Woman's reincarnation is helped by Jordan's reincarnation, a
young man named Nicholas Jordan. As a child he had studied the "Boys'
Book of Heroes" (131). When he reads of this woman living in protest by
a mercury-polluted river, he concludes she must certainly be a hero, one
who "live[s] dangerously for the common good" (159), and so he seeks
her out. Together they burn down the factory—female and male acting
together, true heroes. Through the novel's dual narration by Jordan (son)
and Dog-Woman (mother), in the love between Jordan and Fortunata
that leaves them as separate, complete selves, and in the purifying fire set
by Dog-Woman's reincarnation and Nicholas Jordan, Winterson envisions empowered selves that promise a new society where female and
male can be free and whole.

If imagination is one key to unlocking the self, so, too, is passion. In
Oranges, the narrator says, "I want someone who will destroy and be destroyed by me" (170). In *The Passion,* Henri and Villanelle are destroyed
by the objects of their love; neither is able to destroy their beloved.
Winterson seeks to define passion, not in the sense of setting limits, but
rather, as in music or poetry, by developing multiple refrains, images,
and themes that interweave and rise and fall. In this novel the quest is
for passion rather than for self, yet the two are inextricably bound together. Why does one seek passion? Henri's answer echoes throughout
his and Villanelle's tales: because "We're a lukewarm people. . . . Not
much touches us, but we long to be touched" (7). To escape ourselves, we
seek passion—but tragically in objects not worthy of our obsessions.

Henri's passion is for Napoleon. Henri is individual, a man in love (in
some sense) with another man; he also is universal, a soldier who idol-
ized and fought for Napoleon, representing all those who sacrifice themselves for "heroes." The warmth of the people contrasts to the ice of
Napoleon: "Why would a people who love the grape and sun die in the
zero winter for one man? Why did I? Because I loved him. He was my

passion and when we go to war we feel we are not a lukewarm people anymore" (108). War fails to satisfy the yearning for passion and, worse, destroys us. In the "zero winter" of Russia, Henri's friend Domino, no longer able to speak because of the pain of freezing and starvation, writes "FUTURE" (86) and then crosses the word out. Henri realizes that that is war's result: the destruction of the future. The Napoleonic Wars serve as a paradigm for the misdirection of human passion in war throughout history and the hopelessness of changing the cycle. Henri predicts—as has come to pass—that peace is only a brief relief from the war to come. "War will always be in the future" (108)—unless, Winterson warns, we trust such stories and learn.

The failure of religion to satisfy the human need for passion is apparent when Henri attends Christmas mass. Henri enters an icy cold cathedral, seeking the fire of religion to warm his war-chilled soul. Initially he finds warmth and comfort in the presence of others whose faith melts his "unbeliever's heart," and he glimpses "God through the frost" (41). But even during this momentary thaw, Henri feels apart from God. He thinks of his mother and the honest, faithful people of her village worshiping in a barn, "making a church out of themselves" (42). Yet this image is undercut by the knowledge that in their meekness, the people, like cattle, are asleep to the truth that they are meat to be slaughtered for war. As Henri receives communion, the wafer scorches his tongue, and the wine tastes of the two thousand men drowned by Napoleon's callous indifference; he sees in the priest's face the freezing prostitutes with their "blue breasts" (42). Henri grips the chalice so tightly that it leaves an imprint on his palms, a stigmata, and thinks that if he and every soldier bled for every comrade lost, no soldiers would remain (42). Instead, because the truth is too painful, the soldiers refuse to feel; their hearts are frozen.

While Henri's story portrays love in the form of hero worship, Villanelle's story portrays sexual love. Both characters recognize the need to take risks in order to find what is valuable: "You play, you win, you play, you lose. You play" (43). Gambling with what one loves is "irresistible": "*what you risk reveals what you value*" (43, emphasis added). These latter words are a refrain in *The Passion*. Villanelle makes her living as a gambler in Venice's casinos, and gambling operates in this novel as a metaphor for the risks individuals take to escape being "lukewarm people." Gambling is a corollary of freedom.

Villanelle risks her most treasured possession—her heart. She risks it with a mysterious, masked woman, the "Queen of Spades" (52), who gambles and wins when Villanelle, dressed as a male, deals the cards. As their passion grows, Villanelle ultimately gambles losing this love by revealing her female identity. Villanelle wins: the Queen of Spades has known of her female identity and still returns her passion. Villanelle loses: she has lost her heart to a married woman. Winterson portrays Villanelle's passion as a metaphorical journey over an unknown terrain. Unlike those who travel by choice or explorers who are prepared for their journeys, those "who travel along the blood vessels, who come to the cities of the interior by chance," go unprepared: "Somewhere between God and the Devil passion is and the way there is sudden and the way back is worse" (68).

Winterson transforms the cliché of losing one's heart from the figurative to the literal, first in Henri's story and then in Villanelle's. On the march in the "unimaginable zero winter" (80) through Russia, Henri sees soldiers, insane from cold and hunger, cut off their own limbs and cook them. He admonishes that the heart should be cut out first to deaden the pain: "To survive the zero winter and that war we made a pyre of our hearts and put them aside for ever" (82). The heart betrays because we risk our lives to satisfy its needs. Yet we betray the heart, seeking disastrous substitutes for love.

The figurative loss of heart becomes literal when Villanelle asks Henri to break into her former lover's home to retrieve her heart. The dumbfounded Henri touches and listens for her heart but can feel and hear nothing. Loving her, he sets out on this quest and, searching her lover's house, finds an almost completed tapestry depicting a female figure sitting, legs crossed, with a pack of cards before her—Villanelle (119). About to abandon his search, he hears a muffled sound and discovers a throbbing jar wrapped in blue silk. Henri carries this "valuable, fabulous thing" to Villanelle, hears "terrible swallowing and choking noises" (120), and, placing his hand on her breast, incredulously feels her heartbeat (121). Villanelle pales in terror when she hears of the tapestry, knowing that if it had been completed and her heart woven in, she would have been captive forever. Later, when her husband tries to recapture Villanelle, Henri kills him in the struggle to protect her—cutting out the heart of the heartless meat man and offering it to Villanelle (121).

What are the lessons of these terrible "heart stories"? One lesson is that one must gamble, take risks, in order to discover what one values. Villanelle chastises the "Hopeless heart" because it "plays roulette with anything precious," but she recognizes that we must "play," that "Gambling is . . . an expression of our humanness" (73). A second, more complex lesson involves freedom. The reclaiming of Villanelle's heart represents reclaiming her freedom, but even so she affirms her willingness to gamble it again (151). When Villanelle would rescue Henri from the prison for the criminally insane, where he has been sent for her husband's murder, Henri chooses to remain. At the novel's conclusion, Henri is the sane madman, the wise fool. He says we seek freedom as if it were the Holy Grail, forgetting that Perceval, by remaining still, found it where others had overlooked it (154). Henri concludes that freedom is the ability to love, forgetting one's self in that love: "We are lukewarm people and our longing for freedom is our longing for love" (154). Henri is left growing roses on a rock island, suggesting that despite the frequent barrenness of the human heart, love is still possible.

Creating stories—the fictive act—is Winterson's central device, enabling characters to come to understand the world and themselves. Within each novel—itself a story—the characters tell their tales. In *Oranges*, when the narrator is hospitalized as a child, her mother's friend Elsie comforts her with stories and the poetry of Swinburne, Blake, Christina Rossetti, and Yeats, those who understood the power of imagination: "stories [help] you to understand the world" (29).

The Bible, a collection of God-stories, serves as a fictive frame for *Oranges* as the narrator tells her life story in chapters patterned on the first eight books of the Bible. For example, "Genesis" tells of the narrator's adoption by her mother, while "Exodus" portrays the narrator's awareness of a kind of exile from the ordinary world resulting from their evangelical life. In "Joshua," the walls of the narrator's world come tumbling down as her love for Melanie is discovered; in "Judges," she is judged and exiled. In "Ruth," the novel's final chapter, the structural device draws a shadowy parallel between Ruth's story and that of solitary women bonding in friendship and summoning the courage to travel unknown paths to foreign lands where they create new lives. Winterson's structuring of *Oranges* as a counterpoint to the first eight books of the Bible is a victory of the creative, imaginative self. In the constricted world of the narrator's home, the Bible is one of the "walls," separating good and evil; the narrator's mother uses the Bible to categorize the

world: "There were friends and there were enemies" (3). Winterson crea-
tively transforms this symbol of limiting strictures into a structure for
exploring and expanding the self.

While the Bible's "Deuteronomy" is the book of law, in *Oranges* it is
a defense of fiction. Here Winterson articulates her principles for storytelling. First, a story makes sense of the world without imposing limitations, "explaining the universe while leaving the universe unexplained"
(93). Second, a story, free of the boundaries of time and space, is a way
of "keeping it all alive, not boxing it into time" (93), and she deplores the
curious habit of separating "storytelling which is not fact from history
which is fact" (93). Third, stories involve multiple perspectives: "Everyone who tells a story tells it differently, just to remind us that everybody
sees it differently" (93). In her novels, Winterson uses a recurring simile
for truth: it is like a "string full of knots. . . . The best you can do is to
admire the cat's cradle, and maybe knot it up a bit more" (93). History is
a kind of game. One creates a pattern of the facts—as in a cat's cradle by
interweaving string—but then the pattern dissolves. Because of their inherent order and balance (95), stories are a means of pursuing the quest
for truth. Finally, to consume only the truths digested by others is "Rot-
ten and rotting" (95). This "book of the law of fiction" concludes that the
storyteller must create her own truth: "Here is some advice. If you want
to keep your own teeth, make your own sandwiches" (95).

In *The Passion*, Winterson knots the "cat's cradle" of history with fiction so that it is impossible to unknot the two. One of *The Passion*'s refrains is "I'm telling you stories. Trust me" (5). Together, the stories of
Henri and Villanelle, because they intertwine history and fable, are ultimately more trustworthy in their representation of the human condition
than either is alone. Truth is not the property of any one person, any one
viewpoint; thus, multiple perspectives, represented in Winterson's fiction
by dual narrators of different genders, are imperative.

In *Sexing the Cherry*, history, satire, fairy tale, fantasy, and myth are
even more "knotted up" than in *The Passion*. Continuing the theme that
multiple perspectives are required to be truthful, this novel, too, uses
male and female narrators, but swiftly alternating and pairing historical
with contemporary counterparts. The two epigraphs Winterson selects
provide a clue to her purpose in her knotting up of time. The first epigraph indicates that the language of the Hopi Indian tribe, a language
as complex as our own, lacks verb tenses; past, present, and future are not

distinguished. "What does this say about time?" Winterson asks. Just as her fiction implicitly argues that history and fiction are false dualities, so she uses the structure of *Sexing the Cherry* to suggest that time, too, is only a convenient construct for shaping human experience, one of the "Hallucinations and Diseases of the Mind" (a title of one of the novel's sections). Human notions of space are equally hallucinatory, the second epigraph suggests. Even though matter seems "solid," from an object held in the hands to the body itself, physicists know matter is primarily "Empty space and points of light." Winterson asks what this tells us about what is real in the world. We experience the world as flat, even though we know it is round; the "Flat Earth Theory" is the title of another subsection. Likewise, we experience the world as solid matter, when we know from physics that it mostly empty space. In other words, our perception of reality is a fiction that we adopt.

Winterson writes that "when the heart revolts it wants outrageous things that cannot possibly be factual . . . heart-food" (*Boating* 66). In her fiction, Winterson leads the heart and spirit on journeys into the world and into the self, creating "sandwiches" of history, satire, fairy tale, myth, and fantasy uniquely her own to produce the "heart-food" we need to change ourselves and the world.

NOTES

1. Reviews of *Written on the Body* are listed below in "Works about Jeanette Winterson." See Annan, Berch, D'Erasmo, Glendinning, Koenig, Marvel, Olshan, Petro, Schulman, Shepard, Stewart, Stuart, Vaux, and Wilson.

2. "The Twelve Dancing Princesses," *The Red Fairy Book*, ed. Andrew Lang (1890; New York: Dover, 1966), 1–12.

3. H. J. Rose, *A Handbook of Greek Mythology: Including Its Extension to Rome* (New York: Dutton, 1959), 113–14.

SELECTED WORKS BY JEANETTE WINTERSON

"All Teeth 'n' Smiles." *New Statesman and Society* 22 Dec. 1989: 32–33.
Art & Lies: A Piece for Three Voices and a Bawd. New York: Knopf, 1995.
Art Objects: Essays on Ecstasy and Effrontery. New York: Knopf, 1996.
"Blooded with Optimism." *Sight and Sound* May 1991: 33.
Boating for Beginners. London: Methuen, 1985.

Fit for the Future. London: Pandora Press, 1986.

"Garden Books: Soil for the Spirit" [reviews]. *New Statesman and Society* 24 Nov. 1989: 33–34.

"God the Sod: The Book of Job Translated from the Hebrew by David Rosenberg and Interpreted by Harold Bloom." *New Statesman and Society* 10 May 1991: 37–38.

"Great Moments in Aviation" and "Oranges Are Not the Only Fruit": Two Filmscripts. 1990. London: Vintage, 1994.

Gut Symmetries. New York: Knopf, 1997.

"Imagining a New and Greater London." *Guardian* 14 Oct. 1991: 21.

Interview. *Times* (London) 26 Aug. 1992: 5a.

"Only the Best for the Lord." *New Statesman* 19/26 Dec. 1986: 46–47.

Oranges Are Not the Only Fruit. New York: Atlantic Monthly Press, 1985.

"Orion." *Sudden Fiction International: Sixty Short-Short Stories.* Ed. Robert Shapard and Thomas James. New York: Norton, 1989. 178–84.

"Outrageous Proportions." *Sight and Sound* Oct. 1992: 26–27.

The Passion. New York: Vintage, Random House, 1989.

Passionfruit: Romantic Fiction with a Twist [ed., short story collection]. London: Pandora, 1986.

"Personal View." *Sunday Times* (London) 14 Feb. 1988: G6a.

"Psalms." *New Statesman* 26 Apr. 1985: 27–29.

Sexing the Cherry. New York: Vintage International, Random House, 1989.

"Stories and Histories." *Harper's* Sept. 1987: 22–23.

"Who's Reading Whom." *Sunday Times* (London) 28 Jan. 1990: H2c.

World and Other Places. New York: Knopf, 1999.

"The World and Other Places." *Grand Street* 9.4 (1990): 164–71.

Written on the Body. New York: Knopf, 1993.

Selected Works about Jeanette Winterson

Annan, Gabrielle. "Devil in the Flesh." Rev. of *Written on the Body. New York Review of Books* 4 Mar. 1993: 22–23.

Anshaw, Carol. "Into the Mystic: Jeanette Winterson's Fable Manners." *[Village] Voice Literary Supplement* June 1990: 16–17.

Berch, Bettina. "Briefly Noted." Rev. of *Written on the Body. Belles Lettres* 8.3 (1993): 42.

Birch, Dinah. "Looking for Magic." Rev. of *Sexing the Cherry. London Review of Books* 14 Sept. 1989: 19–20.

"Books: Briefly Noted." Rev. of *Sexing the Cherry. New Yorker* 21 May 1990: 95.

Boston, Anne. "Living in the Clouds." Rev. of *Boating for Beginners. Sunday Times* (London) 12 Jan. 1986: 45.

Brown, Rosellen. "Fertile Imagination." Rev. of *Sexing the Cherry. Women's Review of Books* Sept. 1990: 9–10.

Brunt, Rosalind. "True to the Heart." Rev. of BBC adaptation of *Oranges Are Not the Only Fruit. New Statesman and Society* 12 Jan. 1990: 46.

Chernekoff, Janice. "Big Equals Powerful." Rev. of *Oranges Are Not the Only Fruit. American Book Review* Oct.–Nov. 1992: 9, 15.

Clute, John. "Paradise Lost." Rev. of *Oranges Are Not the Only Fruit. New Statesman* 12 Apr. 1985: 25.

Del Mar Asensio, Mari. "Subversion of Sexual Identity in Jeanette Winterson's *The Passion.*" *Gender, I-Deology: Essays on Theory, Fiction and Film.* Ed. Chantal D'Arcy, Gentille Cornut, Landa Garcia, and Angel Jose. Amsterdam: Rodopi, 1996. 265–79.

D'Erasmo, Stacey. "A Lover's Discourse." Rev. of *Written on the Body. Village Voice* 23 Feb. 1993: 85.

Duchene, Anne. "After Marengo." Rev. of *The Passion. London Times Literary Supplement* 26 June 1987: 697a.

Eyres, Harry. "Unpeeling the *Orange* Psyche" [interview]. *Times* (London) 10 Sept. 1990: 17.

Fisher, Emma. " . . . and Before." Rev. of *Boating for Beginners. London Times Literary Supplement* 1 Nov. 1985: 1228c.

Gerrard, Nicci. "The Prophet" [interview]. *New Statesman and Society* 1 Sept. 1989: 12.

Glendinning, Victoria. "Body Snatcher: *Written on the Body* by Jeanette Winterson." *Vogue* Feb. 1993: 128–30.

Gorra, Michael. "Gender Games in Restoration London." Rev. of *Sexing the Cherry. New York Times Book Review* 29 Apr. 1990: 24.

Greenwell, Bill. "Only Make Believe." Rev. of *Boating for Beginners. New Statesman* 25 Oct. 1985: 31.

Hinds, Hilary. "Fruitful Investigations: The Case of the Successful Lesbian Text." *Women: A Cultural Review* 2 (Summer 1991): 128–33.

———. "*Oranges Are Not The Only Fruit:* Reaching Audiences Other Lesbian Texts Cannot Reach." *Immortal, Invisible: Lesbians and the Moving Image.* Ed. Tamsin Wilton. London: Routledge, 1995. 52–69.

Hornaday, Ann. Rev. of *Oranges Are Not the Only Fruit. Ms.* Oct. 1985: 32–33.

Innes, Charlotte. "Gender Adventure." Rev. of *Sexing the Cherry. New Directions for Women* Sept.–Oct. 1990: B17.

———. "Rich Imaginings." Rev. of *Sexing the Cherry. Nation* 9 July 1990: 64–65.

"Jeanette Winterson." *The Feminist Companion to English Literature: Women Writers from the Middle Ages to the Present.* Ed. Virginia Blain, Patricia Clements, and Isobel Grundy. New Haven: Yale UP, 1990. 1176–77.

Kakutani, Michiko. "Britain's Writers Embrace the Offbeat." *New York Times* 5 July 1990: C11, C15.

Kaveney, Roz. "With the Lord Wigan." Rev. of *Oranges Are Not the Only Fruit. London Times Literary Supplement* 22 Mar. 1985: 326b.

Keates, Jonathan. "Depression over Ireland." Rev. of *Oranges Are Not the Only Fruit. Observer* 22 Dec. 1985: 19.

Koenig, Rhoda. "Luck of the Irish." Rev. of *Written on the Body. New Yorker* 25 Jan. 1993: 60–61.

Krist, Gary. "Innovation without Tears." Rev. of *Sexing the Cherry. Hudson Review* 43 (Winter 1991): 691–98.

LaFaille, Gene. "Science Fiction Universe." Rev. of *Sexing the Cherry. Wilson Library Bulletin* May 1991: 128–29.

Lainsbury, G. P. "Hubris and the Young Author: The Problem of the Introduction to *Oranges Are Not the Only Fruit.*" *Notes on Contemporary Literature* Sept. 1992: 2–3.

Lodge, David. "Outrageous Things." Rev. of *The Passion. New York Review of Books* 29 Sept. 1988: 25–26.

Lynch, Lee. "Laughing Lesbians." Rev. of *Sexing the Cherry. Women's Review of Books* Feb. 1986: 8–9.

Mackay, Shena. "The Exotic Fruits of Time." Rev. of *Sexing the Cherry. London Times Literary Supplement* 15 Sept. 1989: 1006a.

Marvel, Mark. "Affairs of the Heart." Rev. of *Written on the Body. Mademoiselle* Feb. 1993: 52.

———. "Jeanette Winterson: 'Trust Me. I'm Telling You Stories.'" *Interview* Oct. 1990: 164–65, 168.

Messud, Claire. "The Body Politic" [interview]. *Guardian* 26 Aug. 1992: 92.

Miller, Lucasta. "Ways of Writing." Rev. of *Sexing the Cherry. New Statesman and Society* 12 Oct. 1990: 44–45.

Millett, Kate. "What Writers Are Reading." Rev. of *Oranges Are Not the Only Fruit* and *Sexing the Cherry. Ms.* July 1991: 84.

O'Dair, Barbara. "The Color Orange." Rev. of *Oranges Are Not the Only Fruit. Village Voice* 24 Nov. 1987: 65.

Olshan, Joseph. "Picks and Pans." Rev. of *Written on the Body. People Weekly* 8 Mar. 1993: 27.

Onega, Susana. "Jeanette Winterson's Politics of Uncertainty in *Sexing the*

Cherry." *Gender, I-Deology: Essays on Theory, Fiction, and Film.* Ed. Chantal D'Arcy, Gentille Cornut, Landa Garcia, and Angel Jose. Amsterdam: Rodopi, 1996. 297–313.

O'Rourke, Rebecca. "Fingers in the Fruit Basket: A Feminist Reading of Jeanette Winterson's *Oranges Are Not the Only Fruit.*" *Feminist Criticism: Theory and Practice.* Ed. Susan Sellers, Linda Hutcheon, and Paul Perron. Toronto: Toronto UP, 1991. 57–69.

Page, Kathy. "Heart and Stomach." Rev. of *The Passion. New Statesman* 26 June 1987: 26–27.

Petro, Pamela. "Bold Types." *Ms.* July 1992: 66.

——. "A British Original." Rev. of *Written on the Body. Atlantic* Feb. 1993: 112–15.

Picardie, Justine. "Making Things Up" [interview]. *Independent Magazine* 5 Sept. 1991: 44–46.

Pickering, Paul. "Passionate about Life" [interview]. *Sunday Times* (London) 7 June 1987: 52e.

Rev. of *The Passion. Idler* May–June 1988: 53–55.

Rev. of *Sexing the Cherry. Malahat Review* Dec. 1990: 122.

Rev. of *Sexing the Cherry. Publishers Weekly* 23 Feb. 1990: 204.

Rev. of *Sexing the Cherry. Quill and Quire* Apr. 1990: 29.

Rev. of *Written on the Body. London Review of Books* 24 Sept. 1992: 18.

Rev. of *Written on the Body. Los Angeles Times Book Review* 21 Feb. 1993: 3.

Rev. of *Written on the Body. New Statesman and Society* 18 Sept. 1992: 57.

Rev. of *Written on the Body. Observer* 6 Sept. 1992: 51.

Rev. of *Written on the Body. Women's Review of Books* May 1993: 21.

Rev. of *Written on the Body. Spectator* 19 Sept. 1992: 34.

Rev. of *Written on the Body. Times Literary Supplement* 4 Sept. 1992: 20.

Rev. of *Written on the Body. Yale Review* Oct. 1993: 124.

Rieff, David. "Previews: Jeanette Winterson." *Interview* Apr. 1988: 50.

Sage, Lorna. "Weightlessness and the Banana." Rev. of *Sexing the Cherry. Observer* 10 Sept. 1989: 51.

Schulman, Sarah. "Guilty with Explanation." Rev. of *Written on the Body. Lambda Book Report* Mar. 1993: 20.

Scott, Suzanne, and Lynne M. Constantine. "*Belles Lettres* Interview." *Belles Lettres* 2.5 (May–June 1987): 5, 15.

Seaboyer, Judith. "Second Death in Venice: Romanticism and the Compulsion to Repeat in Jeanette Winterson's *The Passion.*" *Contemporary Literature* 38.3 (Fall 1997): 483–509.

Shepard, Jim. "Loss Is the Measure of Love." Rev. of *Written on the Body. New York Times Book Review* 14 Feb. 1993: 7.

Shrimpton, Nicholas. "Emperors and Mermaids." Rev. of *The Passion. Observer* 14 June 1987: 23.

Spark, Muriel. "Books: A Winterson Tale." Rev. of *The Passion. Vanity Fair* May 1988: 54–58.

Stewart, Lucretia. "No, No Jeanette." Rev. of *Written on the Body. Harper's Bazaar* Feb. 1993: 74–76.

Stuart, Andrea. "Terms of Endearment." Rev. of *Written on the Body. New Statesman and Society* 18 Sept. 1992: 37–38.

Suleiman, Susan Rubin. "Mothers and the Avant-Garde: A Case of Mistaken Identity?" *Femmes Frauen Women.* Ed. Françoise Van Rossum-Guyon. Amsterdam: Rodopi, 1990. 135–46.

Thompson, Alice. "Passionate Apostle for the Lexicon of Love" [interview]. *London Times Supplement* 26 Aug. 1992: 5.

Tremain, Rose. "Banana Skins." Rev. of *Sexing the Cherry. Listener* 14 Sept. 1989: 29.

Vaux, Anna. "Body Language." Rev. of *Written on the Body. Times Literary Supplement* 4 Sept. 1992: 20.

Wilson, A. N. "The Narrator That Dare Not Speak Her Name." Rev. of *Written on the Body. Spectator* 19 Sept. 1992: 34.

Wilson, Leigh Allison. "Getting Physical." Rev. of *Written on the Body. Book World [Washington Post]* 14 Feb. 1993: 6.

"Winterson, Jeanette." *Contemporary Authors.* Ed. Susan M. Trosky. Detroit: Gale, 1992. 449–51.

Winterson, Jeanette, and Helen Barr. "A Conversation between Jeanette Winterson and Helen Barr." *English Review* 2 Sept. 1991: 30–31.

14
Sea Changes: African-Caribbean and African Women Writers in England

Laura Niesen de Abruña

An analysis of the black woman writer's experience as émigré in England can be initiated through the examination of the writing of the two major groups of immigrants, women from Africa and women from the Caribbean.[1] Whereas the black American experience of racism differs significantly from that of the black British experience, the émigrés from the Caribbean and Africa do[2] have some similar experiences which should be compared to one another rather than to black American writers. The original black immigrant community in Britain gained significant numbers in the 1950s and 1960s when large numbers of black women from Africa and the Caribbean began to settle in Britain.[3]

Many critics and readers are aware of what Susheila Nasta terms "exile novels" (26) documenting the immigrant experience in Britain. Samuel Selvon's *Lonely Londoners,* published in 1956, was the first of a trilogy concerning these exiles in Britain and their difficulties in confronting the new culture. The problems they experienced originated with the unwillingness of British society to find a place for them socially, politically, or economically. This novel is an ironic watershed because it points to a development of consciousness available only after one has left the native country. As Nasta points out, "The explicit portrayal of the vitalizing growth and recognition of a specifically West Indian consciousness and identity is one of the novel's definitive features. Interestingly, this occurs after departure from the various islands and after arrival in the city" (26). However, until recently, the exile novel signaled the work of male writers such as Samuel Selvon, Austin Clarke, George Lamming, Andrew Salkey, and V. S. Naipaul. Yet the last two decades have marked a tremendous increase in the creative energy and productivity of African and Caribbean women writers in the United States, Canada, the Caribbean, Africa, and England. In fact, the productivity of the African and Caribbean women writers since the 1970s has been called by many critics a kind of "blossoming" or "flowering." And while this observation is surely true, it is also true that women have been writing prior to this time and simply have not been heard until recently because they were denied access to publication by the prestigious presses in Europe and the United States. So it is disingenuous to speak of a "flowering" of women's literary art as if no women had been writing before this time. As Timothy Brennan has observed, the fiction that dominated the publishers' lists in the past two decades did not present a feeling for the experience of other English-speaking regions, or a sense of tension between England and its former colonies, the feeling of a "flooding in and out of contact with the centre" (xi). There was no sense of the experience of the black community either in the West Indies or in England (xii). One must add Africa to Brennan's list.

Even during the early years of the "blossoming" of black women writers, some of the women writing in England had to publish with presses in the United States or the West Indies. Recently, in England, a very strong group of writers has been publishing with Virago Press and The Women's Press. As Lauretta Ngcobo notes in her 1987 study *Let It be Told: Black Women Writers in Britain,* many women have published work now well known to those who follow literary developments in the African and African-Caribbean communities (15). Young people are especially active, and their efforts are supported by groups such as the Afro-Caribbean Education Authority (15). The winner of one of their annual awards for the best Young Black Writer was Accabre Huntley, who wrote her first collection of poems, *At School Today,* when she was ten years old, and her second collection, *Easter Monday Blues,* at sixteen (15).

A writer well known, or at least familiar, to the interested audience is Amryl Johnson, who was born in Trinidad and came to England at age eleven. Her collections include *News for Babylon* (1983), *Long Road to No-*

where (1985), *Facing the Sea* (1986), *With a Poet's Eye* (1986), and *Watchers and Seekers* (1987). Johnson has published a memoir, *Sequins for a Ragged Hem* (1988), that gives an account of her trip "home" to the Caribbean in 1983. She describes a feeling common among those who return: a sense of dislocation both in England and, after many years, also in Trinidad. Barbara Burford has written a collection of short stories, *The Threshing Floor* (1986), that offers the reading public an insight into the black lesbian community in England. In addition, the story concerns the great love that the main character, Hannah, an artist who specializes in glassblowing, shares with her lover, Jenny, a poet. The fact that one woman is black and the other white is not as important to the story as the exploration of the depth of Hannah's love and the grief that eventually ensues. Grace Nichols, an important woman writer from Guyana, has become well known for her fine poetry concerning black women. Nichols, born in Guyana in 1950, has lived in Britain since 1977. She has written two children's books, *Trust You, Wriggly* (1981) and *Baby Fish and Other Stories* (1983). She has also published a novel, *Whole of a Morning Sky* (1986), and is best-known for her poetry appearing in *i is a long memoried woman* (1983) and *The Fat Black Woman's Poems* (1984). Beryl Gilroy's *Frangipani House* (1986) makes an important contribution to Caribbean literature by examining the psychological state of an elderly woman, while *Boy Sandwich* (1989) explores the experiences of a young man growing up in England. Jan Shinebourne was born in Guyana and lives in London. She has written two novels—*Timepiece* (1983) and *The Last Plantation* (1988)—that are notable for their analyses of the characters' mixed Indo-Chinese backgrounds.

Three of Joan Riley's novels—*The Unbelonging* (1985), *Waiting in the Twilight* (1987), and *Romance* (1988)—focus on three stages of development in women's lives: children arriving from the West Indies in Britain; adolescents between two worlds; and adults who still suffer from a sense of "unbelonging" in their new world. Riley has written a fourth novel, *A Kindness to the Children* (1992), which focuses on corruption in contemporary Jamaica, especially the abuse of women and children. In addition, there have been at least two widely known anthologies of creative writing by black women in England, many of whom are Caribbean. The first is edited by two Caribbean critics, Rhonda Cobham and Merle Collins. Their 1986 anthology *Watchers and Seekers* broke new ground in terms of the availability and presentation of British-African-Caribbean women writers. The second, *Let It Be Told: Black Women Writers in Britain,* edited by Lauretta Ngcobo, surveys West Indian and African women's writing and offers extracts from creative writers. In addition, the nonfiction collection of writings from Bryan, Dadzie, and Scafe, *The Heart of the Race* (1985), provides a sociological perspective on the problems experienced by black women émigrés to Britain.

Any discussion of these writers would begin with the roles of Caribbean and African history and geography as partial determinants of identity in specific colonial contexts. Insightful analyses of this type have been made by Gordon Lewis, Kenneth Ramchand, O. R. Dathorne, Eric Williams, Bruce King, and Patrick Taylor. The postcolonial context of recent English-language writing has been explored by Bill Ashcroft, Gareth Griffiths, and Helen Tiffin in *The Empire Writes Back: Theory and Practice in Post-Colonial Literatures* (1989). Henry Louis Gates's theories of signifying explicated in *The Signifying Monkey* (1988) can also be applied to postcolonial African and Caribbean literatures. As these critics and others have argued, to the issues of history and geography must be added the concerns of racism, color-shade prejudice, classism, and the effects of poverty, patterns of family formation, family violence, language patterns, and, of course, gender. West Indian and African literatures render these variables as part of what Brennan calls a "submerged" neocolonial history (xiii).

Since the late nineteenth century, identity and colonialism, two of the major issues of the submerged history, have been explored by such West Indian writers as George Lamming, C. L. R. James, V. S. Naipaul, E. R. Braithwaite, Wilson Harris, Garth St. Omer, and Earl Lovelace. Those writers who returned to the "mother country," England, in some ways occupied the most complicated and difficult position because they had to negotiate their sense of displacement in the very country from which they had been forced to draw a great deal of their heritage and their language. They experienced culture shock and an insidious racism and dislike of foreigners. They felt unwelcome, despite the postwar recruiters' propaganda. The British simply wanted a new source of cheap labor. As Gordon Lewis has explained it, the "neocolonialist economic order still requires . . . cheap, unskilled labor" (238), and in this case, class and race would ensure that the old oligarchy that blacks experienced in the West Indian plantocracy system would be replicated in England. Thus, the West Indians' deep sense of betrayal by the "mother country" made their experience different from the experiences of émigrés to the United States or Canada. In England, black families found that they were no longer a racial majority but a marginalized and victimized minority.

In Britain, all of the black women coming from Africa and the West Indies faced a formidable phalanx of issues, including racism, classism, and sexism. Ngcobo states in her introduction to *Let It Be Told:* "As a group we suffer the self-perpetuating psychological mutilation of oppression: a battered self-image, which has undermined our confidence; diminished possibilities for self-expression, linked with poor educational opportunities; internalized images of ourselves as depicted by others; and countless self-inflicted wounds" (1). The authors of *The Heart of the Race* have commented in an essay in *Let It Be Told* that they have been aware, when writing *Heart of the Race*, that this work was "the first public record of Black women's lives in Britain" (125). The book, based on about one hundred interviews with black women, tried to render some account of their experiences in Britain. Writing not as individuals but as a collective, these three women testified to the difficulties that black women have in writing. One of the major practical problems is finding the time to write. In addition to performing paid work and fulfilling family commitments, these women must find the energy and motivation to write that comes from a conviction that the experience of black women is important and needs to be recorded. As the contributors state, "Perhaps more Black women will begin to articulate some of their experiences, knowing that whatever the commitments, preoccupations or constraints, we can write. We must do this; in order for our presence here to become more visible we must set down what we have done. We must consider our gains, examine, honestly, some of the contradictions within our community and make links with our sisters about what has to be done" (132). Lately, many women writers have published their work, thereby adding further richness to the experiences of these women. This trend has recently produced an important anthology of Caribbean women writers, *Green Cane and Juicy Flotsam: Short Stories by Caribbean Women,* edited by Carmen C. Esteves and Lizabeth Paravisini-Gebert, which also adds stories from the Dutch-speaking Caribbean. Esteves and Paravisini-Gebert argue that Caribbean women writers were in part "silenced" in the Caribbean until the late 1960s. This silence resulted from an emphasis on the issues of colonial history and national identity that inherently led to a conscious or unconscious devaluation of women's writing that failed to focus on issues of national formation such as "political development, agricultural reform, breaking the race barriers to education and the professions" (xvi).

Often, women writers chose not to explore these issues because they were predicated on experiences that women were not permitted to have. In her important and recent book *Working Miracles: Women's Lives in the English-Speaking Caribbean* (1991), Olive Senior investigates the major issues that confront Caribbean women during the life cycle. Drawing on the information provided by the Women in the Caribbean Project of the University of the West Indies, she states: "While recognizing that Caribbean women can and do act independently of official policy to improve their situation . . . their ability to do so is considerably hampered by a gender ideology which consistently ascribes low status to their activities" (188). Senior adds the point that women are in practice excluded from many areas of activity.

Black women living in England have similar problems, but issues of exile, race, and class assume even more importance than gender discrimination. Some of the concerns in the literature written in England, as noted by Rhonda Cobham in her introduction to *Watchers and Seekers*, include the tradition of orature, the use of dreams and visions, and the struggle against oppression (1). In terms of psychology, Cobham also notes a focus on bonding among women characters, especially among family members. Betty Wilson and Pamela Mordecai point to a greater confidence in the power of these literary "voices" (xi). The focus of most of the women's writing has been on the ordinary concerns of the impoverished or suffering (xiii) or on a "community of caring" (xiv).

Women writers from England present, from a female point of view, at least four major areas of experience: racism, economic exploitation, family violence and abuse, and discrimination in British society. Bryan, Dadzie, and Scafe's *Heart of the Race* shows the many problems black women have had to face, including the false promises made to immigrant women about job opportunities in England, the systematic discrimination against them in their jobs, the relegation of their children to special classes for the retarded because of their accent, the scorn of their so-called "broken" English, and their problems with finding adequate housing and education for their families. The book also explores the breakdown in family relationships and the lack of communication among family members, arguing that the adherence to traditional male-female gender roles shreds family commitments. These issues are raised by Amryl Johnson, Beryl Gilroy, Grace Nichols, Barbara Burford, and Joan Riley, although, in addition to the shared themes, each of these writers has her own contribution.

One of the influential women writers from Africa is Lauretta Ngcobo, who was born in South Africa and moved to London as a young adult. In addition to *Let It Be Told,* she published a novel in 1981, *Cross of Gold,* which takes place in South Africa, and another novel, *And They Didn't Die,* in 1990. The latter examines South Africa during the 1950s and 1960s and explores the effect of apartheid on an impoverished community. The major character, Jezile, is compelled to work in a white household where she is mistreated by the woman and raped by the man, whose child she bears. In *Let It Be Told* Ngcobo articulates the experience of "unbelonging": "I am an exiled South African and, although I have lived in several parts of the world for the past twenty-odd years, I remain an exiled South African. The fact of exile in itself, the reluctant choice to live away from one's country of birth, impels me to remain, in my heart of hearts, none other than a South African. I think South African, I feel South African and I write South African. Therefore, on the British scene, I remain an immigrant writer" (133). She points out that although she will always be a South African writer, her own country would not give her the freedom or opportunity to write. Although Ngcobo feels out of place in Britain, her experience there proves less bitter than the British experience of other women from Africa because of the brutality of the South African political system.[4] So in one sense, because she has been able to write in Britain, she does consider herself a British writer. In South Africa, the Publications and Entertainments Acts of 1963 made any subject that black Africans chose to write about off-limits (135). The Bantu Education Act of 1953 had the effect of attempting to limit black South Africans to a level of education that would lead to low-status jobs in the community. In addition to these very powerful limiting forces, Ngcobo states that she was living in a country where women are devalued: "I learned to accept that there was no validity in what women thought and said. Men met regularly in places where women were not expected to attend and they discussed community issues to the exclusion of women" (136). Ngcobo claims that the effect of this discrimination appears in her fiction, in which men are initiators of ideas while women are often wrapped in silence. Because of the migrant labor system, however, women are called upon to be very strong and independent in spite of their silence.

One of the most notable diaspora writers living in England is Buchi Emecheta, the author of over a half dozen novels, an autobiography, and several children's books. In a number of the novels, and in her auto-biographical novels *In the Ditch* (1972) and *Second-Class Citizen* (1974) and her autobiography *Head above Water* (1986), Emecheta consistently points out the ways in which African traditional culture constrains women's lives. She has written a large number of works, including *Kehinde* (1994), *The Bride Price* (1976), *The Slave Girl* (1977), *The Joys of Motherhood* (1979), *Destination Biafra, Naira Power, Double Yoke,* the two "young adult novels" *The Moonlight Bride* and *The Wrestling Match, Gwendolen* (1989) (entitled *The Family* in the British, George Braziller edition), and *The Rape of Shavi,* as well as a number of children's books (*Titch the Cat, Nowhere to Play*) and two plays, *A Kind of Marriage* and *Juju Landlord.* In 1980 she was a Senior Research Fellow in the Depart-ment of English and Literary Studies at the University of Calabar, Nigeria, and has been a Fellow at the University of London. Emecheta's works are feminist in the sense that they validate women's experiences, such as raising children, while insisting that women should not be de-fined against their wills into certain social roles, nor should they be con-fined in ways that lessen their human dignity or, in modern terms, their ability to self-actualize.[5]

In many of her novels, and in her autobiography *Head above Water,* Emecheta represents the way Nigerian women are made to feel that their worth depends on bearing a large number of children. In addition, she evokes the sense that the male children are far superior to the fe-male children. In Nigeria there is a proverb that reflects the way in which the extended family and even extended society help to raise children: "It takes a whole village to raise a child." But émigrés to Britain find that no village exists and that the British slum proves an inadequate substitute for the extended family. In fact, both the individual family and some-times the single women must bear responsibility for raising each child, in terms of both time and money. One of the effects of this cultural dif-ference on the male émigrés is a deterioration of the few remaining ves-tiges of their power and control over the people in their society. Be-cause it was written relatively early in her career and because of its half-ironic title, *The Joys of Motherhood* has already received significant examination.[6] At least one male literary critic, Lloyd Brown, has written about Emecheta's early work and taken her to task: "The effectiveness of Emecheta's protest is often undercut by her shortcomings as a writer. All three works [*In the Ditch, Second-Class Citizen,* and *The Bride Price*] suffer from lapses into banal statement and into what is, quite simply, sloppy writing that deserves more careful editing than it apparently received" (36). Clearly, Brown is claiming that the criteria that function well for white male writers from the West provide the basis for his judgment of Emecheta's work. He criticizes her for not writing about subjects that he would consider important. Yet, having read Emecheta's work and having some knowledge of the cultural context, a critic should understand that motherhood and the raising of children are not "banal" subjects that attract Emecheta's "banal" writing.

Indeed, quite the opposite is true. Emecheta writes from the richly textured context of black women writers in England. In her novels that represent a woman who has moved to England from Nigeria, she foregrounds the issues concerning the struggle of black women to establish an individual identity. In *Kehinde,* for example, husband and wife Albert and Kehinde manage fairly well in England after having moved there from Nigeria. Emecheta presents the difficulty of raising children in England and contrasts it with raising children in Nigeria. In England, Albert feels chagrin when Kehinde becomes pregnant, and cajoles her into aborting the fetus. Whereas abortion might provide fairly limited trauma for a Western women, for Kehinde the accepted practice in England is fraught with difficulties. Her culture's tradition teaches that children embody the spirit of one's ancestors. Thus, in killing one's child, one might be refusing to allow one's father to return to the world. This concept forms the basis of Kehinde's dream during the abortion: "The child I just flushed away was my father's *chi,* visiting me again. But I refused to allow him to stay in my body. It was a man-child" (32). This breakdown in their relationship leads to the end of her feelings for Albert: "He had nothing to offer her" (33).

When Albert's relatives insist that he return to Nigeria, Kehinde stays behind because she has a high-paying job that will help her to support their two children. Eventually, Kehinde returns to Lagos despite Albert's protests. His reluctance to have her return, as Kehinde discovers, is the result of his having taken a second wife. When Kehinde does return, she cannot adjust to the customs of the country. She does not wish to be the "senior wife" in a polygamous family. Her "co-wife," Rike, is in an even less advantageous position. Despite having a Ph.D. and a teaching job at the university, Rike still feels the necessity of being a second wife in order to have a family. Kehinde's sister, Ifeyinwa, tries to encourage Kehinde to accept this situation: "This is nothing that has not been seen or heard of before. It happens all the time. My husband has two other wives and we all live in two rooms. At least here you have a whole house, and Albert is in a good job" (71).

Kehinde must also cope with the fact that even though Albert had had her abort their son, he had, once back in Nigeria, married Rike when she produced a "man-child." When Albert decides to take yet a third wife, Kehinde finally returns to England because there at least she can be her own person and escape the humiliation of polygamy. Later her son Joshua arrives in England to claim the house as his, since by Nigerian law every house belongs to a man. Kehinde finally tells him not to expect to obtain the house in her lifetime. Significant to this story is Kehinde's ability to transcend the strictures of her upbringing. As she says at the end of the novel, "Claiming my right does not make me less of a mother, not less of a woman. If anything it makes me more human" (141).

In *Gwendolen,* Emecheta presents a woman who, raped by a family friend in Jamaica, moves to England only to face further abuse at the hands of her father, a man whose self-esteem has been eroded by the humiliations of poverty in England. Melba Wilson has written an important new work, *Crossing the Boundary: Black Women Survive Incest* (1993), in which she discusses the issue of incest and its effect on women as reflected in the literature about black women. Wilson has written the book because she believes that incest, as well as child sexual abuse, has been an issue that has been silenced in our communities, but especially in the black community. She states in her introduction: "I am an incest survivor. Let me qualify that—I am black, female and approaching middle age. I have reached a point in my life where I feel that sharing that information may be useful for those who are also black, female and have survived child sexual abuse" (1). She believes that the silence on this important issue is more destructive than the airing of dirty laundry for the white community to see. Her metaphor for breaking the silence is clear in the title phrase, "crossing the boundary." Through speaking of this problem and placing it in its social, political, and economic contexts, she successfully presents it from the victim's point of view. For the sake of the victims, speaking out about the subject relieves the guilt and self-mutilation that can accompany these problems. The book aims to "move beyond abuse" (3), and in this sense it facilitates our understanding the role of incest in Emecheta's *Gwendolen*.

Wilson provides only the beginning point of such a discussion because she offers no analysis of the text. She gives a brief plot summary focusing on the incest and pointing out the importance of survival for Gwendolen through the friendship and support that she receives from her boyfriend, Emmanuel, and her mother's Nigerian friend Gladys. Gwendolen lives in rural Jamaica with her entire family until her mother and father move to England to find new economic opportunities. They leave Gwendolen with her Granny Naomi with the promise that they will send for her later when the financial situation improves. When she is nine, she is raped by her "Uncle" Johnny, a friend of the family. During most of the time that she endures the abuse, Gwendolen remains silent because the family has no money and Uncle Johnny contributes to Granny Naomi's household expenses. However, after Gwendolen tells her grandmother about the abuse, Granny believes her and thus the community of women takes a stand against Johnny. Eventually, though, the men in the community begin to wonder why Gwendolen allowed the abuse to continue for so long, and Granny Naomi begins to resent Gwendolen because, through her, Granny has lost a source of economic support. Finally, Gwendolen moves to England, but only because her parents have had other children and wish their eldest daughter to return as a sort of governess. When Gwendolyn's mother returns to Jamaica for an extended visit, the father attacks Gwendolen and expresses surprise and disgust that she does not resist. When she becomes pregnant, Gwendolen runs away and is confined in a mental institution for her failure to speak, or even to give her name. She remains silenced with anger and guilt, a silence that in fact constitutes her very form of resistance to the abuse that she has endured. Gwendolen finally begins to heal when she leaves her family's house and begins to live a new life with the help of many of her friends.

Joan Riley, another writer in the Caribbean community, was one of the first black Caribbean women writers to examine the émigré experience in Britain. She writes of some issues that are similar to

Emecheta's—and some that are very different. Riley discusses the break-down of the family in Britain, especially when young female children, left behind in the Caribbean, are then brought to Britain at a later time. She discusses that longing for the homeland and the consequent disillu-sion when someone returns and finds her memory both an illusion and an impediment to coping with emigration's stresses. Emecheta speaks, most of all, of the way various problems affect women and children. Two similar issues in Riley's and Emecheta's works are the relative status of women in their societies and the societal preference for men.

In Jamaica, according to Perry, the worst possible luck is to be poor and to lose the support of a male. Women are willing sometimes to ac-cept being beaten just to keep their man (272). For the same reason, women also accept the practice of concubinage among men: "Concubi-nage is very strong in Jamaica. You talk about outside children—it's al-most an institution" (273). Male children are clearly preferred to females, since the boys are able to carry on the father's name (273). Riley asserts that in Jamaica women are sometimes believed to be unimportant and that brutal treatment is not unknown, especially among people ravaged by poverty: "Who isn't safe are my nieces, my little cousins. Those are the people who are not safe. My favorite aunt was raped when I was very young, and she had a child, and she was kicked out of home. She's going mad now because what happened was that during the troubles they tied her up and shot her son through the mouth and left her with his body. It was about two days before they found her. So this is the Jamaica you never hear about" (278).

Riley's novels involve the most complex vision of the problems en-dured by West Indian women who have emigrated to England. As Donna Perry points out in her interview, Riley feels a specific responsi-bility generated through her status as one of a few black women writing and publishing in Britain (262). Her novels deal with three life periods: *The Unbelonging*, the first novel, treats the life of a child through her late adolescence; *Romance* presents a young woman moving from relative im-maturity to full sensitivity to adult responsibilities; and *Waiting in the Twilight* focuses on the life of an elderly woman in her sixties up until her death. Her fourth novel, *A Kindness to the Children*, focuses on the abuse of women and children in contemporary Jamaica, particularly the abuse that leads to madness in some of the women characters. In it, the character Jean leaves Jamaica at age eighteen and receives an education in Britain. Yet she carries with her old childhood luggage of rape and brutalization. She actually goes mad. In addition, Riley coedits, with poet Briar Wood, an anthology entitled *Leave to Stay,* a collection of fiction and poetry by those writers, white and black, who have left one country for another. Thus, Riley covers the entire female life span and investigates issues of family violence, child abuse, incest, rape, gender relations, marital relations, sexism in the workplace, economic oppression of black women, attitudes toward children, and the erosion of respect for older women. She has experienced some negative criticism of her novels, especially *A Kindness to the Children,* because, according to Riley, "Negativism is seen as reactionary and a betrayal of the revolution" (263). Her novels vary in literary quality and in the degree to which the major character is primarily presented as victim. Much of the writing constitutes a wrenching indictment of the insidious racism and betrayal of blacks in England, as well as of the way that hatred is displaced onto women and children, the most vulnerable and therefore the most common scapegoats.

I view Riley's first novel, *The Unbelonging,* as one of the best examples of the social, economic, and gender issues most commonly presented in West Indian women's writing in England. The novel begins with a poem, "Memories," that argues that the West Indian woman has neither a place nor a space where she belongs. Even feelings of safety engendered by dreams of the past are sentimental since Hyacinth, the central character, cannot return to a romanticized past. The first chapter begins with a memory of a safe green cave where Hyacinth felt secure and the world seemed beautiful to her. She is with two friends, Cynthia and Florence, who accept her as an important playmate. These memories and dreams provide an escape and a defense mechanism for a young woman who is forced at age eleven to leave the safety of her Aunt Joyce's home in Kingston and join her father, Lawrence, and her stepmother, Maureen, in London. Unhappy in her new surroundings, Hyacinth dreams she escapes England, and each time she dreams this she wets the bed.

Inside the house, Hyacinth lives very unhappily with her father, who uses her as a housekeeper, and her stepmother, who hates her as a rival for the father's money and affection, which she believes should go to her own children. More disturbingly, however, Lawrence hovers on the brink of incest, something the girl is too young to understand. Outside the house, she has the problem of her outsider status in a racist and hostile country. Even the other black children do not want to know her because she comes from Jamaica and speaks with an unfamiliar accent. Most of these reactions are responses to Hyacinth's color.

In presenting Hyacinth's father, Riley does not intend to present this male figure as odious. In fact, Lawrence represents the first generation of victimization in his society, the first member of the family to face racism and discrimination. A pathetic, alcoholic, broken man with little to do, Lawrence has no self-confidence and no friends of his own. He beats his second wife, Maureen, and seems to hate her. In turn, Maureen hates Hyacinth and relishes the details of all her beatings. As Hyacinth herself understands, her father's job on the railway has been a disappointment. Like many West Indians, he had thought that his skills and experience would have guaranteed him a better position in England. To compensate for disappointment and humiliation, he has become an alcoholic with a decided propensity for violence. Unfortunately, his abuse takes a vicious and incestuous turn when Hyacinth begins to menstruate. At this point, Maureen overcomes her own oppression to give her presumed rival a warning: "You must watch your father. . . . You are old enough for him to trouble you like he did with your cousin" (45). Again, Hyacinth does not understand the meaning of the word "incest," but she feels the evil symbolized by the word.

Despite their oppression, the women in the novel have a strength that Evelyn O'Callaghan calls their "toughness." Maureen takes a courageous step in standing up to her husband. After experiencing another brutal beating, she decides that she must leave or Lawrence will kill her. She offers to take Hyacinth with her, but Hyacinth feels too bitter to accept an offer that has transcended Maureen's former posture of rivalry. Nevertheless, Hyacinth, now thirteen, understands that her father's attempt to rape her is wrong and manages to escape and telephone the police.

Hyacinth's contact with the police begins a new round of humiliations faced by black children who become wards of the British government. The police send her to an institution, but Hyacinth, never placed with foster parents, is forced instead to live with white children just as abusive as her former schoolmates. By calling the white police, she escapes the personal oppression in her family but none of the causes of that oppression in the larger society. Again, she longs for Jamaica as compensation for the nightmare of oppression. Generalizing about her father's violent treatment of her, she comes to believe that all blacks are violent and tries to dissociate herself from them.

Such generalizing and distancing are unhelpful defenses whose damage is compounded by Hyacinth's escapist reading of romance books and by fantasizing that she has blond hair and blue eyes. Real experiences with men, especially black men, remind her too much of her father and are accompanied by guilt and shame. The image of her father penetrates and spoils any erotic feelings she may experience. At university she meets several Jamaicans, including a close female friend, Perlene, who attempts to introduce her to Caribbean politics. Specifically, Perlene explains the importance of class and the idea that class interests divide the black population in Jamaica. Hyacinth attends lectures on pan-Africanism and the connection between racism in England and in the Caribbean. Yet she resists political awareness because her defense system requires that Jamaica remain an area of perfection to which she could escape from her personal oppression. She refuses to believe that racism exists in Jamaica. Despite this resistance, and despite her desire to view herself as different from other blacks, Hyacinth begins to understand her father's situation from a lecturer at the university: "She found herself sitting forward as he talked about discrimination in schools and housing, remembering the squalor of her father's house with fresh understanding. It brought back other memories too. The teachers turning a blind eye to her misery, the abuse and assaults at the children's home, and, even more painful, her stay in the hostel for young offenders" (116). Whereas Hyacinth begins to gain perspective on her father's social and economic context, her experience as sexual victim remains very difficult to overcome. She finds her first sexual experience very painful, and it reminds her of her father. Even when Hyacinth is an adult, no sexual experience can occur without reminding her of her father's abusiveness.

Hyacinth's return to Jamaica encompasses both an awakening and a tremendous disappointment. Disgusted by the impoverished area where she had grown up, she finds the people there hostile to her because she now represents a different class. She arrives well dressed, carrying packages, and speaking with an English accent. She rejects her Aunt Joyce and their old house. Her sense of "unbelonging" reappears when Florence tells her to return to where she came from—meaning, ironically, England, where Hyacinth had felt so unwelcome. At least she can now put away her dreams of Jamaica and begin to see the real problems of that country, acquiring the political awareness Perlene has been encouraging for many years.

However, Hyacinth's personal awareness will not be so easily resolved. In this respect, the questions of race and class become less important than the issues of sexual abuse and gender. Riley does not present a simplistic positive resolution to childhood incest. Ironically, Melba Wilson, who provides an analysis of the novel in *Crossing the Boundary*, criticizes Hyacinth because she assumes too completely the role of victim:

> I found it difficult to relate to Hyacinth, *because* she wore the badge of victim with such ferocious determination. Her refusal to recognise reality was alien to me. Her inability to let go of a past that was so apparently hopelessly out of the bounds of her reality or any reality (apparent that is, to everyone except Hyacinth) was almost too painful to bear. It was perhaps her way of managing the brutality which she found upon her arrival in the strange country of whites, but the shroud of her pain left no room for anything else. (57)

In effect, however, Riley remains true to her perception of the damage that early childhood abuse and neglect inflict on women. In an interview with Donna Perry, Riley states that she has received many letters from black women who say they have read *The Unbelonging* and have experienced similar situations but, until reading Riley, believed that nobody wrote about them (263). For these and other women, Wilson's call for literature that ends the silence about incest and child sexual abuse finds an answer in Riley, albeit not as positive an answer as Wilson might wish. This division seems rooted in the two writers' slightly differing perspectives on some of the problems in contemporary society. Riley would agree with Wilson that it is unhealthy to create an imaginative world that revolves completely around oppression. And Riley has stated that one of the problems facing the characters in her novels is their inability to come to terms with the past and to create new memories that will allow them to cope with the present:

> In *Unbelonging* the past is handicap, just as it is for so many people here. It's something that stops them from going forward because they've never actually come to terms with exile. It is as much exile if you emigrate as if you came because you had to, particularly

for young people who came in their preteens. They had no choice. (Perry 269)

Some of the events in Riley's *Unbelonging* actually happened to her, and some happened to women she met while employed as a social worker in London. As a student, Riley worked in children's homes and saw firsthand the number of black children who suffered neglect and very poor self-images (267). Riley attempted to contextualize Hyacinth's story of abuse as part of the dislocation that families experienced in moving from the Caribbean to Britain. Under conditions of enormous stress, the family's structure can be skewed, as Riley knew had happened to one of her acquaintances:

> I met one person who had come to England at eleven, which most of them did. And because the parents who were here had new, British families, these arrivals were never seen as children of the family. Because there was this breakdown in relationship, a lot of black girls were inappropriately treated. And she was. The story [*The Unbelonging*] is loosely her story. (Perry 268)

However, one has difficulty imagining a representation of Hyacinth that would not fully explore the pain, humiliation, and guilt resulting from experiences such as those endured by Hyacinth. Riley's depiction does not seem to fit into Wilson's call for full representation of the psychological aftermath of sexual and emotional abuse. In fact, a quick recovery from Hyacinth's experiences would mean falling into the stereotype of black women as strong survivors of any abuse. Riley chooses to end the story with the same dream sequence with which it begins. Hyacinth is in a "secret cave" with her friends, safe from the outside world. Again, this defensive, escapist maneuver shuts out political analysis. The novel's ending clearly demonstrates that Hyacinth cannot put her feelings about Jamaica into a significant political perspective unless she can deal with her personal problems:

> Why had she not listened to the other girl? Perlene knew. She belonged. . . . And always, behind it all, her father waited, crouching in the shadows, beating at her with all the horrors she had faced, laughing and mocking all her attempts at escape. And inside her, deep down, buried inside her woman's body, trapped and bleeding

in the deepest recesses of her, a young girl screamed. As the scream echoed in her mind, the tears seeped out and Hyacinth knew she would never be free until that child had healed. (143)

Hyacinth will never gain political clarity because she needs a pure, imaginative space that her father cannot destroy. Her psychological bargain not only protects her from fully experiencing her own anger but also masks the real problems of self-esteem and political corruption she sees in Jamaica. Thus Riley brings together in a very compelling manner the personal and the political concerns of the young West Indian black woman.

Hyacinth's story is poignant because she experiences a number of the many humiliations that black women have endured. Yet Maureen and Hyacinth overcome obstacles so that they are not purely victims. The text leaves open the possibility that the "child will be healed," yet without glossing over the difficulty of that process. Hyacinth's story, the woman's side of the story, is replete with images of resistance and survival. Possibly, Hyacinth will bring together the various parts of her experience that make her a black woman from Jamaica living in England and dealing with a personal history of abuse.

Notes

1. Margaret Prescod-Roberts and Norma Steele have written an informative work examining immigration among black families, and in particular the role of women in the emigration process. See *Black Women: Bringing It All Back Home.*

2. Lauretta Ngcobo's *Let It Be Told: Black Women Writers in Britain* (1987) is one of the first works to study the importance of émigré black women writers in England. In her introduction, Ngcobo indicates that many black women from the Caribbean and Africa came to England during the 1950s and 1960s, although there were areas in England in which black communities had lived for centuries previous to this time (viii).

3. Many critics of Caribbean literature will also associate the immigration novel with George Lamming, whose two works *The Emigrants* (1954) and *Water with Berries* (1972) explore the problems associated with West Indians moving to Britain.

4. Ngcobo is not being overly positive in her estimation of the experience of black women from South Africa in Britain. She is, however, pointing out the fact that women from a country like Nigeria might feel that their experience is more painful because of the differences in the originating countries. As Ngcobo states in *Let It Be Told:* "The impact of the British experience falls on a padded cushion and often I am aware that this experience is not as raw for me as for many of my people here—nothing in the world can be as devastating as South Africa, so the British experience seems mild by comparison. What I feel most acutely is that Britain is not my place" (140).

5. In one of the earliest and best-known works of literary criticism on African writers, *Women Writers in Black Africa,* Lloyd W. Brown states that, outside of Bessie Head, Emecheta is "the most sustained and vigorous voice of direct, feminist protest," by which he means a writer who protests inequality and dependency (35).

6. Carole Boyce Davies, in her essay "Motherhood in the Works of Male and Female Igbo Writers," discusses the novel in the context of Emecheta's awareness of the importance of motherhood to African women, on the one hand, and the ways in which women's being defined completely through the role is, on the other hand, a kind of enslavement. The trope of slavery runs through Emecheta's works, notably in the title of her novel *The Slave Girl.* In *Let It Be Told*'s introduction, Lauretta Ngcobo discusses *The Joys of Motherhood* as a novel that demonstrates how traditional African culture constrains women's lives (6). Ngcobo claims that the importance of the novel is that it breaks the taboo of silence about women's experiences in order to tell the whole truth about those experiences (6).

Selected Works by Buchi Emecheta

The Bride Price: A Novel. London: George Braziller, 1980.
Destination Biafra. London: Allison & Busby, 1982.
Double Yoke. London: George Braziller, 1985.
The Family. London: George Braziller, 1990.
Head above Water (African Writers Series). New York: Heinemann, 1994.
In the Ditch. New York: Schocken Books, 1980.
The Joys of Motherhood. London: George Braziller, 1979.
Kehinde (African Writers Series). New York: Heinemann, 1994.
The Moonlight Bride. London: George Braziller, 1983.

Nowhere to Play. New York: Schocken, 1980.
The Rape of Shavi. London: George Braziller, 1985.
Second-Class Citizen. London: George Braziller, 1975.
The Slave Girl. London: George Braziller, 1980.
The Wrestling Match. London: George Braziller, 1983.

WORKS BY JOAN RILEY

A Kindness to the Children. London: Women's Press, 1992.
Romance. London: Women's Press, 1988.
The Unbelonging. London: Women's Press, 1985.
Waiting in the Twilight. London: Women's Press, 1987.

SELECTED WORKS ABOUT AFRICAN AND CARIBBEAN WOMEN WRITERS

Ashcroft, Bill, Gareth Griffiths, and Helen Tiffin. *The Empire Writes Back: Theory and Practice in Post-Colonial Literatures.* London: Routledge, 1989.

Bazin, Nancy Topping. "Venturing into Feminist Consciousness: Bessie Head and Buchi Emecheta." *The Tragic Life: Bessie Head and Literature in Southern Africa.* Ed. Cecil Abrahams. Trenton, NJ: Africa World Press, 1990. 45–58.

Brennan, Timothy. *Salman Rushdie and the Third World: Myths of the Nation.* New York: St. Martin's, 1989.

Brodzki, Bella. "'Changing Masters': Gender, Genre, and the Discourse of Slavery." *Borderwork: Feminist Engagements with Comparative Literature.* Ed. Margaret R. Higgonet. Ithaca: Cornell UP, 1994. 42–60.

Brown, Lloyd W. *Women Writers in Black Africa.* Westport, CT: Greenwood, 1981.

Bryan, Beverley, Stella Dadzie, and Suzanne Scafe. *The Heart of the Race: Black Women's Lives in Britain.* London: Virago, 1985.

Cobham, Rhonda, and Merle Collins, eds. *Watchers and Seekers: Creative Writing by Black Women.* London: Women's Press, 1986.

Corhay Ledent, Benedicte. "Between Conflicting Worlds: Female Exiles in Jean Rhys's *Voyage in the Dark* and Joan Riley's *The Unbelonging.*" *Crisis and Creativity in the New Literatures in English: Cross Cultures.* Ed. Geoffrey V. Davis and Hena Maes Jelinek. Amsterdam: Rodopi, 1990. 499–510.

Davies, Carol Boyce. "Black British Women Writing in the Anti-Imperialist

Critique." *Writing New Identities: Gender, Nation, and Immigration in Contemporary Europe.* Ed. Gisela Brinker-Gabler and Sidonie Smith. Minneapolis: U of Minnesota P, 1997. 100–17.

——. "Motherhood in the Works of Male and Female Igbo Writers: Achebe, Emecheta, Napa, and Nzekwu." Davies and Graves 241–56.

Davies, Carol Boyce, and Anne Adams Graves. *Ngambika: Studies of Women in African Literature.* Trenton, NJ: Africa World, 1986.

Emecheta, Buchi. "Head above Water." *Kunapipe* (Aarhus, Denmark) 3.1 (1981): 81–90.

——. "That First Novel." *Kunapipe* (Aarhus, Denmark) 3.2 (1981): 115–23.

Emenyonu, Ernest N. "Technique and Language in Buchi Emecheta's *The Bride Price, The Slave Girl* and *The Joys of Motherhood.*" *Journal of Commonwealth Literature* (London) 23.1 (1988): 130–41.

Esteves, Carmen C., and Lizabeth Paravisini-Gebert, eds. *Green Cane and Juicy Flotsam: Short Stories by Caribbean Women.* New Brunswick, NJ: Rutgers UP, 1991.

Fishburn, Catherine. *Reading Buchi Emecheta: Cross-Cultural Conversations.* Westport, CT: Greenwood Press, 1995.

Gates, Henry Louis, Jr. *The Signifying Monkey: A Theory of Afro-American Literary Criticism.* New York: Oxford UP, 1988.

Gohrisch, Jana. "Crossing the Boundaries of Culture: Buchi Emecheta's Novels." *Anglistik-and-Englischunterricht* 60 (1997): 129–42.

——. "Some Remarks on Writing by Black Women in Britain: Joan Riley's Novels." *Working Class and Feminist Literature in Britain and Ireland in the Twentieth Century.* Vol. 2. Ed. Hanna Behrend and Isolde Neubert. Berlin: Rektor, Humboldt University, 1990. 115–19.

Griffin, Gabriele. "'Writing the Body': Reading Joan Riley, Grace Nichols, and Ntozake Shange." *Black Women's Writing.* Ed. Gina Wisker. New York: St. Martin's, 1993. 19–42.

Iyer, Lisa H. "The Second Sex Three Times Oppressed: Cultural Colonization and Coll(i)(u)sion in Buchi Emecheta's Women." *Writing the Nation: Self and Country in the Post-Colonial Imagination.* Ed. John C. Hawley. Amsterdam: Rodopi, 1996.

Kenyon, Olga. "Alice Walker and Buchi Emecheta Rewrite the Myth of Motherhood." *Forked Tongues? Comparing Twentieth-Century British and American Literature.* Ed. Ann Massa and Alistair Stead. London: Longman, 1994. 336–54.

King, Bruce. "The New Internationalism: Shiva Naipaul, Salman Rushdie,

Buchi Emecheta, Timothy Mo, and Kazuo Ishiguro." *The British and Irish Novel since 1960.* Ed. James Acheson. New York: St. Martin's, 1991. 192–211.

Lewis, Gordon K. "The Contemporary Caribbean: A General Overview." *Caribbean Contours.* Ed. Sidney W. Mintz and Sally Price. Baltimore: Johns Hopkins UP, 1985. 219–50.

Mordecai, Pamela, and Betty Wilson, eds. *Her True-True Name: An Anthology of Women's Writing from the Caribbean.* London: Heinemann, 1989.

Nasta, Susheila. "Samuel Selvon: *The Lonely Londoners.*" *A Handbook for Teaching Caribbean Literature.* Ed. David Dabydeen. London: Heinemann, 1988. 26–34.

Ngcobo, Lauretta, ed. *Let It Be Told: Black Women Writers in Britain.* London: Virago, 1987.

O'Callaghan, Evelyn. "Feminist Consciousness: European/American Theory, Jamaican Stories." *Journal of Caribbean Studies* 6.2 (1988): 143–62.

Oko, Emelia. "The Female Estate: A Study of the Novels of Buchi Emecheta." *Feminism and Black Women's Creative Writing: Theory, Practice, and Criticism.* Ed. Aduke Adebayo. Ibadan, Nigeria: AMD, 1996.

Opara, Chioma. "Clothing as Iconography: Examples of Ba, Aidoo, and Emecheta." *Feminism and Black Women's Creative Writing: Theory, Practice, and Criticism.* Ed. Aduke Adebayo. Ibadan, Nigeria: AMD, 1996.

Oriaku, Remy. "Buchi Emecheta: If Not a Feminist, Then What?" *Feminism and Black Women's Creative Writing: Theory, Practice, and Criticism.* Ed. Aduke Adebayo. Ibadan, Nigeria: AMD, 1996.

Perry, Donna. *Backtalk: Women Writers Speak Out: Interviews by Donna Perry.* New Brunswick, NJ: Rutgers UP, 1993.

Prescod-Roberts, Margaret, and Norma Steele. *Black Women: Bringing It All Back Home.* Bristol, England: Falling Wall Press, 1980.

Riley, Joan. "Writing Reality in a Hostile Environment." *Kunapipe* (Aarhus, Denmark) 16.1 (1991): 517–52.

Senior, Olive. *Working Miracles: Women's Lives in the English-Speaking Caribbean.* Bloomington: Indiana UP, 1991.

Sougou, Omar. "The Experience of an African Woman in Britain: A Reading of Buchi Emecheta's *Second Class Citizen.*" *Crisis and Creativity in the New Literatures in English: Cross Cultures.* Ed. Geoffrey V. Davis and Hena Maes Jelinek. Amsterdam: Rodopi, 1990. 511–22.

Steady, Chioma Filomina. *The Black Woman Crossculturally.* Cambridge, MA: Schenkman, 1981.

Taiwo, Oladele. *Female Novelists in Modern Africa.* London: Macmillan, 1984.

Umeh, Marie. "Buchi Emecheta." *Postcolonial African Writers: A Bio-Bibliographical Critical Source Book.* Westport, CT: Greenwood, 1998. 148–63.

Wilson, Melba. *Crossing the Boundary: Black Women Survive Incest.* Seattle: Seal, 1993.

Yongue, Patricia Lee. "'My Mother Is Here': Buchi Emecheta's Love Child." *Women of Color: Mother-Daughter Relationships in 20th-Century Literature.* Ed. Elizabeth Brown-Guillory. Austin: U of Texas P, 1996.

15
Muriel Spark: Beginning Again

John Glavin

Some not really humdrum people think a quote from Foucault can justify any sort of critical eccentricity. I'm not one of them. But if I were, I'd have begun this essay by quoting that passage from "The Masked Philosopher" where Foucault dreams of "a criticism of scintillating leaps of the imagination [that] would not be sovereign" but would "catch the sea-foam in the breeze and scatter it."[1] "Not . . . sovereign" I can manage. And I'm really good at "scatter." But it's the "scintillating" that gets me down. Still, I like the idea of criticism by leaps, criticism in waves, criticism that is always, like Spark herself, beginning again.

BEGINNINGS

Muriel Spark *is* always beginning again. (Some synonyms for that, as we shall see, can be "transfiguration" and "conversion.") Before she became a novelist, at close to forty years of age, she had been a poet and editor, a well-known London-based essayist and literary critic, a critic who looked upon the novel as a highly suspect genre. And before she was a literateur she had been a spy, a "scrambler" of messages. And before that she had been an émigré. Before that a bored, abused colonial wife, married to a sadist she calls S.O.S., and a mother. Before that—well, you get the picture. There are no real beginnings where nothing follows up. Not for a writer who, like the protagonist of her latest novel, *Reality and Dreams,* repeatedly seems to inquire: I fell off my perch. Now I want a divorce from my past ideas. How do I achieve this?[2]

The writer who is constantly falling, because she is pushing herself off her perch, calls no place her own. That means, among other things, that every word, every page Spark ever wrote simply loathes each beautifully phrased tittle and jot in Virginia Woolf's *A Room of One's Own.* I can go even further than that. Her entire career insists that a room of one's own can never be a room with a view worth savoring. What "One" really needs—if one is a writer—is a room of somebody else's, a room one might rent for a while with ease, and then just as easily abandon, divorce. A room, unburdened by one's past, in which a writer can always begin again. (I point this out here, in this collection of essays, merely as a kindness. The reader who believes that all worthwhile twentieth-century fiction by women must somehow affiliate to Woolf, and to Woolf's own room, will give this chapter a pass.) No room of one's own, and no time of one's own.

Perhaps I might have started off on the right foot if I had begun with her uncommon, unconventional short stories. That's at least where Spark herself probably would have preferred me to start: in 1995 she told me to teach the short—not the long—fiction in a course devoted to her prose. And if I had decided to begin this essay with the short stories, I should doubtless have begun with the short story that ought to have begun her career as a writer of fiction, her prize-winning Christmas tale "The Seraph and the Zambesi" (1951).[3] Yet "The Seraph" didn't really begin her career as a fiction writer. As her autobiography *Curriculum Vitae* (1992) makes painfully clear, despite her prize Spark continued to endure years of deprivation, indeed of starvation to the point of breakdown, before *The Comforters* (1957) furnished the real beginning to her career in fiction. And at the same time, she continued to write and publish poetry, as she still does. See: even at the so-called but inevitably spurious start, this curious, defining rhythm, beginning only to have to begin again, only to find that all her beginnings seem somehow to turn out mysteriously preliminary. And "The Seraph" marks a misleading beginning in another way also. It's a story about writing and inauthenticity—not surprising, since it is a Christmas story, and therefore about incarnating a word—but also about writing as inauthenticity. The slender plot focuses on a comic confrontation over staging a pageant during a stifling African Christmas, a contest between two sorts of writers, a false, fleshy alcoholic, Samuel Cramer, and a truly sublime author, the Seraph, their contretemps witnessed by the author's anonymous persona, a (let's make the leap) would-be writer.

"My masque," said Cramer.
"Ah, no, mine," said the Seraph. "Yours won't do." ("Seraph" 82)

In the story, Cramer emerges as a sodden, self-besotted, failed talent, what she'll later call a *pisseur de copie*. But a year or so earlier, the poet Muriel Spark had deployed Cramer as her highly sympathetic, indeed heroic emblem, in "The Ballad of the Fanfarlo." There, Cramer, borrowed from a Baudelaire *nouvelle*, figures the strong poet's steadfast resistance to postwar London's meretricious vacuum. Within a year, within her fiction, he has suddenly, inexplicably, been rejected. And that rejection is further complicated by her story's ambivalent identification of Cramer with the kind of crude colonial male she had fled when she escaped from her marriage and Africa. Cramer is now not only everything she herself has just been, and admired, but also and at the same time everything she still loathes.

But if Cramer is both the self and the past that Spark the fiction writer wants to divorce, the Seraph scarcely prefigures what she now prefers to become. As the tale concludes, her narrator can only watch the Seraph "ride the Zambesi away from us" (84), leaving her behind to gape in a degraded landscape of commonplace metamorphoses "among the rocks that look like crocodiles and the crocodiles that look like rocks" (84). "I was right," the narrator proclaims, but right about what? Right, it would seem, only about where you can find the vapor trail which the supremely evanescent, inimitably authentic writer leaves behind. There's little left of the Seraph for this new writer of fiction besides "the mute flashes of summer lightning" (84) that illuminate the empty Falls. If Cramer is exactly the sort of writer she hates to have been, his alternative, the Seraph, is exactly the sort of writer she can never even hope to begin to be.

If, then, we choose to stake out this initial story as some sort of scene of instruction, what I still can't figure for myself is: what's here to learn?

One answer to that question won't come from the philosopher Arthur Danto. Very sweetly, he titles his 1981 "Philosophy of Art"[4] as a sort of homage to Muriel Spark, *The Transfiguration of the Commonplace*. The title of course refers to the book of the same name written by the central character of *The Prime of Miss Jean Brodie*, Sandy Stranger, after she becomes a cloistered nun hence known as Sister Helena of the Transfiguration.

That title haunts Spark criticism, and with good cause. Since Jean Brodie is so broadly based on Spark's own Edinburgh childhood, particularly on her own Miss Brodie, Christina Kay, and since Spark, like Sandy, converted as a young woman to Roman Catholicism and then became famous as a writer, it's no great leap to read the novel a clef and to claim Sandy's book and theme as Spark's own. Especially after Spark went on to publish in the mid-1960s *The Mandelbaum Gate*, where the plot turns on a mysterious line of changes set in motion on Mount Tabor, the site of the New Testament's paradigmatic Transfiguration, changes that begin on August 6, the (old style) feast of the Transfiguration. And Spark even seems to have confirmed all this when, answering an inquiry from Danto, she replied that Sister Helena's book "would have been about art, as she herself practiced it" (Danto vi).

But then I think Danto gets it wrong. He interprets Spark's admission to refer to what he takes to be her "practice . . . in transforming commonplace young women into creatures of fiction, radiant in mystery: a kind of literary caravaggism" (v). But isn't that exactly what Spark doesn't do? Indeed, isn't that kind of "transforming" the very opposite of "transfiguration"? The whole point about transfiguration seems to be that it is not transformation, or that it's a sort of transformation-manque at least when you're referring to a notion derived from *the* Transfiguration. In the New Testament narrative, the onlooking apostles glimpse Christ as he must look in Eternity, conversing with Moses and Elijah, and then, before they can do anything about it except hide their eyes, he's back among them looking very much as he always has. And telling them to keep it all to themselves. Transfiguration is literally unspeakable. It is evanescent, momentary, elusive, and illusionary. It may mark a difference epistemologically, but it doesn't, can't, make a difference ontologically. Just the reverse: this sort of transfiguration is always about the poignant gulf between what we may from time to time chance to see and what we, all the rest of the time, do and are.

In that sense, transfiguration is about Spark's own artistic process as long as we do not think she's claiming that she transforms the commonplace into the extraordinary. On her pages the commonplace continues deeply common and quite firmly in place. Transformation, Danto's cara-vaggism, names his, not her, philosophy of art, his ideal, just as it is, ironi-cally, Sandy Stranger's. Sandy Stranger can't forgive Miss Brodie for not producing transformation. The little girl feels her magical teacher open-ing a world entirely different from that of her petit bourgeois mother, an extraordinary world that can transform the child's life into some-thing mysterious and romantic. In other words, she thinks Jean Brodie is Danto's version of Muriel Spark. But all Miss Brodie can produce is the occasional glimpse into that glamorous landscape, hardly an access, merely a recurring narrative, a set of images. Pig-eyed Sandy remains sadly commonplace and, as she enters adolescence, intelligent enough to know, and be angry about, her persistent banality. Indeed, she finally gets angry enough to ruin her former teacher exactly because Miss Brodie has *not* for naught transformed her, as she goes on to transform herself into the mysteriously inaccessible, ineffably wise Sister Helena of—of course—the Transfiguration.

From all this Spark remains tartly aloof. Her books, unlike her char-acter's, tend to be made not from transformations but from something very much like those "mute flashes of summer lightning," fugitive, witty illuminations—sudden, unexpected, discontinuous glimpses into the cu-rious way in which most of the time mounting-up doesn't mean leading-to. It's an art made from sequences of closer, deglamorizing views that take us up and almost immediately thereafter let us down. An art para-digmatically exemplified in the momentary transfiguration that shapes the Zambesi Seraph's transitory, exhilarating, disappointing manifesta-tion. A manifestation that leaves the viewers not transformed but comi-cally stranded, in steadfast commonness amongst the rocks, the drunks, and the crocodiles.

We seem now to have secured a foothold here, so perhaps we can ac-tually begin here. Spark's second-best-known book is called *Memento Mori* (1959)—that is: remember to die. But if we wanted to name a "way" through her work, it might better be to replay that title as *Memento Con-vertere,* that is: remember to convert. Or better still: remember to begin yet again, and again. Or best yet: remember to convert constantly, or at least frequently (beginning again and again) in order not to die. Mori, memento?

This works because Spark turns out to be a sort of professional convert. Conversion is as much the key to her career as confession is to Rousseau's. She is without exaggeration a genius at converting. Don't get me wrong. I'm not referring merely to her notorious conversion to Roman Catholicism in 1954, the conversion that followed her somewhat less notorious, slightly earlier conversion to Anglicanism. (She comes from a mixed Jewish and Christian ancestry, and until her early thirties seems not to have been at all religious.) No, this goes beyond religion. Spark converts for the sake of converting, she converts to stay not dead.

Earlier I offered a list of her jobs. Here's a list of her convertible fictions:

—(1957–61) from *The Comforters* through *The Bachelors:* witty, theological parables of small-scale evil and good set in a physically dilapidated, morally shabby postwar London (except for *Robinson,* which converts Defoe's tale to the same sort of moral allegory).

And then, just after (and because?) she had perfected that form

—(1962–63) *The Prime of Miss Jean Brodie* and *The Girls of Slender Means:* sly, tender evocations of her own earlier life.

Only to be followed next by

—(1965) *The Mandelbaum Gate:* a big—her only big—novel, a mysterious multi-character, multi-plot book about transfiguration set in the then divided Jerusalem and its environs. It met with remarkable success; at no point perhaps has her reputation been higher. Reviewing it, Frank Kermode more or less suggested it was to this century what George Eliot's *Middlemarch* was to the preceding era.

And immediately, after it, of course, she set about converting all her energies into writing the absolutely opposite sort of book.

—(1968–73) laconic, very short satires, almost anti-novels, mostly concerned with the excesses of the expatriate wealthy or (in the inimitable *The Abbess of Crewe*) the powerful in both church and state. (These include my favorite among her books, the glorious and perfect *The Hothouse by the East River,* for my money the finest comedy in English after Oscar Wilde's *The Importance of Being Earnest.*) These books seem not only to unwrite but actually to write against everything established and claimed by *The Mandelbaum Gate.*

And then

—(1976–79) in *The Takeover* and *Territorial Rights* she returns to conventionally plotted and characterized novels about abuse of trust and fatuous self-indulgence in la dolce vita Italy. Indeed, *Territorial Rights* quite boldly sets out to rewrite Henry James's novella *The Aspern Papers*, and one adjective for these novels is certainly Jamesian, not a term one might have thought applying to any of her earlier work.

But then unexpectedly,

—(1981–1990) beginning with *Loitering with Intent* she sets about fictionalizing her own history, but here in a new manner that conflates the anti-novel style of her late-1960s satires with the subject matter of her earlier, heavily autobiographical books, *Miss Brodie* and *Girls of Slender Means*. This period feels, at least now, like a coda, in which Spark revisits not only her own earlier life and methods but even her own earlier fiction—for example, quite explicitly rewriting her first Job story, and first novel, *The Comforters,* as the much darker, unflinching tale of terrorism among tourists, *The Only Problem.*

Why? Why this perpetual beginning again? Why this insatiable compulsion to convert? Why this flight?

But to answer that question, I find I have to begin yet again, in quite a different mode, with some selected short views.

Short Views

Given Spark's emergence in that era we quite properly call the Audenesque (and because next to Spark, I admire Auden the most), I've shaped this second part from lines in his 1946 Phi Beta Kappa poem, "Under Which Lyre":

> Between the chances, choose the odd;
> Read *The New Yorker,* trust in God;
> And take short views.

Here then follow a few short views of some of Spark's very best books— short views that divide among early, middle, and late Spark.

For a short view of the early work there are two ways we might read *The Girls of Slender Means.* First, read Joanna Childe as the novel's martyr-heroine—a sort of Saint Joan—whose heroic, prayerful selflessness converts the poetaster Nicholas Farringdon from ineffectual flaneur to missionary and martyr. Read this way, the novel quite clearly is setting out to revise [convert?] Hopkins's "Wreck of the Deutschland," the poem Joanna is forever reciting. She certainly does echo in words and actions the tall nun praying at the peak of the catastrophe. And Farringdon turns out to be very like the Jesuit poet himself, "the disappointing son of a good English family," Oxbridge-educated, an unpublished avant-garde writer and "a bit of a misfit" (61). Just as Hopkins thrills to the story of the nun, the "spectacle" of Joanna's psalm-chanting death "galvanizes Nicholas's religious sense, fixes his life" (Kemp 89). (In the publisher Rudi Bittesch, Farringdon even gets his own Robert Bridges, the post-humous editor of his work.) Let's call this the novel's Catholic reading.

Second, we may read Joanna's antithesis Selina Redwood as a feminist antiheroine, acting out "the code of female survival," "Triumphantly deny[ing] facile male humanitarianism in favor of the emblem, myth, and vision of a female world" (Auerbach 178). When she abandons her companions trapped in the fiery club, choosing instead to save the Schiaparelli evening dress, "her apparent betrayal is also an act of salva-tion: in stealing the dress and leaving the girls to burn, Selina has res-cued the symbol of their community, a truer memento of the Club than any individual member would have been" (Auerbach 178). That is Nina Auerbach's reading, which means, a priori, it is formidable, smart, and to be reckoned with. However, I buy neither the first nor the second read-ing. I'd rather read the novel as an "ingenious," "Savage" fiction about being co-opted to write, despite oneself, a culturally mandated fiction that devastates women.

In the first reading, Hopkins thinks the nun's dying call, "Come Lord Jesus," signals an English apocalypse. But Joanna heralds no transform-ing revelation; she beckons toward no renewal of faith. Her attenuated dying is merely utter, bitter, and unredeemed loss, "circling round, vaguely wobbling," "puzzled," reciting psalms "compulsively," groping, "partially blind," missing her chance to escape when "half-way up" (159–61). In the end, unlike the nun, her voice "really has been wiped out" (164), and with her the "house sank into its centre" (161). In response Nicholas does not become an undervalued, eccentric, proto-avant-garde poet of almost the very first rank, but an ineffectual crank, the subject of gossip, not gospel.

In the second reading it seems too much to speak of Selina's safe ne-gotiation of "the 'danger-zone' between domesticity and war" (Auerbach 177–78). Early on, the novel can scarcely distinguish her from the mad girl Pauline Fox. "Down the staircase [Selina] floated, as it were even more realistically than had the sad communer with the spirit of Jack Buchanan [Anne Fox] a few moments ago floated up it. It might have been the same girl" (19). By the time the novel ends, even that "might have been" is canceled. The last we hear of Selina, she can't stop screaming, hastily married to a crooner in Clarges Street (171–72). The last we see of her, she is carrying "the fairly long and limp" dress from which the "coat-hanger dangled . . . like a head-less neck and shoulder" (154). If Joanna is Hopkins's nun, then perhaps we're not far off in seeing Selina here as Michelangelo's St. Bartholomew, patron of massacre, his grotesque, flayed face and skin draped over an arm at the bottom of the Sistine Last Judgment.

Of course, each girl does represent, in her own way, a May of Teck ideal, the best of the girls of slender means. But admiration from the May of Teck seems to mean you end up either mad or dead. Those outcomes emerge, quite literally, because the club's managers have bricked in its skylight. I know that's obvious. If the skylight had not been bricked in, then all the girls could have easily climbed out in time to save their lives and their minds. But what does that blocked access "mean"? That's certainly a question Spark seems intent that we raise. She does begin the novel, after all, by claiming that this is a world in which "windows . . . had accumulated much meaning" (4–5). What meaning, then, we seem to be invited to ask, has this particular window, this curiously blocked window, "accumulated"? In the club's grotesque erotic economy, no significant difference emerges between lover and attacker, between visitor and burglar. The skylight has been blocked "by someone's hysterical order" because "a man had penetrated" it "to visit a girl" (144). The interloper was either "a burglar or a lover" who "attacked or merely confronted unexpectedly, or found in bed" his lover. Or was she merely his victim? Or even his accomplice? Or all three (32–33)? It's all so over-interpretable, so plurally explained, at once so simply traumatic—a man penetrated a girl—and so full of alterity—or are we dealing here with some kind of primal scene? At least as Ned Lukacher would define primal scene: the "ontologically undecidable intertextual event that is situated in the differential space between historical memory and imaginative reconstruction, between archival verification and interpretive free play," whose "indeterminant temporality precipitates the temporal ordering of subsequent events" (24, 387). I think that means that, ultimately, it doesn't matter what may actually have originally happened. What does matter is that the women in the club, the women in the novel, women as Spark imagines them, are haunted, harrowed by the primal violence inescapable in men, all men, the individual sexual violence of a burglar-lover, the organized, mass violence of the war, the violence epitomized in the composite of those two kinds of brutality, the "seaman" (surely a pun) who slides "a knife silently between the ribs of a woman who was with him" outside the Palace as victory is declared (174). The break-in from the roof. The bomb concealed in the garden. It's all one.

And the club—that is: the way the "nice" classes in Britain organize women's sexuality—actually exacerbates this omnipresent terror by its insistence on immuring young women in a system of idealization that makes them more rather than less vulnerable to the outrage lurking just above or beneath the apparently placid surface of bourgeois mating rituals. The May of Teck club is, and not very covertly, a machine of devastation. Memorializing the common legend of many "screams in the night" (171–72), it has locked—or bricked—in all the women, denying their access to the roof, to the sky, to freedom, and, for Joanna, to life.

Trying to save those it idealizes, nice Britain merely leaves them entrapped, because its ideals are, in the long run, just those that please men most. (How odd it feels to write this sentence just after the funeral of the Princess of Wales.) Either the girls please men as dutiful daughters—Joanna, the "proclaiming statue" (16) echoes her father's voice, and the voices of the poets and "those theologically minded curates" (23) to whom she listens "obsessively" (24); literally bound by their words, she "pressed down her feelings" (23) and decides "to enter maimed into the Kingdom of heaven" (26)—or they please as sexual conquests: Selina must trade sex for food and, even more crucially, for clothing coupons that produce that "Elegant dress" (57) on which her well-being depends and for which she ultimately and literally—the Schiaparelli—has to trade her self-respect. But whether sacred or profane, pious or poised, girls in this club are narrowed to means far too slender either to save or to free themselves, denied any history but the scream-punctuated "legend," immured in scenarios in which they are never adequate to define or free themselves. "Nicholas said, 'The men are coming to open the skylight'" (151). But of course they never do, or they never do in time. Why should they?

What's more, and worse, the novel—I warn you: here's where things get especially grim—seems to side with the club. Readers find themselves persuaded to idealize Joanna or Selina, to idealize the whole concept of the May of Teck, because the novel itself keeps on doing exactly that, despite its acute awareness of the club's constricting, destructive agenda. Repeatedly, we find the novel making some claim like: "it was not an unjust notion, that [the club] was a miniature expression of a free society, that it was a community held together by the graceful attributes of a common poverty" (13). Its girls are regularly "delightful . . . ingenious . . . movingly lovely" (16). Membership in its precincts enlists one in "a desirable order of life" (1). Of course, the novel is not the club, though the club's qualities also mark Spark's own style: gracious, centered, frugal, witty, self-disciplined, tolerant. But the novel also sees beneath the club's attractive features the ways in which it ensnares, disables, and even destroys its adherents. Clearly, the novel would like to abandon the club. Just as clearly, it can't. It knows no worse, but it knows no better.

I think that means we've arrived at a scene primal not only to *The Girls of Slender Means* but to the entire shape of Spark's fiction, the whole "ordering of subsequent events" that we've been calling from the beginning "beginning again." It is Spark's own trauma, her own primal scene, that the club is primarily constructed to enclose and delimit. She underwrites the club's necessity, all the while deploring its tendency to destroy those very women she cherishes, because she can uncover no better shield against those primal "many screams in the night."

In the first reading, this primal memory conceives male sexuality as inherently brutal, naturally duplicitous, and always a threat, perhaps even a deadly threat—exactly the way sexually active men do appear in Spark's fiction almost without exception (I actually can't think of a single exception, but I'd better cover my flank). The only nice men in Spark, the only reliable ones, are those who are clearly sexually unavailable. In the second, for women, heterosexuality must always open into nightmare. In fact, you can't find a conventionally successful heterosexual romance in her novels before 1988—about which exception more below.

So now, perhaps, we begin to grasp more clearly what we began noticing to start, but which then only befuddles us. If a woman begins again, over and over, she just might avoid being entrapped in the conditions heterosexuality commonly places on her sex. She can never escape those conditions entirely. There's no chance of transformation, obviously, because there is no way to transform men. The only chance of escape seems to lie in regular, brilliant, startling transfiguration, always only becoming, leaving behind every course just before it fully forms. Continually converting her energies, her identities, her endeavors, to new forms, in new fields, she keeps alive at least the energy for self-fashioning, even if she must finally acknowledge that a fully emancipated, independent self is an asymptote, always beckoning, never attained. What's more—and even more important—she can thereby keep herself out of the deadly hands of men. Not within the novels, perhaps, but as a novelist, obviously.

The Girls was early Spark. Now for middle. Early Spark seems to last from The Comforters (1957) until The Mandelbaum Gate (1965), a long series of wittily fictive variations on the motif of transfiguration. But then something radically changes. The extraordinary, grotesque, bizarre novels that follow, The Public Image (1968) through The Hothouse by the East River (1973), "arrange the plot as death might" (Kermode 425). Each of them returns in one way or another to the central figure of a woman incarcerated in a narrative she desperately, and without much success, strives to undo. Together they form "a study in a way of self-destruction," Spark's description of their epitome, The Driver's Seat ("Keeping It Short" 412). In her own self-destruction, I would argue. "I frightened myself by writing [Driver's Seat], but I just had to go on . . . I had to go into hospital to finish" (413).

What necessity impels that willing oneself into illness, that self-hospitalizing, that recurring brush with death? Typically, before the narrative begins in these novels, a young woman takes up a public image fundamentally at odds with the truth of her private history. She does this, more or less innocently, or perhaps just thoughtlessly, in order not to disturb her chances for prosperity, for success, or merely for survival. However, as the novel begins she discovers herself only apparently in her story's driver's seat. In fact, there's a terrible fraud at the core of her being, a hothouse of artificial and dangerous psychic growth that saps not only her integrity but also in large part her sanity. Only by pulling up that fraud by the roots, killing off the public image, can she hope to free herself from the moral and psychic rot that has overtaken her life. Unhappily, killing the public image may mean, as it certainly does in The Girls, killing the essential self also. In this middle period, then, the victim has become indistinguishable from the killer-lover. And her murder is no less terrible or final because the intruder "stabs with a turn of his wrist exactly as she instructed" (Driver's Seat 117).

Middle Spark, then, seems to mean that early Spark got it wrong, so fundamentally—no, that's too watery—so fatally wrong, that middle Spark can not merely not undo, but is itself undone in trying to get it right. Middle Spark is saying, in effect, writing these novels is killing me; killing me is why I write these middle books. *Memento Mori* has become the only book she can write, but it is no longer a story of the moribund and superannuated, but of the woman who once thought she could chronicle their story at a safe distance.

By 1981, however, everything is changed again. It is now late Spark, and late Spark mercifully bears little resemblance to early Spark, and—thank goodness—none to middle. Look, she has come through! We begin all over again, just as we thought we were about to wrap up.

After three novels of social satire, the first scintillating, the second and third crepuscular, she rejoices to rediscover "what a wonderful thing . . . to be a woman and an artist in the twentieth century" (*Loitering* 181), and that joy literally enlivens and (what else) transfigures this and all her subsequent work (63). What has happened? In a word, she has discovered an innate and all-defining agamy.

"Agamy" refers literally to the absence or nonrecognition of the marriage relation. I've enlarged on that meaning—because I can't find another word that quite does the job—to characterize a certain kind of imagination, often but not always an artistic imagination. (It is quite frequently a religious imagination, where it is often accompanied by willed or imposed celibacy; *agamy* is the Greek word for celibacy.) The agamous personality chooses originality over mutuality, knows that he or she doesn't need an, or any, other to become fully or satisfactorily the self, and in fact reacts with horror to any sort of regular coupling. Agamy, to be successful, thus requires heroic narcissism. Not the ordinary, just-look-around-you type of narcissism, which is about the selfish love of lovely or unlovely one. The narcissism that insists on a room of one's own, a large room, with a really nice view. (Vide: those Woolfs.) No, this is a narcissism refined, deepened, focused, a narcissism targeted to what one does rather than who one is, and therefore largely unselfish, generous, and often even self-abnegating. (For more on this positive vision of narcissism you might want to look at Heinz Kohut's *Self Psychology and the Humanities* [1985],[5] especially "Forms and Transformations of Narcissism" and "Thoughts on Narcissism and Narcissistic Rage." A caution: "agamy" is my word, not his.) If you want some pedigree think of agamy as the driving force in Emily Brontë (but not in Charlotte—which is of course why it's Emily and not Charlotte who absorbs Spark's book on the Brontës). And it's also the force driving Dickens.[6]

Agamy is also the force driving Benvenuto Cellini, that supremely committed artist, the key figure in Fleur Talbot's refiguring of her life in *Loitering with Intent*. Cellini's autobiography seems to Fleur to be "sheer magic" (123), no overstatement since its fortuitous discovery literally transforms, not just transfigures, her life. She finds in those pages the figure she will immediately set out to copy. Change genders and material, from sculpture to prose, and Fleur's summary of Cellini's life virtually echoes her own plot: "his love for the goblets and the statues he made out of materials he adored, his imprisonments, his escapes, his dealings with his fellow goldsmiths and sculptors, his homicides and brawls, and again his delight in every aspect of his craft" (123). Well, perhaps not homicides, though there are several deaths mysteriously attached to her tale. What Fleur discovers in Cellini, entirely missing in the work of her earlier hero, Newman, is a life that enjoys, a life that is essentially composed of, and by, "a long love affair with his art" (124). The discovery that such a lifelong affair can generate the deepest satisfaction suddenly makes it joyfully clear, to Fleur Talbot and, a little less suddenly, I think, to Spark (this is an admittedly, indeed intensively, autobiographical novel), that neither woman has either reason or obligation to tell or to relive the conventional scenarios of union. The creating self and its craft are enough for any life to be full of "chance grace." "And so, having entered the fullness of my years, I go on my way rejoicing" (217).

Writing back through her own life becomes the way to release late Spark from endlessly fleeing the primal scene. It is as though she has at last accumulated sufficient experience, and confidence in that experience, to dislodge the version of herself that she cannot bear to write—in favor of a story of herself she delights to tell. Spark started off by revising all those inherited narratives, from *Job* and *Robinson Crusoe* through *The Aspern Papers* and *The Golden Bough,* as though she could never get beyond playing a sort of dodge-em with the master's tales. Repeatedly, inevitably playing Cramer to the Seraph. Now, *mirabile dictu* (she's a very fine Latinist, by the way), she has realized she's not only a first-rate storyteller—she always knew that—but a first-rate story in the telling.

Here then, from Fleur Talbot's meditations on her early novel *War-*

render Chase, is a passage we can cut and paste as a kind of Spark manifesto for agamous style:

(1) "I wasn't writing poetry and prose so that the reader would think me a nice person, but in order that my sets of words should convey ideas of truth and wonder" (8).

(2) "I treated the story of Warrender Chase with a light and heartless hand as is my way when I have to give a perfectly serious account of things" (81).

(3) "I've come to learn for myself how little one needs, in the art of writing, to convey the lot, and how a lot of words, on the other hand, can convey so little" (82).

(4) "I didn't go in for motives, I never have" (83). In other words: the agamous writer refuses ever to be nice, that is, to fulfill any sort of conventional expectation. She tells instead her own truth, a truth at which conventional people can only *wonder.* The *nice* are habituated to treat the *perfectly serious* as weighty and full of feeling. The agamous are free to treat the perfectly serious as *light* and *heartless.* They know that a *lot* of life can be discarded to focus on the *little* that really signifies, the *little* that refuses the imperatives of both the unconscious and the social collective, both alike the breeding ground of *motive.* It's *motive* that always overdetermines. But agamy values instead those spontaneously realized *light, heartless,* wonderful sets of words that suit exactly and only the agamist's needs. Narcissistic, yes. But terrific, right? And agamous, certainly.

Although the surrender to agamy appears first in *Loitering with Intent,* it's in a subsequent novel, *A Far Cry from Kensington* (1988), that Spark works out her discovery most fully. From that novel's elaborate (over-elaborate?) argument I want to select two points on which to concentrate, points which bring my own argument almost to a stopping place.

First, rewriting her self, Spark returns in *A Far Cry* to the postwar London that provided the setting for *The Girls of Slender Means;* indeed, she returns explicitly to the site and the subject of the earlier novel, the rooming house lives of unattached women. Here Wanda Podolak's death echoes Joanna Childe's of almost thirty years earlier, just as Nick Farringdon's moving in the world of corrupt publishers anticipates *Kensington*'s far nastier Hector Bartlett, the *pisseur de copie,* and the novel's shady firms of the Ullswater Press and Mackintosh & Tooley. And each novel ends with an explosion; the bomb-ripped May of Teck contrasting the ruined premises of the Highgate Review (*Far Cry* 185). What's different in the later novel—startlingly different—is the distance the narrator, Nancy Hawkins, can keep between herself and the story of men abusing women that we earlier took to be her inventor's primal scene.

In *A Far Cry* it is Wanda, the narrator's antithesis, who suffers the horrors of devastation. Her ambiguous lover, the *pisseur,* sneaks into the boardinghouse, doubly disguised as cousin and seminarian, using sex to betray her, reducing her to the (sadly inevitable) screams in the night: "That cry, that cry" (148), and finally to death, not by fire this time, but by drowning. (Even closer to Hopkins's nun, then.) Curiously, and wonderfully, Mrs. Hawkins is thereby freed to recollect the primal scene in her own life, a scene that no longer has the power to terrify her but seems merely an unhappy, rather dingy fragment of a now no longer relevant past. And of course it goes without saying that Mrs. Hawkins's recollection parallels with painful clarity Spark's disclosures in *Curriculum Vitae* of her own abusive marriage to S.O.S.

Mrs. Hawkins's recollection of her marriage retains the outline of the common primal scene outlined in our discussion of the early Spark. A criminal/lover (he is AWOL) at the top of a rooming house suddenly turns on the woman, now his wife, and tries to kill her, (exactly as Spark's own newly wedded husband began, in the confines of their ship's cabin, to beat her on their honeymoon journey to Africa). But Nancy Hawkins survives that onslaught, with only a "great bruise on my forehead" and "a cut on my neck" (127). The experience even yields her a sort of bluff, practical wisdom: "It is my advice to any woman getting married to start, not as you mean to go on, but worse, tougher, than you mean to go on. Then you can slowly relax and it comes as a pleasant surprise" (127).

Of course, I think Mrs. Hawkins, unlike Joanna and all the earlier Joanna-like heroines, escapes the pain of the primal scene because her inventor has refounded her own life firmly on agamy. Nancy Hawkins takes what comes, as it comes, confident in her ability to make the best she can out of what transpires. Celliniesque, or perhaps we should say Fleur-esque, she moves haphazardly from job to job, taking work when it is offered, gracefully accepting her first and then her second unmerited firing. She delights in solitariness and self-reliance. For most of the narrative she lives perfectly content in a rooming house, driven by no need of her own space or for companions of her own choice and taste, easily associating with all sorts. "You can decide to think," she insists, so that "the weight of destiny no longer [bears] on the current problems of . . . life" (5).

This leads me to the one glaring thing that doesn't work in this novel—and thereby proves me, I think, right about this agamy business. Unexpectedly, in the middle of this novel, Mrs. Hawkins suddenly sleeps with, and later marries, William Todd, a shadowy figure, one of the boarders in the Kensington rooming house. I accept the fact that they go to bed together; its lack of motivation fits perfectly into this add-a-pearl sort of plotting. At the end of an exciting, unexpected evening, what better way can the two of them find to top off the day? What I can't accept—nor has any reader of the book I've ever questioned—is that they then go on not only to romance but marriage. Nothing in either character or in the novel makes sense of that kind of commitment. And the writing goes completely flat; it has none of the heartless edge, the heedless dazzle of the rest of the book.

For whatever conventional reason, Spark found herself committed to writing a prosaic romantic union into the novel. But she doesn't, she can't, carry it off. There's no force, no passion, behind that plot. She can still remember the pain inflicted by lovers like Bartlett and Hawkins. She knows intimately what it is like to be that divine novelist, Emma Loy, full of talent and taste, and yet enmeshed in an unhappy affair dragging out a now dead past. She can remember, that is, the pain that produced the earlier fiction, and the constant re-conversion that pain generated. But what she cannot create, because it has no part in her truest and deepest imaginings, is a story that turns on characters being all-in-all to one another, to being, that is, gamous.

So here's where we almost wind up. From beginning to beginning again, Muriel Spark is not an artist of commitment but, instead and always, of moving on, of conversion. For a long time, to start, and in that terrible middle, she wanted to go on because she had to, because to stay meant to suffer, to be trapped in a primal, brutal scene, and in the ways society endorses that scene's renarration. Lately, however, she wants to go on because there's more to see, more to do, more to write, to go on like *Loitering*'s Fleur Talbot rejoicing to be a woman and a writer in the twentieth century. But beginning, middle, late, she is always—has always been—about moving on, not staying with. "The late afternoon sun touched lovingly on the rooftops reminding me of time past and time to come, making light of the moment. I had really wanted to go. Really, I had" (51).

Which leaves us only with the two last, but, we pray, not final, novels: *Symposium* (1990) and *Reality and Dreams* (1997). *Symposium* seems in some ways to return to the international scene of the middle-period Jamesian novels. And *Reality and Dreams* quite explicitly revises *The Public Image*, perhaps the least appreciated of her short grotesque novels of female persecution and destruction. Frankly, these latest books stump me. I can't quite see yet what Spark is doing with them. But that bewilderment, of course, delights me. It means that the process of renewal is still at work, taking the novelist in directions I do not recognize, let alone foresee. After all, how can it be anything but delightful that after all this time and all these books, Muriel Spark is still beginning again?

NOTES

1. From an interview with Foucault found in Lawrence Kritzman, *Politics, Philosophy, Culture: Interviews and Other Writings, 1977–1984* (New York: Routledge, 1988), 323–330.

2. Muriel Spark, *Reality and Dreams* 78

3. Muriel Spark, "The Seraph and the Zambesi," *The Stories of Muriel Spark* (New York: New American Library, 1985).

4. Arthur Danto, *The Transfiguration of the Commonplace: A Philosophy of Art* (Cambridge: Harvard UP, 1981).

5. Heinz Kohut, *Self Psychology and the Humanities* (New York: Norton, 1985).

6. For additional observations and information, see John Glavin, *After Dickens: Reading, Adaptation, and Performance* (New York: Cambridge UP, 1998).

SELECTED WORKS BY MURIEL SPARK

The Abbess of Crewe. 1974. New York: Viking Penguin, 1977.
The Bachelors. New York: Putnam, 1984.
The Ballad of Peckham Rye. 1960. New York: Putnam, 1982.

Child of Light: A Reassessment of Mary Wollstonecraft Shelley. Hadleigh, Essex: Tower Bridge, 1951.

The Comforters. New York: New Directions, 1994.

Curriculum Vitae. New York: Houghton Mifflin, 1993.

The Driver's Seat. New York: Knopf, 1970.

Emily Brontë: Her Life and Work. With Derek Standford. London: Owen, 1953, 1975.

A Far Cry from Kensington. Boston: Houghton Mifflin, 1988.

The Girls of Slender Means. New York: Knopf, 1963.

The Go-Away Bird and Other Stories. Harmondsworth: Penguin, 1958, 1984.

The Hothouse by the East River. 1973. New York: Viking Penguin, 1977.

John Masefield. 1953. Rev. ed. London: Hutchinson, 1992.

Loitering with Intent. New York: Coward, McCann & Geoghegan. 1981.

The Mandelbaum Gate. 1965. New York: Avon, 1992.

Mary Shelley. 1987. New York: Trans-Atlantic Publications, 1993.

Memento Mori. New York: Putnam, 1959.

A Muriel Spark Trio: "The Comforters," "The Ballad of Peckham Rye," "Memento Mori." Philadelphia: Lippincott, 1962.

Not to Disturb. New York: Penguin, 1972.

The Only Problem. New York: Putnam, 1984.

Open to the Public: New and Collected Stories. New York: New Directions, 1997.

The Prime of Miss Jean Brodie. New York: Dell, 1961.

The Public Image. New York: New Directions, 1968.

Reality and Dreams. New York: Houghton Mifflin, 1997.

The Stories of Muriel Spark. Ed. Muriel Spark and Joe Kanon. New York: New American Library. 1985.

Symposium. New York: Random House Value Publishing, 1992.

The Takeover. New York: Viking, 1976.

Territorial Rights. 1979. New York: Penguin, 1991.

Tribute to Wordsworth; A Miscellany of Opinion for the Centenary of the Poet's Death. London: Wingate, 1950.

The Very Fine Clock. New York: Knopf, 1968.

Voices at Play. New York: St. Martin's, 1961.

Selected Works about Muriel Spark

Auerbach, Nina. *Communities of Women: An Idea in Fiction.* Cambridge: Harvard UP, 1978.

Barreca, Regina. "The Ancestral Laughter of the Streets: Humor in Muriel Spark's Earlier Works." *New Perspectives on Women and Comedy.* Ed. Regina Barreca. Philadelphia: Gordon and Breach, 1992. 223–40.

Bold, Alan, ed. *Muriel Spark: An Odd Capacity for Vision.* Totowa, NJ: Barnes & Noble, 1984.

"The Deliberate Cunning of Muriel Spark." *The Scottish Novel since the Seventies: New Visions, Old Dreams.* Ed. Gavin Wallace and Randall Stevenson. Edinburgh: Edinburgh UP, 1993. 41–53.

DeVoize, Jeanne, and Pamela Valette. "An Interview with Muriel Spark." *Journal of the Short Story in English* 13 (Autumn 1989): 11–22.

Edgecombe, Rodney Stenning. *Vocation and Identity in the Fiction of Muriel Spark.* Columbia: U of Missouri P, 1990.

Frankel, Sarah. "An Interview with Muriel Spark." *Partisan Review* 54.3 (Summer 1987): 443–57.

Glavin, John. "Muriel Spark's 'Unknowing' Fiction." *Women's Studies: An Interdisciplinary Journal* 15.1–3 (1988): 221–41.

Halio, Jay L. "Muriel Spark: The Novelist's Sense of Wonder." *British Novelists since 1800.* Ed. Jack I. Biles. New York: AMS, 1987. 267–77.

Hynes, Joseph. "Muriel Spark and the Oxymoronic Vision." *Contemporary British Women Writers: Narrative Strategies.* Ed. Robert E. Hosmer, Jr. New York: St. Martin's, 1993. 161–87.

"Keeping It Short—Muriel Spark Talks about Her Books to Ian Gilham." *Listener* 24 Sept. 1970: 411–13.

Kemp, Peter. *Muriel Spark.* London: Elek, 1974.

Kermode, Frank. "Sheerer Spark." *Listener* 24 Sept. 1970: 425, 427.

Little, Judy. "'Endless Different Ways': Muriel Spark's Re-Visions of the Spinster." *Old Maids to Radical Spinsters: Unmarried Women in the Twentieth-Century Novel.* Ed. Laura L. Doan. Urbana: U of Illinois P, 1991. 19–35.

———. "Muriel Spark's Grammars of Assent." *The British and Irish Novel since 1960.* Ed. James Acheson. New York: St. Martin's, 1991. 1–16.

Lukacher, Ned. *Primal Scenes: Literature, Philosophy, Psychoanalysis.* Ithaca: Cornell UP, 1986.

McBrien, William. "The Novelist as Dandy." *Twentieth-Century Women Novelists.* Ed. Thomas F. Staley. Totowa, NJ: Barnes and Noble, 1982. 153–78.

Murray, Isobel, and Bob Tait. *Ten Modern Scottish Novels.* Aberdeen: Aberdeen UP, 1984.

Parrinder, Patrick. "Muriel Spark and Her Critics." *Critical Quarterly* 25.2 (Summer 1983): 23–31.

Pearlman, Mickey. "The Element of the Fantastic and the Artist Figure in the Novels of Muriel Spark." *Contours of the Fantastic: Selected Essays from the Eighth International Conference on the Fantastic in the Arts.* Ed. Michele K. Langford. New York: Greenwood, 1994. 149–61.

Randisi, Jennifer Lynn. *On Her Way Rejoicing: The Fiction of Muriel Spark.* Washington, DC: Catholic U of America, 1991.

Richmond, Velma Bourgeois. *Muriel Spark.* New York: Ungar, 1985.

Schieff, Stephen. "Muriel Spark between the Lines." *New Yorker* 24 May 1993: 36–43.

Shaw, Valerie. "Muriel Spark." *The History of Scottish Literature.* Vol. 4: *The Twentieth Century.* Ed. Cairns Craig. Aberdeen: Aberdeen UP, 1987. 277–90.

Todd, Richard. "The Crystalline Novels of Muriel Spark." *Essays on the Contemporary British Novel.* Ed. Hedwig Boc and Albert Wertheim. Munich: Max Hueber, 1986. 175–92.

Contributors

Laura Niesen de Abruña is Associate Professor of English at Ithaca College and the recipient of several awards, including a Fulbright Lectureship. She is author of *The Refining Fire: Herakles and Other Heroes in T.S. Eliot's Works* (1992) and has published articles on numerous British, Caribbean, and West Indian women writers, including Jamaica Kincaid, Paule Marshall and Jean Rhys. She has also written on American authors ranging from Mark Twain to Edith Wharton.

Regina Barreca is Professor of English at the University of Connecticut. Her numerous books include *Last Laughs: Perspectives on Women and Comedy* (1988), *Sex and Death in Victorian Literature* (1990), *They Used to Call Me Snow White—But I Drifted: Women's Strategic Use of Humor* (1991), *New Perspectives on Women and Comedy* (1992), *Perfect Husbands (And Other Fairy Tales): Demystifying Marriage, Men, and Romance* (1993), *Fay Weldon's Wicked Fictions* (1994), *Untamed and Unabashed: Essays on Women and Humor in British Literature* (1994), *Sweet Revenge: The Wicked Delights of Getting Even* (1995), and *The Erotics of Instruction* (with Deborah Denenholz Morse, 1997). She has also edited numerous collections, most notably *Women of the Century: Thirty Modern Short Stories*

(1993), *Desire and Imagination: Classic Essays in Sexuality* (1995), and *The Penguin Book of Women's Humor* (1996).

KATE FULLBROOK is Associate Dean for Academic Affairs in the Faculty of Humanities and Professor of Literary Studies at the University of the West of England. She is the author of *Katherine Mansfield* (1986), *Free Women: Ethics and Aesthetics in Twentieth Century Women's Fiction* (1990), and, with Edward Fullbrook, *Simone de Beauvoir and Jean-Paul Sartre: The Remaking of a Twentieth-Century Legend* (1993) and *Simone de Beauvoir: A Critical Introduction* (1998). She is also the editor, with Judy Simons, of *Writing: A Woman's Business* (1998).

JOHN GLAVIN is Professor of English at Georgetown University. He is author of numerous articles and essays on British writers and has recently published *After Dickens: Reading, Adaptation, and Performance* (1999). He is Associate Director of The Dickens Project (University of California, Santa Cruz) and is currently working on a collection of essays, *Dickens and Screen,* to be published by Cambridge. John Glavin is also a playwright. His plays have been staged by The Philadelphia Company and by the Contemporary Arts Theatre Company.

DEE GOERTZ is Associate Professor of English at Hanover College. She researches and writes on twentieth-century women writers, both British and Canadian, and on James Joyce. Her current project is a study of symbolism in the works of Carol Shields.

CLARE HANSON teaches English literature at Loughborough University, U.K., where she is Professor of English. Her specialist areas of teaching and research are women's writing and feminist literary theory. She has published numerous articles on these topics and is also the author or editor of *Katherine Mansfield* (with Andrew Gurr, 1981), *Short Stories and Short Fictions, 1880–1980* (1985), *The Critical Writings of Katherine Mansfield* (ed., 1987), *Re-reading the Short Story* (ed., 1989), and *Virginia Woolf* (1994). Her most recent book, *Outside the Canon: The 'Woman's Novel' in the Twentieth Century* will be published in 2000.

PHYLLIS LASSNER is Senior Lecturer in the Women's Studies, Jewish Studies, and Writing Programs at Northwestern University. She is the author of *Elizabeth Bowen* (1990), *Elizabeth Bowen: A Study of the Short Fiction* (1991), and *British Women Writers of World War II: Battlegrounds of Their Own* (1998). She has also published essays on such twentieth-century British women as Beryl Bainbridge, Maureen Duffy, Storm Jameson, Phyllis Botto, Rose Macauley, and Stevie Smith.

DEBORAH DENENHOLZ MORSE is Associate Professor of English and University Distinguished Professor for Teaching Excellence at The College of William and Mary. She has written numerous articles on British and American writers from Anne Brontë, Elizabeth Gaskell, and Anthony Trollope to Kay Boyle, Maxine Hong Kingston, and Mona Simpson. Author of *Women In Trollope's Palliser Novels* (1987) she is also editor of *The Erotics of Instruction* (with Regina Barreca, 1997).

ERIC NELSON is Professor of English at St. Olaf College, where he teaches British literature. He is author of a recent book on the place and impact of shopping malls on American culture, *The Mall of America* (1998), and has a particular interest in detective fiction. He is currently working on a novel set in the south of France.

JUDIE NEWMAN is Professor of American and Postcolonial literature at the University of Newcastle Upon Tyne. Her publications include *Saul Bellow and History* (1984), *Nadine Gordimer* (1988), *John Updike* (1988), an edition of Harriet Beecher Stowe's *Dred: A Tale of the Great Dismal Swamp* (1992), and *The Ballistic Bard: Postcolonial Fictions* (1995), as well as numerous essays on American and Postcolonial novelists. She was the Chair of the British Association for American Studies, 1995–1998.

JAN ROSEMERGY is Director for Communications and Community Relations at the John F. Kennedy Center for Research on Human Development at Vanderbilt University. She is author of numerous articles and essays on British and American women writers.

SUSAN ROWLAND teaches nineteenth- and twentieth-century British literature at Greenwich University. She is the author of *C. G. Jung and Literary Theory: The Challenge from Fiction* (1999) and of articles on Saul Bellow, among others. Her research interests include detective fiction, especially the novels of Sara Paretsky, and the influence of C. G. Jung and literary theory on the works of Michèle Roberts, Nicholas Mosley, Saul Bellow, Lindsay Clarke, and Doris Lessing.

PATRICIA JULIANA SMITH, Lecturer in English at the University of California at Los Angeles, has been the recipient of several awards and fellowships. She has written extensively on issues of opera and gender and has authored numerous articles on such modern British writers as Brigid Brophy, Angela Carter, and Virginia Woolf. She is the author of *En Tavesti: Women, Gender Subversion, Opera* (with Corinne E. Blackmer, 1995), *Lesbian Panic: Homoeroticism in Modern British Women's Fiction* (1997), *The Book of Gay and Lesbian Quotations* (1999), and *The Queer Sixties* (1999).

MARY ROSE SULLIVAN retired in 1996 as Professor of English, University of Colorado at Denver. She is author of *Browning's Voices in "The Ring and the Book"* (1969) and editor of *The Letters of Elizabeth Barrett Browning to Mary Russell Mitford, 1836–1854* (with Meredith B. Raymond, 1983), *Women of Letters: Selected Letters of Elizabeth Barrett Browning and Mary Russell Mitford* (with Meredith B. Raymond, 1987), *Crime Classics* (with Rex Burns, 1990), and *Elizabeth Barrett Browning: Selected Poetry and Prose* (with Meredith B. Raymond, 1992). She has also written numerous articles on the Brownings and on such contemporary writers as Sean O'Faolain and Marilyn French.

ABBY H. P. WERLOCK is Associate Professor of English at St. Olaf College, where she teaches British and American literature. She is the author of *Tillie Olsen* (with Mickey Pearlman, 1990) and editor of *The Facts on File Companion to the American Short Story* (2000). She has published numerous articles on twentieth-century American and Canadian writers from James Fenimore Cooper to Kay Boyle, William Faulkner, Ernest Hemingway, Sandra Birdsell, and Carol Shields and is President of the Edith Wharton Society.

MARILYN C. WESLEY is Babcock Professor of English at Hartwick College. She has written articles on such nineteenth- and twentieth-century fiction writers as Mary Rowlandson, Sarah Orne Jewett, Anne Hebert, and Joyce Carol Oates and is author of *Refusal and Transgres-*

sion in Joyce Carol Oates' Fiction (1993) and *Secret Journeys: The Trope of Women's Travel in American Literature* (1998).

ROBERTA WHITE, Luellen Professor of English at Centre College, has published articles on British and American writers including Margaret Atwood, John Berryman, James Joyce, and Sue Miller, among others. She is currently working on a book-length study of fictional portraits of the woman artist.

Index